CHILDREN'S ILLUSTRATED
ENCYCLOPEDIA
EXPLORING HISTORY

THE
HISTORY
ENCYCLOPEDIA

FOLLOW THE DEVELOPMENT OF HUMAN CIVILIZATION FROM PREHISTORY TO
THE MODERN WORLD, WITH OVER 1500 PHOTOGRAPHS AND ILLUSTRATIONS

SIMON ADAMS | PHILIP BROOKS | JOHN FARNDON
WILL FOWLER | BRIAN WARD

ARMADILLO

CONTENTS

ANCIENT CIVILIZATIONS.....72

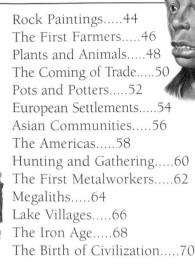

WORLD RELIGIONS.....130

EXPLORATION AND DISCOVERY.....188

SCIENCE AND TECHNOLOGY.....246

THE STORY OF MEDICINE.....304

ANCIENT WEAPONS.....362

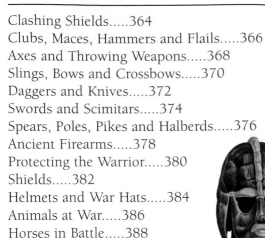

MODERN WEAPONS AND WARFARE.....420

Reaching for the Future

Human beings have rarely been prepared to accept life as it is. Throughout history, we have sought to investigate our world and to understand it. The world today is the point we have reached in a process of civilization that began in prehistoric times. The study of history allows us to discover how we got here. It is a look deep into ourselves and what made us. By looking at how human beings have developed since earliest times, what drove us and the achievements we made, we can begin to understand the complex process that created the modern world.

Prehistoric Peoples

The story of history begins with the emergence of the first people, our ancient ancestors. They had to learn skills to enable them to survive. By trial and error, they learned which plants and fruits were good to eat, and how to make weapons so that they could hunt animals.

Gradually, groups of families joined together. There was safety in numbers, and large groups were less likely to suffer attacks from wild animals or other tribes. People also began to learn that there were advantages to co-operation. They could share the new skills that they mastered, for example how to use fire. Working together made it possible to hunt for larger game, such as elephants. Later, people began to specialize in making weapons and other tools, or in looking after the children of the clan or tribe. In return for these jobs, they would receive a share of the food gathered or hunted by other members of the group.

Co-operation and experience led slowly to a more comfortable life. Humans were free to embark on their first artistic efforts and spiritual searches. Roaming tribes of hunter-gatherers later learned that they could plant seeds to ensure reliable crops of vegetable foods. They could also raise herd animals for a ready source of meat. This led to the first permanent villages, which grew up on the banks of rivers, where there was a constant supply of fresh water and also fish to catch. Light, easy-to-work soil was also important, because the tools for the first farmers were very basic.

As the early villages expanded and became towns, society developed further. The towns grew into cities and some people specialized in trades. Potters, tool and weapon makers, brick makers, spinners, weavers and priests could now rely on their trades to receive sufficient food and housing. They did not need to hunt or farm. These were the beginnings of civilization, which began in different parts of the world at different times.

RELIGION
Most ancient religions involved the worship of many different gods, but often one particular god was in charge of all the others. For the Romans, Jupiter was the chief of the gods.

HUNTERS' TROPHY
Hunting took a lot of effort, so people made sure they used every last bit of the animal. The flesh provided meat and the bones were carved to make simple tools. This woman is cleaning an animal skin. It might be used to make clothes or a rug.

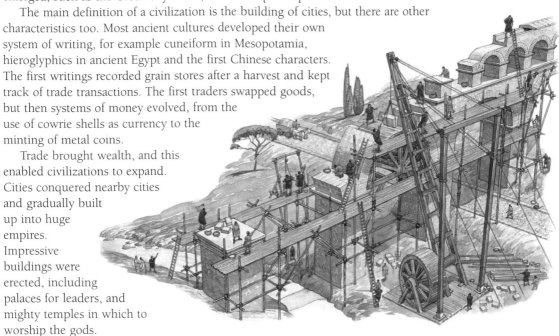

Ancient Civilizations

The development of villages into towns and then into cities, the process of civilization, gathered momentum. Town leaders started to take nearby regions under their own control. Civilization started at different times in various parts of the world. However, in areas that could not support intensive farming, such as the Great Plains of North America and the dry regions of the Middle East, Far East and Africa, civilization never gained a real foothold.

THE COMING OF WEALTH
With civilization came trade and wealth. This palace was built by an Etruscan nobleman in the last millennium BC. The Etruscans were western Europe's first wealthy civilization. They had trade links with the Phoenicians and Greeks.

Geography and climate dictated the nature of the civilizations that emerged. In North Africa and the Middle East, for instance, great rivers such as the Nile in Egypt and the Tigris and Euphrates in Mesopotamia allowed the development of large and increasingly complex civilizations. In other regions, agriculture and transport were limited by mountains, deserts and other barriers. There, different types of civilizations emerged, such as the Greek city-states, or the unique empires of Central and South America.

The main definition of a civilization is the building of cities, but there are other characteristics too. Most ancient cultures developed their own system of writing, for example cuneiform in Mesopotamia, hieroglyphics in ancient Egypt and the first Chinese characters. The first writings recorded grain stores after a harvest and kept track of trade transactions. The first traders swapped goods, but then systems of money evolved, from the use of cowrie shells as currency to the minting of metal coins.

Trade brought wealth, and this enabled civilizations to expand. Cities conquered nearby cities and gradually built up into huge empires. Impressive buildings were erected, including palaces for leaders, and mighty temples in which to worship the gods.

FEATS OF ENGINEERING
The Romans of Italy were champion builders in the ancient world. Many of the aqueducts, bridges, roads and buildings they constructed all over their vast empire can still be seen to this day.

World Religions

Since earliest times, humans had tried to investigate all aspects of the human condition and to make sense of the world. Religion emerged as early people thought about the nature of the world and their position within it. Aspects that could not readily be understood were said to be the actions of superior beings, such as spirits or gods. This led to the development of belief systems and religions. The rituals associated with these became more complex as civilizations developed. Temples were built where people could worship their gods and communicate with them by means of prayer.

Early religions were based on the idea that there were many spirits or gods, who had varying degrees of interest in humankind. Many of the gods worshipped by different cultures had similar characteristics. However, between 2000BC and 1BC, religions emerged around the Middle East that were based on belief in a single god. These are known as monotheistic belief systems, as *mono* means 'single' and *theistic* means 'related to God.' The first was Judaism. Christianity (based on the teachings of Jesus of Nazareth) and Islam (based on the teachings of Muhammad) are the world's other main monotheistic religions. In China, Buddhism, which is more a spiritual way of life than a true religion, developed as people started to follow the teachings of the Buddha (the enlightened one).

Belief in a single god has been the most successful type of religion in the Arab and Western worlds. However, Hinduism and other religions based on multiple gods are still very strong, especially in Asia.

MANY GODS
The goddess Lakshmi is one of many gods worshipped by Hindus. In Asia, belief in religions based on multiple gods is very popular.

HOLY TEACHER
Many of today's major religions developed from the teachings of a single founder. Guru Nanak founded the Sikh religion in the 1400s. He was born a Hindu but did not agree with the ritual and religious wars of the time.

Exploration and Discovery

Religion and other aspects of human culture spread as people set out to explore their world. The great civilizations of the ancient world, such as the Egyptians, Phoenicians, Greeks and Romans, were all skilled boat-builders. They set sail around the Mediterranean to create new trade links and to conquer new territories.

STEAMSHIPS
For centuries ships had to rely on strong oarsmen or on the wind in their sails. In still weather, a ship could be becalmed for days. Then, in the 1800s, the first steamships were built and sea transport became much more reliable.

Later, races such as the Vikings probed through and round Europe as well as west toward North America, while the Chinese explored eastern Asia and the Polynesians roamed through much of the Pacific.

From the 1400s, exploration became a major force in expanding countries. The Europeans set sail in search of sea routes to the Far East, where they could trade for silks and spices. The major maritime explorers were the Portuguese, Spanish, English, French and Dutch. Within 100 years explorers had created maps of most of the world. For this reason, the period from the 1400s to the 1700s is known as the Age of Exploration.

After this time there were still gaps to be filled, and explorers probed into the land areas of North and South America, Africa, Asia and Australia. The trader, the soldier and the priest followed the explorer, and by about 1850, most of the world had been mapped. This was not the end of the exploration story, though. Trade links were established, but there was much left to discover, for the advancement of science. Exploration of inaccessible areas has continued right up to the present, particularly in the snowy polar wastes, the deepest parts of the ocean, the most remote rainforests and, of course, into space.

MAORI CANOES
The Maoris of New Zealand were skilled seamen. They rowed in fleets of intricately carved canoes that were able to carry up to 100 warriors.

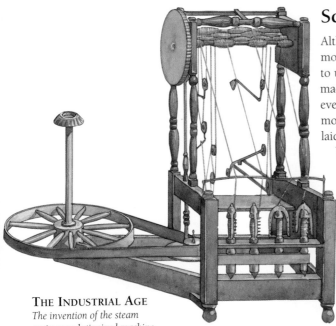

THE INDUSTRIAL AGE
The invention of the steam engine revolutionized machine technology. The first factories were built and the industrial age began. This machine for spinning cotton was adapted to run on steam power in 1771.

Science and Technology

Although science and technology seem very modern ideas, human beings have been striving to understand how things work and inventing machines to help them make their lives easier ever since they first walked the Earth. However, most of the foundations of modern science were laid by Greek thinkers, such as Archimedes, and by the engineers of the Roman Empire.

During the Middle Ages, alchemy emerged, which was the 'science' of trying to turn base metals into gold. This practice paved the way for the development of modern chemistry during the 1600s. The 1700s are often known as the Age of Enlightenment. Men and women thinkers refused just to accept what had been handed down as fact. They demanded rigorous proof before they would accept any information as truth. This approach was the real forerunner of scientific method. It allowed the creation of the instruments and thought processes that enabled scientists to look ever deeper into our world. It also led to a desire to look beyond the Earth and examine the workings of the universe in order to see how humans fit into the bigger picture.

The Story of Medicine

One of the most exciting aspects of science is the investigation into treating human illnesses and ailments. At its very earliest stages, medicine was a matter of herbal remedies found by trial and experiment. Medicine was not regarded as something to do with the body alone. It also involved a spiritual, magical or religious element. Illness was a sign that the body was out of balance, or that a person had fallen foul of the spirits or gods. Treatment involved philosophical or religious aspects as well as physical ones.

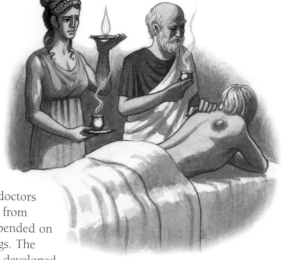

From around 500BC, Greek thinkers and doctors came to the idea that illness resulted from natural causes, and that cures depended on healthy living and the use of drugs. The Chinese and Indians had already developed their own systems of medicine. Further advances came around AD1000–1500, largely from physicians living in the Islamic world. They relearned the discoveries of the Greeks and then built on it to analyse disease and create medicines. The growing Islamic interest in alchemy led to the creation of purer chemicals and better drugs, but it wasn't until the 1500s that medicine began to develop in the West.

ELEMENTARY MEDICINE
Many Greek and Roman doctors believed that disease was caused by an imbalance between the four 'humours' (elements or qualities) in the body. Using heat was one way to draw out excess humours.

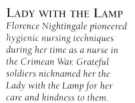

During the Renaissance, the study of anatomy helped medical pioneers to understand how the body functions. Then, from around 1850, medical developments really started to accelerate. One reason for this was an acceptance of scientific method after the Industrial Revolution. Doctors and researchers gained increased understanding of the human body and were able to make more sense of the biological and chemical principles that make it work.

LADY WITH THE LAMP
Florence Nightingale pioneered hygienic nursing techniques during her time as a nurse in the Crimean War. Grateful soldiers nicknamed her the Lady with the Lamp for her care and kindness to them.

Ancient Weapons

A less welcome part of human history has been the growth of warfare. As early people banded together to form tribes and clans and build villages, they also acquired valuable possessions such as food stocks and animals. For the first time, weapons were needed, not just for hunting, but for defending against and attacking other humans. Later, rulers of the first civilizations often wanted to take over a nearby state. This might give them control of a vital river, rich farmland, or raw materials. Many societies gave warriors a place of special privilege.

SPECIALIST WEAPONRY
The knife or dagger was one of the earliest and simplest weapons of all. However, even dagger design became highly specialized. The notched blade of this 17th-century dagger was designed to disarm an opponent during a sword fight.

Warfare spurred the development of technical skills such as metalworking. Soldiers saw the advantage of bronze weapons over copper ones, and then the advantage of iron over bronze. As civilizations grew larger, so did their armies and this called for increased numbers of better weapons.

The development of weapons did not end when the ancient civilizations fell. The centuries after the end of the Roman Empire are sometimes known as the Dark Ages. Many parts of the world lost some features of civilization, but warfare continued, for example in the raids of the Vikings. Then, in the Middle Ages, people began to relearn ancient skills, such as building in stone. New types of weaponry appeared, including steel-bladed swords, cannons and gunpowder. At the same time, new methods of warfare emerged, such as the use of soldiers on horseback.

Modern Weapons and Warfare

The modern age of weaponry really began in the period after the Industrial Revolution. Radical new materials and manufacturing capabilities allowed the creation of weapons that could be mass-produced. The rapid developments in physics and chemistry that accompanied industrial advancement also allowed designers to understand more clearly how weapons worked. They could improve the speed and power of ammunition, for example, by making explosive-filled shells rather than iron cannon balls. New explosives were also developed to replace gunpowder. These and other advances helped make weapons longer-ranged, more accurate and more devastating in their effect.

By 1901, the machine gun had been invented, the submarine was on the verge of becoming a practical weapon, and powered, heavier-than-air craft were about to take to the air. These processes accelerated in World War I, which saw the introduction of the tank and of chemical weapons.

During World War II, existing weapons were refined and tanks and aircraft carriers came to the fore. New technologies included radar and jet propulsion. Most decisively of all, the first atomic weapons were used. Military technology has continued to develop with great speed ever since and, as in every other area of human activity and civilization, including science and medicine, warfare has been transformed by the computer revolution.

FIGHTING AXES
A Native American swings his tomahawk, ready to throw it at an enemy. Hand axes, such as the tomahawk, were used as weapons from the earliest times. They could be used to hack enemies in hand-to-hand combat and could also be thrown.

BOMBS FROM THE SKY
These B-17 bombers were flown during World War II. The ability to drop missiles accurately from the air changed the nature of warfare forever. It increased the number of civilian casualties.

SMG
Sub-machine guns, or SMGs, were first used during World War I. Both world wars forced rapid advances in weapon technology.

PREHISTORIC PEOPLES

BY PHILIP BROOKS

From the moment when ape-like hominids first walked on two legs, the story of humans began. This section looks at how prehistoric people survived, how they mastered hunting, fire and metalworking, and how they made the first art.

First Steps

IN THIS SECTION WE WILL LOOK BACK to the very beginnings of the human story. It starts at a time when people lived in caves and sheltered under cliffs, when the only tools were made of stone, when everyone had to hunt or forage for their own food, when clothes had to be made from animal skins. There were no cities, no large buildings, none of the comforts of modern life, and no one had worked out how to write.

The term "prehistory" means the time before people were able to write their history down. Writing developed at different times in different parts of the world, so the date when the prehistoric period ended varies from one place to another. In Mesopotamia in South-west Asia, for example, writing came around 3000BC. In western Europe by contrast, widespread use of written scripts coincided with the Roman conquerors around 3,000 years later.

Prehistoric life can sound grim. Life was hard, travel must have been difficult, and many people died young without the benefits of effective medicine. Yet the period sees the beginnings of the very things that make humanity what it is today. Technology was simple, but it made possible amazing monuments like Stonehenge. Artists had only basic materials, yet they produced masterpieces on their cave walls. People cared for their

▲ HOMINIDS
The first human-apes appeared about four million years ago in Africa. They came down from the trees where they lived and began to walk on the ground on two legs. Scientists call them australopithecines.

▼ KEY DATES
How humans and human society developed in different parts of the world.

▼ CAVE ART
It seems that humans have always felt the urge for artistic self-expression. During the Ice Age, people lived in caves. Wall paintings from that time show people's skill in making their homes bright and attractive.

	4–1 MILLION YEARS AGO	1MYA–400,000BC	400,000–30,000BC	30,000–12,000BC
AFRICA	Early hominids, the first human-apes, are alive in eastern Africa.	*Homo erectus*, a type of early human, use stone handaxes as a multi-purpose tool.	*Homo sapiens*, humans, appear in various places south of the Sahara.	
MIDDLE EAST & ASIA	*Homo erectus* are established in both Java and China, and have probably mastered the use of fire.		Neanderthals and "modern" humans are living side by side in Mesopotamia.	*Rock painting*
EUROPE		First known settlement of *Homo erectus* in Europe.	Neanderthals and "modern" humans are present, and may breed, but Neanderthals die out.	Europe freezes in the Ice Age. Artists make great cave paintings in France and Spain.
AMERICAS			*Sabre-toothed cat*	The first settlement of North America begins as men and women cross the Bering land bridge from Siberia.

Skull of Homo habilis

MYA = Million years ago

▲ MAMMOTH SHELTER
Homes were built from whatever materials were available. Remains of mammoth bones suggest they were used to build massive shelters almost 3m/10ft high.

▶ FISH CARVING
After the Ice Age, food supplies were much better. Fish carvings found in Europe suggest that fish had become part of the staple diet.

sick, using medicines made from plants, and some illnesses were cured this way.

This section of the book looks at prehistoric life all over the world. It begins with the origins of the human race in Africa and how people spread out around the world. It tells how people developed simple tools, survival skills such as hunting and food gathering, and the ability to make clothes and simple shelters. Gradually, human activities such as art, religion and ceremonies developed, signs that social groups were becoming more complex.

Next, we examine the enormous progress made by early peoples, starting with the invention of pottery and the beginnings of farming, which helped men and women control their food supply. Trade then enabled more people to travel and new ideas to spread around the world. The next "revolution" was when people learned how to use metals, by working copper, making bronze and smelting iron. Finally came the invention of writing, the development of large cities and societies, and the end of the prehistoric period. Throughout this period, people overcame tremendous obstacles, such as the huge climate changes of an Ice Age.

▼ WATCHTOWER
Eventually people began building permanent settlements. The walled city of Jericho dates from about 7000BC and is one of the earliest cities discovered so far. It had watchtowers like this one, which were more than 9m/30ft high.

12,000–9000BC	9000–6000BC	6000–4000BC	4000–2000BC	2000BC–AD1
Japanese pot	*Auroch, an early bull*	The climate of what is now the Sahara Desert is very wet. Cattle herding is common in many parts of the region.	*Cuneiform writing from Mesopotamia*	
The dog is domesticated in the Middle East. The first pottery is produced in Japan.	Farming is established in the Fertile Crescent.	Trading towns such as Çatal Hüyük, Turkey, begin to develop.	Potter's wheel invented; bronze-working begins; writing develops. Cities built in Mesopotamia.	
The great ice sheets begin to thaw as temperatures increase. Sea levels rise.	*Clovis points*	Farming spreads to eastern Europe, probably from Turkey.	Stone circles and other megalithic monuments become common in western Europe.	First ironworking transforms tools and weapons.
People in Chile build houses from wood and skins – the first evidence of shelters in the Americas.	The Clovis culture: on the Great Plains people hunt using stone-pointed spears.	*Cotton plant*	The farmers of Mexico domesticate the maize plant. Other crops spread North America.	The Olmec people of Mexico build the region's first large cities.

Finding the Evidence

▲ BURIAL URN
Some prehistoric peoples cremated their dead by burning the bodies on a funeral pyre. The ashes, and sometimes the bones, of the dead person might then be buried in a pottery urn like this one.

Finding evidence about prehistory is like doing a gigantic jigsaw puzzle with most of the pieces missing. Often very little is now left of the prehistoric peoples who lived thousands of years ago. Archaeologists study every scrap of evidence they can find for clues as to how ancient peoples lived. Sometimes all that remain are a few bits of broken pottery, the foundations of some houses, or the occasional tool or weapon. Archaeologists have to learn what they can from fragments such as these.

Even when there is a big site, a stone circle, for example, or the remains of an ancient town, there are often more questions than answers. What were stone circles used for? Who ruled the first towns? How did people find out how to make bronze? Why did the cave artists paint their pictures? Questions like these still baffle archaeologists. They can suggest answers, but there are no certainties.

Graves can often give archaeologists some of the most fascinating clues about prehistory. They can be almost like time capsules. In many periods, it was the custom to bury a person with some of their possessions. Archaeologists call these items grave goods. These objects can tell us a great deal about the dead person's lifestyle, job and wealth. They can also reveal something about the beliefs of the time. This is because grave goods were usually intended for use in the next world. Such finds suggest that people believed in life after death in prehistoric times. Some of the best evidence, though, comes from the bodies

◀ CHAMBERED TOMB
This type of tomb, common in prehistoric Europe, often contains several burials. These reveal a lot about ancient society. For example, the grave of a ruler or chief was usually treated differently than the others. It might be more carefully constructed or contain richer goods.

DEATH AND BURIAL
Archaeologists rarely know what they will find when they excavate a grave. There may be only a skeleton, or there may be lavish grave goods as well. Whatever they find, it will probably be very fragile if it has been in the ground for thousands of years.

▶ GRAVE GOODS
Items in graves often reveal evidence about the spread of technology. For example, these grave goods from a cemetery at Varna in Bulgaria, show that their owners had discovered how to work metal.

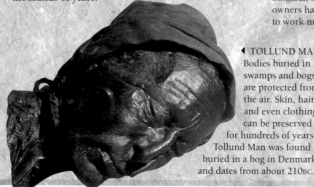

◀ TOLLUND MAN
Bodies buried in swamps and bogs are protected from the air. Skin, hair and even clothing can be preserved for hundreds of years. Tollund Man was found buried in a bog in Denmark, and dates from about 210BC.

▲ PASSAGE-GRAVE BURIAL MOUND
Many passage graves dating from around 3,000BC have been found in northern Europe and Ireland. A passage leads to the tomb at the mound's heart.

themselves. By looking at a skeleton, for example, a trained observer can tell roughly how old the person was at their time of death, and whether that person was male or female. It is also possible to measure how tall the dead person was, and to determine quite a lot about build, physical development and strength. Often, archaeologists can find out about a person's diet, by studying the teeth and doing chemical analyses of the bones. Sometimes they can even say why a person died, as some illnesses, such as arthritis, can be detected from the bones.

Studying the features and contents of an ancient grave can provide enough evidence to work out the approximate date when the person was buried. Factors such as the condition of the bones, the way the person was buried, and the type of grave goods that are found with the skeleton, can help to date the burial. How deep the body lies in the ground is also a clue. The deeper it is buried, the older it is likely to be. Archaeologists working in a vertical trench, for example, can often see layers of objects in historical order, from the oldest to the most recent, almost like a timeline.

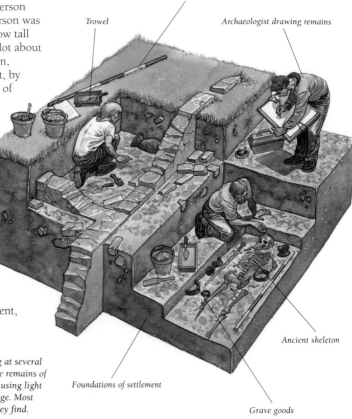

Trowel

Measuring pole

Archaeologist drawing remains

Ancient skeleton

Foundations of settlement

Grave goods

▶ ARCHAEOLOGICAL DIG
Archaeologists excavate an ancient site. They are working at several different levels. The skeleton is on an earlier level than the remains of the settlement above it. The archaeologists' dig with care, using light tools, such as trowels and brushes, to avoid causing damage. Most importantly of all, they record in detail everything that they find.

▼ EXCAVATING GRAVES
Archaeologists have to be very careful when excavating dead bodies. This is not just because they are delicate. These are remains of real people, and they should be treated with respect. At this grave at Les Eyzies in France, archaeologists have worked slowly to remove the bones, which are at least 10,000 years old.

Dates and Dating

Prehistoric people lived thousands or even millions of years ago. However, because these people left no written records, archaeologists have to rely on other evidence to work out the dates of the remains they find. They have many ways of doing this, from studying the site of the find to using chemical analysis. Even so, nearly all the dates can only be approximate. The older the remains are, the less precise the dates are likely to be.

The abbreviations used with dates in this book are:

- MYA indicates "Million Years Ago". It is used for very ancient dates, a million or more years ago.

- BC indicates the number of years "Before Christ". Jesus Christ lived about 2,000 years ago, so you can work out a "number of years old" by adding 2,000 to a BC date.

The Toolmakers

▲ PEBBLE TOOL
Early hominids chipped away the sides of pebbles to make simple, sharp-edged tools.

PROBABLY THE BIGGEST prehistoric mystery of all is how the human race began. Many scientists think that modern humans evolved, millions of years ago, from creatures that looked rather like apes. They hoped to find a missing link, part-ape and part-human, between modern humans and our animal ancestors. No one has found this missing link. But palaeontologists (people who study fossils, the preserved remains of animals and plants) have discovered the remains of a group of creatures called early hominids. These are animals that share many features with humans. Hominids looked rather ape-like, and had smaller brains than modern humans, but they walked on two legs and could make simple stone tools. Our ancestors were probably rather like ancient hominids.

No one has ever found a complete skeleton of an early hominid. Often all that remains is a fragment of bone or a single tooth. Scientists have tried to find out all about the hominids from such meagre evidence. However, they often disagree about which species of hominid a particular find belongs to, and how the various species relate to each other.

The earliest hominids, which lived in Africa around eight million to one million years ago, are called the australopithecines (meaning southern apes). They stood and walked upright, but were shorter than modern humans, standing 1–1.5m/3–5ft tall. Their bodies had a similar shape to humans, but their flat-nosed faces looked ape-like. Their brains were much smaller than human brains, but larger than those of today's chimpanzees and gorillas.

Australopithecines probably spent most of their time on the ground. Like modern gorillas and chimpanzees, they climbed

◀ *PARANTHROPUS ROBUSTUS*
Stocky and ape-like, this hominid probably spent some of its time living in trees, but it came down to the ground from time to time to search for food. Like the modern chimpanzee, it probably ate plants most of the time.

HOMO HABILIS

Since Louis Leakey discovered the first specimen of *Homo habilis* in 1964, many similar remains have been found in Africa – especially in the fossil-rich beds of Kenya and Tanzania. Although it is not certain whether these creatures are direct human ancestors, they are definitely our close relatives.

▼ PREDATOR
Early hominids had to guard against fearsome meat-eaters like this sabre-toothed cat. Sometimes the best escape from dangerous animals such as this was to take to the trees.

▲ A LARGER SKULL – A LARGER BRAIN
Homo habilis had a much larger brain than the australopithecines. This was one reason why its discoverers decided that it should be included in the genus *Homo*, just like modern humans. *Homo habilis* lived 2.1 to 1.5 million years ago.

▼ A FIRM GRIP
Homo habilis had a hand that could grip objects firmly. This, together with its brain size, meant that the creature could make simple stone tools and may have been able to build basic shelters from tree branches and leaves.

Pebble tool

Simple brushwood shelter

trees to hide from enemies or to shelter from the rain. Remains of their teeth suggest that they ate mainly plants, plus a little meat. They probably also used the first simple tools.

In 1964, palaeontologist Louis Leakey announced the discovery of the fossilized remains of a previously unknown hominid. It had a larger brain than the southern apes, so Leakey decided to place it in the genus *Homo*, the same as our own species. The fossil was 1.75 million years old, making it our oldest close relative. Stone tools were found near the remains, so Leakey named the fossil *Homo habilis* (handy man).

Like people today, the *Homo habilis* people probably ate quite a lot of meat, but no one knows whether they hunted animals for food or ate the remains left by other animals. Archaeologists have found remains of stone tools next to animal bones, such as simple choppers and hammers made from pebbles. They were probably semi-nomadic, staying in an area for a little while before moving on to a new area for food. When they moved, they left their tools behind.

▲ ROBUSTUS SKULL
The robust australopithecines had heavy skulls with massive jaws and strong ridges of bone across the brows. There were also flanges (areas of bone sticking out from the cheeks) on either side.

▲ AFRICANUS SKULL
Although Australopithecus africanus *had a more lightly built skull than* Paranthropus robustus, *it still had a heavy jaw bone. No one is certain exactly how these two species were related.*

▶ "ARDI"
The most complete set of bones from an early hominid species belonged to Ardipithecus ramidus, *which lived more than four million years ago. Archaeologists have nicknamed her "Ardi". The bones, which include most of the skull, teeth, pelvis, hands and feet, show that Ardi was female and stood up to 1.2m/3ft 11in high. She weighed about 50kg/110lb and could walk upright, but may have used all four limbs when moving through trees.*

Hominid uses its upright stance to gather berries

▲ OLDUVAI GORGE
One of the most important hominid sites is Olduvai Gorge in Tanzania, on the Serengeti Plains of East Africa. Fossils of several hominids, including *Homo habilis*, have been found there, making this one of the great hunting grounds in the search for human origins. The gorge contains fossilized remains ranging from 100,000 to around 2 million years old, the older fossils embedded in the deepest rocks. Scatters of tools, from crude pebbles to stone axes, lie near the bones of their makers.

Key Dates

- 7MYA *Sahelanthropus tchadensis* is present in Chad, in Africa. It may be a common ancestor of humans and chimpanzees.

- 4.4MYA *Ardipithecus ramidus* lives in Ethiopia. The most complete early hominid fossil, nicknamed "Ardi", is a member of this species.

- 3.9 to 2.9MYA *Australopithecus afarensis* inhabits East Africa. The most complete example of this species, dubbed "Lucy", was discovered in Hadar, in Ethiopia.

- 2.5MYA Kenya is home to *Paranthropus aethiopicus*, a robust australopithecine.

- 2.1 to 1.5MYA *Homo habilis*, the oldest known member of our genus, exists in Kenya, Tanzania and South Africa.

The Coming of Fire

AROUND 1.6 MILLION YEARS AGO, A GROUP OF hominids mastered a completely new skill. They learned how to use fire, which must have brought about a huge change in their lives. Suddenly, they were able to cook food instead of eating raw meat and plants. They could keep their draughty caves and rock shelters warm in winter. The heat and flames could even be used as weapons against enemies. Fire probably meant that they had a safer and more comfortable life than the earlier hominids had enjoyed.

The hominids who mastered fire were about 1.5m/5ft tall. They had bigger brains and longer limbs than previous hominids, more like those of modern humans. Scientists called them

◀ FIRE STICK
One way early people made fire was to put dry grass on a stick called a hearth. Then they rubbed another stick against the hearth to make a spark and set the grass alight.

FOOD AND RESOURCES

With their larger brains, *Homo erectus* people were probably better at hunting and finding new types of food than previous hominids. Their travels across Africa may have been to search for new sources of food. As well as hunting animals and gathering plants, they probably killed injured animals or scavenged meat left by other predators.

▲ HACKBERRIES
Gathering nuts and fruit, such as these hackberries, provided a large part of the diet of *Homo erectus*. They had to learn by trial and error which berries were good to eat and which were poisonous.

◀ WOOLLY RHINO
The *Homo erectus* people tried eating whatever meat they killed. They may have eaten large creatures like this woolly rhinoceros, hunting them in groups and sharing the meat.

▲ EAST TURKANA
Close to the mountains and lakes of Kenya, the site of East Turkana was one of the first homes of *Homo erectus* around 1.5 million years ago.

Homo erectus (upright man). The *Homo erectus* people were more advanced in other ways. They made better tools than the earlier hominids, and developed a handaxe, a pointed flint tool with two sharp cutting edges. Handaxes were useful for cutting meat, so the *Homo erectus* people could butcher animals more efficiently. As a result, they may have had more incentive to develop their technology, for example creating smaller tools such as cutting blades.

Homo erectus people probably had more advanced social skills than earlier hominids. They may even have developed a simple language which would have enabled them to talk to and cooperate with each other. This meant that they could perform tasks as a group, such as hunting large animals. They may have used fire in their hunting. Some archaeologists think that they lit bush fires to drive large animals into an ambush, where the creatures could be killed by a hunting group.

Fire also meant they could survive in colder

climates. This encouraged *Homo erectus* people to travel more widely than earlier hominids. Like *Homo habilis*, they were probably always on the move, making temporary camps as bases for hunting and gathering. Some of these homes may have been seasonal, occupied during the spring or summer when fruit, nuts and leaves were plentiful. But *Homo erectus* people also ventured beyond their native Africa, and were probably the first hominids to settle in Europe and Asia.

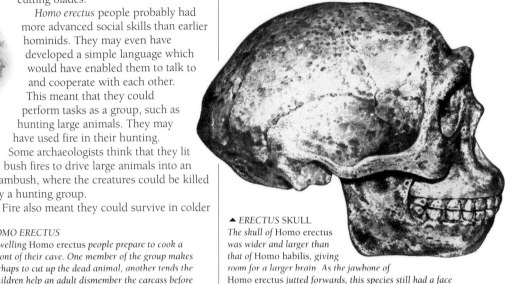

▲ ERECTUS SKULL
The skull of Homo erectus *was wider and larger than that of* Homo habilis, *giving room for a larger brain As the jawbone of* Homo erectus *jutted forwards, this species still had a face that looked more like an ape's than a modern human's.*

◀ HOMO ERECTUS
Cave-dwelling Homo erectus *people prepare to cook a meal in front of their cave. One member of the group makes stone tools, perhaps to cut up the dead animal, another tends the fire and two children help an adult dismember the carcass before it is cooked on the hot fire.*

Map

Sites of
◆ *Homo habilis*
● *Homo erectus*

N

White Nile
Omo
East Turkana Koobi Fora
R. Congo
L. Victoria
Olduvai Gorge
Indian Ocean
L. Tanganyika
AFRICA
L. Nyasa
Zambezi R.
MADAGASCAR
Sterkfontein
Atlantic Ocean

0   Kilometres   1500
0   Miles   1000

◀ EARLY HOMINID SITES, EAST AFRICA
Most of the early remains of *Homo habilis* and *Homo erectus* have come from a cluster of sites in Kenya and Tanzania in East Africa. The structure of the rocks there has helped preserve these fossils. For example, at Olduvai Gorge, hominid bones and tools were left by the shores of a lake, later to be covered by mud and volcanic lava and preserved. Still later, geological faults caused the rocks to move, making the fossils visible.

Key Dates

- 2.6MYA The Pleistocene period begins. Animals such as horses, cattle and elephants appear.

- 1.8MYA The earliest *Homo erectus* ever found comes from Georgia, in Eurasia. Variations between skulls found here have led some scientists to suggest that *Homo rudolfensis*, *Homo habilis* and *Homo erectus* are actually all the same species.

- 1.7 to 0.5MYA Some *Homo erectus* (known as Yuanmou Man) have now reached China.

- 1.6MYA *Homo erectus* camp at Chesowanya in the Kenya Rift Valley. This shows possible evidence of the use of fire.

The Spread of Hominids

AROUND 2 MILLION years ago, the world's wildlife was on the move. Many tropical animals started to travel northwards and eastwards. Gradually, they moved away from the sweltering jungles towards cooler parts of the globe. Food was often difficult to find for the early hominids, so the *Homo erectus* people followed the tropical animals to places with more moderate climates. In doing so, they covered great distances, from modern Africa as far as present-day Turkey, India, Sri Lanka, China and Java.

▲ A PLACE TO SHELTER
At Terra Amata, southern France, there is evidence that hominids made a camp with simple shelters. These small huts were made out of tree branches, weighted down with stones.

In Europe and Asia, *Homo erectus* people set up camps to which they returned year after year. One of the most famous of all is a series of caves at Zhoukoudien, China. Hominids stayed here for thousands of years (from about 700,000 to about 200,000 years ago), and archaeologists have found the remains of more than 40 *Homo erectus* people at the site. In the caves the archaeologists found a variety of tools, including choppers, scrapers, awls, points and cutters, most of which were made from quartz. The more recent in date the tools, the smaller and more finely worked they are. There is also evidence of fire in the Zhoukoudien caves. Similar remains have been found in *Homo erectus* sites in Europe and South-east Asia. They reveal a people who gathered leaves and berries, but were also cunning enough to hunt large mammals. The people moved around from one season to the next. If they could not find caves, they built simple shelters from branches and stones. They probably wrapped animal skins around themselves to keep warm in the winter.

One mystery is that many surviving *Homo erectus* skulls have had their bases removed. Some scientists think that this was done so that survivors could take out the brain. Perhaps these people were the first cannibals? There may be other reasons, such as to make containers to carry water.

Another puzzle is how *Homo erectus* died out. There are no *erectus* remains later than about 200,000 years ago. It is not known whether they perished because other hominids killed them, because their food supplies ran out, or because of ill health.

ANCIENT CULTURE

The *Homo erectus* people were able to produce a wider variety of tools, weapons and other items than the earlier hominids, although the only objects to survive in large numbers are their stone tools. They were skilled flintworkers, creating implements with razor-sharp edges for butchering meat, cutting plant food and scraping hides. They were probably also woodworkers, using wood to build simple shelters and make weapons such as spears and clubs.

◀ HANDAXE
The double-edged stone tool was *Homo erectus*' most common and useful implement. It fitted comfortably into the hand, and was easy to carry around. The two sharp edges could be used for cutting or chopping.

▶ PAINT
Stones marked with red ochre, a natural earth pigment, have been found at Becov in Bohemia, Europe. These finds date to 250,000 years ago, and suggest that people may have decorated their bodies or items that they made. They may have mixed the ochre with fat to make a form of paint.

◀ UPRIGHT MAN
Homo erectus people looked very like modern humans, except for their ape-like faces. But they were not as tall as most people today.

▼ ON THE HUNT
A group of Homo erectus *people have worked together to trap three elephants in a swamp. They are now about to move in on one of the animals, to attack it with wooden spears and clubs.*

Swampy ground

Wooden spear

Wooden club

▲ *HOMO ERECTUS* SITES
This successful hominid spread from Africa to both Asia and Europe. As well as sites in China, there are also many places in Europe with early hominid remains. In the case of most of the European sites, experts are uncertain whether the occupants were *Homo erectus* or an early form of our own species.

Key Dates

- 1.5MYA *Homo erectus* has reached Ubeidiya, by the Jordan and Yarmuk Rivers, Israel.

- 1.2MYA *Homo erectus* living in Olduvai Gorge, Tanzania.

- 1.1MYA *Homo erectus* settles in Europe.

- 1 to 0.7MYA *Homo erectus* is present in central Java. The hominids' long-distance movements show them adapting to different environments.

- 700,000–200,000BC *Homo erectus* living at Zhoukoudien Cave, near Beijing, China.

Neanderthals

▲ CAVE WOMAN
Neanderthals like this female may have been the first hominids to care for the sick and disabled. This prolonged the lives of individuals who would otherwise have met painful early deaths.

A TYPICAL CAVE MAN IS usually portrayed as a stocky creature with heavy bones, a thick ridge across the brows and a blank expression on his face. As far as we can tell, the Neanderthals, who lived in Europe and the Middle East 70,000 to 35,000 years ago, did look rather like this. They are our closest relatives among the hominids, and were intelligent with brains a similar size to our own. In fact, the Neanderthals were so similar to modern humans that some scientists place them in our own species, giving them a sub-species (*Homo sapiens neanderthalensis*). Others give them a species of their own (*Homo neanderthalensis*).

The Neanderthal people used their intelligence to develop tools and technology. Although their tools were still made of stone, they now had specialized items such as chisels and borers. They made these tools by chipping small flakes off carefully selected cores, or lumps, of flint. To chip off a flake of the right size and sharpness, a Neanderthal flintworker needed skill, patience and a very great deal of practice.

Some of the most fascinating evidence about the Neanderthals comes from their burial sites. Several of these have been discovered, from the Dordogne, France, to the Zagros Mountains in Iran. They reveal the bodies placed carefully in their graves. Items such as animal horns or bones were deliberately placed around them, probably as part of a burial ritual. Sites like these have led modern archaeologists to believe that the Neanderthals were the first hominids to develop burial ceremonies. The burial sites also provided a great deal of evidence that enabled scientists to work out what these people looked like, from

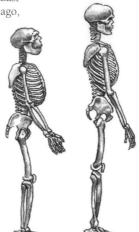

Neanderthal   Modern human

◀ SKELETONS
Stockily built and with a large head, Neanderthals were strong hominids with brains about as big as our own. Modern humans were taller and more upright.

NEANDERTHAL LIFE

During much of the Neanderthals' lifetime, Europe and Asia were in the grip of an ice age. The Neanderthals had to adapt to the cold, making clothes from skins and finding whatever shelter they could. This necessity, together with their large brains, made them inventive and adaptable.

chopper

scraper

borer

◀ NEANDERTHAL TOOLS
The Neanderthals developed different tools for scraping, cutting, butchering and boring holes in hides. These flint-working skills have been perfected over many generations.

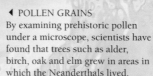

◀ POLLEN GRAINS
By examining prehistoric pollen under a microscope, scientists have found that trees such as alder, birch, oak and elm grew in areas in which the Neanderthals lived.

▲ NEANDERTHAL GRAVE
Skeletons from this grave at La Chapelle-aux-Saints in France, were found to be deformed and stooping. This could mean the people suffered from arthritis.

Flower offerings

Bone offerings

Animal horns

◀ BURIAL
A group of Neanderthals bury one of their dead. As mourners look on, two members of the group make offerings of pollen and flowers, which are placed carefully on and around the deceased's body. Animal horns are positioned to mark the grave. Rituals like this are the earliest known ceremonies.

their stocky build to the size of their heads and brains.

Some of the skeletons showed signs of bone diseases, such as arthritis, that must have developed over many years. Any individual who developed such a disease would not have been able to hunt and gather food. Other members of their family group must have fed them and looked after them. So as well as being intelligent, the Neanderthals may have been the first carers, helping relatives who were not able to fend for

themselves. The Neanderthals died out around 35,000 years ago, but it is not certain why. They may have perished through disease, or have been killed by Cro-Magnons, *Homo sapiens* who lived at the same time. New evidence is now being found to suggest that Neanderthals interbred with Cro-Magnon people.

▲ NEANDERTHAL SITES
The homeland of the Neanderthals stretched from France and Germany to Mesopotamia in the east. The eastern and western populations were separated during ice ages, but both groups produced similar tools and buried their dead in a similar way.

Key Dates

- 120,000BC Neanderthals living from Europe to Mesopotamia.

- 100,000–40,000BC Neanderthals develop stone tools for several different purposes.

- 100,000BC Neanderthals and *Homo sapiens* both living at Qafzeh, Israel.

- 50,000BC Remains of a burial site of this date found at Shanidar Cave, northern Iraq.

- 40,000BC Skull of this date found at Monte Circeo, Italy, had been smashed to remove the brain.

- 35,000BC Neanderthals die out.

Wise Man

▲ FIRE
The discovery of fire by Homo erectus was an enormous technological advance that Homo sapiens would have inherited.

B Y THE TIME OF THE Neanderthals, members of our own species, *Homo sapiens*, or "wise man" were also living in many parts of the world. In some places, Neanderthals and humans lived close together, which suggests that Neanderthals could not have been our direct ancestors. If they lived together, we could not have evolved from both species. If this is correct, who were they?

Homo sapiens may have evolved from *Homo erectus*, or from another similar hominid that has not yet been discovered. Hominid bones, found in sites all over the world, seem to share features of *Homo erectus* and *Homo sapiens*. Although similar in size to ourselves, these hominids have bone ridges above the eyes and flattened skulls rather than dome-like heads. They mostly date from around 150,000 to 120,000 years ago and are classified by archaeologists as archaic *Homo sapiens*.

Some remains of *Homo sapiens* date from not long after these "archaic" bones.

◀ HUMAN FORM
The first members of Homo sapiens *were similar in appearance to modern people, except that they were generally rather shorter in height. Their upright build made them well adapted to walking on two legs.*

▶ COUNTING STICK
Lengths of bone with small notches cut into them have been found at some Homo sapiens sites. These may have been counting devices, or an early form of writing. They may have been used to record a person's share of food.

◀ EARLY HUMAN SKULL
Early humans had broad skulls that contained large brains. Their faces were flat, so they did not have the ape-like appearance of hominids like Homo habilis *or the Neanderthals.*

THE EARLY HUNTERS
The search for food was the most important part of life for early *Homo sapiens*. Some groups hunted herds of antelopes on the grasslands. Others went into the hills after wild sheep and goats, or to the coast in search of seals and seafood.

◀ SEALS
For northern people who lived near the sea, such animals as seals were a valuable quarry. The animals provided a supply of meat, skins, bones (for tool-making) and blubber.

▲ BONE CARVING
Among the hominids, humans are the only artists. Early hunters liked to carve the creatures they chased, and animal bone was an ideal material – soft enough to carve but hard enough to last.

▲ SKULL, QAFZEH, ISRAEL
This is one of several skulls that have puzzled archaeologists. Experts are not sure if it is a Neanderthal or human. The latest tests suggest that the two species lived together and bred, so specimens like this may have had a parent from each species.

Some experts think humans evolved in one area of Africa and then spread gradually across the world. This idea, which archaeologists refer to as the "Out of Africa" theory is backed up by research based on DNA. This is the chemical in *Homo sapiens* bodies containing genes.

Other scientists believe that modern humans evolved separately in different parts of the world. For example, the population in South-east Asia could have descended from *Homo erectus* people on Java. Europeans could have evolved from hominids from the Middle East that had interbred with Neanderthals.

By 100,000 to 90,000 years ago, modern humans had evolved in southern and eastern Africa. From here they moved northwards, crossing the Sahara and reaching the Middle East. For thousands of years the Sahara was wetter than it is today, and it was covered with grasslands cropped by grazing mammals.

Hominids could cross this green Sahara with ease. By 75,000 years ago there were modern humans in eastern Asia. Later still, they would reach and settle in Europe.

As our ancestors spread across the globe, they settled in many different environments, from the warm African grasslands to the cold forests of northern Europe. They used their skills to adapt to each new place, using local materials to make clothes and huts, finding out about plants and animals, and learning how to fish. These early people were highly advanced compared to many species.

▶ PREPARING SKINS
A hunted animal was not just a source of meat. The skins of larger creatures were removed, scraped clean, and trimmed. Then they were made into clothes, coverings for shelters, and simple bags and containers.

◀ EARLY HUMAN SITES
By 35,000 years ago, early humans had spread across most of Africa. They developed different lifestyles and tools to cope with the different conditions and materials that they found. The people of northern Africa, for example, produced quite finely worked flint scrapers and handaxes, similar to those made by the Neanderthals in Europe. In the south, however, many of the tools were much less finely chipped stone points and scrapers, but they were still sharp and effective.

Map labels:
Mugharet el-'Aliya
Jebel Irhoud
Nazlet Khatir
Sahara Desert
AFRICA
Singa
Dire Dawa
Omo
L. Victoria
Homo sapiens sites, Africa
L. Tanganyika
Indian Ocean
L. Nyasa
Atlantic Ocean
Kalahari Desert
Pietersburg
Florisbad
Klasies River Mouth
N
0   Kilometres   2500
0   Miles   1500

Key Dates

- 150,000–120,000BC Archaic *Homo sapiens*, the most ancient form of our own species, appears.

- 100,000BC Modern humans begin to evolve in Africa.

- 100,000–70,000BC African sites south of the Sahara show signs of modern human occupation. *Homo erectus* is still alive, but is slowly replaced by *Homo sapiens*.

- 100,000–40,000BC The Sahara is cooler than today. Hominids cross it to reach northern Africa.

- 75,000BC Ice sheets in the northern hemisphere begin to get larger.

The First Europeans

LIFE WAS HARD FOR THE first humans who lived in Europe. The climate was colder than it is today. Food could be difficult to find and dangerous animals lurked in the forests. People survived by adapting, and by becoming skilled at making things, such as tools and shelters. Slowly, over many thousands of years, they perfected the essential skills for survival.

The early Europeans are often called Cro-Magnons, after a site in the Dordogne, France. Cro-Magnon people kept themselves warm by making clothes from animal skins. They sheltered in caves when they could, but natural shelter was not always easy to find. They learned how to make simple homes, using whatever materials they could find. Tree branches provided a framework, and was covered with turf or animal skins to keep out the wind and rain. Another solution was to make a framework from the massive bones of woolly mammoths they had killed.

The Cro-Magnons were skilled toolmakers. Their best and sharpest tools were made from flint, which they could work into small points for spearheads and knives. They also used materials such as bone and deer antler to make tools. Small pieces of bone could be carved to make pointed needles, and antlers could be adapted to make tools such as hammers.

Wood was another useful material. Small flakes of flint could be wedged into a twig to make a knife with a handle. The shafts of spears were also made of wood. It is likely that wood was used in many other ways too, such as making simple containers, but all evidence of this has perished with time.

The greatest achievement of the early European people was in their art. It ranged from sculpture to cave painting and tells us a great deal about everyday life. Pictures of

◀ KALEMBA ROCK SHELTER
About 35,000 years ago, hunter-gatherers used this natural shelter at Kalemba in Zambia. Like other similar shelters all over Africa, it provided a good resting place for people out hunting animals or searching for plants to eat.

GROWING SKILLS

The remains and tools of early *Homo sapiens* seem primitive, but early humans were in fact very intelligent. They were using their abilities to adapt to all sorts of different environments. Human language must also have been developing during this period, but unfortunately no record of it exists.

◀ BEZOAR GOAT
This species of goat was a popular quarry for hunters in the rocky, mountainous regions of the Middle East. Groups of hunters would drive a herd into a canyon. Then they could kill as many as they needed and share out the meat between a large number of people.

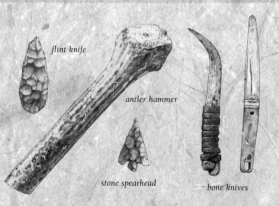

flint knife

antler hammer

stone spearhead

bone knives

▲ TOOLS
People learned to use several different materials to make tools. If no good stone was available, people used bone and antler for knives and points, as well as for tools like hammers.

◀ HUNTERS' CAMP
Early hunters covered quite long distances looking for food, but returned to regular camps at places where there was shelter and a water supply. A campsite could be used by members of the same tribe or group for thousands of years.

animals show the creatures they hunted, from woolly mammoths and rhinoceroses to wild oxen and deer. It is also possible to make out the skin clothing they wore. Female figurines suggest that the people worshipped a mother goddess or goddess of fertility. People who were intelligent enough to produce the art and tools of the early Europeans probably also had quite an advanced society. Although they lived in family-based bands, it is quite likely that these small groups may have come together at certain times. They probably joined together to hunt, or for religious ceremonies celebrating important times of the year.

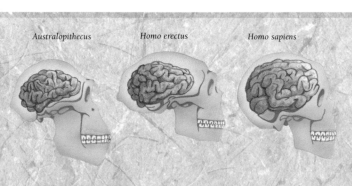

Australopithecus   *Homo erectus*   *Homo sapiens*

▲ THE GROWING BRAIN
Studies of early *Homo sapiens* show that their brains were similar in size to those of modern humans, and much bigger than those of the earlier hominids. The australopithecines, which were the size of modern chimpanzees, had brains with an average cubic capacity just over half that of *Homo erectus*. Even the brain of *Homo erectus* was little over half the total volume of *Homo sapiens*' brain. Human inventiveness, creativity, language and social skills are all the result of our bigger brains.

Key Dates

- 43,000BC *Homo sapiens* established in Bulgaria.
- 40,000BC Humans in western Europe living alongside Neanderthals.
- 35,000BC The Neanderthals die out. *Homo sapiens* is the only human form in Europe.
- 20,000BC French and Spanish flint-workers find out how to bake flints so they can be pressure flaked to make very fine shapes.
- 16,000–12,000BC Human settlement in Russia and Siberia. Mammoth-bone huts built at Mezhrich.
- 6000BC Europeans develop microliths, tools made of tiny fragments of flint.

The Ice Age

▲ CARVING
This head is carved from a piece of mammoth tusk, a material often used for sculpture during the Ice Age.

THE EARTH'S WEATHER IS ALWAYS changing. For the last two million years, the temperature of the planet has see-sawed up and down. This has produced a series of warm periods with cold ice ages in between. The last of these ice ages reached its peak about 18,000BC. The time around this peak (30,000 to 12,000BC) is so important in human history that it is always known as the Ice Age.

Humans had spread over much of the world by the beginning of the most recent Ice Age. All that time, the ice sheets had pushed down from the north, covering huge areas of the globe. Places such as Scandinavia, Siberia and northern Britain, became unfit for humans.

During this period, much of northern Europe was covered with sparse tundra. Large parts of Spain, Greece and the Balkans covered in forests. The area north of the Black Sea in Russia was a vast grassland. These varied habitats were a challenge to early people, and they had to adapt to different conditions. Big-game hunters moved across the Russian plains. Hunter-fishers lived on the tundra and at the edge of the ice sheets. Hunters and food gatherers took shelter in the forests. People had to devise different tools, hunting techniques and social skills to suit these varied lifestyles.

Ice Age tools are more varied than those of previous peoples. People in the Ice Age still used stone for their knives and choppers. But they used more bone and

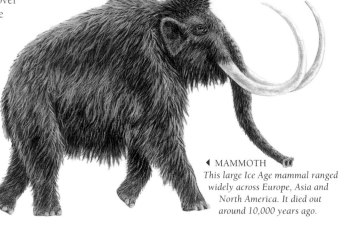

◀ MAMMOTH
This large Ice Age mammal ranged widely across Europe, Asia and North America. It died out around 10,000 years ago.

ICE AGE LIFE

The Ice Age made life difficult in many places. The cold was not just uncomfortable, it meant that some food plants could not survive. In addition, many areas had few or no trees, meaning that people had no wood to make shelters. These difficulties forced people to find new ways of life. They had to experiment with new foods (such as fish) and new materials (such as, bones and antlers).

▼ MAKING FIRE
In a cold, damp climate, fire became even more important as a source of warmth. Making fire by rubbing sticks together to create a spark may have spread across Europe during the Ice Age.

◀ REINDEER
There are many surviving tools, harpoons and carvings made from antler. This shows that reindeer-like animals were hunted across Europe during the Ice Age. Reindeer provided tasty, nutritious meat, as well as hides, bone and antler.

▲ HARPOON POINTS
Ice Age hunters used harpoons for killing animals such as seals and for fishing in the rivers for salmon. The points took a long time to carve from deer antler and were prized possessions.

▶ MAMMOTH HUNTING
Large, fierce and with two powerful tusks, woolly mammoths were an awesome sight for the people of the Ice Age. But these dangerous creatures were such a good source of meat, skins, bones and ivory that the people risked injury or even death hunting and trapping them.

antler than before. They discovered how to use antler to make strong handles for stone blades and axeheads. They carved bone to make needles, which were essential to sew together hides and furs for warm clothes.

People still hunted large mammals such as the woolly mammoth. They also learned how to track and hunt animals that live in herds, such as reindeer. This gave them a rich source of hides, meat and antlers.

Because resources were scarce, Ice Age people probably became the first traders, swapping food and materials. Flints and furs, for example, could be traded for food in times of shortage. People moved about more, they met other groups and they probably found out about new sources of food. Contact with other tribes was an aid to survival. When different groups met it became necessary to have a leader to act as spokesman. This was also a time when personal adornment first became important. A bone pendant or bright body paint could mark out the leader of a group.

▲ ICE AGE WORLD
Lower sea levels meant that the world's continents were larger during the Ice Age, and some landmasses that are now separate were joined together. But the ice sheets in Europe, Asia and the Americas made vast areas of this land unfit for human life.

Key Dates

- 32,000–28,000BC Aurignacian culture in western Europe produces flint scrapers and sharpened blades.

- 30,000–12,000BC Main period of last Ice Age.

- 24,000BC Hunter-gatherers in Europe build permanent dwellings.

- 20,000BC Hunters in western Europe develop spears and spear-throwers. Hunters in Poland use mammoth-tusk boomerangs.

- 18,000BC Peak of Ice Age.

- 18,000–12,500BC People settled near Kebara Cave, Israel, make grinding stones. This suggests they were gathering and processing grains.

Images of the Ice Age

▲ MAMMOTH CARVING
Ice Age art was not always realistic, and carvers often made striking, stylized shapes. In the case of this mammoth, the shape of the animal reflects the shape of the bone from which it is carved.

THE PREHISTORIC CAVE paintings of Europe show a wide variety of creatures. These include groups of wild horses, herds of reindeer and wild oxen, wild cats, birds and mammoths. The animals are shown in action, galloping and running across the cave walls as if they are being chased by human hunters. They are dramatic action pictures, yet they were produced in dark, damp conditions in chilly caves.

Ice Age artists also made sculptures and figures from clay. They engraved cave walls and carved antlers and mammoth tusks into models of animals.

The paintings and sculptures are often hidden so deep in underground caverns that many of them were not rediscovered until the 1900s. It is not known why the paintings were hidden away like this. In fact, no one really knows why the pictures were produced at all. Most experts agree that there was probably some religious reason for the

paintings. They may have been used in magic ceremonies designed to help hunters, or to promote fertility. Sometimes there are several different outlines in the same place, one drawn over another. This makes some cave paintings and engravings very difficult to see. Experts have spent many hours redrawing them in

▲ PAINTING TECHNIQUES
Artists used brushes or pads of animal hair when painting on cave walls. They sometimes put on the paint with their fingers, or created a bold outline by drawing with charcoal.

ICE AGE ART

Because we do not know why Ice Age artists made their pictures and sculptures, it is difficult to decide what their work means. It does show how important animals and the natural world were to them. The cave paintings show the kind of animals these people hunted and ate, and also which creatures they thought were the most powerful. These images, and the small carvings of the time, also provide some clues about Ice Age beliefs.

◄ ANTLER SPEAR-THROWER
A spear-thrower helped a hunter hurl his spear faster and farther than he could unaided by acting as an extension of his arm. This made it easier to kill swift creatures such as deer. Hunters prized their spear-throwers, which were usually made of antler. This material lent itself to carving, and spear-throwers are often beautifully decorated. Swift-running animals like the horse shown here were popular subjects.

◄ VENUS FIGURINE
Carvings of female figures, with their hips and bellies enlarged, have often been found at Ice Age sites. Archaeologists think they are fertility goddesses, and so have named them "Venus" figures, after the Roman goddess of love.

▶ IVORY HEAD
This female head from France, carved in ivory, shows a goddess. Goddess figures have been found in most areas of Europe, from France to Russia, so goddesses were probably the most important deities in Ice Age religion.

▲ CAVE PAINTING, LASCAUX
The caves at Lascaux, France, contain perhaps the most brilliant of all the known prehistoric paintings. Discovered in 1940, they show a variety of animals, including reindeer and horses. These finely drawn, bright paintings began to show signs of damage during the 1960s because the atmosphere in the caves was affected by so many visitors. The caves were closed to the public, who now visit a replica called Lascaux II.

their notebooks to try to make the outlines clearer. For the prehistoric artist, the act of making the image seems to have been more important than the finished result. Perhaps the actual process of painting or engraving was part of a religious ceremony.

Ice Age painters used chalk to make white, charcoal for black, ochre, a kind of earth, for yellow, and iron oxide for red. Sometimes artists used minerals that they could heat to make other pigments. These were mixed with water and applied with fur pads, animal-hair brushes or just with the artist's fingers.

Another technique involved spitting the paint out of the mouth or a reed to make a simple spray effect. The artists used oil lamps to light the caves and sometimes built crude wooden frameworks to gain extra height while working. With these simple techniques, Ice Age artists produced images that were surprisingly complex for such a simple society.

◄ ANTELOPE
This painting from a cave at Font de Gaume, France, shows the skill of the ancient artists. They caught the outline of the creature's head and horns, and cleverly shaded the animal's hide to create a sense of its bulk.

▶ MAKING PAINT
Artists found their pigments in the earth and rocks. They mixed soils and minerals that they found with a medium such as water or animal fat. This produced a type of spreadable paint. They could also draw directly on to the rock surface with pieces of charcoal (burnt wood) or chalk.

iron oxide

brushstrokes   chalk   charcoal

◄ LAMP
Many cave paintings are hidden in dark, underground caverns. The artists needed light to see what they were doing, so they used fires, flaming torches or stone lamps like this one. The animal fat was burnt in the lamps, to give a bright, but rather smelly, flame. Several hundred Ice Age lamps have been found by archaeologists.

Key Dates

- 30,000BC Earliest European cave art.

- 30,000BC European musicians make flutes from lengths of animal bone.

- 23,000BC First cave paintings made in the Dordogne, France.

- 23,000BC Venus figurines made in France and central Europe.

- 18,000–8000BC Main period of cave painting in caves at Lascaux, France, and Altamira, Spain.

- 16,000BC Antler and bone carving reaches its peak. Finely engraved and carved spear points and spear-throwers made.

- 11,000BC Cave painting ends.

The First Australians

▲ ENGRAVINGS
These patterns were cut into rocks at Panaramitee, Australia, thousands of years ago. They may be the world's oldest rock engravings.

DURING THE ICE AGE, the sea level was much lower than it is today. The channels separating Australia from islands such as Timor in Indonesia were far narrower. As a result, groups of islanders took to the sea in bamboo rafts or simple boats in search of fish and shellfish. Some time before 32,000 years ago some Indonesians found themselves on the coast of what is now Australia. No one knows whether they deliberately looked for new land, or whether they were blown off-course on one of their fishing trips. They moved inland and became the first humans to inhabit the Australian continent.

The remains of early settlement in Australia are quite patchy. The

people were spread over a wide area and must have covered vast distances both by sea and on foot. Stone tools, hearths, shell debris, fish bones and other remnants point to a scattered population between 32,000 and 24,000 years ago. Important sites include Devil's Lair Cave near Perth, Western Australia, a rock shelter near the Cleland Hills in Northern Territory and Koonalda Cave in South Australia.

At Devil's Lair, archaeologists found several items that were probably used in religious ceremonies. There were some stone plaques and a pit with human teeth that had been removed by sharp blows. At Koonalda Cave, the inhabitants engraved lines on the rock walls. Native Australians carried on making rock engravings into the 1900s. The finds dating from prehistoric times show how far back a rich native Australian culture goes.

Many early Australian sites were occupied for thousands of years. This can also make exact dating

▶ DUG-OUT CANOE
Early sailors, like the people who first crossed from South-east Asia to Australia, may have hollowed out and smoothed wooden logs to make simple dug-out canoes.

A SCATTERED PEOPLE
The first Australians walked vast distances across their country to find food and good campsites. When they settled, they spread out thinly across the country. Sites in the south, which were well away from their original landing places, seem to have been most popular. The settlement process probably took place very slowly, spreading across the country over thousands of years.

◀ NECKLACE
People wore necklaces made of shells and animal teeth. Ornamentation like this may have been a sign that the wearer was an important person. Such necklaces have been found in Asia as well as Australia. This indicates that the two regions were linked by a common people.

◀ HAND STENCILS
Stencils like this were probably made by spitting paint around and over the artist's hand. This type of art has been produced in Australia since at least 22,000BC. The images, which are on the walls of rock shelters in southern and eastern Australia, show the importance of art to the island continent's earliest people.

of the art and artefacts difficult for archaeologists. One rock shelter, at Puritjarra, was used for nearly 7,000 years.

People had reached the island of Tasmania at the south-east tip of Australia by 32,000 years ago. They remained there even when the final Ice Age was at its coldest, when much of the island was covered by tundra and grassland. They lived in caves and rock shelters, and survived by hunting the local animals, mainly the kangaroo and the wallaby. The new Tasmanians developed their own style of art. They painted hand stencils on cave walls, and made tools

from a natural form of glass that they discovered in a crater formed by a meteorite from space.

The native people of Australia developed a lifestyle long ago that has lasted in some places to the present day. Over the millenia they adapted as their environment changed, from the chill Ice Age to the hot, dry climate of today.

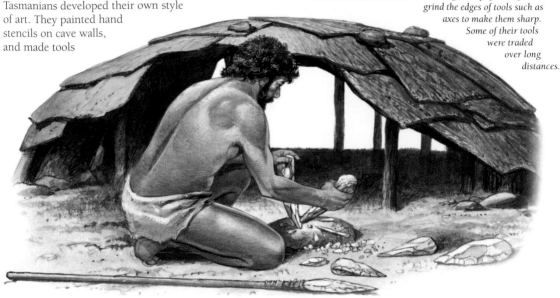

▼ MAKING TOOLS
Early Australians became expert stoneworkers. They could chip away stones to make tools that were the right shape for the job and grind the edges of tools such as axes to make them sharp. Some of their tools were traded over long distances.

◀ EXPLORERS' MAP
Because the sea level was lower, larger pieces of land were above water, so the first people to travel to Australia had a shorter sea journey than navigators would have to make today. They probably crossed from places such as Java or the Celebes, sailing from island to island until they reached the north-western coast of Australia. Even for such short trips, they needed to be good sailors and navigators. They probably built up their sailing skills over many years fishing off the South-east Asian coasts.

Key Dates

- 30,000BC Human settlement of Australia probably begins.

- 29,000BC People are living in Tasmania, which is linked to the Australian mainland by a land bridge.

- 25,000BC Puritjarra Rock Shelter, near the Cleland Hills, Northern Territory, is occupied.

- 24,000BC Signs of human occupation near Lake Mungo, New South Wales.

- 22,000BC Traces of human settlement at Koonalda Cave, on the Nullaboor Plain, South Australia.

- 10,000BC The population of native Australians is about 300,000 people.

Early Americans

THE FIRST AMERICANS probably came from the extreme north tip of Asia, which is now Siberia. In the Ice Age the two continents were connected by a land bridge. The first peoples to cross this narrow neck of land found themselves in North America's bleakest, coldest spot. There would have been little vegetation. Most of their food came from hunting and fishing. They were well prepared for this, because the climate in Siberia was similar to that in North America. Many moved south in search of better weather and more plentiful food.

Archaeologists disagree about exactly when the first Americans arrived. The earliest firm evidence of

▲ THE JOURNEY FROM SIBERIA
It was a long, hard journey from Siberia across the land bridge to North America. We do not know what made people start this journey, but perhaps the harsh Ice Age conditions made them want to look for a place where food, warmth and comfort were easier to find.

humans dates to between 15,000 and 12,000 years ago. However, in the same period, there is more widespread evidence for a hunting people who lived in central North America. Archeologists called them the

THE GREAT MIGRATION
How do we know that the first Americans came from Siberia? One clue lies in the way the early Americans made tools and weapons. Many chipped tiny flint blades from bigger lumps of stone. They jammed these flints into grooves along the edge of a piece of bone to make a spearhead. Spearheads with this design have been found in both Siberia and North America.

▲ CLOVIS POINTS
North American mammoth hunters fitted these finely worked sharp stone points to their spears. They made these points out of several different types of stone.

▲ WEAVING
A few fragments of twine have survived at Guitarrero Cave, Peru, to show that people could weave 10,000 years ago. These pieces may have been part of a bag or similar container.

▼ MAMMOTH TUSKS
These fossilized tusks are among many mammoth remains preserved at the Hot Springs mammoth site, South Dakota. They show that the first American hunters were catching the same quarry as their ancestors in Asia.

Clovis people. They left behind finely worked flint spearheads, now called Clovis points after the city where the tools were found. These have been found at several places near the bones of large mammals such as mammoth and bison, particularly in Arizona and New Mexico. Clovis people probably hunted solitary animals, driving them into swamps where they could be killed.

As the ice melted, the large mammals became extinct, although no one really knows why. The Clovis people vanished as a variety of new environments, from vast woodlands to arid deserts, developed in North America. People learned to adapt to each environment, evolving into distinct societies, whose lifestyles changed little until recent centuries.

In South America there is also evidence for human settlement by 12,000 years ago. At Monte Verde, Chile, the cremated remains of humans have been found in a cave. This site also contains remains of two rows of huts with wooden frames that supported a covering of animal skins. The huts had clay-lined pits for cooking and there were larger, communal hearths outside.

It is just possible that human life began in South America much earlier than the

◀ SPEARHEAD
Spears, with notched bone spearheads bound tightly to wooden shafts with animal sinews, were used by early American hunters.

▶ MONTE VERDE
The huts at Monte Verde, Chile, made of wood covered with skins, provide the earliest evidence in America for man-made shelters. The remains were preserved in peaty soil, along with items such as a wooden bowl and digging sticks.

huts at Monte Verde. At Pedra Furada Rock Shelter, Brazil, there are areas of painted rock which some scientists date to around 32,000 years ago. Not all authorities agree with this dating, or with similar dates for some of the stone tools found at Monte Verde. If the early dates are correct, it is likely that settlement also began much earlier in North America, but that the people left no surviving remains.

◀ NEW ARRIVALS
The first North Americans worked their way between the two main ice sheets. The Bering Land Bridge was created between Siberia and Alaska because the sea level was some 100m/300ft lower than it is today. Some people may also have come along the west coast on boats or rafts, stopping every so often along the edge of the Cordilleran Ice Sheet. When they finally reached beyond the ice, they found a vast empty land. Some people quickly moved east and west, while others pushed on further south.

Key Dates

- 13,000BC Hunters from Siberia cross the Bering Land Bridge.

- 12,500BC Humans at Meadowcroft Rock Shelter, Pittsburgh, Pennsylvania – the earliest known settlement in North America.

- 11,000BC People living at Monte Verde in southern Chile.

- 9000BC Clovis people hunting on the Great Plains.

- 8000BC Human settlers are accompanied by dogs.

- 7500BC The people of the Sloan site, Arkansas, bury their dead. This cemetery is the earliest discovered in North America.

The Thaw Begins

FISH CARVING
Stone carvings of fishes, like this one, were found at Lepenski Vir on the River Danube. They may have portrayed a fish god.

A T THE END OF THE ICE AGE there was a massive change in the world's climate. In much of Europe, Asia and North America, the ice melted, making the sea level rise and causing floods in flat areas near the sea. The land bridge between Siberia and Alaska disappeared, cutting off North America from Asia. Britain, which had been joined to Europe, was now cut off by the North Sea. Large areas of land were lost around the coasts of Denmark and Sweden.

The change must have been terrifying at first. Many people fled the floods to settle in new areas. Their way of life changed. At the same time, the warmer weather transformed the landscape. In many places, ice and tundra were

▶ THATCHED TENTS
The Middle Stone Age settlement of Lepenski Vir was home to around 100 hunting and fishing people. They lived in tent-like houses made of wooden poles which were probably covered with thatch.

replaced by thick woods of birch and mixed forests in northern Europe, and deciduous woods in the south. People soon realized that these changes gave them new types of food. Among the woods lived animals such as wild pig and deer. Near the coast there were seals, waterfowl and, in many places, shellfish. Food was more plentiful because the climate was warmer.

People developed new methods of hunting and fishing. These new techniques were more efficient than previous methods, so they did not have to move around so much to hunt for food. They set up special camps where food of a certain type was plentiful, or where they could mine flint to make their tools and weapons.

Most settlements in this period were by rivers or near the sea, where the people could usually rely on a good food supply. Rivers and coastal waters were the highways of the Stone Age. Rivers provided a way to get through the dense forests. People paddled along in their dug-out canoes, perhaps exchanging valuable goods, such as furs or flint tools, with other people they met along the way.

LIFE DURING THE THAW

As the ice melted, some people moved inland, but for many the sea was too useful to leave behind. Such shellfish as oysters and whelks supplied tasty, nourishing food, so many people returned to the coast for at least part of the year.

scrapers, blades and points from Star Carr

FOREST FRUITS
The trees and shrubs of the new woodlands and forest edges yielded fruits such as blackberries to feed European gatherers.

▲ WILD BOAR
This woodland animals thrived in Europe after the thaw. It became a preferred target for many European hunters.

▲ TOOLS FROM STAR CARR
Hunter-gatherers camped regularly at Star Carr, near a lake in Yorkshire, England, at the end of the final Ice Age. They left behind many stone tools, such as scrapers, which they must have used to prepare animal skins, and smaller sharp cutting blades for butchering meat.

The new lifestyle meant that the people who lived in Europe after the Ice Age were on the whole better fed and more comfortable than their ancestors. They were more settled, so they had time to develop more advanced toolmaking skills. This made them more successful still. As a result, many more of their children began to survive to become adults. The total number of people began to rise and the population began to spread, finding better places to settle and new sources of food.

▼ PINCEVANT

These round tents, held up with wooden poles, were the summer homes of people at Pincevant, France, at the end of the final Ice Age. All that was left to show modern archaeologists that tents had been pitched there were the rings of stones that had held the edges in place, together with hearths and some animal bones.

Spread of broadleaved forest
- up to 11,000BC
- 11,000-8,500BC
- 8,500-7,500BC
- 7,500-5,000BC

N

Scandinavia

EUROPE

Atlantic Ocean

Mediterranean Sea

AFRICA

0   Kilometres   800
0   Miles   500

◀ SPREADING FORESTS

As the ice melted, forests spread slowly across Europe, covering the area in broadleaved trees. The spread of the forests began in the south, working its way north over a period of about 6000 years towards Poland and Scandinavia, where mixed conifer and broadleaved forests grew. This new pattern of forests and woodland provided large areas of Europe with their typical landscape, one which survived for thousands of years. It still survives in some parts of Germany, central Europe and Scandinavia.

Key Dates

- 13,000BC The ice thaws, sea levels rise and lowland areas flood.

- 11,000BC The dog is domesticated in the Middle East.

- 8000BC Temperatures reach roughly their present levels in Europe.

- 8000BC The Mesolithic period, or Middle Stone Age, begins in Europe.

- 7500BC Red deer hunters settle at Star Carr, Yorkshire, England.

- 6500BC Britain is cut off from Europe.

- 5500BC Denmark is cut off from the rest of Scandinavia.

- 5000BC Deciduous forests cover much of Europe.

A Better Food Supply

▲ MATTOCK HEAD
Deer antler was a good material to make a heavy tool such as a mattock. This was used by gatherers for loosening soil and cutting away plant roots for food.

MANY THINGS CHANGED IN North America at the end of the Ice Age. People were suddenly much freer to go where they wanted in search of food and raw materials. They found a range of different regions, from the grassy Great Plains to the drier areas of the southwest, all of which could be settled. At first they moved south, following the mammals, and hunting them with their stone-pointed spears. They also spread out east and west across the continent, finding more and better sources of flint for tools and weapons. Archaeologists have traced many of the stone tools to where they were first made. Some of them were carried hundreds, or even thousands, of kilometres, which shows how far the hunters journeyed.

It took several thousand years for the climate and vegetation to settle down into the pattern that still exists today. As this happened, species such as mammoths became extinct, and people turned to smaller animals for food. The hunters also developed lighter, more accurate spears, which meant that they could bring down game without having to ambush it first. On the grasslands there were still large creatures, such as bison. These provided hunters with a number of different products, such as meat to eat, hides to make leather and bones for tools. From around 9000BC, the people of the plains, like those of other regions in North America, began to develop a lifestyle that would continue, with very little change, for many thousands of years.

The people of Asia, like the Europeans, took advantage of a better, more reliable food supply. They were healthier and their population began to increase. However, they still relied on many of their old techniques for survival and shelter. In some places, people started to settle down and build permanent huts. Elsewhere, hunters still built temporary shelters from branches or mammoth bones and hides.

As the ice thawed in Africa and the Middle East, many areas

◀ ANTLER HEADDRESS
Archaeologists found this unusual antler headdress at the British Stone Age site of Star Carr, Yorkshire. It may have been used in a religious ceremony or as a disguise when hunting deer.

HUNTERS' WEAPONS
By the late Ice Age, weapons had improved. Although spearheads and harpoon points were still made of stone, antler and bone, they were carefully carved so they worked well whenever they were used. When food was scarce, a hunter could not afford to lose his quarry because a blunt spear allowed an animal to escape.

▶ ANTLER POINTS
Hunters used deer antler to make deadly harpoon points. By carving away notches along one edge, then sharpening one or both ends, they made a barbed point. The advantage of this was that when a weapon was thrown at an animal it went in easily, but would not slip out as the creature ran away. Barbed points are still used by Arctic hunters.

◀ REPAIRING SPEARS
Stone spearheads such as North American Clovis points are virtually everlasting. But wooden spear shafts often break or split, so hunters had to fit their points to new ones. They fixed the points by splitting the shaft, jamming in the head, and binding animal sinew around the joint.

▼ HOME OF SKIN AND BONE
Like the people of the Ukraine, Siberian hunters built homes out of large animal bones and tusks, covered with skins and reinforced with timber if they could find it. Stones weighted down the skins on the ground. The people may have learned how to build these tents in the Ukraine before moving eastwards to their new homes.

that had been desert were covered with vegetation. Plants began to flourish in the Nile Valley and the eastern Mediterranean. This was a land of wild grasses, and people began to gather their seeds, grind them into flour and make bread to eat. One group of people who we know did this were the Natufians, a people who lived near the Wadi en-Natuf, in what is now Israel.

These cereal gatherers were learning a lot of vital information about the various kinds of corn. For example, which provided the tastiest grain, when best to harvest them and the most effective tools to use. Later, they would put this knowledge to good use, changing to a settled way of life and becoming some of the world's first farmers.

Removing flakes from the flint.

Carefully shaping the edge. The hand is protected by animal skin.

Putting the point into the cleft stick.

◀ MAKING A POINT
A hunter hit a lump of flint with an antler hammer, removing bits from either side until the piece was the right thickness and shape. Then he took a pointed piece of antler and worked around the edge of the point, removing chips to produce a razor-sharp edge. Next he put the point in a cleft stick and wrapped it around with sinews to protect it. He then hit the base of the point with his hammer, to remove a flake and make a fluted shape to fit the shaft.

Key Dates

- 10,000BC The Natufian culture develops in western Asia. Its people build round stone huts, herd goats, and gather wild emmer wheat.

- 9000BC Population levels begin to rise in Asia, encouraging people to take up new lifestyles such as herding.

- 9000BC People in America begin to hunt a wider range of smaller mammals. At the same time, a more settled lifestyle begins to evolve.

- 5000BC Tools in America become more specialized, and grindstones are created for processing plant foods.

- 3500BC People in North America begin to live in permanent villages.

Rock Paintings

UNLIKE CAVE PAINTINGS, which were hidden deep underground, rock paintings were made on rocks and cliff faces out in the open air. Some of these drawings are engraved into the rock with a sharp stone tool. Others are painted with natural pigments in a similar way to the cave paintings of the final Ice Age. Rock art occurs all over the world, from Africa to Australia. The drawings are usually easier to find than the cave paintings of western Europe, and in some places they are quite common. Some rock drawings date from 8000BC, but others were made as recently as the 1800s. The more recent pictures are often similar in style to the ancient images. This makes them difficult to date, but it also shows how the art and lifestyles of many peoples altered little until

▲ SAN HUNTERS
This modern rock painting by the San people, or bushmen, from the Kalahari Desert shows hunters chasing their quarry. It is one of many recent rock paintings done in a style similar to that used in prehistoric times.

the early 1900s. Rock art can tell us a great deal about the lives of the people who created it – especially the creatures they hunted and farmed, because animals appear in these paintings more than any other subject.

Some of the most interesting and best preserved rock art is found in Africa. In the Saharan region, the types of animals in the pictures show how different the area was compared with the desert of today. After the final Ice Age, when the Sahara was covered in grasslands and dotted with oases

◀ HAND PAINTING
One method used by rock artists was to take some paint into the mouth and spit it on to the rock to produce a stencil of the hand.

THE VARIETY OF ROCK ART

The most common subjects in rock art are animals, people and patterns. Although the subjects are similar, the style of the pictures can vary greatly around the world. Some, like the paintings of the Sahara, are very realistic. Others, like the human figures of South America, are more like symbols than pictures of real people.

▶ GAZELLES
Artists from the Tassili Massif in the Sahara drew these gazelles. They were painted over 6,000 years ago. This was before the beginning of farming, when Saharan artists were still drawing the animals they hunted for food.

▲ BISON
The people of Bhimbetka, India, made rock drawings of animals for thousands of years. Bison, antelope and deer, as well as people, were popular subjects, and some, like this example, were filled in with delicate abstract patterns.

▲ HUMAN FIGURE
This rock engraving of a stylized person comes from Venezuela. No one knows what the circles and curves around it are, but they may be symbols of the Moon or Sun.

or shallow lakes, the area was home to wild oxen and gazelles. The local people hunted these animals and drew them on the walls of their shelters. After about 6000BC, they began to draw domestic cattle, showing that the change from hunting to farming near the oases happened around this time.

Other African paintings, such as those of the San people of what is now the Kalahari Desert, show hunters chasing their quarry. They are also shown fishing from their boats and gathering food. Pictures like these are almost certainly more than just decorations on shelter walls. The hunting pictures were probably produced as part of a ceremony performed before the hunt. The people hoped that drawing a successful hunt would make their own hunt turn out well. In a similar way, a picture of a group of men dancing around an antelope was probably intended to transfer some of the real animal's strength to the men of the tribe.

Paintings with a religious or ceremonial purpose are even more common in Australia. Stories of how the world was created have always been important to the native Australians. Each tribe has its own ancestor, usually an animal that is linked with some special part of the landscape. One Australian myth, which tells how the world was made, describes the way in which the rainbow serpent, who came from the sea, slithered on to the shore and created the landscape as he snaked his way inland. Rainbow serpents first begin to appear in rock paintings made by native Australians some 6,000 years ago.

▲ SPIRIT BEINGS

Australian rock painting represents spirits that were believed to be the ancestors of a particular tribe. They formed the focal point of the tribe's religious beliefs. The ancestors of different groups took different forms. Some were said to be animals, others were features of the landscape. They were all regarded with the deepest reverence by their people, as they are today.

◄ HUNTERS

Many rock drawings were made by hunting peoples, like these figures by the San people of the Kalahari Desert. The painted hunters seem to be moving with great agility, almost like dancers.

▶ LEAF

Depictions of plants are rarer in rock art than animals or people. They do occur occasionally, as in this Australian example from a site in the Northern Territory. Plant pictures may be linked to religion or the ancestors, or may have been done simply to create a decorative effect.

Key Dates

- 25,000BC Early inhabitants of Australia may be developing rock art.

- 20,000BC Rock artists may already be active in some parts of Africa.

- 11,000BC Rock art in central India shows hunters and prey.

- 8500BC The earliest rock paintings found in Saharan Africa portray wild animals.

- 8000BC The main period of cave painting ends in Europe. Rock art on cliffs and in shallower caves becomes common.

- 6000BC Saharan rock artists depict cattle, reflecting the change to the herding of livestock.

The First Farmers

▲ WHEAT
Finding a staple crop that provides basic energy needs is an important step in farming. Wheat is one of the most common. Others are millet, rice and maize.

HUNTERS AND GATHERERS were highly skilled at finding food. However, their success was dependent on the weather, local conditions and luck. If the weather turned bad, or the local supplies ran out, people faced starvation. Around 11,000 years ago, a group of people in the Middle East changed this. They began to produce their own food by farming. It was one of the most important developments in the history of humankind.

Farming gave people control over their food supply. They did not have to wander through the countryside looking for food any longer. They could settle in one place, and as a result began to build stronger, more comfortable houses than before. Farming also offered a more reliable supply of food, although in years when the harvest was bad, people had to return to gathering for a while.

The first farmers lived at the eastern end of the Mediterranean (now Israel, Palestine and Syria) and in an upland region north of the

River Tigris in what now forms parts of Iran and Iraq. This region has more rain than the surrounding plains and grasses such as wheat and barley grow there naturally. Because of its climate and its shape on the map, the area is now known as the Fertile Crescent.

The people of the Fertile Crescent had gathered wheat seeds for thousands of years. They knew which types grew most vigorously and produced the best grain. By about 9000BC, they realized that they could plant these grasses and harvest them. At around the same time, they started to herd the wild sheep and goats. These animals provided milk and wool as well as meat. During the next 3,000 years, people also began to keep livestock, pigs and cattle.

In good years, farming gave the people of the Fertile Crescent more food than they

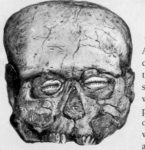

◀ STONE TOWER
Jericho's tallest building was a stone tower. No one knows why the tower was built. It could have been a watchtower, or it might have had some religious purpose.

THE FARMERS' WORLD

Although farming created a lot of hard work, the people of the first agricultural villages did not spend all their time in the fields. In many places, they developed quite complex religious beliefs and ceremonies. They produced new styles of art, including sculptures made from plaster and pottery decorated with striking abstract designs of lines and rectangles. They also started to make larger baskets and clay containers for storing surplus corn.

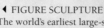

◀ FIGURE SCULPTURE
The world's earliest large-scale human sculptures were produced in Ain Ghazal, Jordan. They were shaped in lime plaster over a skeleton of straw bundles. The eyes were outlined with dark paint. No one knows why they were made.

▶ SPOUTED BOWL
From the early farming site at Khirokitia, Cyprus, came this decorated pottery bowl. It was buried in the grave of an eight-year-old child, and was obviously a well-loved object, as it had been repaired before the burial.

◀ PLASTERED SKULL
Around 6000BC, the religious ceremonies of Jericho involved the use of human skulls. The skulls were covered with plaster, which was shaped to copy the person's ears, nose, mouth and other facial features. Cowrie shells were placed in the eye sockets, and teeth were added.

could eat. They stored the surplus in grain bins or baskets, and traded it for materials, for tools, or items such as pots and furniture.

Gradually, the farmers and craftworkers became rich. They built more and bigger houses clustered together. These groups of houses developed into small towns. The houses were made of mud-bricks, providing warmth in winter while staying cool in summer. One of the first of these towns was Jericho,

built near a spring north of the Dead Sea. The land around the town was good both for growing crops and for grazing herds and flocks of animals, and soon Jericho became prosperous. It was not long before other towns were built in this area.

As farming spread further afield, it was not very long before other regions began to produce their food in a similar way, and the pattern of human life had changed for ever.

◀ EARLY FARMER
To begin with, farming was difficult, back-breaking work – even more so than the toil of hunting and gathering. There were only stone and wooden hand tools to work the soil. Seed had to be scattered by hand and harvesting had to be done in the hot sun with a simple stone sickle.

◀ FARMING IN THE FERTILE CRESCENT
To begin with, farming was most successful where there were light soils. These could be easily worked with basic hand tools. There also had to be plants growing wild that were suitable for cultivating. From its beginnings near the Persian Gulf, the River Euphrates and the eastern Mediterranean, farming spread gradually outwards. Egypt to the south and Turkey and Greece to the north-west were places where farming arrived early.

Key Dates

- 10,000BC Cereal gathering begins in Palestine.

- 9000BC Farming begins in the Fertile Crescent.

- 9000BC The people of Syria and nearby regions sow wheat.

- 9000BC Jericho develops as a small settlement around a spring.

- 8000BC Animal herding is well established in the Zagros Mountains.

- 7000BC Cereal farming is widespread from Turkey to the Fertile Crescent, in the Zagros Mountains and parts of Pakistan.

Plants and Animals

▲ DATE PALM
Early farmers in the Fertile Crescent used the date palm for its fruit, wood, leaves and fibres.

THE FIRST FARMERS DID NOT simply take wild grasses and plant them in rows in their fields. They had to work hard to turn the wild species they found into true cereal crops. To begin with, they had to choose the plants that were the most suitable for food. In Europe and Asia, farmers chose grasses such as wheat and barley. Farmers in eastern Asia grew millet. Tropical African growers cultivated yams. The first farmers in North America selected corn, while those in South America chose potatoes and another root vegetable, manioc.

Farmers watched out for the individual plants that were strongest or biggest. American corn farmers, for example, collected the seed from plants yielding the biggest cobs, and sowed these, to produce a crop with larger cobs next year.

Farmers in the Fertile Crescent had a different problem with their wheat. One species that grew well was wild einkorn wheat. But its seeds tended to break off and fall to the ground when they ripened, making them difficult to harvest. Eventually the farmers noticed that a few plants had seeds that did not fall so quickly, so they bred their crops from these. Soon they had

▼ CATTLE ROCK PAINTING
When the people of the Sahara began to farm, their artists started to paint pictures of cattle. This example shows a herd of cattle, of the type that were kept more than 4,000 years ago. The painting also includes some of the people who herded them. It comes from a site in the Tassili mountains, in the central Sahara.

ON EARLY FARMS
Early farms looked quite unlike modern ones. The animals and plants were different, the farmer and his family usually shared their house with the animals. There were no machines, just simple tools and a lot of hard work. The whole family helped, especially at busy times such as harvest. Even young children lent a hand, which was good training for when they would be farmers themselves.

wild einkorn

domestic einkorn

◀ WILD AND DOMESTIC WHEAT
The main difference between wild and domestic einkorn wheat is the seeds. In the domestic variety these are much larger. The plant's stalk is also stronger, which stops the seeds from falling off before the harvest.

▶ WILD AND DOMESTIC CORN
Modern domestic corn has a larger seed cob than the ancient wild variety. Early farmers probably bred corn cobs that were larger than the wild varieties but not as big as today's giant cobs.

wild corn *domestic corn*

◀ WILD AND DOMESTIC CATTLE
The wild auroch was the ancestor of early farm cattle. Bones found by archaeologists show early domesticated cattle were smaller than the wild ones. But early farmers probably tried different sizes of cattle to see which suited them best.

auroch

cattle

◀ A FARMING VILLAGE
The first farming villages in Turkey were small clusters of mud-brick houses, where people and animals lived close together for safety. In the hot dry summers, the village streets were baked hard and dusty, but in the winter they became a mass of puddles and sticky mud. These farmers kept goats, and cattle descended from the wild aurochs.

developed a new species, domesticated einkorn wheat, with seeds that only broke away during threshing.

Early farmers bred their animals in a similar way, selecting the beasts with the features they wanted, and breeding from them. But the changes to the animal species were less dramatic than with the crops. The pigs farmed in the Fertile Crescent, for example, were much smaller and more like wild boars than modern domestic pigs. Cattle too were smaller than modern cows, and sheep and goats looked like the wild species.

Most early domestic animals were smaller than their wild cousins. This is probably because farmers bred good-tempered, docile creatures that were less aggressive and easier to handle than wild animals. Rather than choosing large specimens, farmers would have selected animals that produced the best-tasting meat or the highest yield of milk. Gradually, the farmers built up knowledge and experience, and must have discovered that the smaller animals often had the features they wanted.

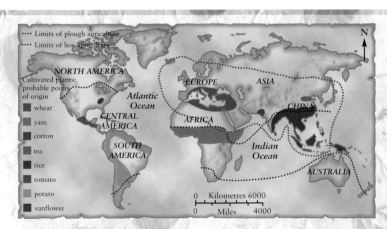

▲ PLANT DOMESTICATION
Farmers in different parts of the world grew different types of crops. In each area, one or two crops became the most commonly grown. They were varieties that were easy to grow in that particular area and provided a good basic crop.

Key Dates

- 9000BC Sheep domesticated in northern Mesopotamia.

- 8000BC First domesticated cereals grown around Jericho.

- 7000 BC Sheep and goats kept in the eastern Mediterranean.

- 7000BC Barley grown in the Fertile Crescent. Emmer wheat in Palestine. Einkorn wheat in Turkey and Mesopotamia.

- 7000BC Pigs are domesticated in southern Turkey.

- 6000BC Cattle kept by farmers in north Africa and the eastern Mediterranean.

The Coming of Trade

▲ DAGGER
This dagger, with its long flint blade and its snake-shaped handle, was probably made for decorative effect rather than use in battle.

FARMING MADE SOME PEOPLE well-fed, rich and successful. They could trade the extra food they produced in exchange for luxury goods. Soon, this became a way of life for many farmers and trading towns began to appear in the Fertile Crescent and in Anatolia (Turkey). Most of these early towns disappeared long ago. As one set of mud-brick buildings fell into disrepair, they were knocked down. People built new houses on top of the old foundations. This happened many times over hundreds of years, and the town's ground level gradually rose as each group of houses was replaced. When a town was finally abandoned, the ruins, with their build-up of floor levels, was left in the form of a mound. In Syria and Palestine this type of ancient mound is called a tell. In Turkey it is known as a hüyük.

One of the most famous of these early town mounds is Çatal Hüyük in central Turkey. When archaeologists began to dig this mound, they found that it concealed an ancient town, occupied by a trading people who lived there between 7000 and

▶ BUILDING WORK
Clay was the main material for building in early trading towns of the Middle East. It could be pressed into brick shapes while wet and left to dry in the sun. Surfaces were plastered to give a weatherproof finish outside and a smooth surface for decoration within.

6000BC. The countryside around the town was rich farming land. Charred remains from the town have shown that the people grew wheat, barley, lentils and other vegetables, as well as eating such fruit as apples and wild nuts such as almonds.

The people of Çatal Hüyük probably traded in food products and raw materials for making tools. A preferred material was obsidian, a black glass, formed naturally in volcanoes. Archaeologists have found a range of different tools and weapons made of flint and obsidian on the site.

The houses of Çatal Hüyük were built of mud-brick. They were square or rectangular, and built close together. One amazing feature of the town was that it had no streets. People entered their houses from the flat

MYSTERIES OF A TURKISH TOWN
There are still many mysteries surrounding the town of Çatal Hüyük in central Turkey in spite of all the work of the archaeologists. No one knows for sure the meaning of the wall paintings in many of the rooms that have been excavated. The bulls, birds, leopards and human figures were probably gods. However, it is not clear what the gods stood for, or how they were worshipped.

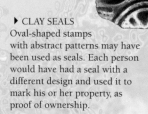

▶ CLAY SEALS
Oval-shaped stamps with abstract patterns may have been used as seals. Each person would have had a seal with a different design and used it to mark his or her property, as proof of ownership.

▲ BULL PAINTING
This mural is from a shrine at Çatal Hüyük. It shows a group of people baiting a gigantic bull. Bulls had religious significance because they were associated with a male god.

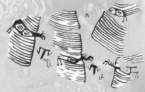

▶ BIRD WALL-PAINTING
These birds are probably vultures. People in some cultures left their dead out of doors, until vultures had picked away the flesh.

roofs, stepping down wooden ladders to the floor below. Defending such places was easy.

Many houses contained at least one room set aside for religious ceremonies. These rooms, or shrines, are decorated with bulls' heads made of plaster and fitted with real bulls' horns. They also have wall paintings of animals and figures. Many of the figures are female, and archaeologists have also found more than 50 small

statues of pregnant women, suggesting that the people worshipped a mother goddess.

In addition, the shrines contain platforms that may have been used as altars in some form of religious ceremony. When residents of Çatal Hüyük died, their bodies were left in the open air, where the flesh was removed by the vultures. Then their relatives brought the bones back into the town and buried them beneath these platforms.

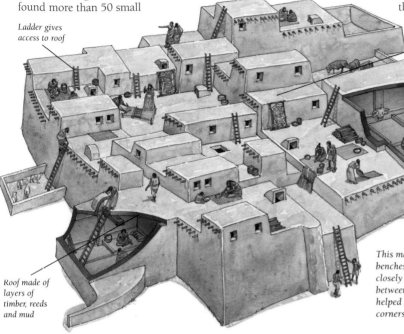

Ladder gives access to roof

Flat roof provides work space and route to adjoining houses

Decorated room used as religious shrine

Roof made of layers of timber, reeds and mud

◀ TOWN HOUSES
Houses at Çatal Hüyük were made mainly from mud-brick. This material was even used for fittings like benches and hearths. The houses were packed closely together with only a few courtyards between them. This made the town compact and helped to make it easier to defend, with few corners where enemies or wild beasts could lurk.

◀ EXCAVATING A SITE
The most common way for archaeologists to dig is to make a trench, a rectangular hole across the site. They can find remains from different periods because they lie in bands like a layer cake, revealing small areas across a broad time span. When there are many remains of buildings and other structures, such as at Çatal Hüyük, archaeologists will sometimes excavate to a shallow depth, over a broader area to cover more of the site.

Key Dates

- 8000BC Trade begins to develops in the Fertile Crescent and Anatolia.

- 7000BC Çatal Hüyük becomes important as a town and trading hub.

- 7000BC Jericho expands; religious rituals include decorating skulls with plaster and shells.

- 6800BC Pottery is widely used in the eastern Mediterranean.

- 6500BC More elaborate burials at settlements such as Çatal Hüyük and Jericho show that some people were more important than others.

- 5000BC Trade links established between Turkey and the eastern Mediterranean.

Pots and Potters

▲ PAINTED POTTERY
The earliest pottery was plain, but potters soon learned how to paint their wares to make them more attractive. This pot is from an early farming community in Europe.

WE TAKE POTTERY, SUCH as cups, bowls, mugs and plates for granted. Before pottery was invented, our earliest ancestors used hollowed out stone containers and woven baskets. The first pottery was probably made around 10,500BC. Pots are made from clay, which was dug from the ground, so they are cheap. They could be made in a variety of shapes and sizes, and hold liquids as well as dry foods. Once people had discovered how to make pots, they never stopped finding new uses for them.

Pottery was probably discovered by accident. Early peoples baked bread and other foods in ovens which they made from earth. They piled up a mound of clay and made a hollow in which they lit a fire. Inside, it became very hot. Eventually someone must have noticed that the sides of the clay oven had hardened with the heat.

It was probably some time before anyone had the idea of using this hardened clay to make containers. The earliest pots so far discovered come from Japan. From Japan, knowledge of pottery may have spread to China, where slightly more recent vessels have been found. However, in the rest of Asia, Europe and Africa, pottery is much more recent. It is possible that it may have been discovered independently, as it was in America.

The first pots were made by the coiling process. The potter made a long, thin sausage of clay and looped it in a circle, working upwards to make the sides of the pot. Another ancient technique was to form pots by using a stone template that was removed when the potter achieved the right shape. Much later, some time after 3000BC, the potter's wheel was invented. This device is still used by potters all over

◀ TERRACOTTA FIGURE
Pottery can be formed into all sorts of shapes, not only containers. People soon realized that they could use it to make small, portable statues. These were common among early farming communities, and archaeologists have excavated shrines with large numbers of these figures.

POTS AND POTTERS

In hunter-gatherer societies, people generally collected food as they needed it. Farming produced a glut of food at harvest time. People now needed containers to store this food, so pottery and farming flourished at the same time. The earliest pottery is unglazed. This means that it absorbs moisture, so that it is best used for dry goods such as grain and other solid foods.

◀ UNGLAZED POTS
Simple unglazed storage jars are still made in many parts of the world. These jars, elegantly shaped and decorated with patterns made by the potters' fingertips, come from Ghana. Pots like this are sometimes given a decorative glaze.

▲ ROUND-BASED POT
This is one of the oldest pots so far discovered by archaeologists. It comes from Nasunahara, Japan, and dates to around 10,500BC. The pot has a beaded pattern in bands around the rim.

▶ JOMON POT, JAPAN
Jomon or cord-marked pottery was produced in Japan around 10,000BC. The clay was coiled into shape and the pots had pointed bases. They were probably hardened by heating on an open fire, rather than by firing in an enclosed kiln like later pots. This pot, used as a storage jar, stands about 23cm/9in high.

the world. The finished pots were fired and hardened in a kiln, which was similar to an ancient oven.

One advantage of pottery is that it is extremely long-lasting, and has survived to provide evidence for archaeologists. Each region and period has its own style of pottery. The shade of the clay, the thickness of the pot, the style of decoration all vary from place to place and time to time. An archaeologist can often tell, even from a fragment of pottery, when and where it was made. They can therefore give a date to the sites where they find pots. Pots of foreign origin also provide clues as to trade and links between various countries.

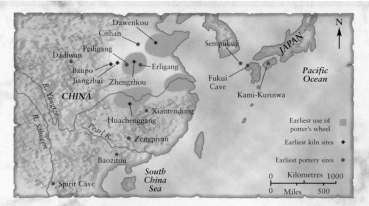

▲ POTTERS AT WORK

The potter in the foreground is making a pot by coiling clay. With help from her daughter, she has prepared long, sausage-shaped pieces of clay and wound them around to build up the shape of the vessel. When she is happy with the overall shape, she will moisten her fingers and rub the surface of the pot to make it smooth. She may then make handles and stick them to the sides.

▲ EARLY POTTERY SITES

Archaeologists have discovered many remains of both early pottery and kilns in China and Japan. These areas continued to be at the forefront of developments in pottery until the 1800s. Kilns, glazing and, much later, waterproof porcelain, were all discovered and first used in the Far East.

Key Dates

- 10,500BC First Japanese pottery.

- 7000BC Unbaked, sun-dried clay vessels made in Syria and Turkey.

- 7000BC Hunter-fishers of southern Sahara are the first potters in Africa.

- 6500BC First European pottery.

- 6000BC Fishing communities in southern China make pottery.

- 3500BC The tournette, a simple device for turning a pot, appears in Mesopotamia and Egypt.

- 3000BC Potter's wheel invented in the Middle East.

- 1500BC Glazed pottery that is resistant to water made in China.

European Settlements

ARMING SEEMS TO HAVE spread to Europe from the east, from around 7000BC. It reached Europe from Turkey and then spread westwards towards the Atlantic coast.

Then, as now, the European climate and landscape varied greatly. In the Balkans, where farming in Europe started, it was dry, and the land was suitable for sheep and goats, as well as for cereal growing. In northern Europe, early farmers led a very different life. The weather was colder, the soil heavier and much of the ground was covered with forest. This was not good country for sheep and goats, so pig-rearing and cattle-herding were more popular. People could grow cereal crops, but the heavier soil was harder to cultivate than in the south. Gradually, over many centuries, the northerners developed strains of cereals that could grow in the heavy soil.

The woods of the north had many benefits. They were good foraging-grounds for pigs, and also provided a variety of food plants for people. They also sheltered animals such as deer and wild boar that could be hunted for both food and skins. The northern Europeans continued to hunt and gather to add variety to the food they produced on their farms.

The plentiful timber was also useful for building. The farmers of central and northern Europe cut down trees to make a stout framework for the walls and roofs

▲ FARMING SETTLEMENT
A small farming village in western Britain consisted of a few round thatched houses clustered together. Next to the houses were fields for animals and crops. A trackway gave access to the fields and connected this village with others.

CRAFTS OF THE FARMERS

With the settled way of life that came with farming, people began to develop their craft skills. Among the most important were building and pottery. These early farmers were skilled woodworkers. They made fences, tools and containers.

face pot, Hungary

Bandkeramik pot, Germany

▲ RAISED PATHWAY
People sometimes built farming villages in marshy land. They made wooden walkways raised on posts so that they could cross the swamps safely.

▲ DECORATED POTS
Potters decorated pots by drawing patterns or simplified faces in the damp clay. Another design was made up of lines and dots in a style known by the German name *Bandkeramik*, meaning "banded pottery".

▲ SEATED FIGURE
This pottery statuette from a farming site in Hungary shows a man holding a sickle. He may be a corn god, or just an ordinary farmer.

of their homes. They used split logs to make the walls and plastered them over with daub, a mixture of mud and straw, to fill the gaps. This helped to keep out draughts. The roofs, which had a steep pitch to throw off snow and rain, were thatched. Some of these houses were up to 45m/150ft in length and are known as longhouses. They were Europe's first sizeable, permanent dwellings. As well as a large room for the family, they usually also contained a store-room

for crops and an area for cattle. Sometimes humans and animals shared the same room. It was cramped and smelly, but people put up with this to make sure their animals were safe.

Farming villages became established in many river valleys. People used the rivers to travel between nearby villages to trade. Along the way, they also exchanged ideas about new discoveries and inventions. As a result, pottery techniques and styles improved and spread, and new ideas about crop and animal cultivation were shared. The people of Europe were developing skills which would stay in use for thousands of years.

◀ EUROPEAN FARMERS
At Langweiler, Germany, farmers build a longhouse for their family and animals. They have constructed the walls and are now thatching the roof. To do this they have gathered reeds from a nearby river. Reeds make a longer-lasting thatch than grass or straw.

Key Dates

- 7000BC Farming reaches eastern Europe, probably from Turkey.

- 6200BC Farming begins in Sicily and southern Italy.

- 5400BC Farming spreads across northern Europe, from Hungary, through Germany to the Netherlands.

- 5000BC Farming communities such as Langweiler are thriving.

- 5000BC Farming has spread across southern Europe and has reached the south of France.

- 4000BC Farming established in most of Europe.

▲ FARMING REACHES EUROPE
From the Middle East and Turkey, farming spread gradually west along coasts and river valleys. The three main areas of farming in Europe were the Balkans, the Mediterranean coast, and north and west Europe, to which farming came last.

Asian Communities

▲ HARPOON
HEADS, CHINA
*Items like these bone
harpoon points from
the farming site at
Banpo, China, show
that hunting and river
fishing were still key
sources of food.*

GOOD SOIL AND USEFUL LOCAL crops encouraged Asian people to begin farming. This is how agriculture began in eastern Asia, in places like the highlands of north-west and central India, and areas around the banks of the Yellow River in China. Both regions had good natural resources and a climate suitable for farming. Archaeologists have found the remains of several early farming villages in both places.

Central India had grassy uplands suitable for cattle grazing and river banks with rich soil for crops. Farming began early here, around 7000BC. Barley was a popular crop, and farmers herded cattle, goats and sheep on the hills. In some places, people gathered together to build villages. One of the first was called Mehrgarh, a cluster of houses by the River Bolan in north-west India. The houses were square or rectangular, and built of mud-bricks plastered with mud. The flat roofs were made of reed thatch supported on long wooden poles. Inside, there were several rooms. Thick walls and small windows kept

▲ RICE FARMER
When the people had worked out how to cultivate the waterlogged fields of southern China and south-east Asia, rice became the staple crop of these areas.

the houses warm in winter and cool in summer. The style remained much the same for the next 1,000 years.

Communities like Mehrgarh grew. People built storehouses for grain to ensure a reserve when supplies became short. Some members of the community grew rich, perhaps by trading. Their graves contain cherished possessions, such as beads of shell or limestone.

Meanwhile, agriculture was developing in China. Here, millet was the preferred crop, and the pig was the

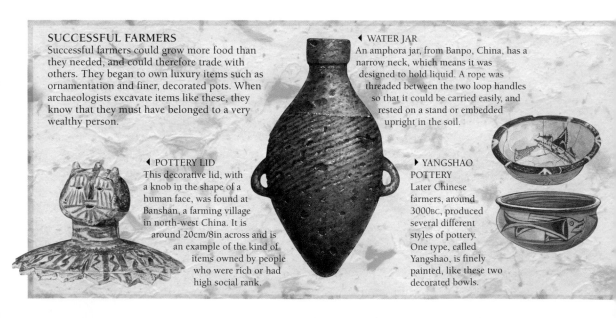

SUCCESSFUL FARMERS
Successful farmers could grow more food than they needed, and could therefore trade with others. They began to own luxury items such as ornamentation and finer, decorated pots. When archaeologists excavate items like these, they know that they must have belonged to a very wealthy person.

◀ WATER JAR
An amphora jar, from Banpo, China, has a narrow neck, which means it was designed to hold liquid. A rope was threaded between the two loop handles so that it could be carried easily, and rested on a stand or embedded upright in the soil.

◀ POTTERY LID
This decorative lid, with a knob in the shape of a human face, was found at Banshan, a farming village in north-west China. It is around 20cm/8in across and is an example of the kind of items owned by people who were rich or had high social rank.

▶ YANGSHAO POTTERY
Later Chinese farmers, around 3000BC, produced several different styles of pottery. One type, called Yangshao, is finely painted, like these two decorated bowls.

first creature to be domesticated. Farmers also grew vegetables such as cabbages, and harvested fruit such as plums. Later, they began to grow rice, which became the staple in most of eastern Asia. Rice was especially successful in southern China, where the ground was wetter.

Chinese farmers quickly learned that their soils needed a rest after a season of cultivation. They developed a method of farming that switched from one field to another. This allowed the land to have a fallow period, where the land was not worked or sown. They found that by leaving a long fallow period between periods of growing, the land could be restored. Much later, around 1100BC, they began to alternate crops of millet and soya beans. The bean plants brought goodness back to the soil, meaning that it was less important to have a fallow period.

Techniques of farming spread steadily across China. Wet farming techniques needed for rice were passed from south to north, along with strains of rice that grew more successfully in the north. China also had contact with Korea and Japan. These two areas had successful hunting and fishing communities. Agriculture did not become established there until much later.

Straw thatch

Plastered wall

Supporting pole

Central hearth

▲ FARMER'S HUT, BANPO
Chinese archaeologists found the remains of a cluster of houses belonging to the early farming community of Banpo in northern China, dating from about 6000BC. The buildings were oblong or round. They were built with a stout wooden framework filled in with a basket-weave of thin branches. This was plastered over to make a smooth, weather-resistant wall. Thatch covered the roofs, but there was a central hole to let smoke escape from the fire in the floor below.

Wooden poles support reed thatch

▲ MUD-BRICK HOUSE
One of India's oldest farming villages is Mehrgarh, by the River Bolan in north-west India. The houses are mostly square, have several rooms and are made of plastered mud-bricks.

▼ BURIAL
The dead at Mehrgarh in north-west India were buried in free areas in the village itself. The bodies were positioned on their sides, their knees bent. Grave goods were placed with them. Rich people's graves contained items such as stone and shell beads.

Key Dates

- 7000BC Barley growing begins in India.

- 6000BC Indian farmers start building storehouses for their surplus food.

- 6000BC Millet is the main crop of farmers in northern China.

- 5500BC Date palms are cultivated in Mesopotamia.

- 5500BC Indian farmers produce their own strains of wheat.

- 5000BC Farmers of the Yangtze Delta area cultivate rice.

- 3500BC Trade networks link the regions of China.

- 3000BC Millet grown in Korea.

The Americas

W HETHER THEY WERE fishing or harpooning seals in the far north, hunting bison on the Great Plains, or gathering food in the south, the people of the Americas followed the food supply. As crops grew in the least extreme weather conditions, they also had to move with the seasons. They became used to a restless life.

▲ DEER FIGURE
People of south-western North America made figures like this split-twig deer. These figures date to a period after 3500BC and are often found near hunters' weapons and equipment.

▲ HUT AND HUNTER
In eastern North America, hunters often built short-term shelters, like this hut. They made a framework of thin wooden poles, joined together at the top. This they covered with grass. Huts like this could catch fire easily, so the hearth was outside.

In Central America, environmental changes were often fast and unpredictable. Torrential rain was followed by baking sun. The people here longed for more control over their food supply, and turned to agriculture before the rest of the Americas. However, they still needed good weather for their crops, which is perhaps why so many of them worshipped gods of rain and sun. The farmers hoped that worshipping these deities would bring them the best conditions throughout the agricultural year.

One of the earliest crops in Central America was corn (maize), a plant which has been important in American farming ever since. It was developed from a local wild grass called teosinte. Farmers tried different varieties, choosing the plants that grew best in local conditions. This proved successful approach, and maize farming spread quite quickly.

Further north, in what is now the south-west USA, the first farmers experimented with various types of gourd and with plants such as sunflower and sumpweed. As the farmers of Central America began to trade more widely, they took their domesticated maize, beans and squash with them, and these joined the local

AMERICAN FARMERS

The Americas contain a variety of different climates and environments, all with their own native plant species. For the early farmers, the challenge was to choose the best plants for their own region. Often this was simply a question of selecting from local species that were known to do well. But sometimes an imported crop, such as cotton in southern North America, was a success.

◀ POTATOES
Between 3000 and 2500BC, farmers in the hills of the Andes were growing the potato. For thousands of years, this useful root crop was grown only in South America, and many varieties of potato are still found only in the Andes.

▲ STONE WEIGHTS
Hunters in Kentucky attached these stone weights to the handles of their spear-throwers. This made their spears travel much farther and faster. As a result, when a spear hit an animal it was much more powerful.

◀ CLAY FIGURINE
Mysterious statuettes like this one have been found in numerous North American settlements. They have little in the way of shaping or facial features, so it is impossible to tell whether they represent male or female figures. They are made of clay and decorated with lines and dots. The clay was not fired, though, it simply became hard with age. No one knows what these figures were for.

plants to become staple crops in the north. For many people in the south-west, the plants were a welcome addition to foraged foods.

In South America people tried to cultivate a variety of crops, including gourds, squashes, manioc, potatoes and various types of bean. In each area, they selected the best plants for local conditions and tried different growing methods over thousands of years. The region where farming caught on most quickly was Peru. In the Andes mountains, hunter-gatherers began to grow crops such as gourds and beans to add to their existing

diet. They carried on using this mixed form of food supply for many thousands of years.

In the coastal areas, rivers had created narrow valleys as they flowed off the mountains to the sea. In the rich soil found in these valleys, people began to grow squashes and peppers, to which they later added maize. They also developed methods of irrigation to bring water from the rivers to their fields.

Animal farming was at first less popular in the Americas than in other parts of the world. There were few native species that were easy to farm. But in the Andes mountains one species, the llama, was valued for its wool and milk, as well as being used as a beast of burden. The people of the Americas developed a variety of crops and farming techniques, but in many places wild foods were still widely available and many groups carried on their lifestyle of hunting and gathering.

▼ RIVER TRANSPORT
Simple wooden canoes provided transport along North America's rivers. There were various ways of making these. They could be "dug-outs", made by hollowing out a log. Another design was made of thin tree bark attached to a wooden frame.

▼ SUNFLOWERS
This giant member of the daisy family is found mainly in North America. Farmers prized it for its seeds, which can be eaten. Later they learned how to extract the oil from the seeds, using it for cooking. Some species also have edible roots.

▶ COTTON
This valuable crop was first cultivated in two separate areas, Peru and Ecuador in South America and Mexico in Central America. From Mexico, traders brought it to the North American south-west, where farmers later began to grow the plant.

Key Dates

- 8500BC Agriculture established in Peru. Crops grown include squash, beans and grasses.

- 7000BC In Central America people gather avocado, chilli, squash and beans. These are plants farmers will begin to cultivate in the next 2,000 years.

- 6300BC Farmers in Peru grow various root crops, such as oca and ulluco.

- 5400BC The use of llamas for wool, milk and transport is common in the Andes.

- 5000BC Mexican farmers grow maize.

- 5000BC Domesticated plants of Central America, such as the bottle gourd, begin to spread to North America.

Hunting and Gathering

Artists painted both farm animals and the hunters' preferred quarry on the walls of rock shelters in the Sahara Desert. The giraffe was one of the creatures that people living in Africa both herded and hunted during prehistoric times.

FARMING WAS NOT FOR everyone. Hunting and gathering can provide a steady, reliable source of food as long as there are not too many people living in a small area. Africa is one part of the world where some peoples made the change to farming, while others continued to hunt and gather for much longer.

After the final Ice Age, the Sahara was a much damper, greener environment than it is today. It became the scene for some of Africa's earliest experiments in farming. Rock paintings show how the people began to herd cattle, together with other local species such as giraffe.

When the Sahara dried out and gradually turned to desert, most agricultural activity was pushed to the south, between the Sahara and the Equator. This was where the climate allowed farmers to develop crops such as yam and

sorghum, a cereal crop that was suited to warm places. This area became the heartland of African farming.

Still further south, people carried on hunting and gathering. They ate a number of local plants, especially various palms and a shrub called bauhinia. In addition, they found out how to use other plants for more specialized purposes. A good example was the bottle gourd, which was suitable for making into containers.

The African hunter-gatherers also improved their tools. To make knives, they used tiny blades of sharp flint, which they glued into wooden handles using natural tree resin. They also carved hooks from bone for fishing. Such uses of the materials around them show how highly adapted they were to their environment.

Australia was another place where the traditional lifestyle of hunting and gathering continued. To begin with,

◄ TRADITIONAL HUNTER
Today, some African peoples still get some of their food by hunting, but now their spears are tipped with metal rather than the stone of earlier times.

USEFUL SPECIES

The early hunter-gatherers of Africa and Australia had a vast knowledge of plants. When they came across a new species they would try it out. This was a dangerous process, as many plants were poisonous. They gradually discovered plants that were good to eat and others that worked as medicines. Modern scientists are still investigating the plant medicines used by the world's hunter-gatherer peoples.

◄ GOURD
Some species of gourd were very useful. When the flesh had been eaten, the outer shells made excellent containers. People made bowls with the larger fruit, while using smaller ones to make items such as dippers and cups.

◄ ALMONDS
Nuts, such as almonds, that are native to North Africa and the Middle East, are a nutritious food. Gatherers made a point of going to the forest when they were in season. They are easy to store and contain plenty of energy-building protein, useful to hunter-gatherers when meat was in short supply.

▶ JUNIPER BERRIES
Gatherers soon knew everything about the plants in their area. They discovered that some plants, though not good to eat, had other useful properties. Berries like juniper, which grows all over the northern hemisphere, were valued for their perfume and their use in medicine.

people stayed near the coast, living on fish, eels and, especially, shellfish. Remains of the shells, left in dumps that archaeologists call middens, have been found along both the north and south-east coasts. As time went on, the native Australians explored the river valleys, moving gradually inland. People discovered that cereal plants such as millet made good food. They developed hunting skills that enabled them to survive when they moved even further inland towards Australia's hot and dry interior.

The early Australians roamed for miles, exchanging tools and shell ornaments, and creating the beautiful rock art, which can still be found all over the country. As they did this, they were also developing a complex series of myths about their ancestry that reflected their hunting and gathering lifestyle. Most important of all are the stories of Dreamtime, the period when the earth and the spirits of people were created. These myths held, and still hold, great religious significance for native Australians, and reveal a people of profound beliefs.

▲ HUNTER-GATHERERS
This group of hunter-gatherers have found an area rich in food and have made a camp with a brushwood shelter that they will occupy for weeks or even months. While two men butcher the antelope they have killed, another group of people returns from gathering vegetables and wood for the fire on which they will cook the meat.

▼ ENGRAVED PEARL SHELL
In societies that did not use metals, all sorts of items were adapted for use as ornamentation. This example, engraved with abstract designs, was made by native Australians from a piece of pearl shell.

◀ BARK PAINTING
A hunter throws his spear at a crane in this bark painting from Australia's Northern Territory. This style of painting is known as "x-ray", because the designs on the crane depict the bird's insides.

Key Dates

- 10,000BC Obsidian, a type of volcanic glass, used to make tools in the Rift Valley area of eastern Africa.

- 9000BC People move into the Sahara region; increased rainfall allows grasslands to grow along the edges of what is now desert.

- 7000BC African communities in the Sahara begin making pottery.

- 6000BC People start herding cattle in some parts of the Sahara region.

- 4000BC Sahara reaches its wettest, most temperate conditions, with Lake Chad at its largest.

- 3500BC Ostrich egg-shell beads become popular as necklaces in eastern Africa.

The First Metalworkers

▲ GOLD BULL
The settlement of Varna, on the Black Sea, was one of Europe's first metal-working sites. Hundreds of gold ornaments, bracelets and beads have been discovered there.

As they created art on to surfaces in caves, ancient peoples must have seen gold. They would also have seen copper, as it has a greenish tinge in the rock. Deposits of metal in rock are rare, and difficult to extract. It was a long time before anyone worked out how to remove the material and then to work it into something useful. Eventually, someone found a place where there was enough metal to remove and found that it could be hammered into shape. Metal was beaten into ornamental objects such as beads, which were soon highly valued.

When craftworkers started to make pottery, they built kilns that could reach temperatures as high as 800°C/1500°F. Before long, they found that heating certain rocks, or ores, in the kiln melted the metal they contained, so that it could be poured off and collected. They had discovered the process called smelting. This made it possible to extract much larger amounts of metal from the ore. People could make all sorts of items out of copper rather than other materials. There was

▲ BRONZE AGE SETTLEMENT
Most of the people of Bronze Age Europe lived in small villages with thatched houses, like those built by the first farmers. An area would be set aside for metalworking away from the houses, so that there was less risk of fire.

THE MAGIC OF METAL
The first metals must have seemed like magic. By heating the ore, the metalworker could make metal appear, apparently out of nowhere. It would first be seen in hot liquid form, then it would miraculously set when it cooled. Copper and gold glittered beautifully in the light, so people found these metals very attractive.

▼ LONG-HORNED OXEN
Small, precious objects were among the first items to be made of metal, because they did not use very much of it. Early metalworkers could produce objects of great skill, as these copper oxen found in Poland demonstrate.

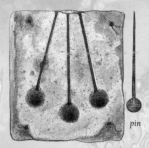

mould

pin

▶ COPPER AND TIN
The first important alloy was bronze, a mix of copper and tin. Tin is not common, so bronze developed slowly where there were good tin deposits – China, the Middle East and parts of France, Germany and Britain.

◀ MOULD AND PIN
A Bronze Age mould and matching pin show how the process of casting could be used to produce a number of items at speed – in this case three pins at the same time. The small holes at each corner would have matched with bumps in the other half of the mould, to ensure a perfect fit.

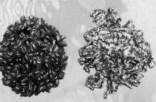

copper

tin

▶ CASTING
Metal items, such as tools and weapons, could be made by casting. The metalworker prepared a stone mould in two parts that fitted together exactly. When joined together and secured with twine, the hollow inside the mould had the shape of the object to be cast. Hot molten metal was poured into the mould through a hole in the top. When the metal had cooled and set, the metalworker took the mould apart to reveal the object. The same mould could be used again and again.

still a problem, however. Metals such as gold and copper were easy to work, but they were soft. They made good adornments, but poor tools. The solution was to combine one metal with another to make an alloy that was hard-wearing. The best alloy discovered in the ancient world was bronze. This was made by mixing copper with a little tin. It was tough, quite easy to work, had a pleasant, golden appearance, and could be sharpened.

Bronze became a popular material for ornamentation, tools and weapons. Sometimes, once a metalworker had smelted some copper and mixed in some tin, he would let the molten metal set into a bar and then hammer it into shape. Liquid metal can also be cast in a mould to produce all sorts of complex shapes. Casting was popular because it was easy to

produce many identical items using the same mould. However, since hammering hardened the metal, this method was still used to make objects like weapons, which had to be very strong.

Metal technology probably began in the Middle East around 3000BC, and spread to other parts of the world during the next 2,000 years. The development of bronzeworking is so important that historians sometimes call this period the Bronze Age. Bronze did not reach all parts of the world. There was no Bronze Age in Australia, South America or many parts of Africa. In such places, although people may have used gold or copper occasionally, they mostly made do with the stone technology they had developed. They had to wait until the coming of iron before they could take full advantage of metals.

▲ THE SPREAD OF COPPER IN EUROPE
In Europe, copper working began in two main areas, Iberia (southern Spain) and the Balkans, where plenty of the metal was available. From these regions, archaeologists have mapped and dated discoveries of bronze objects. This gives a rough idea of how knowledge of the craft spread across the European continent.

Key Dates

- 9000BC Copper used in some parts of Asia for tools and weapons.
- 6000BC Smelting and casting are developed in the Middle East and south-east Europe.
- 4000BC Knowledge of metalworking begins spreading to Europe, Asia and North Africa.
- 3000BC Bronze technology develops in the Middle East.
- 3000–1000BC Better trade routes enable bronzeworking techniques to spread across much of Europe.
- 2000BC Bronzeworking develops in China.
- 2000BC Bronze is used widely in Asia for everyday tools and weapons.

Megaliths

▲ NIGHT SKY
*People have always
looked to the sky in
their religion. Most
stone circles and rows of
standing stones are
arranged to line up with
the Sun, Moon or stars.*

TOWERING STANDING STONES, massive stone circles, and vast rows of stones are the most awesome of all prehistoric remains. Some of them are so huge that no one knows how Bronze Age people ever managed to build them. Because they are so big, they are known as megaliths, a term that comes from two Greek words meaning huge stones.

Another mystery is exactly what these vast monuments were for. Archaeologists think they may have been used for religious ceremonies. The stones are often lined up with yearly movements of the Sun and stars, so the ceremonies were almost certainly linked to the calendar and the seasons. They may have been fertility ceremonies, relating the crop-growing season to the annual movements of the stars.

There are two famous groups of megaliths in Europe, one on England's Salisbury Plain, the other in Brittany, France. Many of the British monuments are

stone circles, the most famous are at Stonehenge and Avebury. The main monument in Brittany is a series of rows, or alignments, of stones near the village of Carnac. In both cases there are many other prehistoric monuments nearby, such as smaller circles and alignments, earthworks, burial mounds and single standing stones. Together these structures make up

▲ BUILDING STONEHENGE
Stonehenge in Wiltshire, the greatest of all the stone circles, was built with the simplest technology. The builders probably used sleds or rollers to move the stones, each weighing about 40 tons, about 25km/15 miles to the site, before heaving them into place with a combination of ropes and levers.

THE CHANGING MONUMENTS

The megalithic monuments of Europe have stood for thousands of years, but they have not always looked the same. Archaeologists have found many holes in the ground where additional stones and wooden posts once stood, making these sites even more complex than they are today. The monuments were also altered throughout prehistory, with the removal of some stones and the addition of others.

◀ DOLMEN
Groups of stones like this are called dolmens. They started out covered with earth as the chambers of prehistoric burial mounds. When the mound was moved or eroded away, the roof and its supports were left.

▲ CALLANISH STONE CIRCLE
This is quite a small circle of 13 tall, thin stones. It is in the Hebrides off Scotland and is at the focal point of lines of standing stones. The stones, some of which are 4.5m/15ft high, were quarried only a short distance away from the site. Archaeologists have calculated that each of the stones could have been dragged along by about 20 people.

▶ FESTIVAL AT AVEBURY
Another British stone circle, at Avebury in Wiltshire, may been the scene of an annual harvest or farming festival like the one shown here. The form of the ritual is unknown, but there were probably processions, offerings and observations of the stars or Moon.

entire regions that would have been known as holy places, landscapes devoted to religion.

The builders of the megalithic monuments had to move and lift huge stones, dig long ditches and pile up enormous mounds of earth. Yet the people of the Bronze Age had no complex machinery, only rollers, levers, ropes and simple hand tools. It must have taken hundreds of people over many years to move the stones. Clearly, a great deal of organization was needed, and probably a ruler with enough power to keep everyone at work on the task. Planning was also important, so that the builders could work out the precise positions for the stones. These vast temples suggest that Bronze Age societies were far more advanced than you would expect, considering the simple tools they had.

◀ MEGALITHIC SITES
Britain, Ireland and northern France are the main areas where megalithic monuments can be found. This probably shows that the people of these three areas were in regular contact, sailing across the English Channel and Irish Sea, when the megaliths were erected. They must have had similar religious beliefs and ceremonies, although we now know very little about these. There were once many more megaliths, but in the 1700s and 1800s farmers cleared away large numbers of these monuments from their fields.

Key Dates

- 4000BC Ditched enclosures common in many parts of Europe.
- 4000BC Long barrows and megalithic tombs become common for high-status burials in Europe.
- 3200BC People in Europe begin to build stone circles.
- 3000BC In Europe, much land is cleared for agriculture.
- 2100BC Stones added to a site originally made up of ditches and earth banks, makes Stonehenge Britain's biggest megalithic site.
- 1500BC The age of stone circles and standing stones comes to an end.

Lake Villages

▲ POTTERY
The lake village people used lots of pottery vessels. Some were narrow-necked, like this jug, which was made for carrying water.

THE SHORES OF ALPINE LAKES in Europe are made up of bogs and marshland. They are difficult to cross and very hard to build on. Yet archaeologists have discovered the remains of several hundred Bronze Age villages in the European Alps. The small settlements with their simple wooden houses were in the middle of swamps by the shores of lakes such as Constance and Neuchâtel, on the borders of modern Switzerland, France and Germany. Why did people put up with damp, boggy conditions?

The lakes themselves were rich in fish, which could be dried or smoked, to preserve them for times when food was less plentiful. Some way beyond the lake shores was grassland, which provided grazing for animals. The foothills of the Alps were thickly forested, offering a good supply of wood for building and fuel. Most important of all, the swampy conditions meant that it very easy to defend the villages against enemies.

Many villages sprang up by the lakes. People cut down trees from the alpine foothills to build their houses. Rooves were thatched with reeds from the lakesides. Each house was raised above the marsh with stout wooden poles rammed deep into the earth. Wood was also used to make pathways across the swamp and to build strong fences around each village. Most villages

TOOLS FOR THE JOB
In prehistoric times, most of the lakeside region of Europe was wooded right down to the lake shores. So, before they could start building homes, the villagers had to clear away some of the trees and prepare logs for building. For this, they needed heavy stone axes with long wooden handles. Once they were settled, they could use lighter metal tools for everyday work in the fields and around the village.

▶ AXE HANDLE
Waterlogged soil near the Swiss lakes has preserved ancient wooden objects, such as this axe handle. This gives us knowledge of craft skills that we lack for most prehistoric peoples.

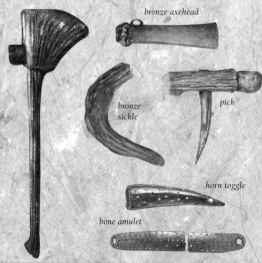

bronze axehead

bronze sickle

pick

horn toggle

bone amulet

◀ TOOL KIT
After about 2000BC, the alpine lake people started to use bronze to make many of their tools. Axes for chopping and sickles for harvesting were two typical metal items. There were also picks with bone or antler handles.

◀ BONE AND HORN
Many items were made of these materials. Animal horn was a good material to make toggles to fasten coats and tunics. Bone could be carved into all sorts of shapes, including fastenings and pierced objects which may have been sacred charms.

were quite small, with up to 20 houses. Eventually, after 30 or 40 years, the wet ground made the poles supporting the houses rot. Either they were replaced, or the people moved on to another site.

Trapped deep beneath the water, however, an amazing amount of evidence of these villages has been preserved. Archaeologists have brought to the surface some of the timbers from the houses and pathways and bronze implements. In some cases even remains of the people's food and clothing have survived preserved in the cold water.

Some of the settlements had at least one large house. This was probably the home of the village chief. Archaeologists have found decorated bronze weapons and ornaments in these houses, showing that these chiefs were rich and powerful.

▼ ON THE LAKESHORE

This view of a prehistoric lake village shows how close the inhabitants were to the resources they needed to live – reeds and fish in the lake itself, timber from the forests, and fertile fields nearby. For communities like this, easy access to these resources made it worthwhile to build in such a difficult, marshy area.

▲ REEDS

For thatched roofs, by far the best material is reed. It is strong, long-lasting and grows in abundance along the edges of lakes.

▼ LAKESIDE VILLAGE

Sites near lakes have always proved popular in places such as Austria, Switzerland and nearby countries. Places such as Zurich, Neuchâtel, Lausanne and Konstanz are all built by large lakes. Many of these modern towns and cities are built on the sites of prehistoric lake villages. The picture shows a lakeside village in the Austrian Alps. Today, many people like to visit lakeside sites because of the stunning scenery.

Key Dates

- 3000BC Trading villages well established on the shores of the Black Sea; the inhabitants work copper and gold and trade along the local rivers.

- 3000BC People settle along the shores of lakes in Europe's Alpine region.

- 2000BC Substantial wooden villages are built by the settlers in alpine areas. The people purposely select sites that are easy to defend and learn how to fortify their villages with boundary fences.

- 1600BC The heyday of the lake villages comes to an end.

The Iron Age

B RONZE WAS A USEFUL METAL, but it was not as hard as stone. Neither was it always easy to find the copper and tin needed to make it. Many people carried on using flint tools and weapons. Then, in around 1300BC, some metalworkers in the Middle East discovered iron.

Iron is a common metal in many parts of the world. It is easy to smelt, providing that the temperature in the furnace is high enough. It can be sharpened easily, and can be strengthened by hammering. When metalworkers first began to smelt iron, they did not realize it was a common material. Because it was new and unusual, it was used for weapons carried by high-ranking men such as chiefs. Soon, however, they saw how common and useful iron was, and began to make iron tools and weapons in large numbers.

Ironworking gradually spread throughout the Middle East and into southern Europe. Iron weapons helped empire-building peoples,

▲ IRON DAGGER
Forged from iron and carried in a bronze sheath, this British dagger probably belonged to an important person such as a chief. It dates from the time when European society was led by warriors.

such as the Hittites of Turkey, to conquer new territory. They helped the Greeks, who were building colonies around the Mediterranean, in much the same way. In India, where the people had found little copper, iron

▼ IRON AGE SETTLEMENT
When the people of Iron Age Europe built a fort, they defended it by building deep ditches. The earth from the ditches was thrown up to make massive banks, giving extra protection. Forts like this covered a huge area, with enough space for people, houses and animals.

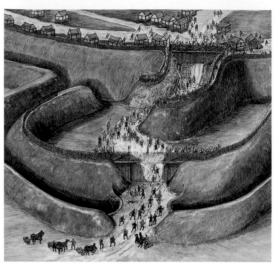

REMAINS FROM THE IRON AGE
Many of the most impressive remains from the Iron Age are actually made of bronze. Iron tools and weapons were made in large numbers, but most have rusted away. Bronze objects, on the other hand, are longer lasting, even if buried in the ground. As a result, many bronze items, buried in the graves of high-ranking chieftains, have survived.

◄ ▼ BROOCHES
Iron Age people fastened their clothes with brooches, which were usually made of bronze and could be very ornate. The fibula style had a long pin that worked like a modern safety pin.

fibula brooch   *spectacle brooch*

▶ LA-TÈNE HORN
The curving, swirling lines of the decoration on the end of this horn are typical of the Celtic La Tène style, which developed during the late Iron Age in Europe. It is one of four horns made of bronze found in an Irish lake.

▲ BRONZE SHIELD
A shield, found in Battersea, London, was decorated by hammering the metal to make raised patterns. Bright glass and stones were added.

detail of trumpet end

made metal technology widely available for the very first time.

In Europe, iron transformed people's lives. It enabled the Celtic people, who lived in western Europe, to become warlike and powerful. They built large hill forts, protected by earthworks and fences, and fought off attackers with iron weapons. A whole village could fit into one hill fort, and these forts became bases for warrior chiefs.

The first phase of the European Iron Age is known as the Hallstatt period, after a site in Austria where a number of iron swords were found. Hallstatt chiefs grew rich, both from trading and from forcing people to pay them tribute. Some chiefs even owned goods imported from as far away as Greece and Italy.

After about the 5th century BC, the Celts began to produce metalwork beautifully decorated in a free, swirling style. This style is called La Tène, after the Swiss lakeside site where archaeologists have found many iron and bronze items.

By the time the Romans were building up their empire in Europe, the Celts were powerful enough to fight the Romans' armies and halt them for a while. The Celtic chiefs issued their own coinage, built strong forts and traded with Rome in times of peace. For several centuries, these men of iron were Europe's strongest and most feared leaders.

▲ IRONWORKERS
In order to produce workable iron, the ore (the rock containing the metal) had to be heated to a high temperature. Early ironworkers made kilns of earth to contain the fire so that it could build up enough heat.

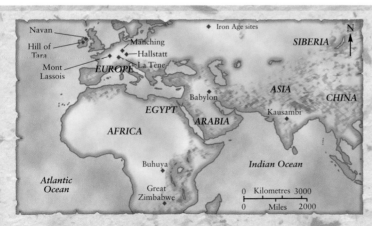

▲ IRON AGE SITES
Although Europe has perhaps the most famous of all Iron Age cultures, people in many other parts of the world discovered how to work iron. Eastern Asia and Africa were two areas that had notable Iron Age societies.

Key Dates

- 1300BC Middle Eastern people discover iron and make iron tools and weapons.

- 1000BC Ironworking established in central Europe.

- 800BC Beginning of Hallstatt period.

- 600BC Iron discovered in China; hotter furnaces mean the Chinese can cast iron, something impossible in the west until much later.

- 500BC Ironworking begins in Africa.

- 500BC Ironworking well established in most of Europe.

- 450–100BC Fine metalwork of the La Tène period made in Europe.

The Birth of Civilization

▲ PAINTED POT
Pottery from the Mesopotamian cities is often of a very high quality, thin, well shaped and with elegant decoration.

WHILE MANY OF THE EVENTS described so far in this book were happening, another development, more earth-shattering than all the rest, was beginning at different points on the globe. Small towns were growing into cities. Their inhabitants were putting up large temples and palaces, inventing written languages and creating complex societies in which there were many different jobs for people to do. There were farmers, craftworkers, priests, governors and kings. This new city-based way of life is what we now call civilization.

The place where civilization first began was Mesopotamia, the land between the Tigris and Euphrates rivers in what is now Iraq. This was part of the Fertile Crescent, where farming had started. It was the reliable food supply produced by farming that made the developments that followed possible.

As the farmers became more experienced, they worked out how to irrigate their fields so that they could bring water to the drier areas. This made the food supply more constant. The farmers could also increase

◀ WOMAN AND BABY
This figure of a mother holding a baby is made of clay. It dates from the 'Ubaid period, which lasted from 5500 to 4000BC. At this time, towns were growing into cities, craftworkers were becoming more and more skilled, and local leaders were gaining in power.

the size of their fields by cultivating previously difficult areas.

At the same time, the people of Mesopotamia began to build large, comfortable mud-brick houses. They created beautiful painted pottery, fine clay sculptures, intricate copper implements and elegant adornments with turquoise beads. People from other areas wanted these items, so the Mesopotamians traded with other cultures, carrying their cargo by boat down the rivers and along the Persian Gulf. Gradually, the traders of Mesopotamia became rich and their towns grew into cities. With cities came more power and more complex government. The priests, who were among the most powerful people, built bigger temples, another mark of civilization. Then came writing. At first, this was only a few simple symbols to show who

ARTS OF CIVILIZATION
One of the features of civilization was that society became more complex. In other words, it was divided into more social classes, with more powerful leaders and more difference between rich and poor. The rich people demanded better, more luxurious goods, from pots to ornamentation, and in Mesopotamia this led to the growth of arts and crafts. Pottery, metalworking, building and sculpture are all crafts which developed quickly at this time.

◀ POTTERY FRAGMENTS
Ancient rubbish heaps are treasure troves for archaeologists. Many pieces of broken pottery have been unearthed from the 'Ubaid period, from 5500BC to 4000BC. They often have striking painted decoration.

◀ WRITING
The scribes of Mesopotamia wrote by making marks in clay tablets with a wedge-shaped reed. This writing is called cuneiform, from a Greek word meaning wedge.

◀ NECKLACES
Mesopotamian necklaces could have thousands of beads in several separate strings. The large one, found at a farming site called Choga Mami, has around 2,200 beads, crudely shaped from clay.

▶ HEAD FROM STATUETTE
Terracotta heads like these show the style of sculpture in Mesopotamia, with some features, such as the eyes, enlarged.

THE BIRTH OF CIVILIZATION 71

owned what. Later people developed more complicated writing systems that people to record stories and religious texts.

The development of writing marks the end of prehistoric society. This happened at different times in different parts of the world. During the lifetimes of some of the prehistoric peoples, civilization was already present in Mesopotamia and other parts of the globe. Civilization came early to the Middle East, Egypt, the Indus Valley in India and parts of China. Elsewhere, in Europe, America and much of Africa, societies based on cities came much later.

In western Europe, for example, it was only with the arrival of the Romans that cities and writing appeared. The Romans took over the area they called Gaul (modern France) in the 1st century BC, some 3,000 years after the first cities were built in Mesopotamia. Today, people in some parts of the world lead successful traditional lifestyles, adapted to their

environment just like their prehistoric ancestors. But even they are affected by the decisions of governments and businesses based in the world's cities.

▼ 'UBAID HOUSE
Houses, like this one in modern Iraq, became larger and more complex in the 'Ubaid Period. They were still made of mud-bricks, but had a large central hall, many smaller rooms, a staircase, and drainage into open gullies outside.

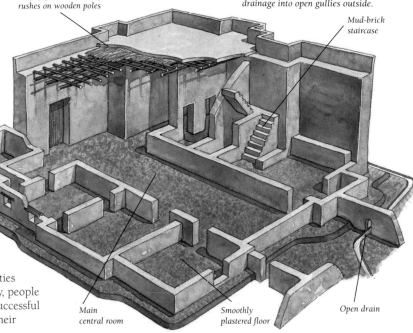

Roof of plaster covering rushes on wooden poles

Mud-brick staircase

Main central room

Smoothly plastered floor

Open drain

▲ MARSH ARABS
These Marsh Arabs live in south-eastern Iraq. They herd water buffalo and build houses out of reeds. This traditional lifestyle of the Marsh Arabs existed alongside the growing cities of Mesopotamia.

▼ ZIGGURAT
A Sumerian ziggurat consisted of a stepped platform made of sun-dried mud bricks. Only priests were allowed to climb to the top. An early example of a ziggurat is the White Temple of Uruk, made of white-washed bricks, which dates back to the late 3000s BC.

Key Dates

- 3500BC The first cities are built in Mesopotamia. Among the most important are Uruk and Ur on the banks of the Euphrates River.

- 3200BC Civilization spreads to Egypt.

- 3100BC Writing is developed in and around the city of Uruk; people write on clay tablets.

- 2500BC The first cities are built in the Indus Valley, Pakistan.

- 2300BC Several of the Mesopotamian cities unite as a single kingdom under Sargon of Agade.

- 1800BC Civilization develops separately in northern China.

ANCIENT CIVILIZATIONS

BY PHILIP BROOKS

*Evidence of the first civilizations can be found
in many forms, from tomb treasures in Egypt to
amazing temples in Mexico. This section goes
back in time to discover the amazing cultures
of the ancient world.*

The Dawn of Civilization

▲ BUILDINGS
The magnificent royal palace of Persepolis was built in ancient Persia's greatest city to reflect power and wealth.

▼ TIMELINE
The civilizations of the ancient world cover a vast time span of about 4500 years: from the first cities of Sumer to the later kingdoms based in Africa.

W HAT IS A CIVILIZATION? The term comes from the Latin word, *civis*, which means "citizen of a city". So a civilization is a group of people living together in a large town or city, who have developed a culture – a way of life with its own special quality. There are several key ingredients in a civilized culture. An early civilization may not have all of them, but it will certainly have some. They include writing, a system of government, organized religion and the ability to construct buildings and monuments on a grand scale. This section of the book describes some ancient cultures that developed along these lines.

Most of the features of civilization began to develop thousands of years ago during the Stone Age. But it took a long time for people to bring all these ideas together and to build cities on a large scale. This happened at different times in different parts of the world, as is shown on the Timeline below.

No one knows why civilizations occurred in some parts of the world much earlier than others. But cities can only grow when the food supply is reliable enough to supply the town-dwellers, who have no way of growing their own food. People had to develop

▲ RELIGION
This stone carving from the Indus Valley civilization may have been a god or a king. As far as we know, all ancient civilizations had some form of organized religion.

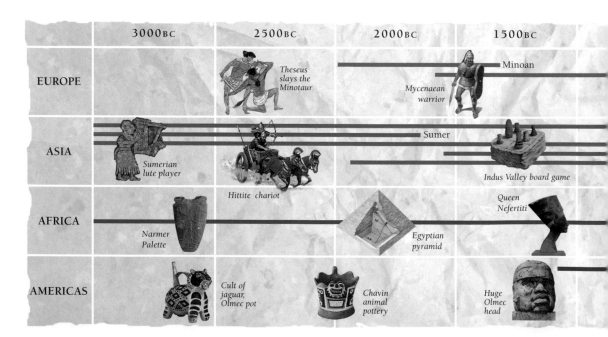

	3000BC	2500BC	2000BC	1500BC
EUROPE		Theseus slays the Minotaur	Mycenaean warrior	Minoan
ASIA	Sumerian lute player	Hittite chariot	Sumer	Indus Valley board game
AFRICA	Narmer Palette		Egyptian pyramid	Queen Nefertiti
AMERICAS		Cult of jaguar, Olmec pot	Chavin animal pottery	Huge Olmec head

efficient farming, and ways of storing and trading food, before they could build large cities. Trade in food also provided a network for trading the products of city workshops – items made of pottery, metal, and wood which city people sold.

Many ancient civilizations built up large empires, either by conquering other settlements in battle or by building up trade networks which allowed them to dominate the surrounding peoples. This meant that many ancient cultures became rich, and their power spread over a large area of the globe. The Roman empire and the empire of Alexander the Great are two examples.

Civilizations such as these have left large amounts of evidence behind them. Archaeologists – people who study the remains of cultures – are still digging up artefacts made by craft workers thousands of years ago. Complex funeral customs, as in ancient Egypt, can tell us a great deal about the civilization. Together with ancient documents and the remains of ancient cities, these things provide a fascinating glimpse of how life was lived thousands of years ago.

▲ WRITING
The marks on this ancient bone are the earliest examples of Chinese script. Writing is a key feature of a civilization.

▶ TRADE
The Romans traded in ships such as this. As civilizations developed and produced a surplus of goods, they set up trading links with others.

▲ FARMING
A civilization can only develop when its food supply is secure and the growing of crops is not left to chance. Evidence shows that rice was cultivated in China around 5000BC. Rice farming arrived in Japan in about 200BC.

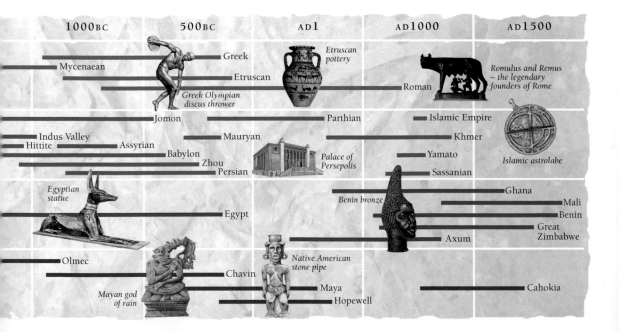

1000BC	500BC	AD1	AD1000	AD1500

Greek
Mycenaean
Etruscan
Etruscan pottery
Roman
Romulus and Remus – the legendary founders of Rome
Greek Olympian discus thrower
Jomon
Parthian
Islamic Empire
Indus Valley
Mauryan
Khmer
Hittite
Assyrian
Babylon
Yamato
Zhou
Palace of Persepolis
Persian
Sassanian
Egyptian statue
Ghana
Benin bronze
Mali
Egypt
Benin
Great Zimbabwe
Axum
Native American stone pipe
Olmec
Chavin
Mayan god of rain
Maya
Cahokia
Hopewell
Islamic astrolabe

The Sumerians

HOME TO THOUSANDS of people and bustling with activity, the world's first cities were built in Mesopotamia, the land between the Tigris and Euphrates rivers in what is now Iraq. The narrow streets and whitewashed mud-brick houses of cities such as Uruk and Ur were home to craftworkers who made pottery and metalwork that were traded as far afield as Arabia and India. People from the region made the world's first wheeled carts and chariots, and invented the world's first known writing system, called "cuneiform" script. For these reasons, Mesopotamia became known as "the cradle of civilization".

One group of people to settle in Mesopotamia were the Sumerians. They arrived in Sumer, the southern part of the area, in about 5000BC. The climate was hot and dry but farmers learned to use water from the rivers to irrigate their fields and grow plentiful crops of wheat, barley, dates and vegetables.

The Sumerians' first city was Uruk, which they built by the River Euphrates. By 3500BC, some 10,000 people lived there. The winding streets of the city surrounded its biggest building, the temple of Anu, the greatest of the Sumerians' many gods. Here the priests worshipped Anu in the hope that he would bring good weather and rich harvests. The people, who knew that they would starve if the harvests were poor, brought generous offerings to the temple. This made the priests some of the richest, most powerful people in the city.

Soon, other cities were founded all over Mesopotamia. They were similar to Uruk, with large temples, called ziggurats, and mud-brick houses. Each city was independent, with its own ruler, priests and merchants. As the cities grew rich from their trade, they competed with each other for power over the whole region.

The Sumerian cities remained independent until about 2350BC. Then the Akkadians, from an area north of Sumer, conquered the area and made it part of their large Mesopotamian empire.

▶ PLOUGH
Sumerian farmers developed the ox-drawn plough in about 4000BC. It was much more efficient than a hand-held plough and meant that they could grow a great deal more food.

◀ LUTE PLAYER
Musicians playing lutes, pipes and tambourines, provided entertainment while people banqueted, drank beer, and watched celebrations. The people of Ur enjoyed music at home and at great festivals such as New Year.

FERTILE LAND
Separate city states made up the Sumerian civilization but there were similarities between them. Each used the Tigris and Euphrates for trade and transport and all had mud-brick buildings. Also, they relied on fertile farmland to produce food. The region was so fertile, it is often called the Fertile Crescent.

▶ GRAVE GOODS
Gold items, such as adornments, were placed in the tombs of the early kings and queens of Ur. Servants followed their king or queen to the grave. After a royal death, the servants walked into the huge tomb, drank poison, and lay down to die next to the body of their royal master or mistress.

▲ STANDARD OF UR
Pictures made from shells and precious stones show a row of Sumerian farmers herding cattle and sheep. Below them, workers carry heavy loads. These pictures, known as the Standard of Ur, may once have decorated a Sumerian musical instrument.

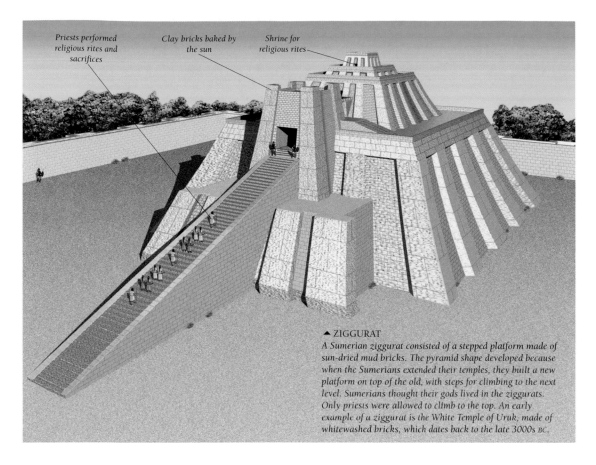

Priests performed religious rites and sacrifices

Clay bricks baked by the sun

Shrine for religious rites

▲ ZIGGURAT
A Sumerian ziggurat consisted of a stepped platform made of sun-dried mud bricks. The pyramid shape developed because when the Sumerians extended their temples, they built a new platform on top of the old, with steps for climbing to the next level. Sumerians thought their gods lived in the ziggurats. Only priests were allowed to climb to the top. An early example of a ziggurat is the White Temple of Uruk, made of whitewashed bricks, which dates back to the late 3000s BC.

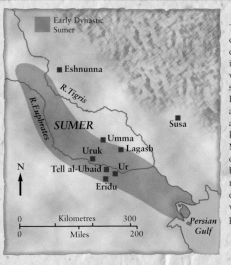

◀ SUMER
The Sumerian civilization consisted of independent, walled city states such as Ur, Lagash, Umma and Uruk. It arose in the area known as Mesopotamia, or "the land between two rivers", which covered much of what is now present-day Iraq.

Key Dates

- 5000BC The Sumerians, a farming people, settle in southern Mesopotamia.

- 4000BC Ox-drawn plough introduced.

- 3500BC Uruk becomes one of the world's first cities. Sumerians develop the potter's wheel and wheeled transport.

- 2900BC Earliest known writing.

- 2500BC Ur becomes a major city.

- 2350BC King Sargon from Akkad conquers the area of Sumer.

- 2100BC Ur is the most important Mesopotamian city, under King Ur-Nammu.

- 1700BC Ur declines, and the city of Babylon gains in strength.

Ancient Babylon

A ROUND 1900BC, the Amorites, a people from Syria, moved into Mesopotamia, the land between the Tigris and Euphrates rivers. They farmed barley, herded sheep and goats and were skilled in all sorts of crafts, from metal working to perfumery and from leather making to beekeeping.

The Amorites made their capital at the city of Babylon, by the Euphrates. During the late 1700s BC, their king Hammurabi conquered the whole of southern Mesopotamia, which became known as Babylonia. The conquered land contained peoples of many different cultures and laws, so Hammurabi decided to unify the laws. They were inscribed on a stone stela, or tablet, for all to see.

Under Hammurabi, Babylon became a great area of science and learning. Babylonian scholars developed a numbering system, based on groups of 60, which is how we get our 60-minute hour and 360-degree circle. The scientists of Babylon were also renowned astronomers, recording the movements of the moon and stars across the night sky.

The rulers of many nearby cultures were jealous of Babylon's power and the wealth the Babylonians earned from trade, and so the city was attacked many times. Hittites, from the area that is now Turkey, raided Babylon, then Kassites, from mountains to the east, invaded and took over the city. They turned Babylon into an important religious area, with a large temple to the supreme god, Marduk.

▲ CLAY LION
A clay lion which stood guard outside one of the Babylonian temples. Its intricate detail shows that the Babylonians were skilled sculptors. The lion was a popular symbol of royal power.

▶ ISHTAR GATE
The Ishtar Gate, decorated with spectacular blue stone, straddled the Processional Way which led into the city of Babylon. Three walls ringed the city, each so thick that two chariots could drive side by side along the top.

SCIENCE AND LAW
Babylon was a sophisticated city and a focal point for science, literature and learning. Scholars studied mathematics and astronomy, the science of the stars. Their ideas continue to influence us today.

◀ THE LAWS OF HAMMURABI
Hammurabi's laws were carved into a stela of black basalt rock. They include laws about money, property, the family and the rights of slaves. According to the law, a wrongdoer had to be punished in a way that suited the crime. The phrase "an eye for an eye and a tooth for a tooth" originates from Hammurabi's laws.

▲ MAP OF THE WORLD
A stone map showing the known land masses surrounded by a ring of ocean. The map was made by Babylonian scholars more than 3,000 years ago. They marked it with wedge-shaped cuneiform writing.

◄ HANGING GARDENS
King Nebuchadnezzar built fabulous hanging, or terraced, gardens for his wife Amytis to remind her of the green hill country of her home in Media. One of the ancient world's great wonders, no one today really knows what the gardens looked like.

▼ DRAGON OF MARDUK
The dragon symbolized Marduk, supreme god of the Babylonians. The Babylonians worshipped many gods. They included the sun god, Shamash, and Ishtar, goddess of war and love.

In around 900BC, the Chaldeans, horsemen from the Gulf coast, invaded Babylon. Their greatest king, Nebuchadnezzar II, rebuilt the city more magnificently than before. He gave it massive mud-brick walls, strong gates and a seven-floor ziggurat. He also built a palace for himself and the Hanging Gardens, which was one of the Seven Wonders of the ancient world.

Babylon became the largest city in western Asia. Trade along the rivers, and via the caravan routes leading eastward to Iran, also made it wealthy once more. Its magnificence survived until it was again invaded, this time by the Persians.

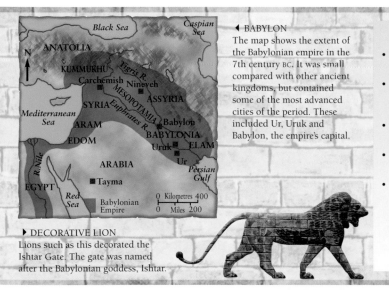

◄ BABYLON
The map shows the extent of the Babylonian empire in the 7th century BC. It was small compared with other ancient kingdoms, but contained some of the most advanced cities of the period. These included Ur, Uruk and Babylon, the empire's capital.

▶ DECORATIVE LION
Lions such as this decorated the Ishtar Gate. The gate was named after the Babylonian goddess, Ishtar.

Key Dates

- 1900BC Babylon becomes the chief city of the Amorites.
- 1792–1750BC Reign of King Hammurabi, law-giver and conqueror of Mesopotamia.
- 1595–1155BC The Kassites rule the city of Babylon.
- 900BC The Chaldeans take over Babylon and begin to rebuild it.
- 605–562BC Reign of King Nebuchadnezzar. He builds the fabulous Hanging Gardens. Babylon is the most sophisticated city in the Near East.

The Hittites

FROM THE COLD, mountainous region of central Anatolia (modern Turkey) came the Hittites, powerful peoples who flourished between about 1600 and 1200BC. A warlike group, they battled constantly with nearby settlements for control over Mediterranean trade.

The Hittites had to master a harsh homeland, finding lands to farm wheat and barley and raise sheep and cattle. They built a huge stronghold at Hattusas, in the heart of their kingdom. From here, they recruited and trained a powerful army. They were among the first to use horses in warfare and developed the chariot as one of the most feared weapons of battle.

They attacked the Mitanni, from northern Mesopotamia, and took over Syria. Their charioteers even threatened the power of the great Egyptian empire. The Hittites also used peaceful means to increase their power. They made treaties with the Egyptian pharaohs, which have been found in clay tablets in the massive royal archives at Hattusas. These show that the Hittites sometimes bought off their rivals with gold.

The Hittites had a strong land army but found it hard to defend their coasts. Invaders from the sea, known as the "Sea Peoples", attacked them constantly. This, together with bad harvests and pressure from Egypt, led to their downfall in around 1200BC.

▲ PRISONER
Egyptian mosaic tile, dating from c.1170BC, shows a Hittite prisoner.

◄ SOLDIER OR GOD?
No one knows for sure whether this armed man is a soldier or a Hittite god. He seems to be flexing his muscles. Placed at the gate of the city, he would have put fear into the hearts of any attacker.

▼ LION GATE
Fearsome-looking lions decorated the stone gateways of Hattusas, the Hittite capital and one of the strongest cities of its time. Set among cliffs and mountains, the city was well protected from enemies.

ARMIES
Both the Hittites and Assyrians had powerful armies but the Assyrian army was the most feared and efficient of its time. Consisting of foot soldiers and heavily armed cavalry, Assyrian armies were huge, several thousand strong. Many of the soldiers were captured people from lands that the Assyrians had conquered.

◄ CHARIOTEERS
Much of the Hittite military success came from their skill as charioteers. Their chariots, which could hold up to three people, one to drive the horses, and two to fight, were feared by all.

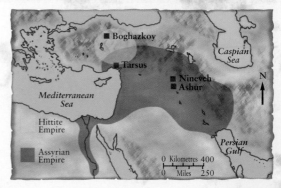

Boghazkoy
Caspian Sea
Tarsus
Nineveh
Ashur
N
Mediterranean Sea
Hittite Empire
Assyrian Empire
Persian Gulf
0 Kilometres 400
0 Miles 250

▲ HITTITES AND ASSYRIANS
The Hittites controlled much of modern Turkey and parts of northern Mesopotamia and Syria. Their real hub of power was around Hattusas and the cities of Alaca and Alisar. The Assyrian empire stretched from the Mediterranean to the Persian Gulf.

The Assyrians

▲ WINGED SPHINX
Massive carved stone sphinxes guarded city gates and palaces. Winged beasts, they had bull or lion bodies and human heads with long beards, like those worn by Assyrian kings. The Assyrians believed the monsters gave heavenly protection and warded off evil wrongdoers.

THEY WERE THE MOST FEARED people of the ancient world. The armies of the Assyrians attacked swiftly, ransacking villages, battering down city walls, and killing anyone in the way. They carried away precious metals, timber, building stone – anything they could use. They took prisoners to work as slaves on building projects in their cities along the upper Tigris river – building luxurious palaces, towering temples, and massive city walls.

The Assyrians seemed unstoppable. They conquered an empire that stretched from the Nile Delta to the ancient cities of Babylon and Ur. They built beautiful cities, such as Nineveh, Nimrud and Khorsabad, which were among the most magnificent the world had ever seen. Their royal palaces were decorated with stone reliefs that portrayed the success and glory of their kings. The reliefs survive today and show us much about the Assyrian kings and their lives – their war triumphs, use of chariots and battering rams, victory celebrations, conquered people bringing them lavish tribute, and hunting scenes.

The main strength of the Assyrians was their army but as Assyria grew in size, the soldiers could not defend the whole empire at once. One conquered city could not defeat the Assyrians but when the people of Babylonia and Media joined forces they could win, and the vast Assyrian empire quickly crumbled.

▼ THE ROYAL HUNT
Assyrian kings enjoyed hunting, particularly for lions, wildest of all creatures. They wanted their people to think their strength was god-like and often had themselves portrayed performing feats of incredible strength and bravery.

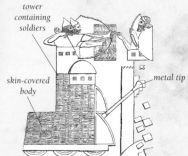

▲ COURT LIFE
A stone relief shows musicians with harps and flutes playing at the palace of Assurbanipal in Nineveh. Reliefs such as this tell us much about court life.

▼ BATTERING RAMS
Assyrian soldiers used a fearsome fighting machine, part battering ram, part tower, to attack and break through the walls of enemy cities. While the metal-tipped battering ram was driven against the walls, soldiers on the tower used picks to break them down.

tower containing soldiers

skin-covered body

metal tip

Key Dates

- c.2000BC Hittite farmers settle in Turkey.
- 1550BC Hattusas becomes Hittite capital.
- 1380–1346BC Hittites flourish.
- 1250BC Assyrians and Sea People attack Hittite empire.
- 1200BC Hittite empire declines.
- 883–859BC Nineveh built.
- 744–727BC Assyria reaches greatest power.
- 721–705BC King Sargon builds Assyrian capital, Khorsabad.
- 664BC Assyrians conquer Egypt.
- 612BC Nineveh destroyed.
- 609BC Babylonians defeat Assyrian army.

The Persian Empire

THEY BEGAN AS A SMALL nation from the region near Babylon. Suddenly, in around 549BC, the Persians seemed to be everywhere. Led by Cyrus the Great (r. 559–530BC), the Persian army pushed west and east, conquering a vast area that stretched from modern Turkey to the borders of India. Cyrus, and the emperors that followed him, gained enormous wealth from their conquests. They built cities with huge palaces, drank from gold and silver vessels, and surrounded themselves with luxury.

The Persian Empire was vast and mountainous and contained many different peoples, who often rebelled against Persian control. To keep order, the Persian rulers had a very effective army. Known as "the immortals", these 10,000 specially trained men were feared wherever they went and moved quickly to put down rebellions.

▲ PERSIAN SOLDIER
Mosaics of Persian soldiers decorated the palace of Susa. They were the keepers of law and order. An elite force of 10,000 warriors were called "immortals" because when one died, he was replaced immediately.

The emperors did not only rely on brute force. They also organized the empire so it could be controlled easily. They divided it into 20 provinces, each governed by a satrap, an official who ruled on behalf of the emperor. Each province raised taxes and tributes. The satraps were extremely powerful in their own right, so the emperor sent spies, known as "the king's ears", to each province to listen out for treachery and to check that the satraps were sending all the taxes to the emperor, not keeping some for themselves. The Persians also built a network of roads to link the corners of their empire. Spies, tax collectors and traders could travel easily around the countryside.

▲ TRIBUTES
Once a year representatives from the provinces came to the royal palace at Persepolis. Everyone brought gifts for the emperor – gold from India, horses from Assyria, two-humped camels from Bactria.

KING OF KINGS
Cyrus the Great belonged to the Achaemenid dynasty. He, and the Persian emperors who followed him, gave themselves the title King of Kings. They lived in grandeur and had absolute power. Below them, and their nobles, most of the population were farmers, craftworkers, serfs and slaves.

▶ SILVER GOAT
A silver ornament in the shape of a goat from the royal city of Persepolis. The Persians loved animals and used many different creatures to decorate all sorts of objects.

▼ PERSIAN NOBLES
A Persian nobleman stands between two soldiers. Nobles were wealthy and educated. Darius appointed his satraps, or provincial governors, from noble-born families.

▲ DARIUS THE GREAT
Emperor Darius I ruled the Persian Empire from 522 to 486BC. He was head of the army and a wise ruler. He also founded Persepolis. During his reign, the empire reached its greatest extent.

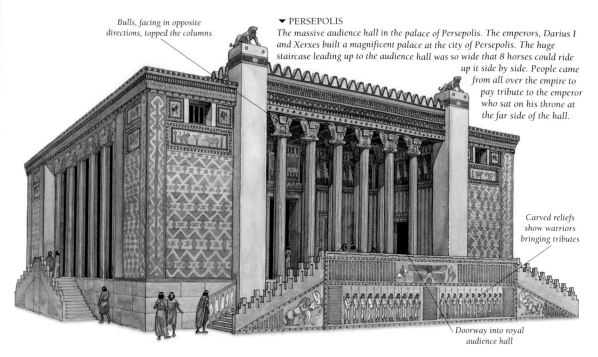

Bulls, facing in opposite
directions, topped the columns

▼ PERSEPOLIS
The massive audience hall in the palace of Persepolis. The emperors, Darius I and Xerxes built a magnificent palace at the city of Persepolis. The huge staircase leading up to the audience hall was so wide that 8 horses could ride up it side by side. People came from all over the empire to pay tribute to the emperor who sat on his throne at the far side of the hall.

Carved reliefs
show warriors
bringing tributes

Doorway into royal
audience hall

The Persians' wealth grew and the emperors brought skilled workers from all over the empire to build cities and palaces. Stone masons came from Greece, brickmakers from Babylon and goldsmiths from Egypt. The Persians also imported raw materials such as cedar wood from the Lebanon and ivory from Ethiopia.

Some people did fight off Persian invasions. The Scythians, fearless horsemen from the north, held back Persia's army, and the Greeks fought off two invasion attempts. The Greeks hated the Persians and eventually Alexander the Great, the famous conqueror from the Greek world, destroyed the Persian empire in 333BC.

▲ THE PERSIAN EMPIRE
The map shows the Persian Empire at its greatest extent in about 518BC. By then, Persia was the largest empire that the world had seen. It stretched from India to the Mediterranean. Susa was the capital. The empire included areas that had previously produced great civilizations: Egypt, Sumer, the Indus Valley and Anatolia.

Key Dates

- 835BC The Medes, from Media, southwest of the Caspian Sea, rule much of Iran.

- 549BC Cyrus becomes leader of the Persians. He conquers Media, Ionia and Lydia, so creating the first Persian empire.

- 522–486BC Reign of Darius I.

- 518BC Darius conquers parts of Egypt.

- 513BC Darius takes over the Indus Valley area.

- 490BC Persians invade Greece but are defeated at the Battle of Marathon.

- 480BC Xerxes leads another attempted invasion of Greece.

- 330BC Persia becomes part of the empire of Alexander the Great.

Parthians and Sassanians

CONQUERED BY THE GREAT Macedonian leader, Alexander the Great, the Persian empire ceased to exist. But after Alexander's death in 332BC, Persian leaders began again to take control of their native land. Once more they created a large empire, uniting diverse people, from sheep-herders in Iran to Mesopotamian farmers, under all-powerful emperors, whom they called the King of Kings.

Alexander, and the Achaemenid emperors before him, had shown the Persians that they needed a strong army to create a great empire. But the new Persian leaders, under two dynasties, the Parthians (240BC–AD226) and the more successful Sassanians (AD226–646), who replaced them, went further. They rebuilt society as a system of rigid social classes: nobles, priests, warriors, high and low officials, and peasants.

◀ PARTHIAN SHOT
Parthian cavalry pretended to retreat, then, unexpectedly, fired arrows backwards with deadly accuracy.

Everyone knew their place. People's whole lives, from the type of job they did to their choice of marriage partner, from how much tax they paid to the type of food they ate, all depended on the class to which they belonged.

This rigid class system kept the country united. At the top of the social tree, and sovereign ruler, was the emperor, the King of Kings himself. The people were reminded of his greatness, because the Sassanian emperors put their own images on everything they created. Their palaces and cites were decorated with stone reliefs and sculptures showing them in battle or enjoying sports such as hunting and horse riding.

▶ ROCK RELIEFS
Sassanian rulers recorded their achievements in stunning reliefs carved on the cliff faces of their native province of Fars. These show subjects such as Persian knights and Sassanian troops.

ZOROASTRIANISM
The Persians adopted Zoroastrianism as their religion. Zoroaster, or Zarathustra as he was also called, lived in about 1000BC. He taught that life was a fight between good and evil. Zoroastrians believed that the source of good in the world was the Wise Lord, a god of light and truth called Ahura Mazda. A sacred fire burned in every Persian temple as a symbol of his light and eternal goodness.

▶ AHURA MAZDA
The chief god of the Persians was Ahura Mazda, source of all goodness. A winged figure, he was the symbol of Zoroastrianism. Priests tended his sacred fire. They were called Magi, from which comes the word "magic".

▲ SACRED BULL
In ancient Persia, the bull was a symbol of power. The Persians also believed it was the first animal to be created and that, after the first bull was killed, all the other animals of the world were born from its soul.

▶ PARTHIAN AND SASSANIAN EMPIRES
The map shows the Parthian and Sassanian empires. They were not as vast as the first Persian empire but these later empires were still large. Parthian lands stretched from the farming area of Mesopotamia, north of the Persian Gulf, to the homelands of herders and nomads in central Iran. The domains of the later Sassians stretched still further east to the Indus River.

◀ CTESIPHON
The capital city, Ctesiphon, stood on the Tigris River, near to present-day Baghdad in Iraq. It grew dramatically in size during the Sassanian period, possibly containing several hundred thousand people. The Sassanians divided the city into two large suburbs. One part was for captives from the Roman empire, and the other was for the emperor and his family. The royal family lived in this large stone-built palace with its great vaulted central hall.

▲ STUCCO PANEL
Part of a decorative border from a Sassanian house. The upper classes loved luxury and their homes were decorated with ornate plasterwork, called stucco. This plasterwork was decorated with guinea fowl.

One of the most important classes was the priests. They were the leaders of the Zoroastrian religion. This faith had been developed in about 1000BC but the Sassanians made it the state religion, although contemporary eastern religions and other cults exerted an influence.

Under these later Persians, trade, industry and the arts flourished. They made developments in farming and improved irrigation systems. The local population rose but farmers worked the land too hard. Crops failed and the region became poor once more. Eventually, the Muslim Arabs invaded, finally ending the later Persian empires.

Key Dates

- c. 240BC–AD226 Parthian dynasty rules lands in Persia.

- AD109 Silk trade links China and Parthia.

- AD224 Ardashir, son of high priest Sasan destroys Parthian power. He founds Persian Sassian dynasty.

- AD226–642 Sassanian dynasty rules Persia.

- AD531–578 Reign of Khusrau Anushirvan. He reforms tax system and improves irrigation in Mesopotamia.

- AD614–628 Reign of Khusrau Parviz, conqueror of Egypt and Syria, the last of the great Sassanian kings.

- AD637 Muslim Arabs invade and destroy Sassanian Empire.

Islamic Empire

▲ MUSLIM WOMEN
Traditionally, many Muslim women cover their heads out of doors, and some wear clothes that cover them completely.

I N THE 7TH CENTURY AD, a new faith appeared that has become one of the world's greatest religions. It emerged in the Arabian peninsula, where the Arab people lived by farming and trading. They had worshipped many gods but in about AD610, the prophet Mohammed, a merchant from Mecca, announced that a new religion had been revealed to him. It was based on belief in a single god, Allah, and he called it Islam, meaning "submission to God's will".

Mohammed and his followers, who are called Muslims, spread the new faith throughout Arabia and beyond. Soon it became the basis of a new and growing empire, which brought learning, art and science to peoples as far afield as Morocco and Persia.

The early Muslims sent out missionaries to convert people. They were followed by Arab merchants, who traversed the desert with processions of camels, known as caravans, trading in luxuries such as

◀ DOME OF THE ROCK
The Dome of the Rock in Jerusalem is the oldest surviving mosque, or place of Muslim worship. It was built at a place where Mohammed was said to have stopped on his journey to heaven.

precious stones, metals and incense.

Next followed armies, led by the caliph, ruler of the Islamic world. Within 30 years of Mohammed's death, they had conquered a huge area, stretching from Tunisia in the west to Persia in the east. Later, Islamic armies pushed even farther afield, conquering Spain and reaching the borders of India.

Islam was based on the Qur'an, the Muslim sacred book. Muslims were expected to learn how to read Arabic so that they could read the Qur'an. This meant that the Islamic empire became highly educated. Schools were attached to every mosque and universities were founded in major cities such as Baghdad. Muslim scholars also collected information from all the conquered countries. Soon the Islamic

SCHOLARSHIP
Baghdad was a focus of culture and learning and Muslim scientists were famous worldwide. Arab scholars studied the stars, mathematics, medicine, engineering, history, geography and philosophy. Islam tolerated other religions so Christian and Jewish scholars were also welcome.

▲ ASTROLABE
Islamic scientists developed the astrolabe. A flat disc with a rod that could be pointed to the sun or stars, it helped Arab sailors find their way.

◀ CALLIGRAPHY
The art of calligraphy, or beautiful handwriting, was one of the many arts that flourished in the Islamic world.

▼ HOUSE OF LEARNING
Islamic scholars study in a mosque, a Muslim place of worship. Arabic textbooks, particularly in medicine, were used in Europe for centuries.

▲ BAGHDAD
Through the centuries, Baghdad has survived repeated damage by wars, floods and fire. Today it is home to millions of Muslims.

▶ SPREADING ISLAM
Arabian merchants blazed new trails across the deserts to spread the new faith. They crossed western Asia and northern Africa.

empire contained the world's finest scientists, doctors and most able writers. The arts also flourished and houses and mosques were decorated with beautiful tiles and stonework.

Religious faith, learning and a powerful army made the Islamic empire successful and long lasting. It survived until the 13th century.

▲ ISLAMIC EMPIRE
The Islamic empire reached its height in AD750, as shown in the map. In some areas, such as Spain, Muslim rule lasted for hundreds of years. In other areas, such as North Africa and much of western Asia, large Muslim communities continue to exist to this day and Muslims can now be found all over the world.

Key Dates

- AD632 Death of Mohammed.
- AD634 The first caliph, Abu Bakr, conquers Arabia.
- AD635–642 Muslims conquer Syria, Egypt, and Persia.
- AD661 The beginning of the Omayyad dynasty.
- AD698 Muslim soldiers capture Carthage.
- AD711 Muslims begin to invade Spain. The empire expands to include northeastern India.
- AD750 Abbasid dynasty founded.
- AD762 Baghdad becomes the Abbasid capital.

Indus Valley Civilization

IN AROUND 2500BC, a mysterious civilization grew up on the plain of the Indus River, in what is now Pakistan. Archaeologists have so far been unable to read their writing, find out what their religion was, or work out why their civilization collapsed. But we do know that the Indus Valley people were very successful. They farmed the fertile soil by the Indus and used clay from the river banks to make bricks. With these they built several huge cities.

Most of what we know about the Indus Valley Civilization comes from the remains of their great cities Mohenjo-Daro and Harappa. They built them on the flood plain of the river. Because the river flooded regularly, they constructed massive mud-brick platforms to raise the buildings above the level of the flood waters.

▲ GODDESS
Small clay figures showing a woman with a decorative head-dress, have been found at Mohenjo-Daro. These were most likely representations of a fertility or mother-goddess.

Each city was divided into two areas. One was where the people lived. Flat-roofed, mud-brick houses were arranged in neat rows along straight streets and alleyways. Most houses had a courtyard, a well for water, and even built-in toilets with drains to take the waste to sewers beneath the streets.

The other half of each city was a walled area containing the larger buildings – a public bath, a great hall, and a massive granary, or grain store, the size of an Olympic swimming pool. Priests and worshippers may have used the baths for ritual washing before religious ceremonies. Near the granaries were large threshing floors where farmers brought their grain to be threshed before selling it to the people of the city.

The Indus civilization continued for about 800 years but then began to decline. Houses fell into ruin and many people left. No one knows for certain why this happened. Bad floods and a rising population may have forced farmers to grow too much food, exhausting the land and causing poor harvests and famine.

◀ GOD-KING
A stone bust showing a man dressed in a patterned shawl. The quality of the carving and the thoughtful expression may mean that the man was an Indus god or perhaps a king.

DAILY LIFE
From the evidence, it seems that Indus Valley cities were full of life and activity. Archaeologists have found weights and measuring sticks, which suggests that they were trading areas. Merchants and traders probably thronged the streets, which also contained skilled craftworkers. Farmers too brought their crops into the cities to sell.

◀ CLAY SEALS
Stone seals, such as this, probably belonged to merchants who used them to "sign" documents and property. Seals featured an animal, such as bull, antelope, water buffalo, or tiger, each of which was found in the region.

▶ CART MODEL
Small clay models, such as this one, pulled by a pair of bullocks, prove that the Indus people used the wheel. They would have used full-size carts to carry grain and other produce.

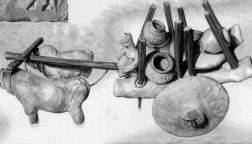

▲ GAME PLAYING
Archaeologists have found board games and toy animals showing that Indus people enjoyed playing games.

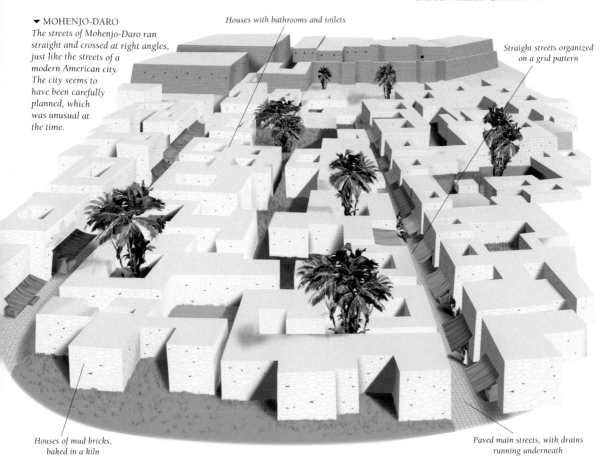

▼ MOHENJO-DARO
The streets of Mohenjo-Daro ran straight and crossed at right angles, just like the streets of a modern American city. The city seems to have been carefully planned, which was unusual at the time.

Houses with bathrooms and toilets

Straight streets organized on a grid pattern

Houses of mud bricks, baked in a kiln

Paved main streets, with drains running underneath

▶ INDUS VALLEY
The map shows the extent of the Indus Valley Civilization. It was based around its great cities, such as Mohenjo-Daro and Harappa, but many people lived in the country in small towns and villages, making their living on the land. They became rich growing corn to trade in the cities, adding to their diet by hunting wild animals. They were also probably the first people to grow cotton as fabric for clothes.

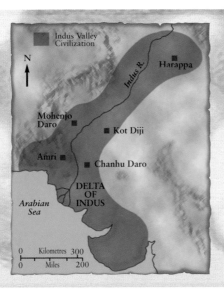

Indus Valley Civilization

N

Indus R.

Harappa

Mohenjo Daro

Kot Diji

Amri

Chanhu Daro

DELTA OF INDUS

Arabian Sea

0   Kilometres 300
0   Miles   200

Key Dates

- 3500BC Groups of farmers settle in scattered communities in the Indus Valley.

- 2500BC First Indus cities built.

- 1800BC Decline of Indus Cities begins. Population falls and cities are poorly maintained.

- 1000BC Much of population has shifted to Ganges Valley.

- c.1500BC Aryan peoples from the northwest invade Indus Valley. Invasions may have been a cause of cities' destruction.

Mauryan India

ORE THAN ONE thousand years after the decline of the Indus Valley Civilization, a new and glorious empire emerged in the Indian subcontinent. It was known as the Mauryan empire, after the Mauryan dynasty, or ruling family. Between 322BC and 185BC, the Mauryan emperors brought peace and Buddhism into war-torn India and united that vast area for the first time.

▲ BATTLE OF KALINGA
A noble Indian warrior. In 261BC, Asoka conquered the kingdom of Kalinga. Hundreds of thousands of people were killed. The cruelty of the battle changed Asoka for ever.

India's huge subcontinent has always been home to a huge variety of peoples with different languages, beliefs and customs. By the 6th century BC, there were 16 separate states in northern India alone. Most were based around mud-brick cities along the Ganges River. The Ganges cities were often at war with each other, competing for fertile land. In the 4th century BC, one kingdom in the northwest, Magadha, emerged as a major power and began to defeat nearby settlements. Its leader was Chandragupta Maurya, a nobleman and warrior.

Chandragupta drove out Greek invaders and built an empire that included the whole of northern India from the Hindu Kush to Bengal. His son continued the expansion but it was under his grandson, Asoka, that the Mauryan empire reached its greatest glory.

Asoka began with further conquests, including the kingdom of Kalinga, but he was shocked by the destruction of war. He decided to become a Buddhist and determined that others should follow his new faith of peace and non-violence.

Asoka sent out missionaries and ordered messages about his beliefs to be put up all over his empire. Buddhist texts and sayings were carved on pillars and specially smoothed cliff faces. They explained his belief that everyone is responsible for the welfare of others. They also instructed people to tolerate the beliefs of others and always to avoid violence.

Inspired by his new faith, Asoka built hospitals and introduced new laws. A network of roads was built that connected towns throughout the empire. Farming improved and trade expanded. The Mauryan empire brought peace and prosperity to many parts of India. However, it needed Asoka's leadership to hold it together. After his death, the empire fell apart when Brihadnatha, the last Mauryan emperor, was killed.

RELIGION
Two of the world's great religions – Hinduism and Buddhism – came from India. Hinduism dates back some 4,000 years. Asoka introduced Buddhism. By the end of the Mauryan period it was the most widespread faith in northern India. Asoka also sent Buddhist teachers to nearby countries, such as Burma, to spread the faith.

◀ COLUMN
Asoka's columns were usually topped with one or more lions. Sayings on the column written in local script told people to avoid violence, eat vegetarian food and respect the beliefs of others. They also reminded everyone of how Asoka's rule helped ordinary people, by building roads, rest houses and wells.

◀ BUDDHA
The founder of Buddhism was Siddhartha Gautama, an Indian prince who was born in 563BC.

▲ RAMAYANA
An Indian miniature shows a scene from one of India's great epic poems, the *Ramayana*. Its hero, Rama, was identified with the Hindu god, Vishnu.

◀ HOLY RIVER
Indians have bathed in the River Ganges for centuries although the temples may not have been there during the time of the Mauryans. To Hindus, the Ganges is sacred. It is believed that bathing in its waters washes away sins.

▲ STUPA
The Mauryans built Buddhist shrines, called stupas, in the form of dome-shaped massive mounds, sometimes known as "temple mountains". Asoka built many stupas. One of the oldest to survive is at Sanchi, in central India.

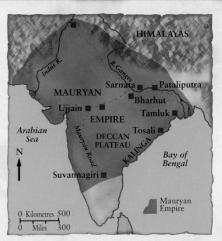

◀ MAURYAN EMPIRE
The map shows the Mauryan Empire at the time of Asoka. His grandfather, Chandragupta, took control of much of northern India, and also made conquests in Pakistan and Afghanistan. Chandragupta's son, Bindusara, conquered large areas of central and southern India, although the southern tip remained unconquered.

Key Dates

- 327–325BC The Macedonian leader, Alexander the Great, conquers the Indus Valley and the Punjab.

- 322BC Chandragupta Maurya takes over the Punjab and founds Mauryan empire.

- 303BC Chandragupta conquers the Indus Valley and part of Afghanistan.

- 301BC Bindusara, Chandragupta's son, comes to the throne and extends the Mauryan empire.

- 269–232BC Reign of Asoka. Buddhism becomes state religion and Mauryan empire flourishes.

- 184BC The death of Brihadnatha, the last Mauryan emperor.

Ancient Egypt

FIVE THOUSAND YEARS AGO, a great civilization – that of Egypt – emerged in northern Africa. Ruled by all-powerful pharaohs, ancient Egypt dominated the region for three thousand years and was one of the most successful of the ancient civilizations.

The Egyptian civilization began with Narmer. In about 3100BC, he unified two kingdoms – Upper and Lower Egypt – and became the first king or pharaoh. The pharaoh was the most powerful and important person in the kingdom and was believed to have the same status as a god. Under Narmer, and the pharaohs who followed, Egypt prospered. To help them wield their power, the pharaohs trained a civil service of scribes or writers. The scribes recorded and collected taxes and carried out the day-to-day running of the kingdom, which was divided into a number of districts. Merchants journeyed to nearby areas such as Palestine, Syria and Nubia, and the Egyptian army followed, occupying some of these areas for a while.

▲ THE NARMER PALETTE *The slate shows Narmer. He was also called Menes, meaning "the founder".*

The land of ancient Egypt was dry and inhospitable and the Egyptians relied on the great River Nile for survival. It was the life blood of the region and provided everything – fertilizer for the land, water for farming and irrigation, and a highway for Egyptian boats, called "feluccas", which were some of the world's earliest sailing craft.

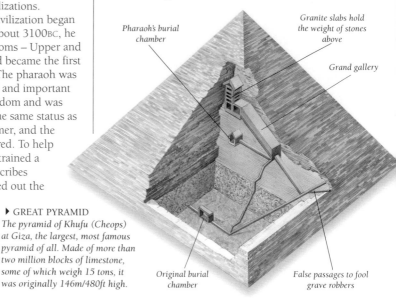

Pharaoh's burial chamber

Granite slabs hold the weight of stones above

Grand gallery

Original burial chamber

False passages to fool grave robbers

▶ GREAT PYRAMID
The pyramid of Khufu (Cheops) at Giza, the largest, most famous pyramid of all. Made of more than two million blocks of limestone, some of which weigh 15 tons, it was originally 146m/480ft high.

AFTERLIFE
The Egyptians believed in life after death. They also believed that their pharaohs were gods, who would continue living after their bodies had died. For this reason they built the pyramids to safeguard their bodies.

▶ THE SPHINX
Half pharaoh, half lion, the great Sphinx at Giza symbolized royal power. Some 18m/60ft high and 55m/180ft long, it was carved out of limestone rock in about 2620BC.

▲ THE GREAT PYRAMIDS
The pyramid of Chephren, pictured above, dates from 2560BC. The top of the original flat casing still survives. Many pyramids had steps on the outside. Tens of thousands of workers were needed to build the great pyramids.

Body wrapped in bandages

Decorated mummy case

Once a year the Nile flooded, its rich silt nourishing the land on either side. All the land watered by the river was needed for cultivation, but during the floods, no one could work the land. This was when all the able-bodied men of the kingdom went to work on large-scale building projects, such as cities and temples to the many gods of Egypt. They also built the great pyramids, the tombs and last resting places of the pharaohs and some of the biggest stone structures ever built. The desert lands were where these burial tombs were built.

◀ MUMMIFICATION
When a pharaoh died, his body was preserved. The inner organs were removed and the body was treated with a chemical and then wrapped in linen bandages. The "mummy" was then put in a decorated coffin and left in the pyramid tomb.

▶ CLOTHING
Egyptian clothes were usually made of linen, woven from flax. The richer the person, the more fine the cloth.

▼ PAPYRUS
The Egyptians invented a kind of paper, called papyrus. They made it from the stems of papyrus reeds that grew beside the Nile. The English word "paper" comes from the word papyrus.

◀ BRICK MAKING
Tomb paintings tell us much about Egyptian daily life. Here Egyptian crafts-people make building bricks using soft clay from the Nile, combined with straw.

▲ HIEROGLYPHICS
The Egyptians invented a form of picture writing, now known as hieroglyphics. There were more than 700 different picture signs, each one corresponding to one sound or word.

Ancient Egypt

▲ RAMESES II
This huge statue of Rameses II, who reigned from 1304 to 1237BC, stands in front of the great temple of Abu Simbel. It was one of many monuments that he had built to remind Egyptians of his power.

PHARAOHS RULED ancient Egypt for the whole of its long 3,000-year history. The later pharaohs, from the period known as the New Kingdom, were the most powerful. They extended the empire, and sent ambassadors all over western Asia. They built huge temples and erected colossal statues of themselves. For about 500 years, New Kingdom Egypt was the world's most magnificent civilization.

The Egyptians believed their pharaohs were gods. To them the pharaoh was both Horus, the falcon-headed sky god, and Amun-Re, the sun god. This god-like status gave the pharaohs absolute power. They appointed the priests, as well as all civil servants and chief ministers. They also controlled the army, which grew large with recruits from conquered regions all the way from Sudan to Syria.

Everywhere they went ordinary Egyptians were reminded of the pharaoh's power. In front of the temples were massive stone statues of the king in the guise of the sun god. Carved inscriptions told anyone who could read of the pharaoh's godly rank. People also read of the pharaohs' victories in Palestine and Nubia and of their peace treaties with the Hittites of Turkey.

▸ TUTANKHAMUN
Pharaoh Tutankhamun was only 18 when he died. However, he is the most famous pharaoh because when archaeologists found his tomb in the 1920s, its contents, including his golden death mask, were still complete.

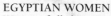

◂ TOMB TREASURES
Most ancient Egyptian tombs were robbed hundreds of years ago, but when Tutankhamun's tomb was opened up, it still contained everything that had been buried with him, including food, furniture, jewels and his glittering gold coffin.

EGYPTIAN WOMEN
Women of all classes in ancient Egypt had many rights, compared to women later in history. They ran the household and controlled their own property. They followed skilled professions; such as midwifery, served as priestesses, and could hold important positions at court.

◂ NEFERTITI
The wife of the New Kingdom pharaoh Akhenaten was Queen Nefertiti. She ruled with her husband, assisted in religious ceremonies, and had a strong political influence.

▲ HUNTING
Egyptians enjoyed hunting. The pharaoh and nobles hunted in the desert, where they caught antelopes, gazelles and wild oxen. They also hunted geese and other waterfowl on the banks of the Nile.

◀ TOMB WORKERS
The workers who built the royal tombs lived in Deir el-Medineh, a village specially built for them in the desert. When they died they were buried in tombs in the cliffs above the village. At work, they were divided into gangs of 60 craftsmen for each tomb. They were supervised by a foreman and worked an eight-hour day, eight or nine days at a stretch but they were well rewarded. Once, they went on strike when rations failed to arrive. It may have been the first recorded strike.

The most famous of the Egyptian pharaohs came from the New Kingdom. They included Rameses II and Seti I, who were renowned military leaders, Akhenaten, who briefly abolished all the gods except for the sun god, the boy-king Tutankhamun, and Hatshepsut, a powerful queen who ruled with all the might of her male relatives.

After the glory of the New Kingdom, Egypt survived numerous invasions and changes of pharaoh. The last ruler of an independent ancient Egypt was Queen Cleopatra VII, famous for her love for the Roman leader Mark Antony. Much Egyptian culture, from its gods to its funeral customs, survived, but after Cleopatra's death in 30BC, Egypt became part of the huge Roman empire.

◀ ANCIENT EGYPT
The map shows the extent of ancient Egypt. Lower Egypt was in the north. The kingdom of Upper Egypt was in the south. Farther south still was Nubia, a source of precious materials such as gold and ivory, which the Egyptians later conquered.

Key Dates

- 3100–2686BC Upper and Lower Egypt are united.

- 2686–2181BC Old Kingdom. The pharaohs build up their power and are buried in pyramids.

- 2182–2040BC The pharaohs' power breaks down and two rulers govern Egypt from separate capital cities, Heracleopolis and Thebes.

- 2040–1786BC Middle Kingdom.

- 1786–1567BC Invasion forces sent to Egypt from Syria and Palestine.

- 1570–1085BC New Kingdom. Egyptian pharaohs rule once more and the civilization flourishes.

- 1083–333BC The empire collapses. Egypt divides into separate states.

- 333–323BC Egypt becomes part of Alexander the Great's empire.

African Civilizations

AFRICA IS A HUGE and ancient continent. Its northern region produced the great Egyptian civilization. But further south, below the Sahara desert that divides the continent, other civilizations and kingdoms also appeared. Many were skilled metalworking cultures that produced tools, beautiful adornments and fine sculptures. They sent merchants on long trading journeys. Some merchants crossed the vast Sahara desert with their camels, braving heat and drought to reach the ports of the Red Sea coast and the trading posts of North Africa.

African civilizations were scattered far and wide across the continent. But there were several main areas. Ghana, Benin, Mali and Songhai were small kingdoms that flourished, at different times, in West Africa. The people were Bantu speakers, descendants of the Bantus, farmers and herders who originated in West Africa about 4,000 years ago. They opened up trade links with the Muslim rulers of North Africa, sending ivory, ebony, gold, copper and slaves northwards and bringing back manufactured goods such as pottery and glassware. They learned how to work iron, perhaps from people in North African cities such as Carthage. As demand for their goods increased, their kingdoms flourished.

There were also numerous trading kingdoms in East Africa. The most famous was on the Zimbabwe plateau. Here the Shona people had fertile land and rich sources of copper and gold. Their merchants reached the east coast of Africa, where they traded with ships coming from

▲ BENIN BRONZES
Craft workers from Benin, in what is now Nigeria, made beautiful cast bronze figures – such as this head of a royal woman.

▶ AXUM
The Ethiopian kingdom of Axum traded with India and the Islamic world. Its rulers built a palace at Takaji Mariam and many stone obelisks, some up to 30m/100ft high. Most people lived in small thatched huts.

EARLIEST CIVILIZATIONS
South of Egypt, the first civilization to emerge in Africa was the kingdom of Kush, which flourished on the Nile from about 500BC to AD350. Its capital was Meroe, an important iron-working area. From about 500BC, metal working spread south to other parts of Africa.

◀ GOLD
Skilled gold workers from the ancient kingdom of Kush made this gold papyrus holder in about 590BC. Much later, African gold workers, especially from Ghana and Mali, became famous all over the world.

▲ ROCK PAINTINGS
Sub-Saharan Africa is rich in rock paintings. This one was painted in the West African kingdom of Mali, which flourished between AD1200–1500.

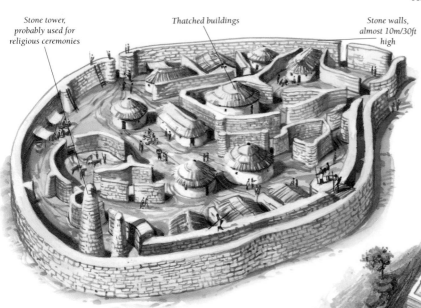

Stone tower, probably used for religious ceremonies

Thatched buildings

Stone walls, almost 10m/30ft high

◀ GREAT ZIMBABWE
The great oval stone enclosure at Great Zimbabwe was the heart of the Shona empire. Its stone walls still stand today and contain the remains of several buildings, possibly the ruler's home.

▼ LALIBELA
Some areas of Africa converted to Islam but Axum became Christian in the 4th century. By the 1200s, local masons had carved entire churches, such as this one, from rocky outcrops at Lalibela, southeast of Axum.

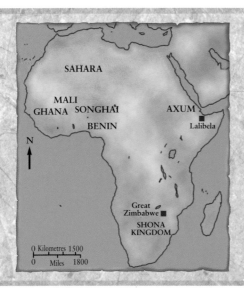

India, the Islamic empire and even China. Further north were still more trading and metalworking kingdoms in what are now Zambia and Ethiopia.

The people of the African kingdoms led lives that were well adapted to their environment. They sought out good land for crops and cattle, and found good sources of metal ore. Their kingdoms lasted a long time and many remained prosperous until the Europeans colonized Africa in the 19th century.

▶ AFRICAN CIVILIZATIONS
The peoples of Africa settled along fertile river valleys and in areas where there were sources of metals such as iron and gold. Soon even the inhospitable Sahara Desert had its settlements, oases and stopping-places for merchants. The Sahara also provided salt, one of the most valuable substances in the ancient world.

SAHARA

MALI
GHANA SONGHAI

BENIN

AXUM

Lalibela

N

Great
Zimbabwe ■

SHONA
KINGDOM

0 Kilometres 1500

0   Miles   1800

Key Dates

- AD320–650 Kingdom of Axum, East Africa.

- AD700–1200 Kingdom of Ghana, West Africa.

- AD1100–1897 Kingdom of Benin, West Africa.

- AD1200–1500 Kingdom of Mali, West Africa.

- AD1270–1450 Great Zimbabwe is capital of Shona kingdom.

- AD1350–600 Kingdom of Songhai, West Africa.

Minoan Crete

▲ FISHERMAN
▲ FISHERMAN
A young Minoan fisherman holds fish caught from the Mediterranean Sea. The Minoans were seafarers. Fishing was the basis of their economy.

JUST OVER 100 YEARS AGO, British archaeologist Arthur Evans made an extraordinary discovery. He unearthed the ruins of an ancient and beautifully decorated palace at Knossos, on the Mediterranean island of Crete. The palace was enormous. It had hundreds of rooms, courtyards and winding staircases. It reminded Evans of the ancient Greek story of the labyrinth, a maze-like structure built by the legendary Cretan king Minos. He did not know who had built the palace, so he called its builders Minoans, after the mythical king.

Remains in the palace gave many clues so today we know much more about the Minoans. They may originally have come from mainland Greece. They migrated to Crete where, for nearly 1,000 years, they created a rich and wonderful culture that reached its height between 2000 and 1700BC. Seas teeming with fish and a rich fertile soil meant that the Minoans had a prosperous and comfortable lifestyle.

The Minoans built many palaces on Crete but Knossos was the largest. The building contained shrines, religious symbols and statues of goddesses. There were several large and lavishly decorated rooms, probably royal throne rooms. Some smaller rooms were full of tall jars, called pithoi, which would have held oil, wine and other produce. Possibly a priest-ruler lived at Knossos, which may also have been an important area for food and trade.

Walls in the Cretan palaces were covered in beautiful paintings, many of which have survived. Some show natural scenes and others show the Minoan people working, enjoying themselves and taking part in religious ceremonies.

◀ WALL PAINTING
The palace at Knossos contained about 1300 rooms. Many were decorated with wall paintings like this one showing a beautiful Minoan woman with long braided hair.

◀ SNAKE GODDESS
A pottery goddess from Knossos wears typical Minoan clothing – an open bodice and pleated skirt. Her snakes may symbolize fertility.

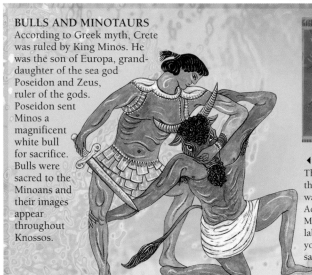

BULLS AND MINOTAURS
According to Greek myth, Crete was ruled by King Minos. He was the son of Europa, granddaughter of the sea god Poseidon and Zeus, ruler of the gods. Poseidon sent Minos a magnificent white bull for sacrifice. Bulls were sacred to the Minoans and their images appear throughout Knossos.

◀ SLAYING THE MINOTAUR
Theseus, the Greek hero, slays the Minotaur, a monster who was half man, half bull. According to Greek myth, Minos kept the Minotaur in a labyrinth or maze. Every year, young men and women were sacrificed to him.

▲ BULL LEAPING
A wall painting shows young Minoan men and women leaping over the backs of bulls. This daring feat was probably part of a religious ceremony that took place in the courtyard at Knossos.

▼ STORAGE JAR
Hundreds of these earthenware storage jars, or pithoi, have been found at Knossos, many as tall as a grown man.

◀ DAILY LIFE
Minoan towns were full of bustle and life. Most were near the coast. Houses were brightly painted and usually two or three levels high. Olive trees grew on the island and olives were used for oil and cooking.

The Minoans were seafarers. They traded with many countries, importing copper from Turkey, ivory and gold from Egypt and lapis lazuli from Afghanistan.

Suddenly, this flourishing culture suffered a disaster. Palace walls collapsed and there were great fires.

Possibly this was due to a massive earthquake or a volcanic eruption on the nearby island of Thera. The Minoans rebuilt their palaces but in 1450BC disaster struck again. Myceneans invaded from mainland Greece and the Minoan civilization was overrun.

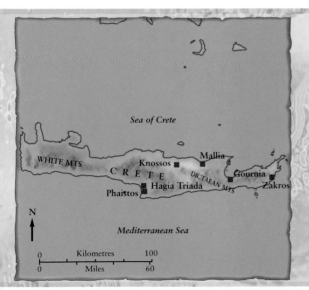

Key Dates

- c.6000BC Mainland Greeks arrive in Crete.

- 2000BC Minoans build palace at Knossos.

- 2000–1700BC Minoans build palaces at Phaistos, Mallia and Zakros. Minoan culture flourishes.

- 1900BC Cretans use potter's wheel.

- 1450BC Minoan civilization collapses with eruption on Thera and the arrival of invaders from Greece.

◀ MINOAN CIVILIZATION
Crete is the largest Greek island and the birthplace of the Minoan culture, one of the first European civilizations. The map shows the extent of this glorious civilization. Apart from the Palace of Minos in Knossos, the Minoans also built fabulous palaces in Mallia, Phaistos and Zakros and established trading posts throughout the Mediterranean.

Mycenae

IN ABOUT 1600BC a warlike group came to power in mainland Greece. They were the Mycenaeans, called after one of their largest strongholds at Mycenae in the northeastern Peloponnese. The Mycenaeans created the first Greek civilization. They lived in massive hilltop citadels or fortified settlements, made stunning gold objects and produced soldiers who were famed for their bravery.

The Mycenaeans probably consisted of several different groups of people, each with their own ruler. Each group was based in its own citadel. Mycenae was the largest but there were others at Tiryns and Gla. The people all spoke an early form of Greek and their massive fortifications were built with such huge stones that people later thought that giants must have hauled the stones into place.

From their native Greek mainland, the Mycenaeans voyaged far into the Aegean and

▲ MASK OF "AGAMEMNON"
This beautiful gold mask would have belonged to a Mycenaean king. When the king was buried, the mask was placed over his face. Archaeologists once thought the mask was a portrait of Agamemnon, a hero of the Trojan War.

Mediterranean Seas. Their merchants went west to Sicily and east to the Turkish coast, where they set up a trading post called Miletus. They also visited many of the Greek islands, trading with local people or setting up colonies. Their greatest conquest was the large island of Crete, where they defeated the Minoans. This conquest gave them access to many new trade routes that Minoan merchants had used.

The ruins left by the Mycenaeans look very bleak today, with their bare stone walls on windswept hillsides. But the kings and nobles did themselves proud, building small but luxurious palaces inside their citadels. Each citadel also contained houses for the king's soldiers, officials, priests, scribes and craftworkers. Farmers settled in the hill country and surrounding plains. They supplied the king and his people with food and sheltered in the citadel during times of war.

The Mycenaean civilization continued until about 1200BC when a great fire destroyed the citadel of Mycenae. Although the Mycenaeans hung on for another 100 years, their power began to decline.

▲ WARRIOR
Mycenaean warriors wore finely decorated helmets and highly elaborate battle dress. They were very important in Mycenaean society.

THE TROJAN WAR
Ancient Greek myths tell of a great war between Greece and Troy. Paris, Prince of Troy, fell in love and ran away with Helen, Queen of Sparta and wife of King Menelaus. King Menelaus, his brother Agamemnon and a huge army beseiged Troy for 10 years, finally capturing the city. Historians believe the legend is based on a real battle involving the Mycenaeans.

▶ THE TROJAN HORSE
The Greeks tricked the Trojans with a huge wooden horse. They pretended to leave Troy, leaving the horse behind. The Trojans pulled the horse into the city. Hidden inside were Greeks. Late at night, they came out of the horse and captured Troy. This modern-day version of the horse was designed by the Turkish architect Izzet Senemoglu and is a popular tourist attraction.

◀ MYCENAE
The Mycenaeans built their huge citadels on the tops of hills, near to the coast. Farmlands stretched back on to the inland plains. Huge walls surrounded the citadels. Some said the walls had been built by Cyclops, the legendary one-eyed giant. Within Mycenae was a palace and many other buildings. A town lay outside the fortification.

▲ SEA CREATURES
The Mycenaeans often decorated objects with sea creatures such as dolphins, or the octopus on this stemmed drinking cup. They valued the sea, which they sailed for trade and conquest.

◀ MYCENAEANS
The map shows the main areas of Mycenaean influence and their extensive trading routes. They lived on sites near to the coast. Many of their major citadels were on the Peloponnese, the large peninsula that makes up the southern part of the mainland. There were also major settlements at Athens and around Lake Kopais. From these strongholds, the Mycenaeans sailed to most of the islands in the Aegean Sea.

Key Dates

- 1600BC Mycenaean civilization begins to develop in groups on Greek mainland.

- 1450BC The Mycenaeans invade and conquer the Minoans of Crete.

- 1200BC Decline of Mycenaean civilization.

- 800BC Homer's epic poems, the *Iliad* and the *Odyssey*, record some of the traditions of the Mycenaeans.

The Etruscans

ONE OF THE LEAST-known early peoples, the Etruscans lived between the Arno and Tiber rivers in western Italy. From the 8th to the 1st centuries BC, they built a series of cities and grew wealthy by mining copper, tin and iron. We do not know where the Etruscans came from originally, and they remain a mysterious people. They could write, but none of their literature has survived, and many of their cities lie beneath modern Italian towns.

The Etruscans' strength came from living near the coast. They established iron mines by the sea, at Populonia and the nearby island of Elba, and used these as the basis for trade. Skilled seafarers, the Etruscans crossed the Mediterranean to trade with the Phoenician settlers at Carthage, North Africa. They constructed ports for their ships but built their cities slightly inland to safeguard against pirate attacks.

They also traded with Greece but the Greeks began to set up rival trading colonies in southern Italy. By the

▲ ETRUSCAN POT
Etruscan pottery was often beautifully decorated with abstract designs or pictures of animals. Many skilled craftworkers lived and worked in the cities.

▲ CHARIOT-RACE MURALS
Etruscans may have been the first people to introduce chariot racing, as shown in this tomb painting from Chiusi. Later, it became a popular Roman pastime.

6th century BC, the Etruscans and Greeks were at war. The Gauls, ancient people of western Europe, were also making raids. Etruscan leaders realized that their best protection was to join forces, and 12 of their cities came together in a league to encourage trade and defend each other from attack.

The Etruscans were also skilled artists. Their art was stongly influenced by the Greeks. The most spectacular Etruscan remains are tombs. Rich families built large

MUSIC AND DANCE
Archaeologists in the 19th century discovered thousands of Etruscan wall paintings and bronze statues. Many of these show that music and dance were an important part of Etruscan culture.

◀ FLUTE PLAYER
Musical instruments, such as these pipes, may have played a part in religious ceremonies, and in entertainment for the noble families.

▶ LYRE PLAYER
Etruscan musicians probably played the lyre, a sort of small harp, to accompany poetry, songs and dancing.

▲ ROOF DECORATION
This brightly painted head dates from the 6th century BC. Made of clay and fired in a kiln, it decorated the roof of a building in the Etruscan town of Veii.

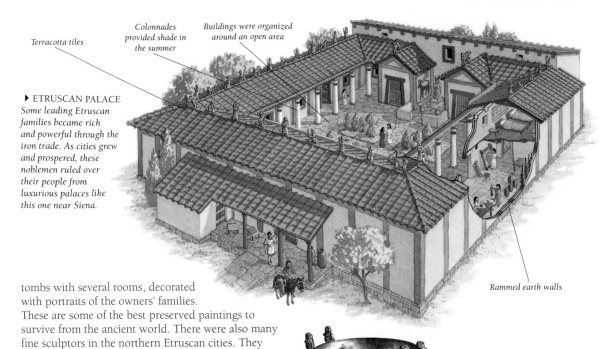

Terracotta tiles

Colonnades provided shade in the summer

Buildings were organized around an open area

▶ ETRUSCAN PALACE
Some leading Etruscan families became rich and powerful through the iron trade. As cities grew and prospered, these noblemen ruled over their people from luxurious palaces like this one near Siena.

Rammed earth walls

tombs with several rooms, decorated with portraits of the owners' families. These are some of the best preserved paintings to survive from the ancient world. There were also many fine sculptors in the northern Etruscan cities. They worked in bronze, producing figurines, statues, and items such as engraved mirrors and decorative panels for furniture and chariots.

The Romans – the Etruscans' final enemies – prized this artwork highly. When Rome and her allies conquered Etruscan cities in the 3rd century BC, they took away thousands of bronze statues.

◀ TRADE
The Etruscans traded with Phoenicia and Greece, becoming the first wealthy civilization in western Europe. With profits from the iron trade, they could enjoy luxuries such as this gold vase.

Original Etruscan Territory

Etruscan Expansion

Greek Colonies

N

CORSICA

SARDINIA

Cortona
Telamon
Vulci
Tarquinii
Caere

Adriatic Sea

Tyrrhenian Sea

SICILY

Mediterranean Sea

0 Kilometres 250
0 Miles 150

◀ ETRUSCANS
The map shows the extent of Etruscan influence and how this grew. Etruria, the land of the Etruscans, stretched from the River Arno to the Tiber. The major Etruscan cities, such as Caere, Chiusi, and Tarquinia, were independent states with their own rulers. Rome, originally a small town on the edge of Etruria, became a city in the time of the Etruscans.

Key Dates

- 800BC Etruscans set up cities.

- 540BC The Etruscans trade with the Phoenician city of Carthage, and forge an alliance with the Carthaginians.

- 524 and 474BC The Etruscans and Greeks battle over trade in Italy. The Greeks, with colonies in southern Italy, are victorious.

- 413BC The Etruscan league of cities makes an alliance with the Greeks.

- 273BC Romans conquer Caere.

- 265BC Romans destroy Volsinii.

Classical Greece

▲ ZEUS
The Greeks worshipped many gods and goddesses. Zeus, above, was supreme. Greeks thought the gods lived on Mount Olympus, Greece's highest mountain.

THE WAY OUR countries are governed, the books we read, the plays we watch, even many of our sports, all have their origins in the classical Greek civilization, which flourished some 2,500 years ago. The Greeks did not have a huge empire. For much of their history their civilization consisted of several separate city-states. But their art, science, philosophy and ways of life have had an enormous influence on our lives.

The Greek countryside is rocky and mountainous. Early Greeks lived near the coast or in fertile plains between the mountains. Gradually, these early settlements became city-states. The Greeks were good sailors and boat-builders and their civilization began to flourish when they sailed to Italy and the eastern Mediterranean to trade with nearby settlements. They also set up colonies in these areas and around the coast of the Aegean Sea.

As their wealth increased the Greeks built fine cities. The largest and richest was Athens. The citizens of Athens enjoyed much leisure time and Athens

◀ PARTHENON
The largest temple on the Acropolis, the Parthenon was built in 432BC. The pillars were marble and its beautiful frieze showed a procession in celebration of the goddess Athene.

became the hub of Greek culture. Greek dramatists such as Sophocles wrote some of the finest plays in western theatre. Their musicians created fine music and architects designed elegant buildings and temples. The Greeks also started the Olympic Games.

Greek education was famous throughout the ancient world. Philosophers, or thinkers, came to Athens to discuss everything from the nature of love to how a country should be governed. The Athenians developed a new form of government, in which people had a say in who ruled them. They called it democracy, or government by the people. Not everyone was actually allowed to vote but their system was the ancestor of modern democratic government.

Athens remained strong for several centuries until the Romans began to take over the Mediterranean world. War with another Greek city state, Sparta, also weakened Athens. In 404BC Sparta defeated Athens.

ENTERTAINMENT

The ancient Greeks believed in enjoying themselves. They enjoyed music and art and went to theatre regularly. Sport too was very important and had religious significance. The first ever Olympic Games were held in 776BC, in tribute to the god Zeus. Like today, they were held every four years.

◀ ATHLETE
A Greek discus thrower. The Olympic Games were only for men. Women were not even allowed to watch. They held their own games, in tribute to Hera, goddess of women.

Actors wore these masks – the one on the left for comedy, that on the right for tragedy.

▲ AMPHITHEATRE
Greek theatres were large, open-air arenas with rows of stone seats. There were regular drama festivals where playwrights such as Aristophanes, Euripides and Sophocles competed for the award of best play.

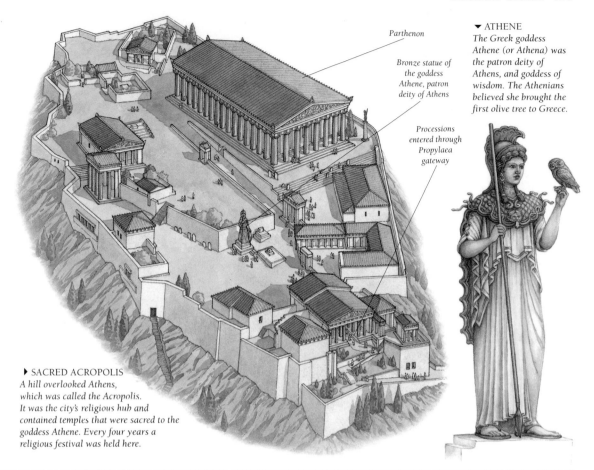

Parthenon

Bronze statue of
the goddess
Athene, patron
deity of Athens

Processions
entered through
Propylaea
gateway

▼ ATHENE
*The Greek goddess
Athene (or Athena) was
the patron deity of
Athens, and goddess of
wisdom. The Athenians
believed she brought the
first olive tree to Greece.*

▶ SACRED ACROPOLIS
*A hill overlooked Athens,
which was called the Acropolis.
It was the city's religious hub and
contained temples that were sacred to the
goddess Athene. Every four years a
religious festival was held here.*

◀ ANCIENT GREECE
The Greeks spread out
from their homeland in
the Peloponnese, setting
up colonies in southern
Italy, Sicily, the Aegean,
and the coasts of the
Black Sea.

▼ ELGIN MARBLES
These marble sculptures,
known as the Elgin
Marbles, were taken
from the Parthenon to England
in 1815 by Lord Elgin.
They remain in the
British Museum.

Classical Greece

THE HEART OF A GREEK CITY was the agora, or market place. This was a central square surrounded by the city's main public buildings – temples, law courts, market halls and shops. Everyone came to the agora to do their shopping, meet friends, listen to scholars, or just gossip. The city council also met in the agora.

Beyond the agora lay streets of private houses. They were usually arranged around a courtyard with overhanging roofs and small windows to keep out the summer sun and winter cold. In the summer, much of the life of the house took place here.

Men and women were not equal in ancient Greece. Women did not have the vote and were allowed little in the way of money or private property. Most women aimed to marry and give birth to a son. Men enjoyed much more freedom. There was even a room in most Greek houses, called the andron, which was used only by the men of the household.

Boys and girls were also treated differently. In the cities, boys went to school from age 7 to 12. They learned reading, writing, music and poetry, as well as sports such as wrestling. Most girls stayed at home with their mothers, where they learned skills such as spinning, weaving and cooking, so that they would be able to run homes of their own.

Life was rather different in Sparta. From early childhood, boys were taught skills to prepare them for fighting and life in the army. All men had to do military service. Girls too were trained for a hard, outdoor life.

When a Greek person died, people believed that he or she would go to Hades, the underworld. The Greeks imagined this as a dark, underground world, surrounded by a river, the Styx. People were buried with a coin, to pay Charon, the ferryman who would row them across the River Styx into the next world.

◀ WOMEN
Greek women wore folded material called chitons, fastened at the shoulder. Few houses had water so, balancing jars on their head, women collected water from the local well or fountain.

◀ VENUS DE MILO
This beautiful statue of Aphrodite is known as the Venus de Milo. Although carved after the time of classical Greece, it still demonstrates the ancient Greek ideal of the perfect body.

LEARNING AND PHILOSOPHY
The Greeks were educated people and valued learning. Western philosophy, which means "love of wisdom" began in ancient Greece. Greek philosophers studied astronomy, science and asked deep questions about the meaning of life.

◀ SOCRATES
The most famous of all the ancient Greek philosophers was Socrates (469–399BC). During discussions, he asked continuous questions, sometimes pretending not to know the answers in an attempt to trip up his opponents.

▲ GOING TO SCHOOL
Boys from rich families were taken to school by a slave called a paidogogos. The tutor used papyrus rolls to teach the child, but the boy would learn to write on a wax tablet, using a pointed tool called a stylus.

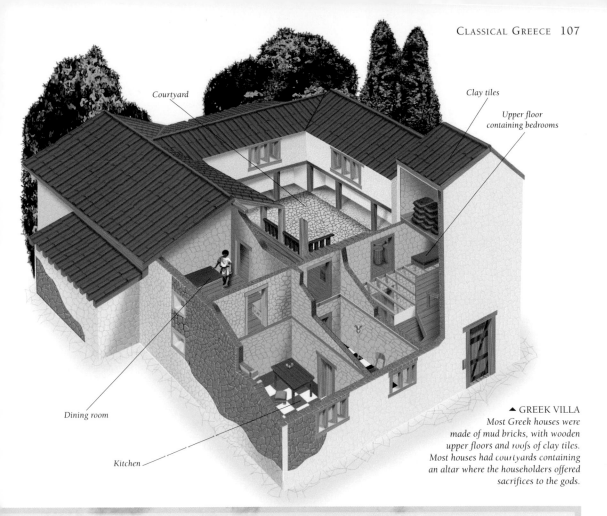

Courtyard

Clay tiles

Upper floor containing bedrooms

Dining room

Kitchen

▲ GREEK VILLA
Most Greek houses were made of mud bricks, with wooden upper floors and roofs of clay tiles. Most houses had courtyards containing an altar where the householders offered sacrifices to the gods.

▶ SPARTA
Spartan footsoldiers were heavily armed. When attacked, they formed a solid line or phalanx, spears pointing outwards. Sparta was far inland. Its people had to be tough to live in their remote mountain region.

◀ COINS
The Greeks used silver coins. Slaves toiled in mines near Athens, digging out silver by hand. Some coins were decorated with an owl, symbol of the goddess Athene.

Key Dates

- 900BC The Greeks begin to trade in the Mediterranean.

- 776BC First recorded Olympic Games.

- 700BC Greek city states develop.

- 490BC Persia attacks Athens but is defeated at the Battle of Marathon.

- 480BC The second Persian war also leads to defeat for Persia.

- 443–429BC Athens flourishes under its greatest leader, Pericles.

- 431BC The Peloponnesian Wars begin between Athens and Sparta.

- 404BC The Spartans defeat the Athenians.

Hellenistic Age

▲ COIN
The head of Alexander the Great (356–323BC), wearing the horns of an Egyptian god appears on this coin. His exploits gained him almost legendary status.

IN 336BC, A YOUNG MAN called Alexander became ruler of the small kingdom of Macedonia, north of Greece. Within just a few years, he and his well trained army had conquered one of the greatest empires of the ancient world. They swept across Asia Minor and marched down the eastern Mediterranean coast to take over Phoenicia (modern Syria) and Judea (modern Palestine). Then they moved on to Egypt, where Alexander was accepted as a child of the Sun God. From there, Alexander and his men went north once more, to take Persia, then the world's greatest empire. Soon Persia too was in Alexander's hands, together with the area of the Indus Valley, on the borders of India. Alexander was preparing to conquer Arabia when he died of a fever, aged only 33.

Alexander was one of the most brilliant generals and powerful leaders the world has known. He was highly educated – his teacher was the Greek philosopher Aristotle – but also a skilled horseman and had boundless energy. After conquering Persia, he would

▲ ALEXANDRIAN LIBRARY
The city of Alexandria contained a fabulous library where many of the works of the great Greek writers were preserved on papyrus rolls. The library burned down in AD391.

have continued into India but his men were exhausted.

By the time he died, Alexander had journeyed 32,000km/20,000 miles on his epic voyage of conquest. Everywhere he went, he took with him the Greek culture and way of life, so spreading it over a huge area. He founded cities, often called Alexandria after him,

◀ BUCEPHALUS
Alexander had a preferred horse, Bucephalus. Legend says the horse was wild and only responded to Alexander.

▶ ALEXANDRIA
The Castle of Qaitbay stands in the present-day city of Alexandria in Egypt. Alexander founded this city in 332BC. He founded others, many of which were named after him.

ALEXANDER
When Philip II of Macedonia was killed, Alexander took over a kingdom that was the strongest in Greece. Philip was about to attack Persia when he died. Alexander inherited his ambition.

▲ DELPHIC ORACLE
The Greeks often consulted an oracle for advice before undertaking a momentous event. The most famous was the oracle at Delphi. Philip II and Alexander consulted her.

◀ BATTLE OF ISSUS
At the Battle of Issus, in 333BC, Alexander with a much smaller force defeated the much larger Persian army under Darius III. It was a tremendous victory, opening Syria and Egypt to Alexander's advance.

▼ TIARA
As the Macedonian army swept across Persia, they took what booty they could carry with them. They especially prized Persian metalwork, such as this gold tiara and other items made from gold and silver worn by Persian nobles.

and left behind workers who filled them with classical buildings – temples, theatres, houses, all in the Greek style. For 300 years, this Greek style remained fashionable all over western Asia. Historians now call this period the Hellenistic Age, after Hellas, the Greeks' own name for their country.

Alexander's vast empire did not survive his death. His generals carved it up between them. Ptolemy, ancestor of Queen Cleopatra, ruled Egypt; Antigonous took over Greece and much of Turkey; Seleucus, founder of the Seleucid dynasty of Persian kings, controlled the area from Turkey to the Indus. Only cities named Alexandria remained to remind people of the great general from Macedonia.

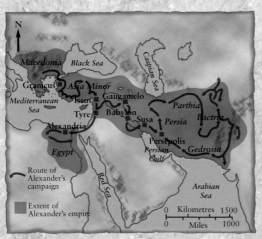

◀ ALEXANDER'S WORLD
The map shows the extent of Alexander's empire and the major routes he took. From its heartland in Greece and the Aegean coast of Turkey, Alexander's empire spread east to the River Indus. The Macedonians founded several Alexandrias in Persia, as well as the more famous one in Egypt.

Route of Alexander's campaign

Extent of Alexander's empire

0 Kilometres 1500
0 Miles 1000

Key Dates

- 356BC Alexander born in Macedonia.

- 336BC Alexander becomes ruler of Macedonia and puts down uprisings in Greece.

- 333BC Alexander defeats the Persians at the Battle of Issus.

- 332BC Macedonians conquer Egypt. Alexander is accepted as pharaoh.

- 331BC Alexander wins the Battle of Gaugamela, the final defeat of the Persians.

- 326BC Alexander and his army reach the Indus River.

- 323BC Alexander dies of a fever. His empire breaks up.

Ancient Rome

TWO THOUSAND YEARS ago a small Italian town grew to become the most important city in the whole of the western world. The name of the town was Rome. Built on seven hills near the River Tiber, Rome was already powerful by the 3rd century BC. It had a well-organized government, a fearsome army and had taken over the whole of Italy. Over the next 200 years, Rome expanded its influence to become the heart of a great empire. By AD117, the Roman Empire stretched from Britain to North Africa, and from Spain to Palestine.

At the heart of this great empire was the city of Rome itself. At the heart of the city was the forum, a market square surrounded by large public buildings, such as temples, baths and stadiums. The Romans took much from the ancient Greek culture. Many of their public buildings looked similar to Greek ones, with classical pillars and marble sculptures.

Beyond the forum were streets of dwelling places. City land was expensive. Poorer Romans could not afford houses so they rented apartments arranged in multi-level blocks, like modern flats. On the ground floor of each block were shops full of goods and craftworkers. Between the shops was an entrance way, leading to the apartments above. Some had larger, more expensive, rooms. Others, further up the building, were smaller and cheaper. Few had their own water supply or proper kitchen.

In the countryside too, many ordinary Romans lived in poverty, working the land to supply food for the cities. Here, land was cheaper and more plentiful so the wealthiest Romans built themselves large, graceful villas, or country houses. These often had their own baths and an underfloor central heating system.

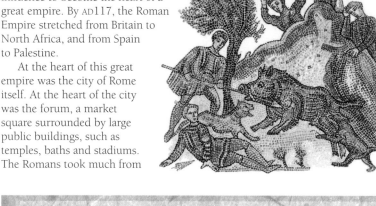

◀ HUNTING
In the countryside, Romans hunted wild boar with dogs. Hunting provided enjoyment and also gave the Romans a more varied diet.

SOCIETY
Roman society was divided into classes, or social groups. At the top were generals, governors, magistrates and other important officials. Further down were bankers and merchants. Below were craftworkers and shopkeepers. Bottom of the social pile were slaves. Romans were either citizens, free people with rights, or non-citizens.

▼ SHIPS
The Romans used ships for war and trade. Slaves worked to drive them forward by means of banks of oars on either side.

▲ AT THE BATHS
Roman cities had large public bath complexes. There were different rooms with baths of different temperatures, and bathers went from one to the other, finishing up with a cold plunge and an invigorating massage. People went to the baths not only to get clean but also to meet friends and socialize.

◀ STREET SCENE

Some of the best preserved ancient Roman houses are in Ostia, the port of the city of Rome. Sand blowing in from the coast covered the houses, protecting mosaic floors and walls. The town was full of blocks of flats with shops and bars beneath.

Poorer people lived in smaller, upper apartments

Craftworkers made and sold wares in workshops on the ground floor

An entranceway led past shops to a stairway going up to the apartments

Lower apartments had larger rooms and were more expensive

▲ CLOTHING

Most Romans dressed simply and according to class. Outside, Roman citizens only wore a toga, a large piece of white woollen cloth, wound round the body. Roman women wore long linen or woollen tunics.

◀ SHOE

Romans wore leather shoes or sandals, which laced part way up the leg.

▼ NEPTUNE

The Romans worshipped the same gods as the ancient Greeks but gave them different names. The Greek Poseidon, king of the sea, became the Roman Neptune, shown here.

Key Dates

- 753BC According to legend, Rome is founded by Romulus and Remus.

- 509BC Rome becomes a republic.

- 146BC Rome defeats Carthage.

- 58–50BC Julius Caesar conquers Gaul.

- 44BC Julius Caesar is assassinated.

- 27BC Augustus becomes first of the Roman emperors.

- AD117 Emperor Trajan conquers Dacia (Romania). Empire is at its largest extent.

- AD324 Christianity becomes the official religion of the empire.

- AD410 Invading Goths conquer and destroy the city of Rome.

Ancient Rome

As ROME'S INFLUENCE grew, so its government changed. The city had once been ruled by kings but in 509BC, it became a republic, governed by elected consuls. A senate advised the consuls. Under the consuls, Rome's power grew until, by the 2nd century BC, only Carthage, the powerful North African trading empire, could stand up to its might. In 146BC the Romans destroyed Carthage. Rome continued to be a republic until 27BC when, after a civil war, Augustus became the first Roman emperor. For the next 500 years, a series of emperors ruled an empire that was the largest in the western world.

There were many reasons for Rome's success. The empire had a strong, well-organized army. The Romans also gained rich spoils whenever the army conquered a new territory. In this way, Rome had access to a wide range of raw materials, including iron from central Europe and gold and silver from Spain. As the Romans conquered new territories, they introduced their own system of government, language and laws into the conquered regions.

◄ AQUEDUCT
The Romans built many aqueducts to bring in water from the rivers in the countryside to the city. Rome had many aqueducts and was the only ancient city with a reliable water supply. Roman aqueducts still stand today in cities as far apart as Nîmes, France and Istanbul, Turkey.

The empire also included many talented engineers, who built bridges and aqueducts as well as the first large domes. The Romans developed concrete. They also built a huge network of long, straight roads across the empire, linking all parts of the empire to Rome. Many of these routes are still used today.

By AD220, the power of Rome appeared complete. The Romans seemed to be able to build anything and their army seemed to be able to conquer any country. But in the end, the empire became too large. Peoples from the lands on the fringes of the empire in central Europe began to rebel, and it was difficult for the army to move quickly and crush their revolts. Rome's vast empire began to fall apart. In AD395, the empire divided into two and within a few years the last Roman emperor was overthrown.

ROMAN ARMY

Without their powerful army, the Romans would have had no empire. The Roman army conquered new territories and defended frontiers. It also worked on huge engineering projects such as bridges and roads.

◄ LEGIONARY
The best-trained soldiers in the Roman army were the 150,000 legionaries. They were highly disciplined, and wore metal battle dress.

▶ JULIUS CAESAR
Caesar was a consul who ruled Rome as dictator. He conquered Gaul (France) and invaded Britain. His enemies assassinated him in 44BC.

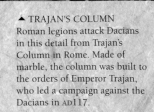

▲ TRAJAN'S COLUMN
Roman legions attack Dacians in this detail from Trajan's Column in Rome. Made of marble, the column was built to the orders of Emperor Trajan, who led a campaign against the Dacians in AD117.

▶ COLOSSEUM
The Roman emperors staged great "games" to win the approval of the Roman people. The Colosseum in Rome, shown here, was the most famous arena. Opened in AD80, it could hold up to 50,000 spectators who crowded in to see gladiators fight.

▼ GLADIATOR
Specially trained, gladiators fought each other to the death or were forced into combat with wild beasts from all over the empire. Slaves and prisoners of war were used as gladiators.

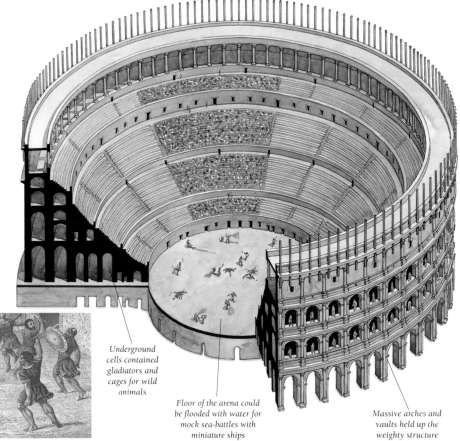

Underground cells contained gladiators and cages for wild animals

Floor of the arena could be flooded with water for mock sea-battles with miniature ships

Massive arches and vaults held up the weighty structure

◀ ROMAN EMPIRE
At its largest extent, in around AD117, Rome's empire stretched right across Europe into western Asia. Hadrian's wall, northern England, was the northern frontier. Egypt was the empire's southernmost point. In AD395, the empire, which was too large, divided. The eastern empire became known as the Byzantine Empire.

Roman Empire

North Sea
BRITISH ISLES
GERMANY
N
Atlantic Ocean
GAUL
DALMATIA
Black Sea
ANATOLIA
ITALY
CORSICA
GREECE
Rome
Antiochia
IBERIA
SARDINIA
Athens
CYPRUS
Jerusalem
Carthage
Mediterranean Sea
NORTH AFRICA
EGYPT
Red Sea

0 Kilometres 500
0 Miles 300

Early Japan

OR THOUSANDS OF YEARS after the last Ice Age, the people of Japan survived by hunting and gathering. Archaeologists call these early people the Jomon. They used tools made of stone and bone and by about 10,500BC, had produced some of the world's first pottery, even though they did not use the potter's wheel. During the 3rd century BC, a new people arrived in Japan, probably from the mainland of Asia. Known as the Yayoi, they were the first people in Japan to grow rice in irrigated fields. They also brought metal working to Japan as well as domesticated animals, woven cloth and the potter's wheel, and established a new, settled agricultural society.

The Yayoi people began farming rice on the southern Japanese island of Kyushu. Soon their farming way of life had spread to much of Japan's main island, Honshu. Yayoi farmers used stone tools, such as reaping knives, and made hoes and spades out of wood. Bronze was used mainly for weapons and finely decorated

▲ POTTERY FIGURINE
Jomon potters showed their skill making figurines like this.

◀ FARMING RICE
Early Japanese cultivated rice in wet paddy fields. Rice farming probably came to Japan from Korea between 500 and 300BC.

IMPORTED SKILLS
Settlers who came from mainland Asia brought important skills to early Japan. These were bronze and iron casting, useful for making effective tools. They also brought the potter's wheel, so the Japanese could make earthenware objects like jugs and pots, and they introduced land irrigation for growing rice.

◀ BRONZE BELL
Bells like this, covered with decorative patterns and simple pictures of humans and animals, were made in both the Yayoi and Yamato periods. Unlike western bells, they did not have clappers, so must have been rung by beating.

▲ GONE FISHING
Japanese fishermen pursue a whale through high seas in this typically stylized image. Early people in northeastern Japan relied on fish and other seafood for much of their diet. Whale meat was an important food source to them.

▼ TOMB HORSE
When a Yamato emperor died, the people surrounded his burial site with thousands of pottery objects, such as this horse. They were meant to protect the tomb and its contents.

◀ SHINTO
A Shinto temple in Nikko, Japan. Shinto is the traditional religion of Japan. It dates back to very early Japan and was based on a love of nature and belief in spirits, called kami.

items such as bells and mirrors. From this evidence, archaelogists believe that only rich or high-status Japanese, such as chiefs, priests and warriors, used metal items. Their owners may have used many of these bronze items, including bells, in ceremonies to celebrate the passing of the seasons or rituals performed during rice planting and harvesting.

By the 3rd century AD, some of the warrior-chiefs had gained power over large areas of Japan. These powerful families became the leaders of the next Japanese culture, the Yamato. They claimed to be descended from the sun goddess and their power soon stretched across the whole of Japan. They led their soldiers on horseback, and copied the government of the Chinese emperors, with large courts and ranks of officials. The Yamato built hill-top settlements to defend themselves and huge burial tombs, surrounded by moats, were also used for protection. These tombs, filled with adornments and weapons, indicate the great power and wealth of the Yamato emperors.

◀ EARLY JAPAN
The Yayoi rice farmers spread northwards from southern Japan. They are named after the section of modern Tokyo where remains of their culture were found. The later Yamato culture began on the Yamato plain in southeastern Honshu. The greatest number of Yamato remains, especially palaces and tombs, is still to be found in this area.

Key Dates

- 8000BC Jomon culture of hunter-gatherers dominates Japan.

- 200BC The Yayoi people begin to introduce rice farming.

- AD250 Rise of the Yamato culture.

- AD350 The Yamato emperor rules the whole of Japan.

- AD538 The first Buddhists to settle in Japan arrive from Korea.

- AD604 After a period of weakness, Prince Shotoku Taishi strengthens imperial power and introduces new forms of government based on Chinese models.

- AD710 The Yamato period ends and the state capital moves to the city of Nara.

The Khmers

▲ GLAZED JAR
This Vietnamese jar was made around the 11th century AD. It has a finely cracked cream glaze, decorated with brown leaf sprays.

DEEP IN THE JUNGLES of Cambodia stand the remains of some of the largest temples and palaces ever constructed. They are reminders of the great civilization of the Khmers, who flourished between the 9th and 15th centuries AD, and were ruled by kings so powerful that their people believed them to be gods.

The Khmers lived in a difficult, inhospitable part of the world. Dense tropical forests covered much of their country and every year the monsoons flooded their rivers, making it difficult to grow crops. But they began to clear the forests and adapted to the rains, growing rice in the flooded plains on either side of the great Mekong River.

As time went on, the Khmers learned how to dig canals and reservoirs, to drain away and store the flood water. Then they could water their fields during the rest of the year, when there was little rain.

While their farmers were busy in the fields, the

▲ ANGKOR WAT
The greatest of all the Khmer temples was Angkor Wat. Started by King Suryavarman II in 1113, it covers a vast area. It contains several courtyards lined with shrines and topped with huge towers. The picture shows a detail from the Elephant's Terrace.

Khmers were opening up trade routes through Siam (Thailand) into India. As a result of these links, Khmer artists and architects copied Indian styles, and the Khmers began to adopt the Hindu religion.

RELIGIOUS TEMPLE

The Khmer kingdom lasted for 500 years. Angkor Wat was its most fabulous achievement. The Khmers were Hindus, who believed in gods such as Vishnu, Shiva and Brahma. Their images appear in reliefs all over the temple. Also at Angkor Wat were statues of Nagas, mythical seven-headed snakes. The Khmers believed they were kindly water spirits.

▶ ANGKOR CARVING
The sculptors who worked at Angkor Wat created fabulous work. This intricate stone carving forms part of a massive gateway to the temple. It has survived for hundreds of years in the Cambodian jungles.

▲ ASPARAS
Carved in relief on the walls and in the courtyard of Angkor Wat, these dancing women were known as *asparas*. Covered in jewels and wearing towering headdresses, they entertained kings.

◀ CUTTING TREES
The Khmers had to clear large areas of tropical forest for farming and to build their temples. They used elephants to move and carry heavy trees. They also used elephants in warfare.

The godly status of the Khmer kings gave them enormous power and made most people eager to work for them. From the 12th century onwards, the kings began enormous building projects – temples covering many acres, surrounded by huge lakes and long canals. Thousands of workers, toiling in groups of 25 or more, hauled massive blocks of stone through the forest to the building sites to create towering temples. They also built hospitals, reservoirs and roads.

The Khmer kingdom lasted until the 15th century, although the people had to fight off several invasion attempts by rival nations jealous of their wealth. Finally, in 1431, an invading army from Siam proved too strong for the Khmers, who fled to a small area in the south of the country.

◀ KHMERS
The kingdom of the Khmers occupied much of modern Cambodia, plus the southern part of Vietnam. Around one million people lived in and around the capital, Angkor. The rest of the population occupied the floodplains of rivers such as the Mekong.

Key Dates

- AD802 The Khmer empire is founded under King Jayavarman II (r.802–850).

- AD881 King Yasovarman I builds the earliest surviving Khmer temple.

- AD1113 Work starts on building Angkor Wat.

- AD1177 The Cham sail up the Mekong River and attack Angkor Wat.

- AD1200 King Jayavarman VII builds a new temple, Angkor Thom.

- AD1431 Siamese invaders destroy Angkor; the Khmer empire collapses.

North American Civilizations

THE EARLY CIVILIZATIONS of North America are famous for their burial mounds, remains of which still exist today. These huge structures contain thousands of tons of earth. Large numbers of people must have worked hard for months or even years to build them. The most famous of the North American civilizations were the Hopewell people, who were based in the Ohio River valley, and the mound builders of the Mississippi area.

Hopewell mounds were gathered together in groups. At Hopewell itself, 38 mounds form a complex of 45 hectares/110 acres. Most are round or rectangular mounds. They contain several bodies. The Hopewell people left offerings and belongings in the graves with their dead. These included tools, beads, jewels and ornaments.

Some of the graves were made from raw materials that came from far away because the Hopewells traded over long distances. They imported sea shells from Florida, obsidian (a naturally occurring form of glass) from the Rockies, and flint from Illinois. In return they made goods such as pipes, pottery figurines and copper ornaments as far as southeastern Canada.

After about AD400, the Hopewell trading network began to break down, and the civilization went into decline. No one knows why this happened. Perhaps the population was too large for the local food supply. The climate became colder which may also have cut down the food supply.

But by this time another mound-building group were living in the Mississippi area. They mainly lived in small settlements but created a large city, of perhaps 30,000 people, at Cahokia. This city consisted mainly

CROPS
The most important crop for the early North American civilizations was maize. Together with beans and squash, it may have come into North America from Mexico. Most early North Americans relied on agriculture, which enabled them to create more permanent settlements.

◀ STONE PIPE
Native Americans may have used this carved stone pipe, dated about 100BC, to smoke various plants, including tobacco. Archaeologists found the pipe in Ohio.

▼ HOMES
Houses made from a framework of wooden poles, covered with thatch, provided homes for early Native Americans in the river valleys of southeastern North America.

▲ MASK
The Kwakiutl, Native Americans from the northwest Pacific coast, carved this elaborate mask. Unlike the Ohio peoples, they relied mainly on fishing for their food.

of wood and thatch houses on the fertile river flood plain. In the central area were more than 100 earth mounds. The largest was the vast Monk's Mound, which was 30m/100ft high and topped by a wood and thatch temple. Cahokia was probably the home of local chiefs, whose period of greatest power lasted some 200 years, from 1050 to 1250AD.

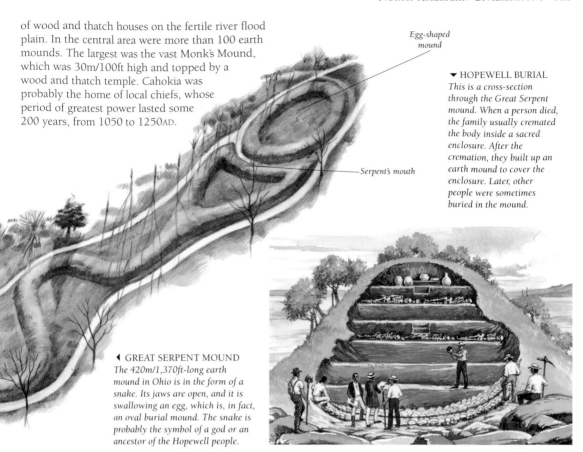

Egg-shaped mound

Serpent's mouth

▼ HOPEWELL BURIAL
This is a cross-section through the Great Serpent mound. When a person died, the family usually cremated the body inside a sacred enclosure. After the cremation, they built up an earth mound to cover the enclosure. Later, other people were sometimes buried in the mound.

◀ GREAT SERPENT MOUND
The 420m/1,370ft-long earth mound in Ohio is in the form of a snake. Its jaws are open, and it is swallowing an egg, which is, in fact, an oval burial mound. The snake is probably the symbol of a god or an ancestor of the Hopewell people.

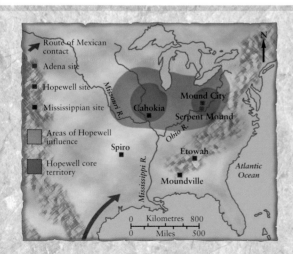

◀ NORTH AMERICA
The Hopewell people had their main areas in Ohio and Illinois. The Mississippi people came from the area where the Mississippi and Missouri rivers joined. But the influence of both peoples spread much farther. Archaeologists have found their goods all over eastern North America, from Florida in the South to Canada in the North.

Key Dates

- 200BC Beginnings of Hopewell civilization.
- AD400 Hopewell civilization declines.
- AD400–800 Maize growing spreads across southeastern North America.
- AD900 Rise of the Mississippi civilization.
- AD1050–1250 Cahokia is a major region of Mississippi civilization.
- AD1250 Power shifts to Moundville, west-central Alabama.

People of the Andes

▲ STAFF GOD
This 4m/13ft-high image, part human, part jaguar, stood in the Castillo, the main temple at Chavín de Huantar.

IT SEEMS AN UNLIKELY PLACE to settle. The high Andes mountains make travel, building and farming difficult. But in the 12th century BC, a group of people started to build cities and ritual areas in these harsh conditions. We know these people as the Chavín, after their city at Chavín de Huantar. During their most prosperous period, their settlements spread for many miles along the coastal plain.

At Chavín, near the Mosna River, they built a large temple complex with a maze of corridors and rooms. Here they hid the images of their gods, who were often beings that combined human and animal features – jaguars, eagles, and snakes. Archaeologists think that people came to the temple to ask the gods about the future, and that priests inside the hidden rooms replied by blowing conch-shell trumpets.

The Chavín were powerful for around 500 years, after which several local cultures sprang up in the region. The Huari people took over much of the Chavín's territory and a civilization of sun-worshippers emerged at Tiahuanaco, Bolivia.

▲ GATEWAY OF THE SUN
The Gateway of the Sun stood at the entrance to the temple at Tiahuanaco, near Lake Titicaca, Bolivia. It was carved out of one enormous piece of stone.

TIAHUANACO

The Tiahuanaco civilization emerged near Lake Titicaca, where they built an extraordinary city and temple complex. On the shores of the lake, the Tiahuanaco people drained large areas of marsh to make farmland to feed the city's population. With the Huari, they controlled the Andes region.

◀ ANIMAL POT
Tiahuanaco's potters were some of the most skilled in South America. They made many of their pots in animal shapes.

▲ TEMPLE WALL
The main buildings at Tiahuanaco included a huge temple whose walls were decorated with stone heads. Tiahuanaco was probably also a bustling city as well as an important ceremonial site.

◀ JAGUAR CULT
Fearsome deities appear in all early Central American civilizations. The jaguar was especially sacred.

The Olmec

THEY WERE KNOWN AS THE PEOPLE of the jaguar. The Olmec came from a small area by the Bay of Campeche in central Mexico. Like the Chavín of South America they worshipped gods that were half-human and half-animal. A jaguar figure seems to have been their preferred, and most feared, deity.

The Olmec were the ancestors of the later Mexican civilizations, such as the Maya and Toltec. Like them, the Olmec cleared the tropical forest to farm maize, squash, beans and tomatoes. Like them too, they built their temples on tall pyramids, expressed

◄ JAGUAR SPIRIT
The image of the jaguar spirit appeared on all sorts of Olmec objects, such as this pot.

◄ COLOSSAL HEAD
Archaeologists have found huge heads, such as this, at many Olmec sites. About 1.5m/5ft tall and carved from a single piece of rock, they were probably portraits of Olmec rulers. Olmec sculptors also used precious materials such as jade to carve human heads.

their beliefs in stone carvings, and were a strong warlike people.

But the Olmec did not use warfare to build a large empire. They probably used their army to protect the extensive trade links they set up in Central America. This trade brought them a plentiful supply of raw materials, especially rocks such as basalt, jade and obsidian. Olmec sculptors used these materials to produce massive carved heads and decorative reliefs showing their gods.

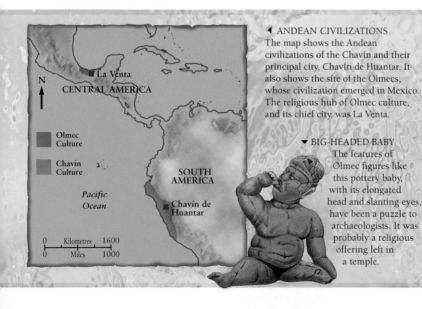

◄ ANDEAN CIVILIZATIONS
The map shows the Andean civilizations of the Chavín and their principal city, Chavín de Huantar. It also shows the site of the Olmecs, whose civilization emerged in Mexico. The religious hub of Olmec culture, and its chief city, was La Venta.

N

CENTRAL AMERICA

La Venta

Olmec Culture

Chavín Culture

Pacific Ocean

SOUTH AMERICA

Chavín de Huantar

0   Kilometres   1600
0   Miles   1000

▼ BIG-HEADED BABY
The features of Olmec figures like this pottery baby, with its elongated head and slanting eyes, have been a puzzle to archaeologists. It was probably a religious offering left in a temple.

Key Dates

- 1200–900BC The Olmecs rule north-central Mexico.

- 850–200BC The civilization of Chavín de Huantar is at its peak.

- 200BC Many small, independent cultures develop in the valleys of the Andes.

- AD500–1000 Civilizations of Huari and Tiahuanaco.

The Maya

▲ CHAC
One of the most important of the many Maya gods was Chac, the god of rain.

During the 19th century, archaeologists in Mexico were amazed when they stumbled across tall, stone-built, pyramid-shaped temples and broad plazas. They belonged to the Maya, an ancient Mexican people. The Maya created wonderful cities and were scholars. They invented their own system of writing and were skilled in mathematics and astronomy. But they were also a violent people. Their cities were continuously at war with each other. They took prisoners, who were later sacrificed to their gods.

The Maya lived in Mexico before 2000BC. But their cities became large and powerful much later, after AD300, in what historians call the "Classic" phase of their civilization. They developed efficient farming, producing maize, squash, beans and root vegetables to feed their rising population of city-dwellers.

By the Classic period, some Maya cities were huge, holding up to 50,000 people. The people lived in mud-brick houses around the outer edges of the cities. Most of the houses had only one or two rooms, and little in the way of furniture – just thin reed mats to sit on and slightly thicker mats for mattresses.

The chief Maya cities included Palenque, Copan, Tikal and Chichen Itza. In the heart of each of the cities was a complex of pyramid-shaped temples. The Maya continually rebuilt these temple-pyramids, adding more earth and stone to make them larger and taller.

The Maya survived for hundreds of years, but eventually constant civil war ate away at their wealth and power. Chichen Itza declined around 1200 and by the 16th century AD, when the Spanish conquered Mexico, only a few small Maya towns were left.

▲ TIKAL
Tikal was one of the largest cities of the Mayan civilization. Its ruins lie in the tropical rainforest of what is now northern Guatemala.

CRAFTS AND SKILLS
The Maya were skilled craftworkers. They produced fine pottery, carved stone reliefs and jade ornaments. They used razor-sharp flints for stone carving. Some flints were highly decorative and therefore buried as offerings to their gods.

◀ COSTUME
A Maya warrior wears a distinctive headpiece and carries a wooden spear. The Maya wove cloth from plant fibres such as cotton, and used plants to produce decorative dyes.

▼ CODEX
The Maya developed a series of picture symbols for writing, called glyphs. They carved these on stone tablets and also wrote them in books, called codices, made of paper, cloth or animal skins. They were the first Americans to develop picture writing.

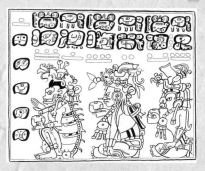

▲ CALENDAR
Astronomers and mathematicians, the Maya also invented calendars. One was a solar calendar, like ours, based on 365 days in the year. The other had a year of 200 days and was used for religious ceremonies.

▲ WALL OF SKULLS
These carvings come from a 60m/200ft-long wall at Chichen Itza. The wall once supported a fence on which heads of sacrificial victims were displayed, skewered on poles.

▲ WARRIOR
The people of Chichen Itza had an army of warriors who were feared all over the Yucatan peninsula. Their prisoners of war were often sacrificed to the gods.

▼ MAYA CITY
The heart of a Maya city contained tall pyramid-shaped temples. Staircases led up each face of the pyramid to a shrine. Special courts were included in the temple complex, including a ball court for playing games.

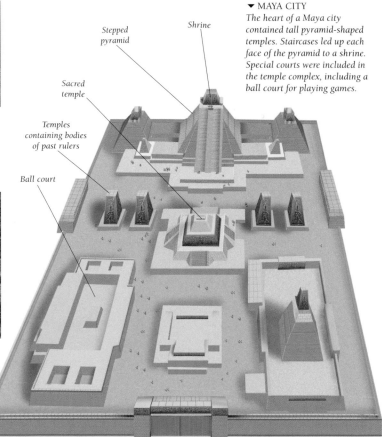

Stepped pyramid

Shrine

Sacred temple

Temples containing bodies of past rulers

Ball court

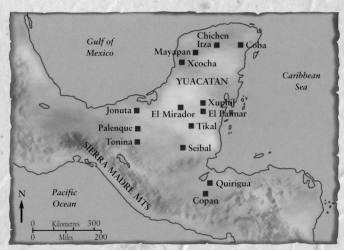

◀ THE MAYA
The Maya came from the Yucatan, the large peninsula that sticks out from the eastern coast of Mexico. They built most of their cities here and in the area to the southeast, now part of Guatemala and Honduras.

Gulf of Mexico

Chichen Itza

Coba

Mayapan

Xcocha

YUACATAN

Caribbean Sea

Xuphil

Jonuta

El Mirador

El Palmar

Palenque

Tikal

Tonina

SIERRA MADRE MTS

Seibal

Quirigua

Copan

N

Pacific Ocean

0 — Kilometres — 300

0 — Miles — 200

Key Dates

- 300BC–AD300 Many of the Maya cities are founded.

- AD300–800 "Classic" phase of Maya civilization flourishes.

- AD900 Most Maya cities are in decline.

- AD900–1200 Cities in the northern Yucatan flourish under the warlike Toltecs, from Tula.

WORLD RELIGIONS

By Simon Adams

*Throughout history, human beings have sought
to make sense of their world through
spirituality, faith and a system of values.
This section explores all aspects of religion,
from shamanism to a belief in one god.*

Faith and Spirituality

▲ OHM SYMBOL
Every religion has its own symbol. This identifies the religion and its believers. Hindus use the Ohm symbol. Jews have the menorah (candlestick), Christians have the cross and Muslims use the hilal (crescent moon and star).

▼ KEY DATES
The panel below charts the history of religion, from the earliest religion of the ancient Egyptians to the new religions founded during the 1900s.

THROUGHOUT HUMAN HISTORY, people have asked questions about life and their place in the world. They have wondered why evil and suffering exist, how the world came into existence and how it might end. Above all, they have asked if there is a god who guides and directs the world, or whether events just roll on for ever without purpose or end.

There is no definite answer to these questions, but people have tried to make sense of their lives through religion. The first religions, such as Hinduism, were pantheistic, that is they involved the worship of many gods. With Judaism, a new type of religion known as monotheism (the worship of a single god) began. Christianity and Islam are also monotheistic religions.

At first sight the teachings of the various religions appear to be very different. In fact, they can be placed into two main groups. The first group includes Hinduism and Buddhism. These religions state that the world is a spiritual place, and that it is possible to escape the endless circle of birth, death and rebirth and reach a totally spiritual life. The second group includes Christianity and Islam. These religions say that the world is essentially good, but that humans make it bad. They urge people to behave well in order to change the world and make it a better place.

All the various religions use similar techniques to put across their messages. They tell stories and myths to explain complicated subjects in a way that is easy to understand. They use symbols that identify the faith and its believers and they use rituals, such as

▲ THE GOSPELS
All religions have their own holy book or books. These contain the words of God or the gods, as told to his earthly prophets (messengers). Jews have the Torah, Christians have the Bible, Sikhs have the Guru Granth Sahib and Muslims have the Qur'an. Many religions also have books of religious laws, such as the Jewish Talmud.

BC

c.3100 Kingdom of Egypt founded. The ancient Egyptians worship many gods.

c.3000 *I Ching* compiled.

c.2166 Birth of Abraham, founder of the Jewish nation.

c.2000 Celtic tribes have a very local religion with their own group of gods.

Tutankhamun's death mask

Souvenir of a Hindu pilgrimage

c.1500 Hindu beliefs spread throughout northern India.

c.1200 Zoroaster lives in Persia.

c.900 Hindu beliefs are written down in the four *Vedas*.

600s Greek city-states link religion with government.

660 Legendary date of the unification of Japan and the start of the Shinto religion.

c.500s Mahavira founds Jainism.

c.500s Life of Lao-Tzu, legendary founder of Taoism.

551–479 Life of Confucius.

539–331 Zoroastrianism is the official religion of the Persian Empire.

Zoroastrian cup for Jashan ceremony

c.500 Jewish *Talmud* (laws) are written down.

c.500 The *Mahabharata*, a Hindu epic, is written.

The Buddha

485–405 Life of the Buddha.

c.250 Buddhism spreads to Sri Lanka and to Southeast Asia.

c.200 The *Ramayana*, the final Hindu epic, is written.

146 Greece comes under Roman rule. Many Greek gods are taken over and renamed by the Romans.

c.6BC–AD30 Life of Jesus Christ, founder of Christianity.

Christian baptism. Finally, religions develop societies that bind believers together. These techniques help worshippers to understand their faith and apply it in their daily lives.

Examining the development of the world's religions is one way to chart the history of humankind. Holy scriptures are the oldest written records we have. Not all the information contained in them need be read as historical fact. However, the latest archaeological discoveries are proving that many stories in the religious texts are based on true events.

At the start of the third millennium AD, the majority of the world's population follow a religion. There are also people, known as agnostics, who are not convinced that there is a god, but do not rule the possibility out. Atheists are people who do not believe in the existence of any god at all. Some people worship nature, while others, known as humanists, believe in the supremacy of human beings and their ability to make sensible decisions for themselves.

◀ A PHYSICAL GOD
Many religions see a human as a form, or manifestation, of their god on earth. Egyptians thought this way about their pharaoh, and some Chinese religions thought that the Emperor (left) was also a god.

▲ WORLD PICTURE
This is mandala, a Buddhist representation of the world through pictures and diagrams. Buddhists believe that it is possible to overcome suffering in the world if people follow guidelines to help them live a good life.

AD

c.30 The first Christian churches are founded.

100s Mahayana Buddhism emerges and gradually spreads to China.

313 Christianity is tolerated throughout Roman Empire. Many Romans convert to Christianity.

Jesus Christ

570–632 Life of Muhammad, the founder of Islam.

600s Islam spreads throughout Middle East and North Africa.

Muslim shahadah *(statement of faith)*

600s Buddhism spreads to Tibet and Japan.

680 Decisive split between the Sunni and Shi'ah Muslims.

800s Vikings spread their Norse religion throughout northern Europe.

1054 Christianity splits into Roman Catholic and Orthodox Churches.

1469–1539 Life of Guru Nanak, the first Sikh guru.

1517 Roman Catholic Church splits as the Reformation gives rise to Protestant churches.

1699 Guru Gobind Singh forms the *Khalsa* (Sikh community).

1830 Joseph Smith translates the *Book of Mormon.*

Modern Rastafarians

1863 The Baha'i religion is founded.

1870s The Jehovah's Witnesses are formed.

1930–74 Emperor Haile Selassie is Black Messiah to Rastafarians.

Israeli flag

1939–45 More than six million Jews are killed during World War II.

1954 L Ron Hubbard founds the Church of Scientology.

1954 Sun Myung Moon founds the Unification Church, or Moonies.

Ancient Egypt

T HE ANCIENT EGYPTIANS lived in the rich and fertile valley of the River Nile, which flowed from Central Africa in the south to the Mediterranean Sea in the north. From around 3100BC they built a great civilization along the river banks which lasted for almost 3,000 years. Ancient Egypt was governed by 31 dynasties (families) of kings, who were known as pharaohs. Pharaohs were believed to be gods on Earth.

Throughout their long history, the Egyptians worshipped many gods, each responsible for a different aspect of daily life. Their main god was Ra, the sun god. He was reborn every morning at dawn and rode across the sky during the day. In the form of the Sun, Ra brought life to Egypt. He made the plants grow and the animals strong. The ancient Egyptians

▲ THE GREAT PYRAMIDS AT GIZA
Some pharaohs were buried in vast tombs called pyramids. About 100,000 people, many of them slaves, toiled for 20 years to build the Great Pyramid at Giza for Pharaoh Khufu. The shape might have been a symbol of the Sun's rays, or a stairway to heaven.

▶ FLOODS OF TEARS
Osiris was the god of farming. After he was killed by his jealous brother, Seth, Osiris became god of the underworld and the afterlife. Egyptians believed that the yearly flooding of the Nile marked the anniversary of Osiris's death when his queen, Isis, wept for him.

AFTER DEATH
The Egyptians believed that a dead person's spirit would always need a home to return to. That is why they took such trouble to embalm (preserve) dead bodies as mummies. The body was treated with special salt so that it would not rot. Then it was wrapped in linen bandages.

◀ MUMMY MASK
Tutankhamun was a pharaoh who died 3,500 years ago. In 1922 his tomb was discovered. The wrapped-up mummy was wearing a solid-gold death mask. The mummy had been placed in a nest of three ornate wooden coffins, inside a stone box called a sarcophagus.

▶ ANUBIS
The god Anubis led the dead person to the underworld. He was also the god responsible for embalming. Anubis was always shown with the head of a jackal, a type of wild dog. As real jackals often lived in cemeteries, the animal had come to be associated with death.

called their pharaohs the Sons of Ra. Pharaohs were said to be immortal, which meant they would never really die. They were buried in vast pyramids and, later, elaborate underground tombs. Special objects and treasures were buried with them, to ensure that they journeyed safely to the afterlife.

The Egyptians believed that everything in life was controlled by the gods. They worshipped them in order to keep them happy and gain their protection. People tried to lead good lives so that, after death, they could enter the next world, which they called the Field of Reeds. They thought this was something like a perfect version of Egypt itself. To get there, first they had to pass through the dangerous *Duat* (underworld). Then they were judged by Osiris, god of the afterlife. If they had lived a good life and passed the test, they would

▲ IN THE BALANCE
In order to get into the heavenly kingdom after death, an Egyptian had to pass a test in a place known as the Hall of Two Truths. The person's heart was weighed to see if it was heavy with sin. If their heart was lighter than the Feather of Truth, the dead person had passed the test and was then presented to Osiris, god of the afterlife. If their heart was heavier, a monster called Ammit ate the heart and the person died forever.

live forever in the Field of Reeds.

The Egyptians placed detailed handbooks in their coffins to help them in this quest. These instruction manuals contained spells for the dead person to recite at each stage of the journey through the *Duat*. The most famous of these manuals is the *Book of the Dead*.

◀ CANOPIC JAR
The liver, lungs, intestines and stomach were removed from the body before it was mummified. The organs were dried out, wrapped in linen and stored in containers called canopic jars.

▶ CAT MUMMY
The Egyptians considered cats to be sacred. Some people even took their dead pet cat to the city of Bubastis, where the cat god Bastet was worshipped. There it would be embalmed and buried in a cat-shaped coffin in the cat cemetery.

▲ EYE OF HORUS
Lucky charms called amulets were wrapped in among a mummy's bandages. The eye amulet stood for the eye of the god Horus, son of Osiris and Isis. Horus lost his eye in a fight with his evil uncle Seth, but it was magically restored. The eye amulet symbolized the victory of good over evil, so everything behind it was protected from evil.

Key Dates

- c.3100BC The Egyptian kingdom is founded.

- c.2630BC First pyramid is built with stepped, not straight, sides.

- c.2528BC Great Pyramid built.

- c.2150BC Last pyramids built.

- 1504–1070BC Nearly all pharaohs, from Thutmose I to Ramses XI (and including the boy-king Tutankhamun), are buried in the Valley of the Kings.

- 332BC Egypt is conquered by the Greek ruler Alexander the Great.

- 30BC Egypt becomes part of the Roman Empire.

The Classical World

THE CIVILIZATION of the ancient Greeks began around 1575BC in Mycenae (southern Greece). The Greeks had no word for religion, yet religion affected every aspect of daily life. People believed that 12 major gods lived on Mount Olympus, the highest mountain in Greece. The god Zeus was their ruler. The gods rewarded good people and they intervened regularly in human affairs.

The Iliad, said to be written by the poet Homer around 800BC, tells the story of the historic siege of Troy by the Greeks. This event from real history is explained and presented as a squabble between the gods. In *The Iliad*, the gods used the Greeks and Trojans to fight on their behalf.

In addition to the pantheon (collection) of 12 main gods, the Greeks believed in the existence of thousands of others. Some gods had more than one role. Athena was the goddess of wisdom and a war goddess, as well as the sacred spirit of the olive tree. She was also the patron (protector) of the city of Athens. Aphrodite was the goddess of love and beauty and also the sacred spirit of the myrtle tree.

The Greeks built temples where they could worship their gods. These were erected in the highest part of a city, which was known as the acropolis. People also built shrines in their homes where they could worship

▲ EARTH AND SKY GOD
Zeus was the king of the gods. As ruler of the sky, he brought rain and storms. As ruler of the land, he took charge of morals and justice.

▶ THE DELPHIC ORACLE
Greeks used to visit the Temple of Apollo in Delphi to consult the oracle. This was the voice of the god Apollo, heard through a young priestess, the Pythia.

ROMAN GODS AND BELIEFS

The city of Rome was founded in 753BC. The Roman Empire grew to one of the largest in the world. When they conquered Greece in 146BC, they added the Greek gods to their own. Often, they changed the gods' names into Latin. By the AD300s, however, many Romans had become Christians and the old gods were neglected.

◀ PAN'S PIPES
Pan was originally the Greek god of the countryside, later associated with the Roman god Faunus. He was usually shown as half-man, half-goat. Pan had many lovers, one of whom, Syrinx, escaped him by turning herself into a reed bed. From these reeds, Pan made a set of musical pipes.

◀ MITHRAIC TEMPLE
The Romans adopted the gods of many peoples they had conquered. Mithras was a Persian god of light and truth. There were Mithraic cults across the Roman Empire.

▶ NIKE
The Greek goddess Nike was known as Victoria to the ancient Romans. She was the goddess of victory. She had a devout following among soldiers in the Roman army.

their preferred gods. This might be a shrine to Hestia, goddess of the hearth (fireplace) and family life. Some gods were worshipped in secret by members of mystery cults. Believers went through a special initiation (joining) ceremony. Once they were in, they took part in elaborate rituals. The two most famous cults were those of Demeter, the goddess of farming and harvests, and Dionysus, the god of wine. Throughout the year, the Greeks celebrated their gods at numerous festivals and ceremonies. In Athens, 120 days of the year were dedicated to festivals.

Stories about the gods and their activities had explained the workings of the world. However, Greek philosophers worked out more everyday explanations. The most famous were Socrates (469–399BC), Plato (c.427–347BC) and Aristotle (384–322BC). As their philosophical ideas took hold, religion became less important to the Greeks and their gods became part of myth and legend.

▲ POSEIDON
Poseidon was god of earthquakes and the sea. He was associated with horses and was said to be the father of Pegasus, the winged horse. Greeks believed that Poseidon was the brother of Zeus and Hades. He was often shown carrying a three-pronged spear, called a trident.

▶ KINGDOMS OF THE GODS
Zeus ruled the land and sky, and Poseidon looked after the sea. Their brother, Hades, was god of the underworld. He ruled there with his wife, Persephone.

▼ JUPITER
The main god of the Romans was Jupiter. Like Zeus, he held supreme power over all the other gods, and showed his power through thunder storms and lightning.

▶ APOLLO
The Greek, and later Roman, god Apollo was associated with light, healing, music, poetry and education.

Greco-Roman gods

These Greek gods were adopted, or adapted, by the Romans. Their Roman names are in brackets.

- Aphrodite (Venus) goddess of love
- Apollo (Apollo) god of healing
- Ares (Mars) god of war
- Artemis (Diana) goddess of hunting
- Demeter (Ceres) goddess of grain
- Dionysus (Bacchus) god of wine
- Hades (Pluto) god of the underworld
- Hephaistos (Hephaestus) god of fire
- Hera (Juno) wife of Zeus (Jupiter)
- Hermes (Mercury) messenger god
- Persephone (Proserpina) goddess of death, queen to Hades (Pluto)
- Poseidon (Neptune) god of earthquakes and the sea
- Zeus (Jupiter) supreme god

Hinduism

▲ OHM
Every Hindu prayer that is said or sung includes the sound 'Ohm.' The part that looks like a '3' stands for the gods of creation, preservation and death. The part that looks like an 'O' is the silence of god.

THE WORD HINDU comes from the Persian word *sindhu*, which means 'river.' It refers to the religion of the people who lived by the River Indus around 2500BC. This ancient civilization was based around the cities of Mohenjo-Daro and Harappa (in modern-day Pakistan). Over the centuries, the religion spread across northern India to the valley of the Ganges River.

In the 900s BC, the Hindu scriptures were written down. Two thousand years later Indian rulers took Hinduism to Sri Lanka and Southeast Asia. Today, it is followed around the world. There are more than 800 million Hindus, 700 million of whom live in India.

Hinduism does not have one central belief. It has evolved slowly over time, drawing in ideas from other religions. There are many different types of Hinduism and many different ways to be a Hindu.

Most Hindus believe that they have four aims in life. The first, *dharma*, is to live a good life by being kind to others and telling the truth. The second, *artha*, is to be wealthy and prosperous in life. *Kama* is to enjoy pleasure and *moksha* is to be freed from the world and its desires.

Hindus also believe that they pass through four stages in life. These are being a student, then a householder, then a thinker and finally an ascetic (someone who is rid of all worldly pleasures). Not everyone achieves these four aims and stages, but if they do, they will be reincarnated (reborn) into a better life. For Hindus, this eternal cycle of life, death and then rebirth into a new life is very important.

◀ BRIDE AND GROOM
A Hindu marriage ceremony contains many religious rituals. At the end of the ceremony, the couple take seven steps, making a vow at each one. The steps represent food, strength, prosperity, well-being, children, happiness and harmony.

HINDU WORSHIP
Worship is an important part of Hindu religion. Hindus worship in temples, at shrines and in their own homes. Most people pray alone, rather than in large groups. Sunrise and sunset are the most popular times of day. Worship can involve singing, prayer and offering up gifts to the gods.

▶ HINDU TEMPLE
Temples have tall, ornate towers and four gateways that represent the four directions of the universe. Hindus visit the temple throughout the day to worship at its main icon (holy image).

◀ SITE OF LIGHT
Varanasi, on the banks of the Ganges, is the most important pilgrimage city in India. Varanasi is known as the City of Light, because it was here that the god Shiva's light reached up to the heavens.

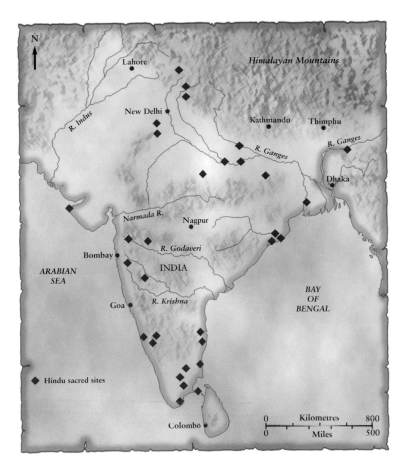

N

Lahore
Himalayan Mountains
New Delhi
R. Indus
Kathmandu
Thimphu
R. Ganges
R. Ganges
Dhaka
Narmada R.
Nagpur
R. Godaveri
Bombay
INDIA
ARABIAN
SEA
Goa
R. Krishna
BAY
OF
BENGAL

◆ Hindu sacred sites

Colombo

Kilometres	
0	800
0	500
Miles	

◀ **THE BIRTH OF HINDUISM**
Hinduism began in the Indus valley in present-day Pakistan. It spread throughout northern India, along the valley of the Ganges. In the early AD700s, Arab conquerors brought Islam to the valley of the Indus River. Over the next seven centuries, Islam spread slowly across northern India and sometimes there was conflict between Hindus and Muslims.

▼ **HINDU PRIESTS**
A brahmin (priest) looks after the temple and acts as a go-between between the worshipper and a god. Wandering priests or holy men are known as sadhus. These men lead an ascetic way of life. This means they give up worldly pleasures and wander from place to place begging for food.

▼ PILGRIMAGE
Going on a pilgrimage is an important part of Hindu worship. Places of pilgrimage include large cities, such as Varanasi and sacred rivers, such as the Ganges. Holy mountains, temples and small, local shrines are visited by pilgrims too.

▲ MEMENTO
To remind them of their pilgrimage, Hindu pilgrims often bring back small mementoes from the shrine they have visited.

Key Dates

- c.1500BC Hindu beliefs spread throughout northern India.

- c.900BC Hindu beliefs are written down in the four *Vedas*.

- c.500BC The *Mahabharata* written down by Vyasa, a wise man.

- c.300BC The *Ramayana* is written down by Valmiki, a poet.

- AD850–1200 Chola dynasty of northern India takes Hinduism to Sri Lanka and Southeast Asia.

- 1900s Hinduism spreads throughout world as Indians settle in Europe, Africa and the Americas.

Sikhism

▲ THE KHANDA
Every part of the Sikh emblem, the khanda, *has a meaning. The double-edged sword in the middle stands for truth and justice. The ring symbolizes the unity of God. The two curved swords at the bottom stand for spiritual and earthly power.*

THE SIKH RELIGION was founded by Guru Nanak. He was born in the Punjab province of what is now Pakistan and northwestern India in 1469. The Sikh holy book, the *Guru Granth Sahib*, was gathered together by the end of the 1500s. Despite persecution by Hindu and Muslim rulers of India, Sikhism slowly gained strength. Today there are more than 20 million Sikhs, mainly in the Punjab but also wherever Punjabis have settled in the world, notably Britain, East Africa, Malaysia, and North America. The word *sikh* is Punjabi for 'learner.' Sikhs see themselves as learning their faith from one true teacher, Sat Guru (the Sikh god). *Gurus* (teachers) reveal God's teachings. The Sikhs recognize 12 *gurus* in total. They are God, ten leaders of the faith, and the *Guru Granth Sahib*, the holy book.

The first *guru* was Nanak. He lived during a period of great conflict between Hindus and Muslims in India. Some Hindus were seeking a god above any religious conflict, and Nanak joined them in their search. "There is no Hindu or Muslim, so whose path shall I follow?" he wondered. Nanak came to believe that there was one God, who created everything, and that everything depended on him. Nanak also believed that God does not appear on Earth but makes himself known through teachers, or *gurus*. Sikh beliefs are summed up in the words of the *Mool Mantra*, the first hymn written by Guru Nanak.

◀ GURU NANAK
The founder of the Sikh religion was born in the Punjab in 1469. Born a Hindu, Nanak did not agree with the religious wars at the time. He also felt that too much ritual made God distant to us.

THE SIKH HOMELAND
Sikhs were often under attack from Muslim, Hindu and Afghan armies so, in 1799, they established their own kingdom in the Punjab. This lasted until British forces occupied it in 1849. When the British left in 1947, the Punjab was split between India and Pakistan. Since the 1980s, some Sikhs have campaigned for the Punjab to become an independent Sikh state. This would be called Khalistan (the land of the *Khalsa*).

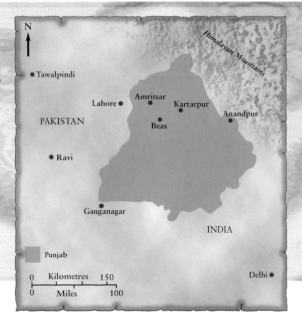

▲ GURU RAM DAS
Ram Das became the fourth *guru* in 1574. He founded the city of Amritsar. His followers dug out the Harimandir Sahib, the vast holy lake that surrounds the Golden Temple.

▶ THE GOLDEN TEMPLE

Guru Nanak saw that it was easy for worship to become a meaningless ritual. He said that God can always be found within oneself. However, as long as Sikhs understand that buildings are not holy in themselves, they can build temples at important holy sites. The Golden Temple at Amritsar, Punjab, is the holiest Sikh shrine. It was built in 1601 and contains the Guru Granth Sahib, the holy book of the Sikhs.

"There is only God. Truth is his name. He is the creator. He is without fear. He is without hate. He is timeless and without form. He is beyond death, the enlightened one. He can only be known by the Guru's grace." Sikhs meditate so that they can understand the *gurus*' teachings.

Nanak ensured that after his death another *guru* would take over and continue his work. Nanak died in 1539. Nine more *gurus* carried Sikhism forward until the death of Guru Gobind Singh in 1708. Guru Gobind Singh chose the Sikh holy scripture, not a person, to be his successor. That is why the scripture is called the *Guru Granth Sahib* and is considered to be the 11th guru. The holy book and its teachings guide the Sikh community to this day.

▼ GURU ARJAN

Arjan became the fifth *guru* in 1581. He collected all the hymns of previous *gurus* with his own contributions and combined them into the *Guru Granth Sahib*, the Sikh holy book. He died in 1606.

▲ GURU HAR KRISHAN

Har Krishan was only five when he became the eighth *guru* in 1661. He died of smallpox three years later. He is the only *guru* to be shown without a beard, because he was too young to grow one.

▼ GURU GOBIND SINGH

Gobind Singh, the tenth *guru*, is the second-most important *guru* after Guru Nanak. He established the *Khalsa* (community of Sikhs) and resisted the Hindu and Muslim rulers of India.

Key Dates

- 1469–1539 Life of Guru Nanak, the first *guru*.
- 1577 Guru Ram Das founds the city of Amritsar.
- 1604 The *Guru Granth Sahib* is installed in the Golden Temple.
- 1699 Guru Gobind Singh forms the *Khalsa* (Sikh community).
- 1799 Maharajah Ranjit Singh founds an independent Sikh kingdom in the Punjab.
- 1849 The Punjab becomes part of British India.
- 1947 The Punjab is split between India and Pakistan.

Sikh Teachings

IN 1699 THE LAST of the ten *gurus*, Guru Gobind Singh, called the Sikhs together at the *mela* (fair) in Anandpur. He called for a volunteer who was willing to die for his faith. One man stepped forward and went into a tent with the *guru*, who came out soon afterwards with a bloody sword. Four more men then volunteered, and they also followed the guru into the tent. Then the *guru* opened the tent and revealed that all the five men were still alive.

This event marks the start of the *Khalsa* (Sikh community) whose members pledge to uphold the Sikh religion and defend all those in need, perhaps even to lose their lives for their faith. In order to make all Sikhs equal, Guru Gobind Singh gave all men the name Singh (lion) and all women the name Kaur (princess).

▲ THE CHAURI
The chauri, *or whisk, is a symbol of authority. Just as a whisk was waved over a guru to keep the flies away in the Punjab, so the* chauri *is waved over the holy book to show respect for it.*

▶ THE GURU GRANTH SAHIB
The Sikh holy book is a collection of teachings by Guru Nanak and other gurus. The book starts with verses written by Nanak, which are recited everyday by Sikhs in their morning prayers.

FESTIVALS

All Sikh festivals are times of meditation and thought. Sikhs hold two types of festival. *Gurpurbs* remember the birth or martyrdom of one of the ten gurus. Sikhs prepare for a *gurpurb* by reading the whole of the *Guru Granth Sahib*, which takes about 48 hours. *Melas* are fairs. They are times of strenuous activity, with sports events, mock battles, and firework displays.

▼ SIKH WEDDINGS
When Sikhs marry, the bride and groom's families are joined together as well. Verses from the *Guru Granth Sahib* are read out, and the couple walk around the holy book after each verse as part of their wedding vows.

▼ GOBIND SINGH'S BIRTHDAY
At the festival to celebrate Guru Gobind Singh's birthday, Sikhs read the *Guru Granth Sahib*, pray, meditate and sing together. People wear traditional costume.

kara

kirpan

kangha

◀ THE FIVE Ks ▶
When the Khalsa *was founded in 1699, Guru Gobind Singh asked Sikhs to wear five symbols to show their allegiance to the Sikh community. These are known as the Five Ks, because their names all begin with the letter 'k.' They are* kirpan *(a curved dagger),* kangha *(a comb),* kara *(a steel bangle),* kachh *(short pants worn as underwear) and* kesh *(uncut hair). Sikh boys and men wear a turban to keep their* kesh *tidy. However, the turban itself is not one of the Five Ks.*

Sikhs become members of the *Khalsa* in an initiation ceremony known as an *amrit sanskar*, which is often performed at the Vaisakhi festival held in April to commemorate the founding of the *Khalsa*. The ceremony is private, and takes place in the local *gurdwara* (Sikh temple). Many Sikhs wait until they are adults before joining the *Khalsa*, although boys as young as 14 do join. Women can join, but it is rare for them to do so. All candidates must be approved by existing members of the *Khalsa*.

At the ceremony, five members of the *Khalsa* each hand over one of the Five Ks to the new recruit. These are symbolic objects that all Sikhs must have. In return,

the young Sikh pledges to defend the faith, serve other people, pray every morning and evening, and not to smoke or drink alcohol. He is then given a sweet drink called *amrit* and says that "The *Khalsa* is of God and the victory is to God." After a few prayers, the new recruit is admitted to the *Khalsa*.

Sikh religious and community life revolves around the *gurdwara*. Its name means 'the door of the *guru*.' This is where the *Guru Granth Sahib* is kept, and were Sikhs gather to sing, meditate and study. There is no holy day of the week reserved for worship as in many of the other religions. Services can take place at any time.

▼ HOLY LITTER
The *Guru Granth Sahib* takes pride of place in any festival procession. It is carried on a litter by five Sikh elders, dressed in yellow and white. The litter is decorated with garlands.

▲ ANANDPUR FAIR
At the time of the Hindu festival of Holi, Sikhs gather for a *mela* (fair) to remember the life of Guru Gobind Singh. They hold athletic and horse-riding events and compete in the martial arts. The greatest of these *melas* is the Hola Mohalla in Anandpur, Punjab.

Sikh Festivals

- December/January – Guru Gobind Singh's birthday.

- February – Hola Mohalla, in memory of Guru Gobind Singh.

- April – Formation of the *Khalsa*.

- May – Martyrdom of Guru Arjan (1606).

- August – Celebration of the *Guru Granth Sahib* (1606).

- October – The Hindu festival of Diwali marks Guru Hargobind's release from prison in 1619.

- October – Guru Nanak's birthday.

- November – Martyrdom of Guru Tegh Bahadur (1675).

Religion in China

CHINA DOES NOT have a single religion. Instead Chinese religion is made up of four separate religions and philosophies (ways of thinking). The three main ones are Confucianism, Buddhism and Taoism. Together, they are known as the *San-chiao* (the three ways). The fourth is the popular folk religion followed throughout the country. The Chinese follow all these religions in their daily lives, picking out those bits that seem most helpful or useful at the time. Few people follow just one.

The first way, Confucianism, is based on the practice of divination (foretelling the future). This is explained in five books, all compiled long before the birth of Confucius. The books are the *I Ching* (*Book of Changes*), the *Shih Ching* (*Book of Poetry*), the *Shu Ching* (*Book of History*), the *Li Chin* (*Book of Rites*) and the *Ch'un-ch'iu* (*Spring and Autumn Annals*). Confucius's own teachings are contained in the *Four Books of Confucianism*. Together these books produce a code of good conduct for people to follow, rather than a formal religion for them to worship. Followers of Confucius can believe in any god or none.

▲ GOOD WORK
Confucius expected farmers to work hard and produce food for their family and country. Many Chinese festivals celebrate farmers' closeness to the land and their success in getting the harvest in.

Confucius tried to balance the opposing forces of *yin* (darkness) and *yang* (light) in the universe. He stressed the need for order and respect on Earth so that there will be a harmonious balance between heaven, Earth and human beings. To achieve this, people have to learn from the past to see how they should behave today. Confucius ignored existing religious beliefs and stressed instead the importance of serving other people. He said

CONFUCIANISM

Confucius was a philosopher and teacher who lived at a time of great disturbance in China. He wanted to bring order and peace to his country and taught that people should respect their ancestors and parents and work hard. *Li* (good conduct) was very important. Confucius taught that if everyone did their duty to the emperor and behaved well, then the country would be strong and at peace.

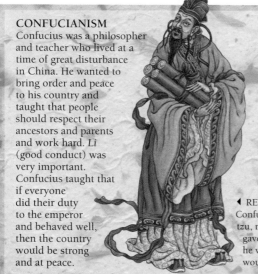

◄ RELIGIOUS RULER
Confucius's Chinese name, K'ung Fu-tzu, means 'master king.' His parents gave him this name because, when he was born, it was foretold that he would be a king without a crown.

▲ CHINESE TEMPLE
Confucius did not found a religion, but throughout China, shrines and temples were erected in tribute to him. Confucianism became the state religion.

▼ LOOKING
FORWARD
*Children are very
important in Chinese
life. They represent the
future of the family. In
the Chinese language,
the character for 'good'
(hao) shows a mother
and child, representing
harmony and fertility.*

▶ CONSULTING
THE I CHING
*The I Ching consists of 64
hexagrams (six lines) made up of
broken (yin) or unbroken (yang)
lines. Users draw stalks from a
container, and throw them to the
ground. Then, they consult the I
Ching, compare the way that their
sticks have fallen to what is in the
book and see what they foretell.*

that people should not do anything to other people that
they would not like others to do to them. Above all, he
taught that it was pointless to worship a god, or respect
your ancestors, if you did not serve other people first.
The second and fourth ways, Taoism and folk religions,

are described on the next page. The third way,
Buddhism, has already been described. Together, all
four ways showed people how to live their lives as
good citizens and therefore keep a balance between
yin and *yang* in their lives.

▲ EMPEROR TEAON-KWANG
The Chinese believed that the very first Chinese
emperors were gods and that their successors had a
mandate (approval) from heaven. Emperors were
worshipped and treated with great respect.

▼ BELL
Once, when Confucius
heard a bell ringing, he
decided to give up worldly
comforts and live on rice
and water for three months
as he meditated. To this
day, the Chinese believe
that bells calm the mind
and help clear thinking.

Key Dates

- c.3000BC The *I Ching* is written
  down by Wen Wang.

- 500sBC Life of Lao-Tzu.

- 551BC Confucius is born.

- c.495–485BC Confucius travels
  to nearby states in the hope of
  realizing his ideals.

- 479BC Confucius dies.

- 221BC China is united for the
  first time under Emperor Qin
  Shi Huangdi.

- 202BC–AD220 Under the Han
  dynasty, Confucianism becomes
  the official religion of China.

- AD100s Buddhism reaches China.

Judaism

JUDAISM IS THE RELIGION of the Jewish people. Jews trace their origins back to Abraham (the Father of Many Nations), who lived in Mesopotamia (modern-day Iraq) more than 4,000 years ago. They believe that God revealed himself to Abraham and promised to make him the father of a great nation. Abraham and his family settled in Canaan (modern-day Israel), and this became the hub of Judaism. As Jews chose or were forced to settle elsewhere, the religion gradually spread. Today there are more than 13 million Jews worldwide, with large numbers in Israel, the USA, and in Russia, Ukraine and other countries of the former USSR.

▲ JEWISH LIGHTS
The menorah, a type of multi-branched candlestick, is a symbol of Judaism. A seven-branched menorah stood in King Solomon's temple in Jerusalem.

Judaism was the first great faith to believe that there is only one God. An important statement called the *Shema* (in the *Tenakh*, the Jewish holy book) says "Hear, O Israel: the Lord our God, the Lord is One."

Jews believe that God is the creator of the world, and that he chose their ancestors, the Israelites, to be his special people. He led the Israelites out of slavery in Egypt and brought them to Canaan, the Promised Land. God's holy name is the Hebrew (Jewish) word *Yhwh*, usually written as

▼ THE FERTILE CRESCENT
Most of the events in the Hebrew Bible took place in the region known as the Fertile Crescent. This is a huge arc of fertile land, stretching from the Tigris and Euphrates rivers in Mesopotamia (modern-day Iraq) and through the Jewish homeland of Israel to Egypt.

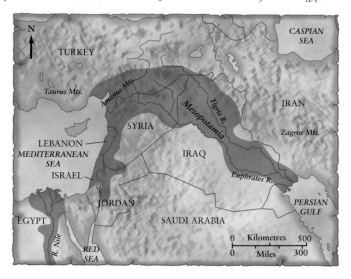

MODERN JEWISH GROUPS

Different customs have evolved in the various Jewish communities around the world. The two main groups are the Orthodox (traditional) Jews and the Reform Jews. Orthodox Jews stick to the traditional way of doing things. They hold their services in Hebrew, follow the ancient food laws, and separate men and women in the synagogue, the Jewish place of worship. Reform Jews reject traditional customs that seem old-fashioned to them. They hold their services in the local language, rather than Hebrew. They modify or discard the food laws, and they allow women to become rabbis.

▶ ETHIOPIAN JEWS
The Falasha are Jews who live in Ethiopia, east Africa. Their ancestors converted to Judaism more than 2,000 years ago. In the 1980s, about 45,000 Falasha emigrated to Israel to escape the war and drought in Ethiopia.

◀ THE TALMUD
Study of the scriptures is an important part of Jewish education. The main books are the Hebrew Bible, or *Tenakh* and the *Talmud*, a book of Jewish laws written in Babylon around 500BC.

Yahweh. Yahweh means 'I am' or 'I am who I am.'

Jews believe that God communicates with people through prophets. The greatest prophet was Moses, to whom God revealed the *Torah*, the first five books of the Bible. The *Torah* contains God's sacred laws, the best-known of which are the Ten Commandments. Keeping these laws is central to the Jewish way of life.

Jews believe that in the future, God will send a Messiah (anointed one), who will right all wrongs, reward good people and punish evil. His arrival will mark the end of history and the beginning of God's kingdom on Earth. Some Jews believe that when this happens the dead will be resurrected (brought back to eternal life). Other Jews believe that when they die their souls will go on living.

▲ THE GREAT FLOOD
According to the Bible, God sent a flood to destroy everything and rid the world of sin. Noah and his family were the only people to survive. Noah built an ark (huge boat), in which he saved his family and the animals.

▶ MODERN ISRAEL
Six million Jews were killed during the Holocaust in World War II. After the war, Jews stepped up their campaign to have their own country, where they could live and worship without threat of persecution. In 1948 the state of Israel was created as a Jewish homeland. Since then, thousands of Jews from all over the world have emigrated to Israel.

▲ RELIGIOUS TEACHER
Rabbis are the spiritual leaders for the Jewish community. They conduct services and teach children about Judaism.

▼ HASIDIC JEWS AT THE WESTERN WALL
Hasidism is a strict form of Judaism that originated in southeast Poland in the 1700s. It was founded by a Jewish scholar called Dov Baer. Hasidic Jews have many special customs. The men wear black suits and hats, and have side curls and beards. *Tzaddiqim* (Hasidic leaders) established new communities after World War II, when many Hasidic Jews were killed. These include the Lubavich sect in New York City.

Key Dates

- c.2166BC Birth of Abraham, the founder of the Jewish nation.

- c.586–537BC Judaism spreads beyond Canaan, when hundreds of Jews are forced into slavery in Babylon.

- c.500BC The *Talmud* is written.

- AD70 The Jewish population spreads throughout the Roman Empire. This is known as the Diaspora (dispersal).

- 1939–45 During World War II, six million Jews are killed by the Nazis during the Holocaust.

- 1948 The state of Israel is founded.

Christianity

THE FOUNDER OF CHRISTIANITY was Jesus Christ, a Jewish teacher and healer who lived in what is now Israel during the first century AD. His followers steadily grew in number. In the AD300s the Roman emperor, Constantine, decreed that Christianity should be tolerated throughout his empire. An important figure around that time was Augustine, who was bishop of Hippo (in modern-day Algeria, Africa) from AD396 until AD430. Augustine developed Christian thought in his *Confessions*, mixing them with Greek ideas. His interpretation of Christianity spread throughout Europe.

From the 1500s, as Europeans explored other continents, they took Christianity with them. Today Christians live on every continent of the globe. They total almost two billion, making Christianity the world's biggest religion.

Christians believe in one God. They believe that Jesus Christ was the Messiah promised in the Old Testament. The Christian God has three parts, known as the Holy Trinity. The Trinity consists of God the Father, God the Son (Jesus) and God the Holy Spirit.

Christians believe that God came to Earth in the form of a man, Jesus. He showed

▲ THE CROSS
Jesus was crucified (put to death on a cross), but Christians believe he rose from the dead. This has made the cross a symbol of Jesus's sacrifice. Christians see it as a symbol of victory and hope, too.

▲ THE VIRGIN MARY
The Bible says that Jesus's mother, Mary, was a virgin. The power of the Holy Spirit made her pregnant, so that Jesus could be born as a human being.

THE CHRISTIAN CHURCH

The first Christian Church was the Catholic (universal) Church, with the Pope at its head. In the AD1000s there was disagreement about the use of icons (holy pictures). This led to a split between the Catholic Church in Rome and the Orthodox Church, based in Constantinople. This is called the Great Schism (split). The Protestant churches were founded in the 1500s. This period is called the Reformation.

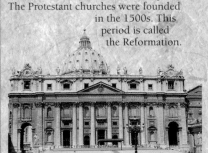

▲ MARTIN LUTHER
Luther was a German monk. He felt the Catholic Church abused its position of power. In protest, he founded the first Protestant church in the 1520s.

◀ ST PETER'S BASILICA
The Pope lives in the Vatican, a tiny country within the city of Rome. The Pope's church is St Peter's, begun in 1506 by Pope Julius II.

▶ JOHN CALVIN
Calvin set up a Protestant church in Switzerland. Like Luther, he tried to get rid of church traditions and simply follow the teachings of the Bible.

▼ ORTHODOX ICONS
Orthodox churches are usually full of beautiful icons. These are religious pictures or statues of Jesus, Mary, or the saints.

people how to confess the things they had done wrong in the past and have a fresh start with God. During his lifetime Jesus gathered a large body of followers. This alarmed the Romans, who occupied what is now Israel, and also the Jewish religious authorities, who feared Jesus was damaging their own power base. Jesus was put on trial and sentenced to death by crucifixion. When Jesus died, followers of Jesus believe that he paid the price for everyone's sins. According to the Bible, three days after his death, Jesus rose from the dead. Christians believe that when they die, they can look forward to eternal life in heaven.

Jesus said in the Bible that he is still with all Christians in spirit, and that he will come back at the end of the world to judge all people. Those who have faith in him will be saved and go to heaven. Those who have not will be banished to hell.

Jesus promised his disciples (followers) that after he was gone he would send a helper for them, the Holy Spirit. Christians believe this Spirit is still active in the world today.

▶ THE ASCENSION
Jesus appeared to his followers on many occasions in the 40 days following his resurrection, when he came back to life. Then one day he was taken up into heaven before his disciples' eyes. This event is known as the Ascension.

Roman Catholic regions
Protestant regions
Orthodox regions

NORWAY
SWEDEN
SCOTLAND
NORTH SEA
Dublin
Hamburg
N
IRELAND
WALES
ENGLAND
R. Rhine
HOLY ROMAN EMPIRE
BOHEMIA
Paris
Vienna
ATLANTIC OCEAN
R. Loire
FRANCE
SPAIN
PORTUGAL
Madrid
Rome
PAPAL STATES
R. Tagus
MEDITERRANEAN SEA
0 Kilometres 750
0 Miles 500

◀ EUROPE IN THE 1500S
During the Reformation, northern Europe became mostly Protestant, while southern Europe remained mostly Catholic. Most Orthodox Christians live in Russia and parts of eastern Europe, such as Greece and the Balkans.

Key Dates

- c.AD30 Birth of the Christian Church. Jesus's disciples start to preach the Christian message.

- AD313 Emperor Constantine grants tolerance of Christianity. It eventually becomes the official religion of the Roman Empire.

- 1054 The Orthodox Church breaks away in the Great Schism.

- 1517 Martin Luther publicly criticizes the Catholic Church and starts the Reformation. Protestant churches are founded.

- 2000 Christians celebrate the millennium, 2,000 years after the traditional birth date of Jesus.

The Life of Jesus

ESUS CHRIST WAS BORN IN about 6 or 7BC in Judah (modern-day Israel), which was then a province of the Roman Empire. His mother was Mary, a young Jewish woman from Nazareth.

According to the Bible, the Angel Gabriel appeared to Mary and told her that she would have a child who would be God's son and the saviour of the world.

We know very little about Jesus' childhood, except that he lived in Nazareth and was brought up as a Jew. The Bible picks up the story when Jesus was in his early 30s. He was baptized in the River Jordan and spent

▲ JESUS
All that we know about Jesus's life comes from the accounts in the four gospels, the books of the Bible written specifically about Jesus.

▶ PARABLES
Jesus often told parables (stories about everyday life) to teach people about God in a way they could understand and remember. One of his most famous parables is the story of the good samaritan. It tells the story of a man who was helped by the one person he thought was his enemy.

WEEKLY WORSHIP
Christians gather together to worship God on Sunday and at other important festivals. They usually meet in a church, but some groups meet in people's homes. The most important form of Christian worship is the service known as communion, mass, or the Eucharist. At holy communion, Christians share bread and wine as Jesus did with his disciples at the Last Supper. Christian worship includes prayers, readings from the Bible, and singing religious songs called hymns.

◀ NOTRE-DAME CATHEDRAL
Huge cathedrals were built in Europe during the Middle Ages. One of the most beautiful is the Cathedral of Notre-Dame (Our Lady), in Paris, which was begun in 1163. It has three stained-glass windows.

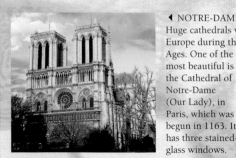

▲ MODERN CATHEDRAL
Not all cathedrals are centuries old. The Cathedral of Christ the King, in Liverpool, England, dates from 1967.

◀ A PARISH CHURCH
Most Christians worship at a small local church, with members of their parish (community).

40 days fasting in the desert in preparation for his work. Then he went around the country, teaching people about God, healing the sick and performing miracles. He was accompanied by a group of 12 disciples (followers). Jesus told people that God's kingdom was coming and that they should ask God's forgiveness so they could be saved. Jesus became very popular and vast crowds of people came to hear him preach. However, he faced opposition from the Jewish religious authorities, who saw him as a threat.

After three years, Jesus journeyed to Jerusalem for the Jewish festival of Pesach (Passover). According to the Bible he rode a donkey into the city, cheered on by crowds who threw palm branches in his path. Later in the week, Jesus and his disciples ate *seder* (the Pesach meal) together. This is now known as the Last Supper. Jesus shared bread and wine with his disciples. Later that night, Jesus was arrested, tried and found guilty by the religious authorities. The Roman governor of the province, Pontius Pilate, sentenced him to death. The following day, Jesus was forced to carry a wooden cross through the streets of Jerusalem to a place outside the city walls, where he was crucified. He died in the afternoon, and was buried by his friends and followers.

Three days later Jesus's followers discovered that his tomb was empty. An angel told them that Jesus was alive again. Jesus himself appeared to his astonished disciples on many occasions over the next few weeks. Forty days later, he was taken up into heaven. This marked the end of his life on Earth, but Christians believe that Jesus is still alive in heaven.

▲ THE WEDDING AT CANA
In the three years of his teaching, Jesus performed many miracles. His first was to turn jars of water into wine at a wedding. Jesus healed many people, and even brought a dead man, Lazarus, back to life. He also used miracles to demonstrate his power over nature, for example by calming a storm.

▲ HOLY COMMUNION
The bread and wine that Christians receive at communion represent the body and blood of Jesus. At the Last Supper, Jesus told his disciples to think of bread and wine in this way.

▼ FORMS OF WORSHIP
There are many styles of Christian worship. The Baptist Church, founded around 1611, is known for its lively services. Baptists celebrate Jesus with joyful singing and even dancing.

Key Dates

- c.6–7BC Jesus is born in Bethlehem.His family flees to Egypt to escape King Herod.

- c.4BC King Herod dies and Jesus's family returns to Nazareth.

- c.AD5–6 Jesus visits the temple at Jerusalem with his family where he is dedicated to God.

- c.AD28 Jesus is baptized in the River Jordan and starts his public teaching.

- c.AD30 Jesus is crucified in Jerusalem, but is resurrected after three days. About forty days later he ascends into heaven.

The Christian Scriptures

▲ GUTENBERG BIBLE
In the Middle Ages, when all books had to be copied out by hand, Christian monks produced some beautiful Bibles. The first printed edition was the Gutenberg Bible of 1455.

THE CHRISTIAN HOLY BOOK is the Bible. Christians believe that although the Bible was written by people, it was inspired by God. It is a collection of books written by different authors. These books are divided into two sections, the Old and New Testaments. The Old Testament consists of the Jewish scriptures. The New Testament deals with the life and teachings of Jesus Christ and the story of the early Christian church. All 27 books in the New Testament were written by early followers of Jesus, roughly between AD45 and AD97.

The first four books of the New Testament are the gospels of Matthew, Mark, Luke and John. The word gospel means 'good news' and refers to the good

news that Jesus was the long-awaited Messiah. Together the gospels tell the story of Jesus's life. All four of the gospel writers were closely involved with Jesus or with his followers. Matthew and John were two of Jesus's disciples. Mark was probably a translator for Peter, another of the 12 disciples. Luke was a friend of Paul. Paul was not a disciple. He was a Jew who had persecuted the Christians but converted to Christianity after seeing a vision on the road to Damascus. After this, Paul journeyed widely spreading the Christian message.

Each of the gospels tells the life of Jesus from a different viewpoint. All four concentrate on Jesus's ministry, his time teaching in Galilee, and on the events of the last week of his life.

The fifth book of the New Testament, *The Acts of the*

◀ ST ANDREW AND ST JAMES
The first four disciples that Jesus recruited were Peter, Andrew, James and John. After Jesus's death, they carried on preaching his message. Some died for their religion. King Herod Agrippa I of Judah had James beheaded around AD44 and Andrew was crucified in modern-day Turkey in the AD60s.

THE CHRISTIAN YEAR

Christians celebrate many festivals. Most commemorate events in Jesus's life. In some churches, saints are celebrated on the particular days dedicated to them. Festivals are marked with special church services and with other customs, such as giving Christmas presents or Easter eggs.

▲ EASTER EGGS
In some countries it is traditional to give and receive eggs at Easter, as a symbol of new life. Easter eggs may be real, or made of wood or chocolate.

◀ THE NATIVITY
At Christmas, Christian homes and churches often display models of the nativity, Jesus's birth in the stable in Bethlehem.

▲ PALM SUNDAY
Shortly before his death, Jesus rode into Jerusalem on a donkey. He was greeted by crowds of people, who laid palm branches in his path. Christians remember this event on Palm Sunday. At some churches, small crosses made of palm leaves are handed out to worshippers.

◀ RUINS AT EPHESUS
Paul was one of the first church leaders to see that the good news about Jesus was meant for all, not just Jews. He went on four journeys around the Mediterranean, telling people about Jesus and founding Christian churches in cities such as Ephesus in Turkey, and Corinth, in Greece.

Apostles, was written by Luke, the author of the third gospel. It tells what happened in the 30 years after Jesus's ascension into heaven. *Acts* describes the missionary work of the apostles, Jesus's specially appointed helpers, the life of the early Christian church, and Paul's travels.

The next 21 books are letters from the early Christian leaders to the newly founded churches, giving them advice and encouragement. Paul is believed to have written 13 of the letters. Other authors include the disciple Peter and Jesus's brother, James.

The final book of the Bible is the *Book of Revelation*. The writer, John, who may be the same John who wrote the fourth gospel, describes what will happen at the end of the world.

▲ A FRANCISCAN FRIAR
Monks or friars try to spread the Christian message by setting a good example. Francis, who later became a saint, founded his order of monks in 1209. The Franciscans live in poverty and in harmony with nature.

▶ PENTECOST
A few days after Jesus had ascended into heaven, his disciples gathered together on the Jewish festival of Shavuot. The Bible says that they suddenly heard a sound like rushing wind. They saw tongues of flame that came to rest on each of them. They were all filled with the power of the Holy Spirit and began to speak in tongues (other languages). Christians celebrate this event at the festival of Pentecost, or Whitsun.

Christian Festivals

- 25 December – Christmas (celebrates Jesus's birth)

- March/April – Lent (a 40-day fast that ends on Easter Sunday)

- March/April – Maundy Thursday (held the Thursday before Easter to celebrate the Last Supper)

- March/April – Good Friday (marks the crucifixion of Jesus)

- March/April – Easter Sunday (celebrates Jesus's resurrection)

- May/June – Pentecost or Whitsun (celebrates when the disciples received the Holy Spirit)

Islam

▲ SACRED SYMBOL
The hilal (crescent moon and star) is the symbol of Islam. It reminds Muslims that they follow a lunar calendar (a calendar based on the movements of the Moon), and that Allah created the stars. The hilal appears on the flags of some Muslim countries, including Pakistan, Singapore and Turkey.

ISLAM WAS FOUNDED by the prophet Muhammad. It began in the cities of al-Madinah (Medina) and Makkah (Mecca) in modern-day Saudi Arabia in about AD620. Muhammad received revelations from Allah (God) and began to preach his message.

Muhammad died in AD632, and within a few years the peoples of the Arabian peninsula had converted to Islam. The new religion soon had followers as far west as the Atlantic coast of Africa and as far east as India. Today, Islam is the world's second-largest religion, with more than a billion followers spread over almost every country.

The word Islam means 'surrender to the peace of Allah.' Muslims (followers of Islam) give themselves up to Allah's will. They believe that Allah is the one God, and that Muhammad was Allah's messenger.

Muslims believe that Allah sent many prophets (messengers) before sending Muhammad. These include holy men recognized by Jews and Christians, such as Adam, Ibrahim (Abraham), Musa (Moses), Dawud (David) and Isa (Jesus). Muhammad received revelations from Allah through the Angel Jibril (Gabriel) from the age of 40. He told his followers about these revelations. They were eventually written down in the Islamic holy book, the Qur'an.

Muslims believe that their faith is the final revelation of Allah. Every aspect of Muslim life is governed by the Five Pillars of Islam, duties that unite Muslims all over the world into a single community.

▶ THE SACRED KA'BAH
The Great Mosque at Makkah is set around the Ka'bah, a square building made of grey stone. In its eastern corner is the Black Stone. Muslims believe this fell to Earth as a sign of the covenant (agreement) between Allah and the prophet Ibrahim. Muslims believe that Ibrahim built the Ka'bah.

THE FIVE PILLARS OF ISLAM

Islam rests on five duties that all Muslims must obey and carry out. These are called the Five Pillars (supports) of Islam. They are based on the Qur'an and the actions of Muhammad. They give a sense of purpose to every Muslim's life.

◀ SALAH
The second pillar is *salah*, the prayers that Muslims say five times a day. Wherever they are in the world, Muslims face towards the sacred Ka'bah in Makkah when they pray.

▼ CHARITY SCHOOL, OMAN
Every Muslim must give one-fortieth of his or her annual income to charities such as this religious school. This is called *zakat*, and is the third pillar.

◀ SHAHADAH
The first pillar is *shahadah*. This is the Muslim statement of faith – that Allah is the one true God, and that Muhammad was his prophet. This belief is stated each day in the call to prayer.

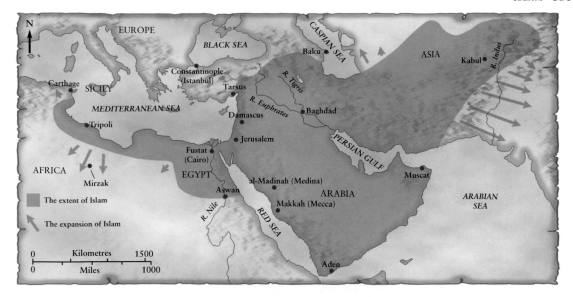

▶ HOLY SITE
Al-Aqsa (the Dome of the Rock) in Jerusalem is where Muhammad ascended into heaven in AD619 to meet Allah. It is sacred to Jews and Christians, too, as the ancient site of Solomon's temple. Other holy Muslim sites are the Great Mosque at Makkah and the tomb of Muhammad at al-Madinah.

▲ THE ISLAMIC WORLD
Islam began in the cities of Makkah and al-Madinah. It became the chief religion of the Arabian peninsula, spreading into Persia (modern-day Iran), Mesopotamia (modern-day Iraq) and North Africa. During the 1100s and 1200s, Christian knights known as Crusaders recaptured Jerusalem from Muslim control, but they failed to hold their gains for long.

▼ ID-UL-FITR
The fourth pillar is *sawm* (fasting). During the month of Ramadan, Muslims do not eat or drink during daylight hours. Muslims celebrate the end of Ramadan with a feast. They call this festival Id-ul-Fitr.

▶ TO BE A PILGRIM
During their lifetime all healthy Muslims must make at least one *hajj* (pilgrimage) to Makkah during the 12th month of the Islamic year. The *hajj* is the fifth pillar.

Key Dates

- AD570–632 Life of Muhammad.
- AD622 Muhammad's hijrah (flight) from Makkah to al-Madinah.
- AD630 Muhammad conquers Makkah.
- AD634 Muhammad's successor, Abu Bakr, conquers Arabia.
- AD638 Arab armies capture Jerusalem.
- AD651 Arab armies overrun Persia.
- AD711 Arab armies reach India.
- AD732 Arab armies conquer Spain.
- 1453 Muslim Ottoman Turks capture Constantinople.
- 1492 Last Muslim armies retreat from Spain.

The Qur'an

CALLIGRAPHY
Muslims are forbidden to depict Allah or Muhammad in paintings. They decorate the Qur'an with geometric or floral designs and with intricate calligraphy (writing). This lettering is the Arabic script for 'Allah.'

MUHAMMAD TOLD his followers all the teachings that Allah had passed on to him through the Angel Jibril. They learned his revelations by heart and dictated them to scribes, who wrote them down in what became the Qur'an, which means 'revelation.' Muslims believe that earlier messages from Allah to his prophets had been corrupted or ignored. They believe that the Qur'an is the true word of Allah. As it was spoken by Muhammad in Arabic, the Qur'an can only be written and recited in Arabic, regardless of the language of the believer. Muslims believe that the Qur'an is perfect and therefore it cannot be translated into any other language, only interpreted.

Copies of the Qur'an are always beautifully illustrated. Muslims believe that making the word of Allah beautiful is in itself an act of worship.

The Qur'an is divided into 114 *surahs* (chapters). It starts by saying that Allah is the one true god. Then it discusses Allah's role in history and Muhammad's role as Allah's prophet. The Qur'an describes Allah's last judgement on his people and the need to help other people. It tells Muslims how to behave, as well as how to treat other people and animals. However, not everything is covered by the Qur'an, so Muslims also study the *Sunnah*, too. This book contains accounts of the words and deeds of Muhammad and his close followers. The *Sunnah* helps Muslims to gain a clear understanding of the Qur'an. Muslim laws are taken from both the Qur'an and the *Sunnah*. These laws, known as the *Shari'ah*,

◄ **PATHWAY TO ALLAH**
Islamic law is known as the Shari'ah. This is an Arabic word meaning a track that leads camels to a waterhole. In the same way, Muslims who obey the Shari'ah will be led to Allah. The Shari'ah guides Muslims on their faith and conduct. It is taught in law schools, such as this one, throughout the Islamic world.

THE SUFIS
Sufis are Muslims, who can be either Sunnis or Shi'ahs. They place complete obedience and trust in Allah. They try to get closer to Allah through dance and music. Sufi beliefs are passed down through the generations by saints and teachers. Many Sufis are involved in education and community work.

▶ **SOULFUL SINGER**
Sufis believe that music is both a path to Allah and a means of spiritual healing. They sing *qawwalis*, trance-like hypnotic songs that build up to an ecstatic climax. *Qawwali* singers such as Nusrat Fateh Ali Khan have achieved international fame.

▲ **DERVISHES**
Some Sufis dance and spin to forget the things around them and get closer to Allah. They are known as Whirling Dervishes.

▲ **A SUFI**
No one really knows how Sufis got their name. The word might come from *suf*, a basic wool garment that early Sufis wore. Sufis turn their back on the world. They do not own many possessions and they often take vows of poverty.

▼ THE QUR'AN
*The Qur'an was prepared in about AD650 by Uthman, the
third successor to Muhammad. Careful study of the book is
important for Muslims in order to gain a deeper understanding
of the philosophy and wisdom of Allah. They consider the book
to be the perfect word of Allah and believe that it lays down the
moral and ethical principles that explain the correct way to lead
their lives. Many mosques have areas in which Muslims can
study the Qur'an.*

provide detailed instructions to Muslims as to how
to lead a good life. Sunni Muslims follow one of
four different schools or interpretations of the
Shari'ah. The Shi'ahs also follow the teachings of
the first *imams,* the spiritual leaders descended
from Ali, Muhammad's cousin. They follow the
teachings of individual thinkers, too. The greatest
religious thinkers are known as *ayatollahs,* which
means 'signs of Allah'. They are extremely learned
in the teachings of the Qur'an and the *Shari'ah* and
are regarded as an authority on Islamic religious
law. They also have a strong political influence.

▶ SHI'AH LEADER
*Muslims interpret the
Qur'an in different
ways. Ayatollah
Khomeini was leader of
Iran between 1979 and
1989. He interpreted the
Qur'an very strictly.
During his decade of
power, he applied its
teachings to every aspect
of political and social
life in his country.*

▼ QAWWALI SHRINE, DELHI
One of the main Sufi shrines, dedicated
to the Sufi saint Nizamuddin Awliya,
is in Delhi, India. Its community of
qawwali singers trace their ancestors
back to Amir Khusrau (1253–1325).
He was the founder of *qawwali* music.

▲ THE SIMURG
Sufis use a mythical bird, the *simurg,*
to symbolize their search for unity with
Allah. Its name is Persian for '30 birds.'
The *simurg's* great variety of feathers
represent every other bird that there is.

The Islamic Year

The Islamic calendar has 12 lunar
months, each with 29 or 30 days.

- Muharram is the first month.
- Muslims celebrate the birthday
  of Muhammad on the 12th day
  of Rabi'I, the third month.
- Ramadan is the ninth month,
  when Muslims fast during
  daylight hours.
- Id-ul-Fitr (the breaking of the
  fast) is celebrated at the start of
  Shawal, the tenth month.
- Dhul-Hijjah, the 12th month, is
  when Muslims make their *hajj*
  (pilgrimage) to Makkah.

Journey Without End

▲ SCIENCE
Explorers in the 18th century set out to record the world they found. Illustrators were taken on expeditions to record the wildlife of the islands that they discovered.

▼ KEY DATES
The panel charts voyages of discovery on Earth, from the first sea voyages in the Mediterranean 3,500 years ago to the conquest of the South Pole in 1911.

EVER SINCE THE FIRST PEOPLE walked on the Earth they have explored the world they lived in. In the beginning, hundreds of thousands of years ago, this was to hunt and gather food; later on it was to find new pastures for their animals. But food was the reason for exploring, and people rarely went far from the place they were born.

When the first civilizations began in the Middle East people began to live in towns and cities. Farmers grew crops and traders bought and sold goods that were not available in their own area. It was these intrepid merchants, from ancient civilizations like Phoenicia and Egypt, who were the first explorers. The Phoenicians sailed out from the Mediterranean into the North Atlantic, while the Egyptians ventured south into the Indian Ocean, looking for opportunities to trade and to establish permanent trading posts or colonies.

Throughout history trade has remained the driving force of discovery. It was the search for a new trade route to China and India that sent da Gama round Africa into the Indian Ocean, and Columbus across the Atlantic. Explorers like Hudson and Bering braved the Arctic Ocean trying to find ways around the top of America and Siberia. And it was trade that sent Magellan round the world and European sailors into the Pacific

▼ CONVERSION
Many European explorers set out to convert the local people they encountered to Christianity.

Caravanserai on the Silk Road

EUROPE

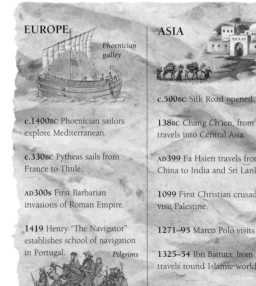

Phoenician galley

c.1400BC Phoenician sailors explore Mediterranean.

c.330BC Pytheas sails from France to Thule.

AD300s First Barbarian invasions of Roman Empire.

1419 Henry "The Navigator" establishes school of navigation in Portugal.

Pilgrims

ASIA

c.500BC Silk Road opened.

138BC Chang Ch'ien, from China, travels into Central Asia.

AD399 Fa Hsien travels from China to India and Sri Lanka.

1099 First Christian crusaders visit Palestine.

1271–95 Marco Polo visits China.

1325–54 Ibn Battuta, from Algeria, travels round Islamic world.

1405–33 Zheng He, from China leads expeditions to South-east Asia.

1498 Da Gama, from Lisbon, Portugal, sails to India.

1549 Xavier, a Spanish Jesuit, goes to Japan as a missionary.

1594–97 Barents, a Dutch mariner, explores Arctic Ocean.

1725–29 Bering, from Denmark, crosses Siberia.

1734–42 Teams of explorers map Siberian coast and rivers.

1878–79 Nordenskjöld, from Finland, discovers the North-east Passage.

Inuit igloo

AFRICA

Timbuktu

c.1490BC Egyptians sail to Punt.

c.600BC Phoenician fleet sails round Africa.

c.500BC Hanno, from Carthage in modern Tunisia, explores coast.

AD1480s Portuguese cross the Equator and sail round Cape of Good Hope.

1768–73 Bruce, from Scotland, searches for source of the River Nile and discovers Lake Tana.

▼ NAVIGATION
The first explorers had little to help them navigate apart from the positions of the Sun, Moon and stars and had to stay close to land. The development of instruments like the magnetic compass, astrolabe and quadrant made navigation easier and more exact.

Ocean to the rich spice islands of South-east Asia.

Explorers also set out seeking fame and fortune and for political advantage – to conquer new lands for their king and country. Many European explorers went out of religious conviction, attempting to convert other races to Christianity. But by the 18th century, it was scientific curiosity that sent Cook into the Pacific Ocean and Bates into the Amazon rainforest.

Today there are few places left on Earth that have not been fully explored. There are unexplored mountains in Tibet and the ocean floor remains largely undiscovered, but now our attention has turned to the skies and space. Unmanned space probes explore the planets of our solar system and the wider reaches of our galaxy of stars, looking for life on other planets. Exploration has come a long way since those early sailing ships left the shores of Phoenicia and Egypt more than 3,500 years ago.

▲ TRADE
The Dutch East India Company was a powerful trading organization. By 1700 they had control of the valuable cinnamon, clove and nutmeg trade in the East. They established trading posts throughout Asia and ruled what is now called Indonesia.

1795–1806 Park, from Scotland, explores the River Niger.

1841–73 Livingstone, from Scotland, explores southern and central Africa.

1844–45 Barth, from Germany, explores the Sahara Desert region.

1858-63 Englishman John Speke discovers the source of the River Nile.

1874–77 Stanley, from Wales, sails down Congo River.

Stanley's hat

AMERICA
and the ARCTIC

AD980s–90s Vikings settle in Greenland and explore parts of North America.

1492 Columbus, from Italy, finds the West Indies.

1497 Cabot finds Newfoundland.

1502 Amerigo Vespucci, from Spain, explores South America.

1513 Balboa sights Pacific Ocean.

1519–33 Spanish conquer Aztecs.

1535–6 Cartier, from France, journeys up St Lawrence River.

1603–15 Champlain explores Canada and founds Quebec.

1610–11 Englishman Henry Hudson searches for North-west Passage.

1680–82 La Salle, from France, sails down Mississippi River.

1800s Several scientific expeditions explore the Amazon.

1804–06 Americans Lewis and Clark explore Louisiana.

1903–06 Amundsen, from Norway, finds the North-west Passage.

1908 Peary, from America, reaches North Pole.

Lewis and Clark

AUSTRALASIA
and the ANTARCTIC

c.1000BC Polynesians settle in Tonga and Samoa.

Boomerang

AD400 Polynesians reach Easter Island and Hawaii.

c.1000 Maoris settle in New Zealand.

1520–21 Magellan crosses Pacific on his round-the-world voyage.

1605 Jansz explores Queensland.

1642–43 Dutchman Tasman discovers New Zealand.

1770 Cook lands in Australia.

1828–62 Interior explored.

1911 Amundsen reaches South Pole.

Egyptians, Phoenicians and Greeks

PEOPLE HAVE BEEN EXPLORING the world since ancient times. The earliest civilizations grew up in the Middle East thousands of years ago. Merchants began to trade with far-off cities so that they could get hold of goods that were not available in their own land. Gold, spices and craftworks were bought and sold. The easiest way to make long journeys to other countries was by sea. The traders had no maps to guide them, so they had to discover the best routes for themselves. They soon learned about the winds and sea currents that would help their voyages, and which seasons were best to travel in.

The ancient Egyptians lived along the banks of the River Nile. They had plenty of

▲ BABOON
The Egyptians brought live baboons and cheetahs back from Punt, as well as leopard skins.

food and other goods, so traders did not venture very far. But eventually the traders wanted to find new markets, and this tempted them to explore further afield. They started to sail ships out into the Mediterranean and the Red Sea.

In 1490BC, Queen Hatshepsut of Egypt ordered a fleet to sail down the Red Sea in search of new lands. The fleet reached a place called Punt (modern Somalia or somewhere further down the coast of East Africa). The sailors returned with ivory, ebony, spices and myrrh trees – a present from the people of Punt. Other expeditions explored the interior of North Africa.

Phoenician sailors began to explore the Mediterranean Sea in about 1400BC. The Phoenicians lived in cities along the coast of what is now Lebanon, at the eastern end of the Mediterranean. They were skilled seafarers and soon started to establish prosperous trading colonies throughout the region. One Phoenician fleet even sailed round Africa on behalf of an Egyptian pharaoh. In 500BC a man called Hanno sailed from Carthage, a Phoenician colony in North Africa, as far as modern Senegal,

▶ A PHOENICIAN SHIP
Phoenician ships were short, broad and strong. They were built from cedar, which grew on the mountain slopes of Phoenicia. A single sail and oars powered the ship along.

SAILING THE MEDITERRANEAN
Phoenicia had little arable land, and so in 1400BC its people turned to the sea for a living. They became excellent seafarers, sailing great distances in search of new markets. They established colonies as far away as North Africa and Spain. Egyptians and Greeks also began to explore by sea.

◀ PHOENICIAN TRADERS
The Phoenicians traded grain, olive oil, glassware, purple cloth, cedar wood and other goods throughout the Mediterranean area. They were rather like mobile shopkeepers.

▼ MUREX SHELL
One of the most precious items traded by the Phoenicians was purple cloth. The dye for the cloth was made from murex shells. Up to 6,000 shells were crushed to make 450g/1lb of dye.

▶ PHOENICIAN GLASS
The Phoenicians were good at making glass items, such as vases and adornments. Sand and soda were mixed to a paste, which was tinted with pigment and fired at a high temperature.

Warehouse

Single sail

▼ EGYPTIAN PORT
In Egypt, shallow-bottomed boats made of reeds, with a single sail, carried goods and passengers along the River Nile. After about 2700BC the Egyptians began to build wooden boats, which were stronger and could cross seas to foreign lands.

a journey of 4,000km/2,500 miles. Other Phoenician traders sailed to Britain, buying tin in Cornwall.

The Greeks also founded colonies throughout the Mediterranean. The Phoenicians were their great rivals, because they were so successful at trading by sea. Greek merchants wanted some of the business for themselves. In 330BC, an explorer called Pytheas sailed to Britain, possibly to try to get access to the profitable tin trade.

▶ PYTHEAS
One of the most amazing voyages of ancient times was made by a Greek astronomer called Pytheas. In 330BC he set sail from Marseille in southern France, which was a Greek colony. He headed round Spain and then north to the British Isles, where he reported that the local people were friendly. Pytheas continued his voyage further north to the land of Thule. Thule was probably Norway or Iceland. Pytheas noted that in Thule the sun never set. (In these countries it does not get dark in summer.)

N

Iceland (Thule?)

Orkney Islands

Norway (Thule?)

North Atlantic Ocean

British Isles

North Sea

Cornwall

Pytheas's travels
•••••➤

EUROPE

Marseille (Massilia)

Rome

Mediterranean Sea

Carthage

0 Kilometres 1000
0   Miles   600

Key Dates

- 1490BC Egyptians sail to Punt.

- 1400BC Phoenician traders explore the Mediterranean Sea and the eastern Atlantic Ocean.

- 1000BC First Phoenician colony established on Cyprus.

- c.800BC Greeks set up colonies in the eastern Mediterranean.

- 814BC Phoenicians found Carthage in North Africa.

- c.600BC Phoenician fleet sails round Africa.

- 500BC Hanno explores the coast of West Africa.

- 330BC Pytheas sails to Thule.

The Polynesians

▲ PELE GOD
Polynesians made statues, as here, of dead ancestors, as they thought their spirits became gods.

THE ISLANDS OF THE South Pacific were uninhabited until about 3,000 years ago. Then the first Polynesians arrived to live there. We do not know much about these people. Historians think that they originally came from Asia or America.

Over the next 2,000 years the Polynesians slowly spread out across the vast South Pacific Ocean. They sailed north to Hawaii, east to Easter Island and, finally, south to New Zealand. They were probably the greatest explorers and navigators in history. When Europeans first visited the region in the 1500s, they got a surprise. They could not believe that the Polynesians, who they thought were a very primitive people, could have developed such advanced skills.

The immense Pacific Ocean is scattered with islands, but these make up only a minute part of its total area and lie hundreds of kilometres apart from each other. The rest is open sea, and it is easy to sail for days without sighting any land. The Polynesians did not have any maps or modern navigation equipment, but they successfully explored the entire ocean in their sturdy canoes. They settled on almost every island, finding them by following migrating birds and by watching changes in wind direction and wave pattern.

The Polynesians gradually built up a detailed knowledge of where each island was and how they could find it again in the future, using the Sun, Moon and stars as navigation aids. They gave each island its own "on top" star. Sailors knew that when this was directly over their boat, they were on the same latitude as the island. Using the position of the Sun, they sailed due east or west until they reached land. Sirius, for example, was the "on top" star for Tahiti.

All this information was passed down

▶ GIANT STATUES
Easter Islanders erected 600 giant carved statues across their small island between AD 1000 and 1600. No one knows what these statues were for, or how the islanders managed to move and erect the huge stones.

ASIAN OR AMERICAN?
Some historians think that the Polynesians originally came from South-east Asia, but there are many similarities between the cultures of Polynesia and Peru. One modern explorer from Norway called Thor Heyerdahl set out to prove that Polynesians could have come from South America. He built a raft like those used by early settlers and sailed from Peru to the South Pacific.

▼ THOR HEYERDAHL
Thor Heyerdahl was born in 1914 and studied zoology and geography at university. He became fascinated by Polynesia and lived for two years in Tahiti.

◀ KON-TIKI
Thor Heyerdahl's raft was called *Kon-Tiki* after the Peruvian sun-god. The god was believed to have migrated to the Pacific islands. The raft measured 13.7m/45ft long and 5.5m/18ft wide, and was made of balsawood and bamboo.

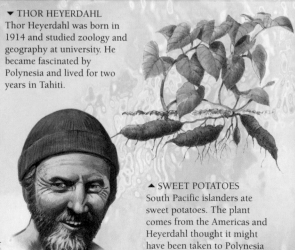

▲ SWEET POTATOES
South Pacific islanders ate sweet potatoes. The plant comes from the Americas and Heyerdahl thought it might have been taken to Polynesia by settlers from America.

▼ POLYNESIAN BOAT
Polynesian canoes were up to 30m/100ft long. They were built with two hulls or a single hull and an outrigger. The sails were made from coconut-palm leaf matting stitched together.

Canoe steered by
single oar

Main hull

Outrigger

▲ PACIFIC ISLANDS
There are about 20,000 islands in the Pacific Ocean. Most are either high volcanic peaks or low coral reefs. Apart from New Zealand, the vast majority are small, some only a few kilometres across.

through the generations and recorded on a chart made of palm sticks tied together with coconut fibre. The framework of sticks represented distance, and shells threaded on the sticks showed where the islands were.

The Polynesians used these simple but effective charts to make accurate voyages across vast expanses of ocean. They took colonists and supplies to newly discovered islands and brought back fish and other goods.

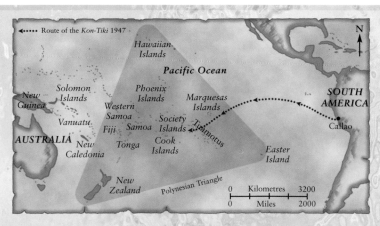

◄••••• Route of the *Kon-Tiki* 1947

Hawaiian
Islands

Pacific Ocean

New
Guinea

Solomon
Islands

Phoenix
Islands

Marquesas
Islands

SOUTH
AMERICA

Western
Samoa

Society
Islands

Tuamotus

Vanuatu

Fiji Samoa

Callao

AUSTRALIA New
Caledonia

Tonga

Cook
Islands

Easter
Island

New
Zealand

Polynesian Triangle

N

| 0 | Kilometres | 3200 |
| 0 | Miles | 2000 |

▲ THOR HEYERDAHL'S VOYAGE
In 1947, *Kon-Tiki* set sail from Peru. It steered westwards, making use of the winds and sea currents. After a voyage of 6,900km/4,300 miles, lasting 101 days, Thor Heyerdahl reached the Tuamotu archipelago in the South Pacific.

Key Dates

- 1000BC Polynesians begin to settle in Tonga and Samoa.

- 150BC Settlers leave Samoa for Marquesas Islands.

- AD400 Polynesians reach Easter Island in the east and the Hawaiian Islands in the north.

- 1000 Polynesian Maoris settle in New Zealand.

- 1000–1600 Statues built on Easter Island.

- 1947 Thor Heyerdahl's *Kon-Tiki* expedition from Peru to the South Pacific.

Wayfarers in Europe

TODAY WE KNOW OF Europe as a busy place with a huge population. However, a thousand years ago Europe was a very different place indeed.

In the year 1000 the total population of Western Europe was fewer than 30 million, which is about half that of modern France. Only a handful of cities, including Paris, Milan and Florence, had more than 40,000 people. Most had fewer than 10,000 inhabitants. Roads were rough and uneven, and much of the countryside was covered in thick forests. Bandits lay in wait to rob the unwary. Yet despite these problems, a surprising number of people ran the risk of getting lost or being robbed and took to the roads.

Pilgrims journeyed in great numbers to holy sites, such as the shrine of St James in Compostela, northern Spain. Some went even further afield, to Jerusalem in the Middle East. Armies of Crusaders assembled to reconquer the Holy Land from its Muslim occupiers. National armies marched off to fight wars on behalf of their kings. Merchants and traders roamed from town to town, buying and selling goods at the increasing number of trade fairs held in northern France, Germany and Flanders (Belgium). Government and church administrators moved from town to town on official business. Scholars often passed from one

▼ PILGRIMAGES
Pilgrims went to the great religious shrines in large groups, telling each other stories and singing songs to pass the time.

THE CRUSADES

Between 1095 and 1444, armies of Christian knights went to Palestine in the Muslim Empire. They intended to secure the Christian holy places against Muslim control. The First Crusade successfully captured Jerusalem. In 1291, the last Crusader stronghold was lost. Later Crusades all ended in failure.

◄ THE CRUSADERS
Crusading knights and soldiers were inspired by religious devotion. They also followed a code of conduct called chivalry, which meant that they pledged to be brave, loyal to their lord, and to protect women.

▲ RICHARD I
Many kings and princes joined the Crusades. Richard I of England (ruled 1189–99) took part in the Third Crusade.

▼ HEIDELBERG
Heidelberg, and other fortified towns throughout Germany, were good places for recruiting men for the Crusades. All types of people went, commoners and knights, to spread Christianity through the Holy Land.

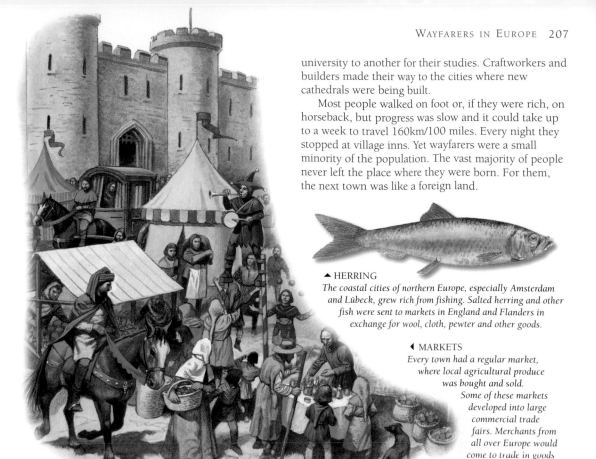

university to another for their studies. Craftworkers and builders made their way to the cities where new cathedrals were being built.

Most people walked on foot or, if they were rich, on horseback, but progress was slow and it could take up to a week to travel 160km/100 miles. Every night they stopped at village inns. Yet wayfarers were a small minority of the population. The vast majority of people never left the place where they were born. For them, the next town was like a foreign land.

▲ HERRING

The coastal cities of northern Europe, especially Amsterdam and Lübeck, grew rich from fishing. Salted herring and other fish were sent to markets in England and Flanders in exchange for wool, cloth, pewter and other goods.

◀ MARKETS

Every town had a regular market, where local agricultural produce was bought and sold. Some of these markets developed into large commercial trade fairs. Merchants from all over Europe would come to trade in goods from Europe, the Arab world and Asia.

▼ KRAK DES CHEVALIERS

The Crusaders built castles throughout Palestine to secure their conquests against Muslim invaders. The most impressive was Krak des Chevaliers, which is in present-day Syria. It eventually surrendered to Muslim armies in 1271.

Key Dates

- 1095 Pope Urban II calls for a Crusade to defend the Church.

- 1099 Crusaders capture Jerusalem and set up Crusader kingdoms throughout Palestine.

- 1187 Muslim leader Saladin retakes Jerusalem and overruns most of the Crusader kingdoms.

- 1189–92 Third Crusade recaptures Acre from Saladin.

- 1241 Hamburg and Lübeck set up the Hanseatic League.

- 1291 Acre, the last Crusader stronghold in Palestine, is lost.

- 1444 Final Crusade.

The Portuguese

▲ DA GAMA
In May 1498 the Portuguese navigator Vasco da Gama (1460–1524) became the first European to reach India by sea.

Portugal is on the extreme west of Europe, facing the Atlantic Ocean. The Portuguese relied on the sea to give them a living. Traditionally, they had fished and traded northwards along the Atlantic coast with France and Britain. But during the 1400s they turned their attention south and started looking at Africa.

The Portuguese wanted to explore Africa for two main reasons. They aimed to convert the Moors (the Muslim people of North Africa) to Christianity. They were also going to search for gold and other riches. To do this they needed better ships than the inshore, open boats they usually sailed. They developed the caravel, which was able to withstand the storms and strong currents out at sea.

Caravels allowed the Portuguese to venture further and further from their own shores. Expeditions boldly set off down the African coast, erecting *padrãoes*, or stone pillars with a Christian cross on the top, to mark their progress. By 1441 they had reached Cape Blanc in what is now Mauritania. By 1475 they had sailed round

▲ CARAVEL
The development of the small but sturdy caravel enabled the Portuguese to leave coastal waters and venture out into the open seas. A caravel was about 20m/65ft long and held a crew of 25.

West Africa and along the coast to the Gold Coast (Ghana) and Cameroon.

By now the Portuguese had an extra reason to voyage south. In 1453 the Ottoman Turks had captured the Christian city of Constantinople, which was the gateway to Asia, and closed the Silk Road to China. Europeans needed to find a new way to get to the wealth of the East. In 1482 Diego Cão was the first

NAVIGATION

The first sailors navigated by sailing along the coast from one landmark to the next. Once out of sight of land, they could not do this! Portuguese sailors learned how to use the positions of the Sun and stars to calculate where they were. With the aid of compasses, astrolabes, quadrants, sand glasses and nocturnals, they were able to navigate over long distances with increasing accuracy.

◄ PRINCE HENRY "THE NAVIGATOR"
Prince Henry (1394–1460) was the son of King John I of Portugal. He was keenly interested in the sea and supported many voyages of exploration. He set up a school of navigation, astronomy and cartography (map-making) to educate captains and pilots. These skills enabled Portuguese sailors to explore the coast of Africa.

▲ NOCTURNAL
The old way of telling the time, by the position of the Sun, did not work at night. The development of the nocturnal during the 1550s solved this problem. By lining it up with the Pole Star and two stars close to it, it was possible to tell the time to within ten minutes.

▶ SAND GLASS
Sailors told the time with a sand glass. The sand took 30 minutes to run to the bottom and it was then turned over. To calculate the ship's speed, they floated a knotted rope beside the ship, and worked out how long it took to pass each knot.

European to cross the Equator. On his second voyage in 1485–86 he sailed as far south as the Namib Desert. He thought that the African coast was endless, and that there was no way round it towards Asia. But in 1487–88 Bartolomeu Dias proved him wrong when he sailed round the stormy Cape of Good Hope into the Indian Ocean. He was the first Portuguese explorer to enter these waters. Although Dias wanted to go on, his exhausted crew made him turn back. Ten years later Vasco da Gama achieved the Portuguese dream. He rounded the tip of Africa with a fleet of four ships. After sailing up the east coast, he headed across the Indian Ocean. In May 1498 he arrived in the busy trading port of Calicut in the south of India. He had discovered a new route to Asia.

The map shows the route to India with the following labels:

Lisbon
Mediterranean Sea
ASIA
INDIA
AFRICA
ARABIAN PENINSULA
Da Gama meets the ruler of Calicut
Elmina trading fortress
Calicut
Statue from the São Rafael
Mombasa
Ships unloading at port
The São Rafael sinks
Padrão set up by Cão
Mozambique (Moçambique)
Walvis Bay
Table Mountain
N   W   E   S
Dias in stormy weather
Mossel Bay
Cape of Good Hope

Cão 1485–86
Dias 1487–88
Da Gama 1497–98

▲ THE ROUTE TO INDIA
By slowly mapping the coast of Africa, the Portuguese discovered a route which took them round the Cape of Good Hope to East Africa and then, using the westerly winds, across the ocean to India. Once the coast was mapped, later voyages could take a more direct route.

▶ USING A COMPASS
The magnetic compass was developed by both the Chinese and the Arabs. It was first used in Europe during the 1200s. By lining up the compass with the magnetic North Pole, sailors could tell which direction they were sailing in. However, early compasses were often unreliable and were easily affected by other iron objects on board ship. As a result, many ships headed off in the wrong direction. By the time of Henry the Navigator in the 1400s, compasses were much improved.

Key Dates

- 1419 Prince Henry establishes a school of navigation.

- 1420s First voyages south to southern Morocco.

- 1475 Portuguese sailors map the African coast from Morocco to Cameroon.

- 1482 Diego Cão crosses over the Equator.

- 1485–86 Diego Cão sails south to Namibia.

- 1487–88 Bartolomeu Dias sails round Cape of Good Hope.

- 1497–98 Vasco da Gama sails round Africa to India.

Christopher Columbus

▲ COLUMBUS
Christopher Columbus (1451–1506) was born in the Italian port of Genoa. He was named after St Christopher, the patron saint of voyagers. His discoveries included Cuba and the Bahamas.

FOR CENTURIES Europeans believed that the world consisted of just three continents – Europe, Africa and Asia. They thought that the whole of the rest of the world was covered by sea.

The traditional route to Asia had always been overland along the Silk Road. During the 1400s, the Portuguese discovered a way of getting there by sea, sailing south and east round the coast of Africa. Then an Italian called Christopher Columbus worked out that it should be possible to get to Asia by sailing west, across the great Atlantic Ocean.

Columbus devoted his life to finding this sea route to the riches of Asia. At first, people thought that it was a stupid idea and Columbus could not get any support. But in 1492 Queen Isabella of Spain agreed to give him money to make the voyage on behalf of Spain. He set out with three ships in August 1492, and after 36 days landed in what we now call the Bahamas. Sailing southeast, he passed Cuba and Hispaniola (present-day Haiti) before returning home in triumph in March 1493.

▼ LANDING IN AMERICA
When Columbus and his crew landed on Watling Island in the Bahamas, he claimed the island for Spain and renamed it San Salvador in tribute to God, "who guided us and saved us from many perils".

Columbus was convinced that he had found a new route to Asia. Although he was disappointed that the new lands were not full of gold, he set off again later in the year to confirm the discoveries of his first voyage.

Columbus made four voyages west across the Atlantic, establishing Spanish colonies on the islands he passed and claiming the region for Spain. Right up to

THE NEW WORLD?
The lands visited by Columbus disappointed him, for he did not find the walled cities and fabulous wealth of China and Japan he expected. Yet he remained convinced that he had sailed to Asia and never realized that what he had discovered was a continent previously unknown to Europeans.

◀ FERDINAND AND ISABELLA
When Ferdinand of Aragon married Isabella of Castile in 1469, Spain became a united country for the first time since the Roman Empire. Isabella sponsored Columbus's first voyage.

◀ NATIVE AMERICANS
The Arawak peoples of the West Indies lived off the abundant fruits and berries of the islands. They lived in shelters that they built out of palm leaves and branches. Most people did not wear anything, although some wore clothes for ceremonies.

▼ TOBACCO
While in Cuba, Columbus saw the Arawak people roll the dried leaves of the tobacco plant into a tube, set light to it and smoke it. Smoking soon became a popular pastime throughout Europe. Below you can see tobacco leaves being dried in a shed.

▼ THE *SANTA MARIA*
Columbus's flagship was the Santa
Maria, *a three-masted, square-rigged
cargo ship capable of holding up to 40
crew. The other two ships, the*
Niña *and* Pinta, *were
much smaller.*

▲ COCONUT PALMS
*During his travels, Columbus saw many crops
unknown to Europeans, including coconuts,
pineapples, potatoes and sweetcorn.*

his death in 1506, he remained
convinced that he had sailed to
Asia, although he failed to find
proof. Because he had sailed
west, the new islands he had
come across became known as
the West Indies.

Few people accepted his
claims. In 1502 Amerigo Vespucci
(1451–1512) returned to Europe from
an expedition down the east coast of South America.
He was certain that the lands were not part of Asia, but
part of a continent unknown to Europeans. He called it
Mundus Novus – the New World. In 1507 a German
geographer, Martin Waldseemüller, renamed it America
after Amerigo Vespucci. What Columbus had actually

discovered was of far greater importance than a lengthy
sea route to Asia. By sailing west, he had stumbled
upon the American continent. As a result, within a few
years the history of both America and Europe was
completely transformed.

▼ THE VOYAGES OF COLUMBUS
Over the course of four voyages, Columbus sailed round most of the Caribbean
islands and explored the coasts of South and Central America, believing that he had
discovered a new route to Asia.

Voyages of Columbus
◄···· 1st journey
◄···· 2nd journey
◄···· 3rd journey
◄···· 4th journey

NORTH AMERICA
Hispaniola
Cuba
Jamaica
Limor
SOUTH AMERICA
Trinidad
North Atlantic Ocean
Portugal
Lisbon
Palos
Azores
Madeira
Cadiz
Canary Islands
Cape Verde Islands
AFRICA

0 Kilometres 1600
0 Miles 1000

1492-1493
1493-96
1502-04
1498-1500

N

Key Dates

- 1492–93 Columbus makes his
first voyage to the West Indies,
finding the Bahamas, Cuba and
Hispaniola.

- 1493–96 His second voyage
takes him throughout the
West Indies. He builds
settlements on Hispaniola
and explores Jamaica.

- 1498–1500 On the third voyage
he sails between Trinidad and
South America and is the first
European to land in South
America.

- 1502–04 Fourth voyage, along
the coast of Central America.

Conquering the New World

I N THE YEARS AFTER THE HISTORIC voyages of Columbus a wave of Spanish explorers descended on Central and South America. They were searching for treasure.

Vasco de Balboa (1475–1519) was one of these adventurers. He was a colonist living in Hispaniola (Haiti), who fled to Central America to escape his debts. In September 1513 he set off into the interior of the country in search of gold. Twenty-seven days later he gazed westwards across a vast sea, becoming the first European to look at the eastern shore of the Pacific Ocean.

In November 1518 a second expedition left the Spanish colony of Santiago in Cuba, bound for Mexico. Previous expeditions had reported that there were vast temples and huge amounts of gold there. The 11 ships and 780 men were commanded by Hernán Cortés, a Spanish lawyer who had gone to

▲ KNIFE
The Aztecs were skilled craftworkers. They used wood inlaid with gems and pieces of shell and turquoise to make the handle of this sacrificial knife. This knife was given as a gift to Hernán Cortés.

the West Indies to seek his fortune. Cortés sailed along the coast for some months, raiding local towns and gaining valuable intelligence, then set off inland to the Aztec capital of Tenochtitlán.

Although the Aztecs were immensely skilled people, they were no match for the Spanish. The Aztecs had no gunpowder, and horses were unknown in the Americas. Cortés enlisted the help of the Aztecs' many enemies, then entered the city and captured its ruler, Montezuma. Cortés finally secured Tenochtitlán in August 1521, with only 400 men. The mighty Aztec Empire now became the province of New Spain.

Soon, word began to circulate about another rich empire, this time in South America. In 1530 Francisco Pizarro set out to conquer it with only 168 soldiers. The Inca Empire he found was weakened by civil war and an epidemic (probably smallpox). Once again, the Spanish soldiers overwhelmed the enemy. By 1532 the vast Inca Empire was defeated and its huge reserves of gold and silver were now under Spanish control.

◀ MONTEZUMA'S HEADDRESS
The Aztecs and Incas hunted tropical birds for their feathers. The quetzal's bright green feathers were highly prized and used in the headdress of Montezuma, the last Aztec ruler.

THE INCAS

The Incas were a hill tribe from Peru. Over the course of 300 years, they came to dominate the whole of the Andes mountains. By 1500 their empire stretched for more than 4,000km/2,500 miles. Although they had no wheeled transport, they built a huge network of roads and large cities of stone. They seem to have had no alphabet, so could not read or write. Despite this, their civilization was as advanced as any in Europe. The Incas were overthrown by Pizarro's small army.

▲ PIZARRO
The Spaniard Francisco Pizarro (1475–1541) went to the Americas to seek his fortune. He was spectacularly successful, crushing the powerful Inca Empire.

▶ QUIPU
Special officials kept records of taxation, population figures and other statistics on quipus. A quipu is a series of vertical knotted strings, of varying length and pigmentation, that hang from a horizontal cord. The length and shade of each string, its position and the type of knot record the information.

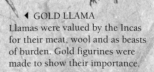

◀ GOLD LLAMA
Llamas were valued by the Incas for their meat, wool and as beasts of burden. Gold figurines were made to show their importance.

◄ TENOCHTITLAN
The Aztecs' capital city had a population of 200,000, bigger than any Spanish city, yet Cortés and his 400 men managed to capture it using trickery and deceit.

Cortés, Pizarro and the other adventurers were *conquistadores,* which means conquerors in Spanish. The conquistadores were brutal and often dishonest. They went in search of wealth, and to convert everyone they met to Christianity. Their conquests stretched the length of the Americas, from Mexico to Chile. Within 50 years of the expedition by Columbus, the Americas were under European control.

▸ MACHU PICCHU
The Incas established the city of Machu Picchu in a strategic position, protected by the steep slopes of the Andes mountains. It was built of stone blocks fitted together without mortar. Temples, ceremonial places and houses made up the 143 buildings. The city was so remote that the Spanish failed to discover it, and it was forgotten until an American explorer found it in 1911. It is located in south Peru.

Key Dates

- 1100s Incas start to dominate central Peru.

- 1325 Aztecs found the city of Tenochtitlán.

- 1430 Incas begin to expand north along the Andes.

- 1450s Incas build Machu Picchu.

- 1500 Aztec and Inca empires at their greatest extent and power.

- 1513 Vasco de Balboa first sees Pacific Ocean.

- 1521 Spanish capture Tenochtitlán and take over the Aztec Empire.

- 1532 Inca Empire conquered and under Spanish control.

Into Canada

▲ JOHN CABOT
The adventurer John Cabot (1450–99) was probably born in Genoa in Italy. He traded in spices with the Arabs before moving to England.

IN ABOUT 1494 AN ITALIAN merchant called John Cabot arrived in England. Like Columbus, he planned to sail west across the Atlantic in search of the Spice Islands of eastern Asia. However, he proposed to make the voyage at a more northerly latitude, making the journey shorter. Cabot needed to find someone to finance his trip. After rejection by the kings of both Spain and Portugal, Cabot took his idea to King Henry VII of England. Henry had previously refused to sponsor Columbus. This time he was aware of the riches of the New World, and was eager to support Cabot so that he could profit from any discoveries.

In May 1497 Cabot set sail from Bristol on board the *Matthew*. A month later he landed in Newfoundland, off the east coast of Canada, which he claimed for England. He had not found Asia,

nor had he found wealth, but he had discovered rich fishing grounds and lands not yet claimed by Spain.

The French set out to explore these new lands. In 1534 Jacques Cartier (1491–1557) sailed from St Malo. Like Cabot, he too was searching for a new, northerly route to Asia. He sailed round the mouth of the great St Lawrence River, returning the following year to sail up it to present-day Montreal. He struck up good relations with the Huron Indians who lived there, who told him about the riches of the kingdom of Saguenay, further west up the St Lawrence. In 1541 Cartier decided to return to find Saguenay. But not surprisingly he failed to do so, because Saguenay was an imaginary place. The Hurons had made up the story about this wonderful kingdom,

◀ MONTREAL
When Cartier sailed up the St Lawrence River in 1535, he got as far as the wooden-walled Huron village of Hochelaga. Cartier climbed the hill behind it, naming it Mont Réal (Mount Royal), the present-day Montreal.

NATIVE AMERICANS
Numerous tribes of Native Americans lived in the woods and plains of the St Lawrence valley. Five of the main tribes – the Mohawk, Onondaga, Seneca, Oneida, and Cayuga – joined together to form the Iroquois League in the early 1600s to protect themselves from other powerful tribes in the area.

◀ A HURON BRAVE
The Hurons welcomed the French to North America, trading furs and other goods with them and acting as guides and advisers. They also enlisted the French to help fight their wars with the Iroquois, who were their deadly enemies.

▼ FUR TRADE
The rivers and woods of Canada teemed with wildlife, providing furs for clothing and meat for food. Animal pelts, particularly from the seal, otter and beaver, were prized by the Europeans. They traded guns and other goods to obtain the skins from the Native Americans.

▲ A SCALP
Fierce warfare between the different tribes was common. The most important trophy a brave could win in battle was the scalp of his opponent. Skin and hair were removed in one piece and then displayed on a wooden frame.

▶ QUEBEC

When de Champlain visited Canada in 1608, he built a wooden fort on a hill overlooking the St Lawrence River at a point where it narrowed considerably. The Native Americans called the place Kebec, and today it is known as Quebec.

Fort built of wood

Balcony for strategic lookout

Cannon positioned for quick firing

Bridge for crossing the St Lawrence

full of treasures, in order to please their French visitors!

Fur traders and fishermen followed Cartier's route up the St Lawrence. But it was not until the next century that the French abandoned their search for a new route to Asia and began to settle in Canada. Samuel de Champlain (1567–1635) explored the east coast of North America and went inland as far as the Great Lakes. In 1608 he founded the city of Quebec, the first permanent French settlement in North America. The continent was now open for European colonization.

▼ EXPLORING CANADA

After John Cabot's exploratory voyage in 1497, the Frenchmen Jacques Cartier and Samuel de Champlain explored the valley of the St Lawrence River and claimed the region for France. De Champlain founded the city of Quebec.

Key Dates

- 1497 John Cabot claims Newfoundland for England.

- 1534 Jacques Cartier explores St Lawrence estuary in Canada.

- 1535–36 Cartier sails up St Lawrence as far as Montreal.

- 1603 De Champlain sails up the St Lawrence to Montreal.

- 1604 De Champlain explores from Nova Scotia to Cape Cod.

- 1608–09 De Champlain founds settlement of Quebec.

- 1615 De Champlain explores Lakes Huron and Ontario.

The North-east Passage

▲ SEALS
Siberian peoples, and explorers seeking the North-east Passage, hunted seals for food. Their skins also had many uses.

WHILE ENGLISH SAILORS concentrated on finding a north-west passage round the north of Canada, the Dutch were seeking a north-east passage to the north of Russia and Siberia. The Dutch were good sailors and their fishing and whaling fleets regularly sailed in the Arctic Ocean, but even so they were unsure whether a north-east passage really did exist.

The Dutch followed in the wake of an Englishman called Hugh Willoughby (1510–54), who had succeeded in sailing as far as the large island of Novaya Zemlya. But on his return journey, he perished in the pack ice off Murmansk on the Kola Peninsula in 1554.

In 1594 the Dutch mariner Willem Barents (1550–97) set sail on the first of his expeditions to find the North-east Passage. He too was unsuccessful, although on his third voyage in 1596 he discovered Bear Island, which got its name after his crew had a fight with a polar bear. He also found the rich fishing grounds of the Spitsbergen archipelago, which was to become hugely profitable for Dutch hunters of whales, seals and walruses. Then Barents's ship became trapped and damaged by the winter pack ice. He set off to row

▲ SIBERIA
The northern coast of Siberia lies inside the Arctic Circle. Here the temperature barely reaches above freezing point in summer and drops far below it in winter. Little grows in such an inhospitable landscape, although animals such as reindeer live there.

and sail the 2,560km/1,590 miles to Kola, but died of starvation at sea. His crew survived and managed to return home once the ship was free.

After the failure of Barents's trip, there were no more expeditions until the Russian explorer Semyon Dezhnev (1605–72) sailed round the eastern tip of Siberia into the Pacific Ocean, proving that Asia and America were not joined. This knowledge did not reach Europe for

THE ARCTIC OCEAN

Although the waters north of Siberia do not freeze over as much as those north of Canada, the Arctic Ocean is still a harsh place. The ice-free summer months are short and ships risk being caught and trapped in pack ice during the winter, which can last for up to nine months.

◀ THE *VEGA*
The 300-ton *Vega* was built in Germany as a whaling ship. It was constructed of oak with an outer skin of tougher wood to protect it against the ice. The ship had sails and a powerful steam engine. Nils Nordenskjöld made the first successful transit of the North-east Passage in it during 1878–79.

▶ WHALES
The first people to explore the Arctic Ocean were whalers (whale hunters) from ports in northern Europe. They sailed the ocean in reinforced ships. Whales were caught for their meat, blubber and bone.

◀ ICE-BREAKER
Today the North-east Passage is kept reasonably free of ice by a fleet of ice-breakers. These specially strengthened ships clear a passage to allow shipping through the pack ice.

Icicles hanging on the bunk beds

Chimney to escape through if snow blocked the door

Turkish bath made of a barrel

◀ AN ARCTIC SHELTER
In the winter of 1596 the ship of Barents and his crew of 20 men was trapped by ice in the Arctic. The men survived by building a hut out of driftwood. It measured 10m/30ft x 6m/20ft and contained a fireplace, with a chimney to escape through if the hut was buried by snow. It even had a primitive Turkish bath made out of a barrel.

many years, and the Arctic Ocean was mainly left to the Siberians to fish. It was not until the late 1800s that there was interest in the North-east Passage again, when Russia and other European countries realized that the great rivers and forests of Siberia might be a rich hunting ground. In 1878 the Finnish polar explorer Nils Nordenskjöld (1832–1901) set out from southern Sweden on board his ship, the *Vega*. Keeping close to the Siberian coast, he voyaged east until ice near the Bering Strait blocked his way. The following July he sailed into the Pacific Ocean. The quest was over and the North-east Passage was now open for commerce.

▲ THE NORTH-EAST PASSAGE
For more than 300 years, explorers sailed north-east from Europe in the hope of finding a way along the top of Siberia and round into the Pacific Ocean. They were looking for an easy way to the riches of Asia.

Key Dates

- 1554 Hugh Willoughby reaches Novaya Zemlya.

- 1594 Barents sails into Kara Sea east of Novaya Zemlya.

- 1595 Barents's second voyage ends in failure in the Kara Sea.

- 1596 Barents discovers Bear Island and the rich fishing grounds of Spitsbergen.

- 1597 Barents dies on the sea that now bears his name.

- 1648 Semyon Dezhnev sails round eastern tip of Siberia.

- 1878–79 Nils Nordenskjöld navigates the North-east Passage.

Exploring Asia

▲ PETER THE GREAT
Peter I (Peter the Great) was Tsar of Russia from 1682 to 1725. Under him, the backward country was transformed into a great European power.

AT THE START of the 1700s Russia had a dynamic ruler, Tsar Peter I. He built up a big navy and army, reorganized the government and constructed the country's new capital of St Petersburg. In previous years Russia had extended its territory right across Siberia to the shores of the Pacific Ocean. However, few Russians had any idea what their new land contained, or whether it was joined to America, so Peter the Great decided to find out.

Vitus Bering (1681–1741) was born in Denmark. He was a superb administrator, and Peter invited him to help modernize the Russian navy. In 1724 Peter appointed him to lead a large expedition across Siberia. The expedition left St Petersburg in 1725 and reached the Pacific Ocean two years later. There Bering and his men built a ship, the *St Gabriel*, and sailed up the coast and into the Arctic Ocean. From what he saw, Bering was satisfied that Siberia and America were not linked and returned to St Petersburg in 1730. In 1732 Bering was put in charge of a huge new undertaking. The Great Northern Expedition consisted of more than 3,000 men, including 30 scientists and 5 surveyors, with 13 ships and 9 wagonloads of scientific instruments. Its task was to explore the entire northern coast of Siberia as well as the seas to its east.

Over the next ten years five teams mapped the northern coast and the great rivers that flowed north through the country towards it. Bering concentrated on the seas beyond Siberia. This time he sailed across the Pacific to Alaska, returning to the Kamchatka Peninsula along the string of islands called the Aleutian Islands.

▲ CROSSING SIBERIA
Wayfarers in Siberia used teams of trained reindeer or huskies to pull sleds bearing food and other provisions. People sometimes wore wide snow-shoes to stop themselves sinking into the snow.

EASTERN ASIA

During the 1500s, Europeans began to travel to China and Japan. Most were Jesuit missionaries, who were trying to convert people to Christianity. However, eastern Asia was still mainly closed to foreigners, and little was discovered about these strange and distant lands.

◀ JESUIT PRIEST
The Jesuits were a Roman Catholic religious order formed in 1534 by Ignatius Loyola. Their main aim was to convert Muslims to Christianity, but they soon expanded their work, opening missions in India and China.

▲ FRANCIS XAVIER
Francis Xavier (1506–52) was a Spanish Jesuit who journeyed around India before visiting Japan in 1549. He admired Japanese people for their sense of respect, and made many converts.

▶ PRAYER WHEEL
Siddhartha Gautama was an Indian prince who became known as the Buddha. The religion of Buddhism is based on his teachings. From about 400BC it began to spread throughout eastern Asia. Many Tibetan Buddhists use a prayer wheel for saying their prayers.

▲ HUNTERS' PREY
The Siberian tiger lives in south-east Siberia, near to the border with China. Its pelt (skin) was much prized by fur trappers.

▶ DEATH OF BERING
In 1741 Bering started the voyage back from the Aleutian Islands off Alaska. He reached an island near the Kamchatka Peninsula, where he died of scurvy and exposure. The island is now named after him.

Bering died in 1741, before the expedition was finished, but he achieved a great deal. His team had mapped Siberia and opened up both Siberia and Alaska to Russian fur traders. By 1800 Alaska was part of the Russian Empire. Although Semyon Dezhnev had discovered a century earlier that Siberia and America were separated by sea, he left no records and few people were aware of his work. Bering confirmed these findings, so in tribute to him, the strait between the two continents is named the Bering Strait.

▶ LHASA
In Tibet, the isolated city of Lhasa was the heart of Tibetan Buddhism. In 1658 the German Jesuit John Grueber (1623–80) and the Belgian Albert d'Orville (1621–62) set out from China to find an overland route to India so as to avoid hostile Dutch ships on the sea route. In 1661 they entered Lhasa – the first Europeans to set eyes on the mystical city with its palaces and great temple complexes.

Key Dates

- 1549 Francis Xavier in Japan.

- 1661 Grueber and d'Orville visit Lhasa in Tibet.

- 1725–29 Bering crosses Siberia and explores the sea between Siberia and Alaska.

- 1732 Bering organizes Great Northern Expedition.

- 1734–41 Bering crosses Siberia and explores coast of Alaska.

- 1734–42 Five teams of explorers map the northern Siberian coast and the Ob, Yenisei and Lena rivers.

Advancing into America

△ JEFFERSON
In 1803 President Thomas Jefferson bought Louisiana from France, more than doubling the size of the United States.

TWO HUNDRED years after Columbus landed in the West Indies, Europeans still knew surprisingly little about the enormous American continent to the north. The Spanish explored Florida and the Gulf of Mexico, the English established colonies on the east coast, and the French sailed up the St Lawrence River and settled in Canada. But the vast lands that lay in between remained a mystery.

In 1541 the Spaniard Hernando de Soto set out to explore Florida and became the first European to set eyes on the wide southern reaches of the Mississippi River. Unfortunately he died soon afterwards and the Spanish failed to explore further. More than a century later, hundreds of kilometres to the north, Louis Jolliet (1645–1700) and the French Jesuit missionary Father Jacques Marquette (1637–75) discovered a route to the Mississippi River from the Great Lakes. They explored the river as far south as Arkansas. However, it was another Frenchman, Robert de la Salle (1643–87), who became the first European to sail down the river to its mouth on the Gulf of Mexico. He claimed the land in

▶ SAGAJAWEA
In 1804 Lewis and Clark were joined by Sagajawea, a member of the Shoshone tribe. She spoke many native languages and acted as the interpreter on the expedition.

this area for his country, naming it Louisiana after the French king, Louis XIV.

Over the next century, European influence in North America changed considerably. The Spanish still controlled Mexico and Florida, but the English had thrown the French out of Canada. Most importantly, the English colonists rebelled against their own country and set up an independent United States that stretched from the Atlantic coast to the east side of the Mississippi River. The west side – Louisiana – still belonged to France, but in 1803 the French sold it to the United States.

US President Thomas Jefferson wanted to find out more about this vast new land he had bought. In 1804 he sent two men to explore it. They were his personal secretary, Meriwether Lewis (1774–1809), and William Clark (1770–1838), a former army officer. Over the

△ CABEZA DE VACA
Alvar Núñez Cabeza de Vaca (1490–1556) sailed with de Narváez around the Gulf of Mexico. The fleet was wrecked off Texas in November 1528, but Cabeza de Vaca was saved by Yaqui tribesmen. He stayed with them for five years, then set out on foot through Texas and across the Rio Grande into Mexico, reaching the safety of Mexico City in 1536.

THE NEW CONTINENT
The Spanish were the first Europeans to explore North America moving northwards from their empire in Mexico. Pánfilo de Narváez (1470–1528) explored the Gulf of Mexico, while Hernando de Soto (1500–42) became the first European to see the Mississippi River in 1541. These were the first of many people to push across this huge new continent.

▶ THE MISSISSIPPI RIVER
The mighty Mississippi River flows south across North America to the Gulf of Mexico. The discovery of its northern reaches by Jolliet and Marquette opened up America to European explorers and settlers.

◀ BISON
For 350 years European settlers hunted the bison herds of the plains almost to extinction, wiping out the Native Americans' main source of food and clothing.

course of two years, they followed the river from St Louis up the Missouri River, over the Rockies, and down the Columbia River to the Pacific coast, before returning via the Yellowstone River to St Louis.

The success of the expedition convinced the US government that Louisiana was suitable for people to live in. Within a generation, settlers were pouring across the Mississippi to start a new life on the Great Plains and the Pacific coast. The expansion of the United States across the American continent had begun.

▲ SHOOTING RAPIDS
Lewis and Clark used canoes to navigate the dangerous Missouri, Columbia and Yellowstone rivers.

▶ GRIZZLY BEARS
Bears were a menace to the expedition. One chased six men from Lewis and Clark's party into the Missouri River.

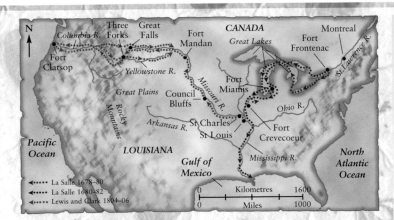

▲ SPREADING OUT ACROSS AMERICA
Robert de la Salle's two voyages around the Great Lakes and down the Mississippi River, and the expedition of Lewis and Clark up the Missouri River, did much to open up North America to traders and eventually to settlers.

Key Dates

- 1527–28 De Narváez explores the Gulf of Mexico.

- 1528–36 De Vaca explores Texas.

- 1541 De Soto is first European to see the Mississippi.

- 1672 Marquette and Jolliet explore the upper Mississippi.

- 1678–80 La Salle explores the Great Lakes.

- 1680–82 La Salle sails down Mississippi to Gulf of Mexico and claims the region for France.

- 1804–6 Lewis and Clark explore the Missouri River and routes to the Pacific.

The Amazon

▲ JAGUAR
Alfred Wallace met a jaguar, a tree-climbing big cat, when he was exploring the River Orinoco.

D URING THE 1700S A NEW TYPE of explorer emerged. While most explorers set out to make their fortune, either by finding gold or by opening up new and profitable trade routes, this new breed of explorer wanted to expand the scope of scientific knowledge.

This was a period of great scientific and intellectual debate across Europe. Scientists such as Galileo and Newton had already worked out the laws of the natural world – the movement of the planets and how motion and gravity worked. Now philosophers began to challenge existing religious beliefs with the power of human reason, or rationality. In France a group of

▶ UNKNOWN TRIBES
Explorers of the Amazon jungle discovered many tribes of people unknown to Europeans. But the arrival of settlers, and exposure to their diseases, soon killed off many of these native South American tribes.

intellectuals compiled a 35-volume *Encyclopédie* of all knowledge. This new thinking was called "The Enlightenment". It influenced explorers, who now searched for knowledge, not for gold or glory.

South America had barely been explored since the Spanish and Portuguese conquered it in the 1500s. Two hundred years later scientists started to examine this rich and varied continent. In 1735 the French mathematician Charles-Marie de la Condamine (1701–74) went to Ecuador to record the shape and size of the Earth – the science of geodesy – by calculating its width at the equator. He was so enthralled by the wildlife there that he stayed for another ten years.

At the end of the century, the German naturalist Alexander von Humboldt (1769–1859) and the French naturalist Aimé Bonpland (1773–1858) trekked up the River Orinoco and along the Andes mountains to study plant life. Over the course of five years they recorded more than 3,000 previously unknown plant species and gathered many samples. Fifty years later two pioneering English naturalists, Henry Bates (1825–92) and Alfred Wallace (1823–1913), ventured into the

---

THE AMAZON RAINFOREST
Even now, scientists have no idea how many different plants and animals live in the Amazon rainforest, as new species are constantly being discovered. Two hundred years ago the first European explorers were amazed at the sheer variety of wildlife they found, and fascinated by the tribes of people they met living deep in the jungle.

▲ ALEXANDER VON HUMBOLDT
German naturalist Alexander von Humboldt journeyed extensively throughout South America, examining plants and wildlife as well as the landscape and climate. The cold sea current that flows up the west coast of South America is named after him.

▲ RECORDING NATURE
In the days before photography, explorers recorded what they saw by drawing it. In his sketchbooks, Henry Bates drew hundreds of the butterflies and other insects he saw on his travels.

◀ CINCHONA
Among the many new plants discovered by Aimé Bonpland was the cinchona tree. Its bark was used to make quinine, a natural cure for malaria, one of the most deadly tropical diseases.

Amazon rainforest. When Bates returned to England in 1859, he took with him more than 14,000 insect and other specimens. Another scientist, Richard Spruce (1817–93), went back to England in 1864 with more than 30,000 plant specimens.

As a result of this scientific activity people became far more aware of the variety of life on Earth. New animals and plants were discovered, and medicines developed from some of the plants. The age of the scientific explorer was now well under way.

▲ RIVER AMAZON
The Amazon in South America is the second-longest river in the world and runs east from the Andes mountains, through Brazil to the Atlantic Ocean. It flows through the world's largest rainforest, which is home to many exotic animals and plants.

▶ TOUCAN ATTACK
Although toucans are normally shy and nervous, they can be aggressive. When naturalist Henry Bates attempted to capture one, he was attacked by a flock of its fellow birds.

◀ COLLECTING RUBBER
Rubber is made from latex, a sticky white liquid drained from the trunk of the rubber tree and collected in pots. Columbus saw locals playing with a rubber ball, but la Condamine was the first European to take rubber back home, in 1744.

▲ TREE FROG
Tree frogs were among the many new and exciting species that European naturalists encountered for the first time in the rainforest.

Key Dates

- 1735–44 La Condamine studies the shape of the Earth at the Equator. He stays there to watch the wildlife.

- 1799–1804 Alexander von Humboldt and Aimé Bonpland study botany along the River Orinoco and in the Andes.

- 1848–59 Amazon explored by Alfred Wallace and Henry Bates.

- 1849–64 Richard Spruce travels up the Amazon, collecting 30,000 plant specimens.

- 1852 Wallace returns to England, but all his specimens are lost in a fire on board ship.

The North Pole

IN 1881 A SHIP, the *Jeannette*, sank off the coast of Siberia. Three years later the wreckage turned up 4,800km/ 3,000 miles away on the coast of Greenland, right on the other side of the Arctic Ocean. This extraordinary event caused great confusion, because everybody knew that the Arctic Ocean consisted of a thick layer of pack ice. How had the wreckage managed to travel such a great distance? And how had it moved through the ice?

The Norwegian explorer Fridtjof Nansen (1861–1930) decided to find out. He calculated that the wreckage could only have been moved by a powerful ocean current which had pushed it along in the ice. Nansen designed a boat, the *Fram*, which he intended to steer into the ice and allow the currents to move it, just as they had the *Jeannette*. He worked out that the currents would

carry him close to the North Pole, in the middle of the Arctic Ocean. For three years, the *Fram* drifted in the ice from Siberia to the Spitsbergen islands to the east of Greenland. Although he failed to reach the North Pole, Nansen did prove that there was no land under the North Pole – it was just ice.

Nansen was not the first explorer to try to reach the North Pole. Between 1861 and 1871 an American, Charles Hall (1821–71), made three attempts on foot, dying after his last journey. But it was Nansen's voyage that raised huge international interest in the North Pole and a race to get there first began.

In 1897 the Swedish engineer Salomon Andrée tried to fly to the North Pole in a balloon, but he perished soon after taking off from Spitsbergen. Robert Peary (1856–1920) was more successful. He was an American explorer who made his first visit to the Arctic in 1886. For the next 22 years he devoted

◀ HUSKIES
Husky dogs have a thick, double coat of fur which helps to keep them warm in the extreme cold and snowy conditions of the Arctic. They can be trained to pull sleds of equipment over the ice.

WHAT'S IT LIKE AT THE NORTH POLE?
The North Pole is situated in the middle of the Arctic Ocean, which is covered with pack ice all year round. Because the ice floats on top of the ocean currents it is broken up and jagged, often rising to ridges 10m/30ft or more high.

▲ PLANES TO THE POLE
Aircraft play a vital role in bringing in supplies to the North Pole. American explorers Richard Byrd and Floyd Bennett reached the North Pole by plane in 1926.

▲ SEALSKIN
The first European explorers in the Arctic wore layers of wool clothes, which failed to protect them from the cold. Later, they learned to wear Inuit-style animal-skin clothes, such as this sealskin hood.

▼ PEMMICAN
An ideal food for a long Arctic expedition is pemmican. It is made from dried, shredded meat mixed with melted fat. It is full of calories and lasts for years.

Icebergs and frozen pack ice pile up either side of the Fram

◀ THE *FRAM*
Nansen needed a very strong ship for his plan. The Fram was specially designed to be frozen into the Arctic ice so that it could then float with the currents across the Arctic Ocean without being damaged. Nansen hoped that the ice-bound ship would drift towards the North Pole. The ship went right across the Ocean, but it didn't get as near to the Pole as Nansen had hoped.

Hull built to withstand the huge pressure of the ice

himself to polar exploration, returning year after year, each time getting closer to his goal of reaching the North Pole. In 1908 he set off up the west coast of Greenland and established a base camp at Cape Columbia on Ellesmere Island. His six strong team set off from there, making a mad dash and reaching the

North Pole on 6 April 1909. They then hurried back to base camp. The top of the world had been conquered.

Some people doubted that Peary had reached the North Pole, since he made the return journey in record time, covering 112km/70 miles in one day. Nowadays most people think that Peary did indeed reach the Pole.

▼ USS *NAUTILUS*
In 1958 a US nuclear-powered submarine, the USS *Nautilus*, sailed under the polar ice-cap. It left Point Barrow in Alaska and sailed the 2,930km/1,820 miles to Spitsbergen in the North Atlantic Ocean in four days. The submarine, which was 90m/300ft long and had a crew of 116, passed directly under the North Pole.

Key Dates

- 1871 Charles Hall sails up the west coast of Greenland and gets nearer to the North Pole than anyone before him.

- 1893–96 Fridtjof Nansen sails the *Fram* into the polar ice and drifts towards the North Pole, but fails to reach it.

- 1897 Salomon Andrée attempts to reach the Pole by balloon, but dies in the attempt.

- 1908–09 Robert Peary reaches the North Pole.

- 1958 USS *Nautilus* sails under the polar ice-cap.

Race to the South Pole

Affter Robert Peary made his successful attempt on the North Pole in 1909, all eyes turned towards the South Pole. Because it was the last unconquered place on Earth, the South Pole held a huge attraction for explorers, but it was a daunting place to visit.

Unlike the North Pole, the South Pole is covered by land. The vast, frozen continent of Antarctica is the coldest place on Earth, with ridges of mountains and large glaciers, making it extremely difficult to traverse. In addition, the land is surrounded by pack ice and icebergs that stretch far into the Southern Ocean. Two people prepared themselves to conquer this icy wilderness. The first was Robert Scott, a British explorer who had visited the region in 1901–4 and came to think of the continent as his to conquer. As his

▶ ROALD AMUNDSEN
Norwegian polar adventurer Roald Amundsen (1872–1928) was a skilled explorer and had three impressive records to his name. He was the first person to sail through the North-west Passage, in 1903–6, the first person to reach the South Pole, in 1911, and the first person to fly an airship across the North Pole, in 1926.

intention to lead an expedition to the South Pole became known, a second explorer, the Norwegian Roald Amundsen, joined the race. He kept his plans secret to prevent Scott speeding up his preparations. Amundsen too was an experienced polar explorer, but he was far better equipped and prepared than Scott.

Both expeditions arrived in Antarctica in January 1911 and spent the winter either side of the Ross Ice Shelf. Amundsen, however, had left two weeks before Scott and was 110km/70 miles closer to the Pole. He was also better prepared, having already made several journeys to leave food stores at stages along the route. His five-strong party made fast progress, climbing the steep Axel Heiberg glacier on to the

◀ PENGUINS
The Antarctic is home to several different species of penguin. Penguins cannot fly, but use their wings as flippers to swim.

SCOTT'S JOURNEY
In 1910 Robert Scott set out for Antarctica on board the ship *Terra Nova*. After spending the winter at Cape Evans, he set out for the South Pole in November 1911. Unlike his rival Amundsen, Scott used ponies as well as dogs to haul the sleds, but the ponies died in the cold. As a result, the party of five made slow progress and were devastated to discover, when they reached the South Pole on 17 January 1912, that Amundsen had beaten them to it. All five died on the return journey.

▲ ROBERT SCOTT
The naval officer Robert Scott (1869–1912) led a scientific expedition to Antarctica in 1901. His ill-fated expedition to the Pole in 1910–12 captured the imagination of the world.

◀ CHEMISTRY SET
Scott's expeditions were scientific as well as exploratory. His team carried this chemistry set with them when they set off in 1910.

▶ SCOTT'S BASE CAMP
Scott established his base camp at Cape Evans, on the east side of the Ross Ice Shelf. Here he and his team spent the winter of 1911, planning their route to the Pole, studying maps and also writing letters and reports.

▶ BATTLING ACROSS A FROZEN LAND
Amundsen and his party were well equipped to endure the cold conditions and were all expert skiers. They used husky dogs to pull their sleds. As food and other provisions were used up and the sleds got lighter, unwanted dogs were shot and eaten, reducing the amount of food required for the expedition. As a result, Amundsen and his team moved far faster than Scott's team.

plateau surrounding the South Pole. They arrived at the Pole on 14 December 1911. Scott set out on 1 November 1911 but encountered far worse weather and made slow progress, finally getting to the Pole a month after Amundsen, on 17 January 1912.

Amundsen's expedition skills and equipment ensured that all his party returned home safely. Sadly, Scott and his team all perished, three of them within 18km/11 miles of a supply depot equipped with food and other life-saving provisions.

The race to the South Pole was over, but although Amundsen claimed the prize, Scott has continued to hold a special fascination for people, because of the tragic ending to his expedition.

▼ RESEARCH STATION, ANTARCTICA
In 1959 an agreement was made to reserve Antarctica for scientific research. Today, 30 nations have scientific bases there to conduct research into the environment, wildlife and weather. In 1987 scientists found a hole in the ozone layer above Antarctica. The ozone layer protects the earth from the harmful rays of the sun.

Key Dates

- 1840 Antarctic coastline visited by James Wilkes and Jules Dumont d'Urville.

- 1841 James Ross from Britain explores the Ross Sea and its vast ice shelf.

- 1901–04 Scott explores the Antarctic coast and Ross Sea.

- 1908 Ernest Shackleton gets within 180 km of the Pole.

- 1911 Roald Amundsen reaches the South Pole.

- 1912 Scott gets to the Pole but the team dies on return journey.

Seas, Summits and Skies

▲ CHARLES LINDBERGH
The first solo flight across the Atlantic was made by 25-year-old Charles Lindbergh in 1927, when he flew the Spirit of St Louis *from New York to Paris in 33 hours.*

WITH THE CONQUEST of the South Pole in 1911, an age of exploration came to an end. All the major undiscovered parts of the world had now been explored. But eight years earlier, in 1903, a new method of transport had made its début. Orville and Wilbur Wright took to the skies over North Carolina in the aeroplane they had built, called the *Flyer*. Powered aircraft created new opportunities for exploration and discovery and in the first 30 years of the 20th century a series of epic flights took place.

Louis Blériot made the first crossing of the English Channel in 1909. The first non-stop journey across the North Atlantic, from Newfoundland to Ireland, followed a decade later. It was made by John Alcock and Arthur Brown. Charles Lindbergh flew solo over the Atlantic in 1927, while Amy Johnson made the first solo flight by a woman, from Britain to Australia in 1930. These and other historic flights opened up the skies to commercial travel, and airlines began regular

▲ BALLOONING ROUND THE WORLD
In 1999 Brian James and Bertrand Piccard became the first people to circumnavigate the world non-stop in their balloon, the Breitling Orbiter 3. *The pair set off from Switzerland and used the jet streams in the upper atmosphere to glide eastwards round the world.*

flights between the major cities of the world. People were now able to travel to faraway places without spending months at sea in order to get there.

As a result, more and more people decided to travel to other countries and explore the world for themselves. The growth in foreign travel led to a change in the nature of exploration. Now explorers took to the

HIGHS AND LOWS

Although nearly three-quarters of the world's surface is covered by sea, we still know very little about what lies beneath the ocean's surface. The development underwater craft enabled explorers to study the seas in greater detail. At the other extreme, the highest places on the earth's surface have similarly fascinated explorers.

▲ THE *TRIESTE*
The *Trieste* bathyscaphe was designed to withstand the great pressure under the sea. In 1960 Jacques Piccard descended 11km/ 7 miles into the Marianas Trench in the western Pacific Ocean, setting a world record that still stands today.

▶ JACQUES COUSTEAU
One of the world's most famous ocean explorers, Jacques Cousteau (1910–97) invented the aqualung in 1943 to help divers breathe under water. It was an air tank connected to a face mask.

▲ DIVING BELL
Edmund Halley invented the diving bell in 1690. It consisted of a watertight barrel anchored to the sea floor by heavy weights. Barrels of air were lowered and connected to the bell to supply the divers with fresh air.

▼ AMY JOHNSON
In 1930 the English pilot Amy Johnson (1903–41) flew single-handed from Britain to Australia in just 17 days. She had only learned to fly two years earlier. Amy went on to become the first woman to fly solo across the Atlantic and also made solo trips to India and Japan.

air, surveying lands by aeroplane and producing detailed maps by aerial reconnaissance. For those expeditions still on foot, supplies and reinforcements could now be airlifted in, and any casualties flown out for medical treatment. As a result, explorers face less physical danger than they used to, and their emphasis has shifted away from exploration from its own sake towards exploration for scientific reasons. Today, teams of scientists investigate the impact of global warming in Antarctica, for example, or the effects of the climate change in the Pacific Ocean. They use highly complex scientific instruments and techniques, and have a support team ready to fly them out of danger at a moment's notice.

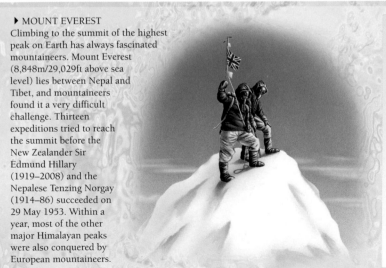

▶ MOUNT EVEREST
Climbing to the summit of the highest peak on Earth has always fascinated mountaineers. Mount Everest (8,848m/29,029ft above sea level) lies between Nepal and Tibet, and mountaineers found it a very difficult challenge. Thirteen expeditions tried to reach the summit before the New Zealander Sir Edmund Hillary (1919–2008) and the Nepalese Tenzing Norgay (1914–86) succeeded on 29 May 1953. Within a year, most of the other major Himalayan peaks were also conquered by European mountaineers.

Key Dates

- 1903 Wright brothers' flight.
- 1909 Louis Blériot flies non-stop across the English Channel.
- 1919 Alcock and Brown cross the Atlantic.
- 1927 Charles Lindbergh crosses the Atlantic.
- 1930 Amy Johnson flies single-handed from Britain to Australia.
- 1953 Everest conquered.
- 1954 Italians climb K2 – world's second-highest mountain.
- 1960 Jacques Piccard descends to record depths below the sea.

Blasting into Space

O N 4 OCTOBER 1957 an aluminium sphere no bigger than a large beachball was launched into space by the USSR. It measured 58cm/23in across and had four antennae trailing behind it. It orbited the Earth once every 96 minutes. This was *Sputnik 1*, the world's first artificial satellite, and it began a period of intense space exploration and discovery that continues to this day.

Modern rocket technology had made it possible to travel out of the Earth's atmosphere and into space. Once there, it became easier to fly to the Moon and to examine other bodies in the solar system. Scientists wanted to find out the answer to some of the oldest questions on Earth – is there life elsewhere in the universe? How and

▲ FLOATING IN SPACE
Astronauts are able to venture outside their spacecraft to do repairs or to help it dock with another craft. They must be tethered to their own craft to stop them drifting off into space.

▲ LAUNCH SITE
A rocket needs huge power to lift it and its load off the launch pad. Once in space, the rocket is no longer needed and falls away, leaving the spacecraft or satellite to continue on its own.

▶ MOON LIVING
Astronauts lived in this lunar module when they landed on the Moon. When they were ready to leave, the module blasted off to rejoin the orbiting main spacecraft.

THE SPACE RACE

The former USSR launched the world's first satellite in 1957, beginning a space race with the USA that lasted until 1969. The Americans feared that the USSR would use space for military purposes, and wanted to prove that the USA was the world's leading superpower. The race ended when the USA landed a man on the Moon. Today the two countries co-operate on missions.

▲ DOG IN SPACE
The first living creature in space – a Russian dog called Laika – was launched into space on board *Sputnik 2* in November 1957 and remained in orbit for two days. Many other creatures, such as monkeys and jellyfish, have made the trip.

▶ SPACE FOOD
Pre-packed, specially prepared food is taken on space missions. It requires heat or water to make it edible. Fresh foods are rarely eaten because they do not keep well.

◀ YURI GAGARIN
The first human to go into space was the Russian cosmonaut Yuri Gagarin (1934–68). On 12 April 1961 he orbited the Earth once on board *Vostok 1*, returning to Earth after 108 mins in space. Gagarin became a hero throughout the USSR and was awarded many national prizes.

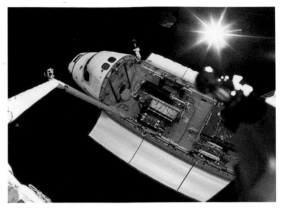

◄ MOON WALK
Neil Armstrong became the first person to walk on the Moon on 24 July 1969. He said, "That's one small step for a man, one giant leap for mankind." Today, only 12 astronauts, including Buzz Aldrin, pictured, have been there.

▼ WORKING IN SPACE
The space shuttle was reusable. It was launched into space like a rocket, but could then return to Earth like a plane. In space the shuttle was used for launching, repairing and recovering satellites and for further scientific research.

when were the Earth, and the universe itself, formed? They also wanted to explore the nearest planets and find out more about them.

This combination of technology and curiosity has sent men to the Moon and unmanned spacecraft to examine every planet in the solar system. Weather, communication and spy satellites now orbit the Earth

in huge numbers. At least two new satellites are launched each week. Orbiting telescopes send back detailed information about distant stars, and permanent space stations enable astronauts to spend many months in space. Gradually a more complete picture is being built up about our solar system and its place in the universe, and new discoveries are made every year.

▼ THE HUBBLE TELESCOPE
In 1990 the *Hubble* space telescope was launched into orbit high above the Earth. It sends back X-ray and other photographs free from interference or distortion by the Earth's atmosphere.

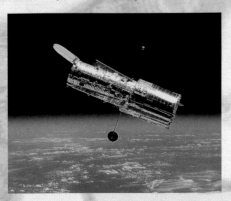

▲ THE GALAXY
The exploration of space has told scientists more about our own galaxy (the Milky Way) and the millions of stars it contains. By observing how these stars are born and die, scientists have begun to understand how the universe itself was formed.

Key Dates

- 1957 Russians launch *Sputnik 1*, the first satellite, into space.
- 1960 First weather, navigation, communication satellites (USA).
- 1961 Soviet cosmonaut Yuri Gagarin is first person in space.
- 1966 *Luna IX* lands on Moon.
- 1969 Neil Armstrong is first person to walk on the Moon.
- 1970 USSR launches *Salyut 1*, the world's first space station.
- 1983 *Pioneer 10* is first space probe to leave solar system.
- 2014 *Philae* lander makes first soft landing on a comet.

The Quest for Knowledge

▲ PYTHAGORAS
Great thinkers such as Pythagoras of Samos (560–480BC) are essential to scientific progress. Without the input of people like Pythagoras, Albert Einstein and Louis Pasteur there would be no scientific advances at all.

▼ KEY DATES
This panel charts the progress of science through the ages, from the invention of the wheel to the creation of the World Wide Web.

Science and technology seem very modern ideas, but humans have been striving to understand the world and inventing machines to help them ever since they first walked on the Earth 30,000 years ago.

The earliest people lived simply by hunting animals and gathering fruit and there was no need for science to be anything but basic. But as people settled down to farm around 10,000 years ago, the first towns and cities were built in the Middle East and life became much more complicated. At once science and technology began to develop apace to meet their varied needs. The Babylonians, for instance, created numbers and mathematics to keep track of goods and taxes. The Egyptians studied astronomy to help them make a calendar. And the astonishing achievements of Greek thinkers like Archimedes and the engineers of the Roman empire laid the foundations of modern science and technology.

Their achievements were almost lost with the collapse of the Roman empire, which plunged Europe

▼ OVERCOMING PROBLEMS
Most of the great explorers had used square-sailed ships, which were limited in their manoeuvrability. The development of new technology, such as this caravel with its triangular sails which could sail almost directly into the wind, opened up new possibilities.

EUROPE

c.3200BC The wheel is invented in Sumeria.

c.2500BC The Ancient Egyptians devise a 365-day calendar.

c.1500BC The Babylonians develop numbers.

c.300BC Euclid writes *Elements of Geometry*.

c.250BC Archimedes establishes the mathematical rules for levers.

221-206BC The Great Wall of China is built.

AD130 Galen writes his medical books.

140 Ptolemy writes *Almagest*.

c.850 Al-Kharwarizmi introduces algebra.

1492 Christopher Columbus sails across the Atlantic.

1543 Copernicus shows that the Earth circles the Sun.

1610 Galileo spies Jupiter's moons through a telescope.

1628 Harvey shows how the heart circulates blood.

1661 Boyle introduces the idea of chemical elements and compounds.

1686 Newton establishes his three laws of motion and his theory of gravity.

1698 Savery invents the first practical steam engine.

1735 Linnaeus groups plants into species and genera.

1752 Franklin shows lightning is electricity.

1783 The Montgolfier brothers' balloon carries two men aloft.

1789 Lavoisier writes the first list of elements.

1804 Trevithick builds the first steam locomotive.

1808 Dalton proposes his atomic theory of chemical elements.

1830 Faraday and Henry find that electricity can be generated by magnetism.

1825 The first passenger railway, from Stockton to Darlington.

▲ FIRST CARS
The invention of the motor car has had a huge impact on transport throughout the world. The slow and noisy early cars have been replaced by quieter, safer and more economical models. Prices have come down, and the range of makes is now greater than ever. The car has, in fact, been so successful that many countries are now trying to limit car ownership because of the impact on the environment.

into the Dark Ages. But scientific thought continued to flourish in the Islamic east, and further east in China. And as eastern ideas gradually filtered into Europe in the 15th century, European scholars began to rediscover Greek and Roman science, and make new discoveries of their own.

The next 100 years brought great shocks to established ideas. First, in 1492, Columbus sailed across the Atlantic to discover a whole new, undreamed of continent. Then, in 1543, Copernicus showed that the Earth, far from being the central point of the Universe, was just one of the planets circling around the Sun.

Deep thinkers realized that ancient ideas could not necessarily be trusted: the only way to learn the truth was to look and learn for themselves. Observation and experiment became the basis of a new approach to science which has led to a huge range of discoveries such as Newton's laws of motion, Dalton's atoms, Darwin's theory of the evolution of life and many more – right up to recent breakthroughs in the science of genetics. Trade and industry, meanwhile, have sparked a revolution in technology which began with the steam-powered factory machines of the late 18th century and continues to gather pace with the latest computer technology of today.

▼ MIR
Despite a number of mishaps, the Soviet Mir spacecraft stayed up in space for 15 years, from 1986 to 2001. It made more than 76,000 orbits of the Earth, and was a temporary home to many astronauts. The Russian Valery Polyakov spent a record 437 continuous days aboard Mir.

1830s Babbage designs his 'Analytic Engine'.

1856 Mendel discovers the basic laws of heredity.

1858 Darwin and Wallace suggest the theory of evolution by natural selection.

1861 Pasteur shows many diseases are caused by germs.

1862 Lenoir builds the first internal combustion engine car.

1862 Maxwell proposes that light is electromagnetic radiation.

1888 Hertz discovers radio waves.

1895 Röntgen discovers X-rays.

1897 Thomson discovers electrons and Becquerel discovers radioactivity.

1900 Planck suggests quantum.

1903 The Wright brothers make the first controlled, powered flight.

1905 & 1915 Einstein's Special and General Theories of Relativity.

1908 Ford's Model T, the first mass-produced car.

1911 Rutherford shows atom has a nucleus circled by electrons.

1923 Wegener suggests continental drift.

1927-9 Hubble realizes there are other galaxies and the universe is expanding.

1928 Fleming discovers penicillin.

1935 Carrothers develops nylon.

1939 Hahn and Strassman split a uranium atom.

1945 The USAF drop atomic bombs on Nagasaki and Hiroshima.

1948 Shockley, Bardeen and Brattain invent the transistor.

1953 Crick and Watson show DNA, the gene molecule in living cells, has a double-spiral shape.

1957 Sputnik is the first spacecraft to orbit the Earth.

1961 Gagarin is the first man in space.

1967 Nirenberg and Khorana show how the genetic code works. Gurdon creates the first animal clone.

1969 Armstrong and Aldrin are the first men on the Moon.

1989 Berners-Lee creates the World Wide Web.

Roman Engineers

▲ ROMAN BUILDINGS
This temple is an excellent example of Roman architecture. To create buildings such as this, the Roman's would use bricks to form a strong and long lasting structure.

ANCIENT ROME HAD few great thinkers of the kind that made ancient Greece so remarkable. However, it had many clever, practical men, and the Romans were the greatest engineers and builders of the ancient world. Their bridges, roads and aqueducts are marvels of ingenious, efficient large-scale construction, and many of them are still standing today, over 2,000 years on. Some, such as the eight aqueducts that supply Rome with water, are still in use, working as well as they ever did. It is hard to imagine many modern structures lasting quite so long.

Much of the Romans' engineering was connected with their military conquests, and engineers went with the armies to build roads and bridges. A sound knowledge of engineering was an essential skill for an officer, and soldiers provided much of the work for the major construction sites. Whenever the Romans conquered a new territory, one of the army's first tasks was to lay out cities to a standard plan, build roads to supply the army and lay on a clean water supply.

The Romans inherited some of their construction techniques from the Greeks and the Etruscans. They added to the Greek knowledge, and pushed Greek techniques to new levels, and added a number of features of their own. One of the keys to Roman engineering was the arch. The arch is a simple but clever way of making strong bridges. A flat piece of stone across two posts can only take so much weight before snapping. But in an arch the stones are pushed harder together when weight is placed on them, so the arch actually becomes stronger.

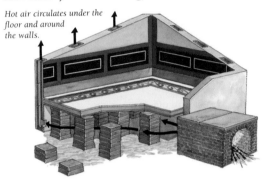

Hot air circulates under the floor and around the walls.

▲ UNDERFLOOR HEATING
We tend to think of central heating as a modern invention, but many Roman villas (houses) had a space under the floor called a hypocaust. Warm air from the hot bricks of a furnace circulated through this space, keeping the floor warm and the house very cosy.

ROMAN ROADS

None of the Romans' engineering achievements has had more impact than their road system. The Romans began building roads in 334BC, and by the time their empire was at its peak they had laid down more than 85,000km/ 50,000 miles of roads, including the famous Appian Way running 565km/350 miles through Italy.

During this time most other roads were simple dirt tracks, which were impassable with mud in winter. In contrast the Romans laid smooth, hard-surfaced roads that cut as straight as an arrow across marshes, lakes, gorges and hills. Using these roads, their soldiers could move around the empire with astonishing speed.

▲ ROMAN ROUTES
Even today, roads in many parts of the world quickly become impassable in bad weather. The Romans, however, built their roads to be used in all seasons. They built strong stone bridges high above rivers, and raised roads above ground that was liable to flooding on embankments called aggers. They even made grooves in the road to guide trucks.

Another feature of Roman engineering was cement. The Romans made bricks on an unprecedented scale, and Roman bridges and buildings are the first great brick structures. At first, the structures were mortared together with a mixture of sand, lime and water. In the 2nd century BC a new ingredient was added: volcanic sand found near the modern town of Pozzuoli in Italy. This ingredient, now called pozzolana, turned mortar into an incredibly tough cement that hardens even underwater. Pozzolanic mortars were so strong and cheap that the Romans began to build with cement only and dispense with the bricks. Eventually, they added stones to make concrete.

With the arch and pozzolanic cement, the Romans could build bridges and aqueducts on a massive scale, such as the famous Pont du Gard near Nîmes in France and the 780m/2560ft-long Segovia aqueduct in Spain. The fact that these bridges have survived almost 2,000 years testifies to both their strength and durability.

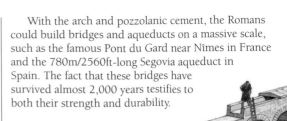

▶ BUILDING AN AQUEDUCT
Building a Roman aqueduct was a massive job involving hundreds and sometimes thousands of men. To build each arch, the engineers constructed a framework of wood on which they laid the stones. Towering scaffolds of wood enabled them to build rows of arches which were 100m/330ft or more high.

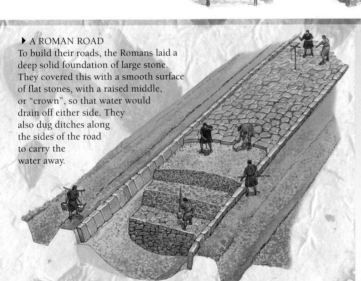

▶ A ROMAN ROAD
To build their roads, the Romans laid a deep solid foundation of large stone. They covered this with a smooth surface of flat stones, with a raised middle, or "crown", so that water would drain off either side. They also dug ditches along the sides of the road to carry the water away.

Key Dates

- c.3200BC The wheel is invented in Sumeria.

- 2800BC The ancient Egyptians build the first pyramid.

- 1470BC Pharaoh Sesostris builds first Suez Canal, linking the river Nile to the Red Sea.

- 480BC Xerxes of Persia builds a bridge of boats across the Hellespont.

- 312BC The Appian Way, the first great Roman road, is built.

- 221–206BC Great Wall of China is built.

- c.AD200 By this time the Romans have built more than 85,000km/50,000 miles of roads.

Where and When

▲ SHIP'S COMPASS
The compasses that ships use utilize a suspended, magnetized needle that aligns itself in a north-south direction with the Earth's magnetic field.

I N THE MIDDLE AGES THE Europeans knew little of the world. Maps were inaccurate and showed Asia to the east only vaguely. To the south, Africa faded off into a mystery land filled with monsters and dangerous peoples. To the west there was nothing at all. It was still not absolutely certain that the world was round. Perhaps the world ended in empty space? Even in Europe itself, charts were so inaccurate and navigation methods so unreliable that ships stayed in sight of land to be sure of finding their way.

Then, in the 14th century, the great Mongol Empire in Asia collapsed. The roads to China and the East, along which silks and spices were brought, were cut off. So bold European mariners set out westwards to find their way to the East by sea. From 1400, ship after ship sailed from Europe. At first they ventured south around the unknown west of Africa in small ships called caravels. The mariners were often Portuguese, sent out by Prince Henry "the Navigator" (1394–1460) from his base at Sagres. They pushed on, cape by cape, until Bartolomeu Dias rounded Africa's southern tip in 1488. Nine years later, Vasco da Gama sailed right round to India. In the

▼ THE CARAVEL
Up until the 15th century, most European ships were square-rigged, which meant they could only sail in much the same direction as the wind. Most of the great explorers, including Columbus, used a small revolutionary ship called a caravel, which had triangular "lateen" sails adopted from Arab dhows. With these sails, a caravel could sail almost directly into the wind.

THE SEARCH FOR LONGITUDE

Finding longitude was for a long time a problem in navigation. In theory you can work it out from the Sun's position in the sky, comparing this to its position at the same time at a longitude you know. However, you must know the exact time. Huygens had made an accurate pendulum clock in the 1670s, but it was too sensitive to keep good time aboard a tossing ship. The solution was the chronometer, a very accurate, stormproof clock made in the 1720s by John Harrison (1693–1776). It used balance springs, rather than a pendulum, to keep time.

◀ HUYGENS' CLOCK
The pendulum clock, invented by Christiaan Huygens in the 1670s, was the world's first accurate timepiece.

◀ HARRISON'S CHRONOMETER
It took John Harrison decades to persuade the authorities that his chronometer was indeed the solution to the longitude problem. This is his second version.

▲ LATITUDE
Latitude says how far north or south you are in degrees. Lines of latitude are called parallels because they form rings around the Earth parallel to the Equator. You can work out latitude from the Sun's height in the sky at noon. The higher it is, the nearer the Equator you are.

▲ LONGITUDE
Longitude says how far east or west you are in degrees. Lines of longitude, or meridians, run from pole to pole, dividing the world like orange segments. You can work out your longitude from the time it is when the Sun is at its highest.

meantime, in 1492 Christopher Columbus took a great gamble and set out west across the open Atlantic, hoping to reach China. Instead, he found the New World of the Americas waiting to be explored. Finally in 1522, fewer than 90 years after the voyages of discovery began, Ferdinand Magellan's ship *Victoria* sailed all the way around the world. Now there could be no doubt; the world is round.

Maps improved vastly as each voyage brought new knowledge, and map "projections" were devised to show the round world on flat paper and parchment. Yet these early projections helped sailors little, since a straight course at sea was an elaborate line on the map. In 1552 Dutch mapmaker Gerhardus Mercator invented a new projection. It treated the map of the world as if it were projected onto a cylinder, which could then be rolled out and lay flat. Although Mercator's projection made countries near the Poles look far too big, it meant that sailors could plot a straight course by compass simply by drawing a straight line on the map.

At the same time, navigation at sea made startling progress. Early sailors had steered entirely by the stars – they had only a vague idea where they were during the day, and no idea at all if the sky clouded over. From the 12th century on, European sailors used a magnetic needle to find north at all times. This however, only gave them a direction to steer; it did not tell them where they were. From the 14th century, sailors used an astrolabe to get an idea of their latitude – how far north or south of the Equator – by measuring the height of a star or the Sun at noon. The great breakthrough came with the invention of the cross-staff in the 16th century. Sailors used it to measure the angle between the horizon and the Pole Star and so work out their latitude precisely. Now the problem was longitude – how far east or west they were. For centuries, the only way to work out a ship's longitude was to guess how far it had come by "dead reckoning". This involved trailing a knotted rope in the water to keep a constant track of the ship's speed. However, this was not very accurate, so the problem of longitude was to tax some of the greatest minds over the next few centuries.

▶ GREENWICH
The great observatory at Greenwich, London, was set up in 1675. Its brief from King Charles II was to map the movements of the heavens so accurately that the longitude problem could be solved. The problem was not solved here, but the observatory sits on the Prime Meridian, the first line of longitude.

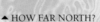

▲ HOW FAR NORTH?
The mirror sextant was developed in the mid-1700s from the cross-staff to measure latitude accurately. It became the main navigation aid for sailors until the days of electronic technology after World War II. It has one mirror that you point at the horizon, and another mirror that you adjust until the Sun (or a star) is reflected in it at exactly the same height as the horizon. The degree of adjustment you need to make to the second mirror gives the latitude. The sextant gets its name from its shape, which is one-sixth of a circle.

Key Dates

- 1488 Bartolomeu Dias sails round the southern tip of Africa.
- 1492 Christopher Columbus sails across the Atlantic.
- 1497 Vasco da Gama sails round Africa to India.
- 1497 John Cabot discovers Canada while trying to find a way to Asia.
- 1501 Amerigo Vespucci realizes South America is a whole new continent.
- 1513 Vasco de Bilboa of Spain sails into the Pacific Ocean.
- 1519 Ferdinand Magellan leads the first voyage around the world.

The Great Anatomists

▲ LEONARDO DA VINCI
*Da Vinci (1452–1519) is best
known for his few master
paintings, such as the* Mona
Lisa *and the* Last
Supper. *His curiosity
led him to study
everything from
human anatomy
to astronomy
with the same
remarkable
insight.*

Nothing is closer to us than the human body, yet it has taken as long to explore it as it has to explore the Earth. For thousands of years medicine was based as much on superstition as on research. The first doctor that we know about was Imhotep, who lived in ancient Egypt 4,600 years ago. People journeyed from far and wide to be treated by him, and after his death he was made a god. The greatest physician of the ancient world was the Roman Galen, born around

▼ DA VINCI'S ANATOMICAL DRAWINGS
*To draw human figures exactly, many artists in the Renaissance
began to study human anatomy for themselves. Some,
such as da Vinci, made their own
dissections, and their knowledge of
the human body often
outstripped that of
physicians.*

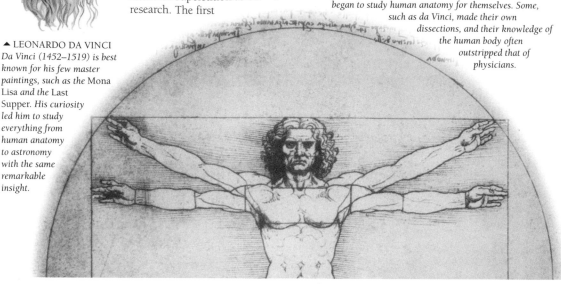

THE POWER OF THE MICROSCOPE

People never suspected that many things were far too small for the eye to see until the microscope was invented in around 1590. Soon, using a simple microscope made with a drop of water, the Dutch scientist Anton van Leeuwenhoek found that the world is full of tiny micro-organisms such as bacteria.

In the 1660s Italian physician Marcello Malphigi (1628–1694) began to use a microscope to study the human body. He made many discoveries of tiny structures such as the tastebuds on the tongue. He did not, however, restrict himself to the study of humans, but he studied plants and animals in great detail as well.

▼ MICROSCOPES
Early microscopes magnified things many times by combining two lenses. One lens, called the objective lens, bends light rays apart to create an enlarged image, but this image is still very small. A second lens, called the eyepiece lens, acts like a magnifying glass to make this tiny image visible.

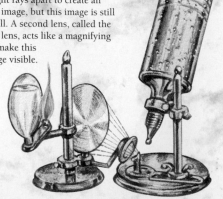

AD130. Like his contemporaries, Galen learned about the body by studying ancient manuscripts, but he also took a scientific approach and cut up animals to see how their bodies worked. He recorded his findings in many books describing the skeleton, the muscles and the nerves. Respect for Galen was so great that for more than 1,000 years, doctors would consult Galen's books rather than look at a body.

During the Renaissance in Italy in the 15th and 16th centuries, physicians began to consider that it might be better to look at real bodies, rather than at Galen's texts. They retrieved dead bodies from graveyards and cut them up to see exactly how they were put together. This is called dissection. The focus of this revolution was the University of Padua, where a brilliant German, Andreas Vesalius (1514–1564), was professor of surgery and anatomy. (Anatomy is the study of the way the human body is put together.) When dissection had been done in the past, it was usually done for the physicians by a butcher. Vesalius, though, began dissecting corpses himself, and asked the Flemish artist Jan van Calcar to draw very accurately what he found. In 1543, Vesalius published his findings in a textbook of anatomy called *De humani corposi fabrica* (On the Structure of the Human Body), which became the most influential medical book ever written.

Inspired by Vesalius's work, other physicians began to make their own dissections. Piece by piece, a very detailed picture of human anatomy began to build up. In the 1550s, for instance, Vesalius's colleague Gabriel Fallopio (1523–1562) discovered the tubes that link a

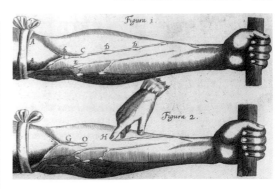

▲ BLOOD CIRCULATION
The English physician William Harvey (1578–1657) was one of the many great scientists who studied at the University of Padua in the 1500s and 1600s. Harvey's great insight was to realize that blood flows out from the heart through arteries and back through veins, making a complete one-way circulation of the blood.

female's ovaries to the uterus. These are now known as the Fallopian tubes. He also identified various other parts of the female reproductive system. Another colleague, Matteo Corti, discovered minute structures in the inner ear.

Gradually, physicians began to learn about physiology too (the science of the workings of the body). In 1590, for instance, Santorio Sanctorius showed how to measure pulse and body temperature. In 1628 William Harvey showed that the heart is a pump, and that blood circulates round and round the body. In this way the foundations for our current knowledge of the human body were built bit by bit.

▶ MALPHIGI
Marcello Malphigi was the first person to apply the power of the newly invented microscope to the human body. He made the first microscopic studies of human tissues, discovering the tiny structures present in the body. In 1661 Malphigi discovered capillaries, the minute blood vessels that were the missing link in Harvey's blood circulation.

Marcellus Malpighius
Medicus Bononiensis mortuus 29 Nov.

Key Dates

- 480BC Hippocrates is one of the first great doctors.

- c.AD130 Galen writes his medical treatises.

- 1543 Vesalius publishes his book *De Humani Corporis Fabrica*.

- 1550 Gabriel Fallopio studies the human body in minute detail.

- 1590 Santorio Sanctorius creates science of physiology, and shows how to measure pulse and temperature.

- 1628 William Harvey shows how the heart circulates blood.

- 1661 Marcello Malphigi sees tiny blood vessels called capillaries under a microscope.

Force and Motion

▲ ISAAC NEWTON
Isaac Newton (1642–1727) showed the link between force and motion in his three laws of motion. He realized that a force he called gravity makes things fall and keeps the planets orbiting the Sun.

THE 17TH CENTURY WAS THE first real age of science, when brilliant men such as Galileo, Huygens, Boyle, Newton, Liebnitz and Leeuwenhoek made many important discoveries. Of all their achievements, however, perhaps none was as important as the understanding of forces and motion.

The philosophers of ancient Greece had known a great deal about "statics" – things that are not moving. Though when it came to movement, or "dynamics", they were often baffled. They could see, for instance, that a plough moves because the oxen pulls it, and that an arrow flies because of the force of the bow. But how, they wondered, did an arrow keep on flying through the air after it left the bow – if there was nothing to pull it along? The Greek philosopher Aristotle made his common-sense assertion that you must have a force to keep something moving – just as your bike will slow to a halt if you cease to pedal.

Yet common sense can be wrong, and it took the genius of Galileo and Newton to realize it. After a series

▼ THE TOWER OF PISA
Galileo was the first to appreciate that gravity accelerates downwards anything falling by exactly the same amount. In other words, things will fall at the same speed no matter how heavy they are. Legend has it that he demonstrated this by dropping two objects of different weights from the Leaning Tower of Pisa in Italy. The two objects will have hit the ground at the same time.

NEWTON AND GRAVITY
No one knew why planets circle round the Sun or why things fall to the ground until one day around 1665, when Newton was thinking in an orchard. As an apple fell to the ground, Newton wondered if the apple was not just falling, but actually being pulled to the Earth by an invisible force. From this simple but brilliant idea, Newton developed his theory of gravity, a universal force that tries to pull all matter to together. Without gravity, the whole Universe would disintegrate.

Newton showed that the force of gravity is the same everywhere, and that the pull between two things depends on their mass (the amount of matter in them) and the square of the distance between them.

▲ NEWTON'S PRINCIPIA
Newton's *Philosophiae naturalis principia mathematica* (The Mathematical Principles of Natural Philosophy), in which he set out the laws of motion, is the most influential science book ever written.

▶ BAROMETER
By the mid-1600s scientists knew about force and motion, and about gravity. The picture of what made things move was completed when they learned about pressure. In 1644 one of Galileo's students, Evangelista Torricelli, showed that air is not empty space but a substance.

In a famous experiment, Torricelli showed that air has so much substance it can press hard enough to hold up a column of liquid mercury in a tube. In this experiment, Torricelli made the first barometer, the first device for measuring air pressure. Before long, he realized the value of the barometer for forecasting weather.

of experiments – notably rolling balls down slopes – Galileo realized that you do not need force to keep something moving. Exactly the opposite is true. Something will keep moving at the same speed unless a force slows it down. This is why an arrow flies on through the air. It only falls to the ground because the resistance of the air (a force) slows it down enough for gravity (another force) to pull it down. This is the idea of inertia. Galileo realized that there is no real difference between something that is moving at a steady speed and something that is not moving at all – both are unaffected by forces. But to make the object go faster or slower, or begin to move, a force is needed.

Further experiments, this time with swinging weights, led Galileo to a second crucial insight. If something moves faster, then the rate it accelerates depends on the strength of the force moving it faster

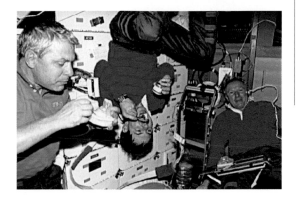

and how heavy the object is. A large force accelerates a light object rapidly, while a small force accelerates a heavy object slowly.

Galileo's ideas made huge leaps in the understanding of force and motion. In 1642, the year he died, another scientific genius, Isaac Newton, was born. It was Newton who drew these ideas together and laid the basis of the science of dynamics. In his remarkable book *Philosophiae naturalis principia mathematica* (The Mathematical Principles of Natural Philosophy), published in 1684, Newton established three fundamental laws, which together account for all types of motion.

The first two laws were Galileo's two insights about inertia and acceleration. Newton's third law showed that whenever a force pushes or pulls on one thing, it must push or pull on another thing equally in the opposite direction (see below). Newton's three laws gave scientists a clear understanding of how force and motion are related, and a way of analyzing them mathematically. Morever, together with Newton's insight into the force of gravity (the pull between two things), these laws seemed to account for every single movement in the Universe, large or small – from the jumping of a flea to the movements of the planets.

◀ WEIGHTLESSNESS

In a spaceship orbiting the Earth, the crew floats weightless. You might think that gravity is not working, just as Newton had predicted. The reality is that gravity is in fact still acting as a force, but the spaceship is hurtling round the Earth so fast that its effects are offset.

▼ THE THREE LAWS

Newton's laws of motion are involved in every single movement in the Universe. They can be seen in action in a frog jumping from a lily pad.

Newton's first law says an object accelerates (or decelerates) only when a force is applied. In other words, you need force to make a still object move (inertia) or to make a moving object slow down or speed up (momentum). To jump from the lily pad, the frog needs to use the force of its leg muscles.

The second law says that the acceleration depends on the size of the force and the object's mass. So the frog will take off faster if it gives a stronger kick (or is less heavy).

The third law says that when a force pushes or acts one way, an equal force pushes in the opposite direction. So as the frog takes off, its kick pushes the lily pad back.

Key Dates

- 1638 Galileo publishes his theories on speed and forces.

- 1644 Evangelista Torricelli demonstrates the reality of air pressure and invents the barometer.

- 1646 Blaise Pascal shows how air pressure drops the higher you go.

- 1650 Otto von Guericke invents the air pump.

- 1660 Robert Boyle shows how the volume and pressure of a gas vary.

- 1686 Newton publishes his work *The Mathematical Principles of Natural Philosophy*. It contains his theory of gravity and three laws of motion.

Factory and Furnace

▲ IRON BRIDGE
Iron was the new material of the Industrial Age. In 1779 the first all-iron bridge was built in Coalbrookdale in Shropshire.

UNTIL 1750, MOST people lived in country villages, raising animals and growing crops. Then two great revolutions started in Britain and changed things forever. A revolution in farming drove poor workers off the land. A revolution in industry saw cottage crafts give way to great factories. People who were driven off the land came to work in the factories, and the first great industrial cities grew up.

These revolutions were driven by the growth of European colonies and trade around the world. Colonies were vast new markets for goods such as clothes and cutlery. In the past people had made things slowly by hand. Now enterprising men realized they could make a fortune by producing huge quantities of goods quickly and cheaply for the new markets. They began to invent machines to speed things up, increase production and reduce the number of people to be paid.

At first, the clothing industry was the main focus. Traditionally, yarn was made by spinning together fibres, such as cotton, with a foot-driven spinning wheel. Cloth was made from yarn by weaving it on a loom by hand.

THE COMING OF WATERWAYS

The traditional horse and cart could not transport all the goods produced by the new factories, and within a few decades thousands of kilometres of massive canals were built across Europe. Using thousands of construction workers these canals were then the biggest, most complex things ever built by humans.

▶ NEWCOMEN'S ENGINE
Newcomen's 1712 beam engine was the first practical steam engine. Steam drove a piston up and down to rock the beam that pumped water from the mines. It was heavy on coal but worked.

◀ SEVERN CANAL
The great canal-building era began in 1761 with James Brindley's Bridgewater Canal from Manchester. Soon the Grand Trunk Canal linked the rivers Mersey and Trent, and the Severn Canal linked the Thames and Bristol Channel. The area around Birmingham became the hub of a national canal network.

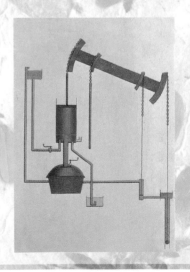

Then in 1733, John Kay built a machine called a flying shuttle. Kay's shuttle wove cloth so fast that the spinners could not make enough yarn. In 1764 Lancashire weaver James Hargreaves created the spinning jenny to spin yarn

▼ THE INDUSTRIAL TOWN
The vast new towns of the Industrial Revolution, such as Birmingham and Leeds, were different from any town before. Noisy, smoky factories loomed over neatly packed rows of tiny brick houses – home to tens of thousands of factory workers. The coming of the railways in the 1840s completed the picture.

on eight spindles at once. This was a machine for home use, but a bigger breakthrough was Richard Arkwright's water frame of 1766. The water frame was a spinning machine driven by a water wheel. In 1771 Arkwright installed a series of water frames in a mill in Cromford in Derbyshire, England, to create the world's first large factory.

The early factories were water powered, but could they be powered by steam? Steam would be more powerful and there would be no need to locate factories by rivers. Thomas Savery had created a steam engine for pumping water out of mines in 1698, and a version developed by Newcomen in the 1720s was installed in many mines. Newcomen's engine was expensive to run, but in the 1780s James Watt created a cheaper engine. It gave power anywhere, and steam engines soon took over in factories.

The success of steam power depended on machine tools to shape metal, such as John Wilkinson's 1775 metal borer, and on iron and coal. Coal produced heat to make, or "smelt", iron. In the past iron had been smelted with charcoal. Then, in 1713, Abraham Darby found out how to smelt with coke, a kind of processed coal. Soon huge amounts of iron were churned out by coke-smelters. The combination of big steam-powered machines, cheap iron and coal proved unstoppable, and the quiet rural ways gave way to the big cities and noisy factories.

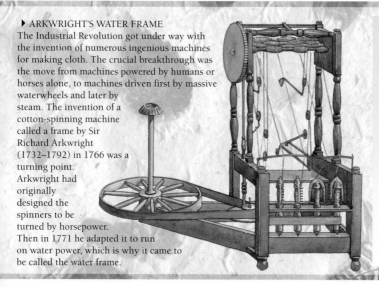

▶ ARKWRIGHT'S WATER FRAME
The Industrial Revolution got under way with the invention of numerous ingenious machines for making cloth. The crucial breakthrough was the move from machines powered by humans or horses alone, to machines driven first by massive waterwheels and later by steam. The invention of a cotton-spinning machine called a frame by Sir Richard Arkwright (1732–1792) in 1766 was a turning point. Arkwright had originally designed the spinners to be turned by horsepower. Then in 1771 he adapted it to run on water power, which is why it came to be called the water frame.

Key Dates

- 1698 Thomas Savery invents the first practical steam engine.
- 1722 Thomas Newcomen improves the steam engine.
- 1713 Abraham Darby smelts iron with coke.
- 1733 John Kay invents the flying shuttle weaving machine.
- 1764 James Hargreaves invents the spinning jenny to spin yarn.
- 1766 Richard Arkwright invents the water frame for spinning by water power.
- 1782 James Watt creates a cheap-to-run steam engine for powering machines.

The Charged World

▲ MICHAEL FARADAY
(1791–1867)
*The son of a blacksmith,
Michael Faraday grew up
to become one of the
greatest experimental
scientists of all time. He
laid the foundation of our
knowledge of electricity
and magnetism.*

I T WOULD BE HARD TO IMAGINE
a world without electricity.
Not only is it the energy that
powers everything from toasters
to televisions, but it is one of
the fundamental forces in the
Universe that holds all matter
together. Yet until the late 18th
century scientists knew almost
nothing about electricity. The
ancient Greeks knew that when
you rubbed a kind of resin
called amber with cloth it
attracts fluff. The word
"electricity" comes from
elektron, the Greek word for
amber. For thousands of years
amber attraction was
considered a minor curiosity.

In the 18th century scientists such as the French
chemist Charles Dufay (1698–1739) and English
physicist Stephen Gray (1666–1736) began to
investigate electricity. They soon discovered, not only
that various substances could conduct (transmit) the
same attraction to fluff as amber, but also that rubbing
two similar substances together made them repel each
other, not attract. This attraction and repulsion came to
be called positive and negative electrical "charge".

▶ THE DYNAMO
*The discovery of the link
between electricity and
magnetism led to the
development of the
dynamo. It could generate
electricity by turning magnets
between electrical coils. In 1873
Belgian Zénobe Gramme built
the first practical generator. By
1882 power stations were
supplying electric power to both
London and New York.*

By the mid-1700s
some machines could
generate quite large
charges when a handle
was turned to rub glass
on sulphur. The charge
could even be stored in a
special glass jar called a
Leyden jar – then suddenly let out via a metal chain to
create a spark. Seeing these sparks, American statesman
and inventor Benjamin Franklin (1706–1790)
wondered if they were the same as lightning. He
attached a metal chain like that of a Leyden jar to a kite
sent up in a thunderstorm. The lightning sent a spark
from the chain – only much bigger than expected – and
Franklin was lucky to survive.

ELECTRICAL PROGRESS
Faraday's and Henry's discovery of a way to
generate electricity may have transformed our
lives more than any other single scientific
discovery. For thousands of years, people had
seen at night by candle light, kept in touch with
messages carried on foot or horseback and heard
music only when someone played an instrument
near them. The discovery of electricity changed
all this.

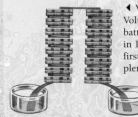

◀ VOLTAIC PILE
Volta's pile, or
battery, was invented
in 1800. It was the
first source of
plentiful electricity.

▲ EDISON'S PHONOGRAPH
The first record player, Edison's phonograph
of 1877, was mechanical. The arrival of
electrical sound recording in the 1920s,
including sound on TV and film, made
sound and music more accessible.

▲ EDISON'S ELECTRIC
LIGHT BULB
The electric light bulb was
invented independently by
Sir Joseph Swan in the UK in
1878, and by Thomas Edison
in the USA in 1879.

▶ FARADAY AT WORK
Michael Faraday spent his life working at the Royal Institution in London, where his exciting and brilliantly clear public demonstrations of the latest electrical discoveries were famous. For one show he built a big metal cage. He stepped inside it with his instruments while his assistant charged up the cage to 100,000 volts – a terrifying crackle of sparks ran around it. Faraday knew that he would be safe inside the cage because the charge courses around the outside. Such electrically safe cocoons are now called Faraday cages.

People were so excited by Franklin's discovery that demonstrations of electrical effects became very fashionable. When Italian anatomist Luigi Galvani (1737–1798) found that a dead frog's legs hung on a railing twitched in a thunderstorm, people wondered if they had found the very force of life itself – animal electricity. Alessandro Volta (1745–1827) realized that it was not the life force that made the electricity to twitch the frog's legs, but simply a chemical in the metal railing. Soon scientists realized that an electrical charge could be made to flow in a circular path from one side, or "terminal", of a battery to the other.

The real breakthrough, however, was the discovery of the link between electricity and magnetism. In 1819, Danish physicist Hans Øersted suggested that an electrical current has a magnetic effect, turning the needle of a compass. Little more than a decade later Joseph Henry (1797–1878) in America and Michael Faraday (1791–1867) in Britain proved that the opposite is in fact true – that it is actually a magnet that has an electrical effect. When a magnet is moved near an electric circuit, it generates a surge of electricity in the circuit. Using this principle – called electromagnetic induction – huge machines could be built to generate large quantities of electricity. The way was now open for the development of every modern appliance from electric lighting to the Internet.

▲ ALEXANDER BELL
Bell (1847–1922) was the Scottish-born American inventor of the telephone and a pioneer of sound recording.

▼ THE FIRST TELEPHONE
When Alexander Bell invented the telephone in 1876, electric telegraphs were already widely used to send messages along an electric cable, simply by switching the current on and off. Bell found a way of carrying the vibrations of the voice in a similar electric signal.

Key Dates

- 250BC Parthians invent the battery.

- 1710s Stephen Gray transmits electricity 100m along a silk thread.

- 1752 Benjamin Franklin shows that lightning is electricity.

- 1800 Alessandro Volta makes the first modern battery.

- 1819 Hans Øersted discovers an electric current creates a magnetic field.

- 1820 Georg Ohm shows that the flow of an electric current depends on the resistance of a wire.

- 1830 Joseph Henry and Michael Faraday discover how an electrical current can be generated by magnetism.

Steam Power

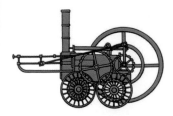

▲ TREVITHICK'S STEAM
LOCOMOTIVE
*The age of modern powered land
transport began in 1804 with
Trevithick's locomotive, the world's
first steam railway locomotive. It
ran on a mine track in Wales.*

FOR TENS OF thousands of years, human beings had managed with the power provided by wind, water or sheer muscle. Then with the Industrial Revolution of the 18th century came the first steam engines, bringing huge amounts of controllable, and reliable power.

The idea of using steam for power dates back to the 1st century AD, to an ancient Greek mathematician called Hero from Alexandria in Egypt. He came up with the idea of using jets of steam to rotate a kettle-like vessel. However, it was not until the 18th century that steam engines became a practical reality.

Most of the early steam engines, including those built by James Watt, were fixed engines, which provided power for working machines and pumps in factories and mines. Then in 1769 a French army engineer called

Nicolas-Joseph Cugnot (1725–1804) built a massive three-wheeled cart that was driven along by a steam engine at walking pace.

The problem with using steam to drive vehicles such as this was that steam engines were incredibly heavy. Weight though, would not be a problem in boats. In 1783 the Marquis Claude de Jouffroy d'Abbans, a French nobleman, built a massive steamboat that churned up the Saone River near Lyon, in France, for 15 minutes before the pounding of the engines shook it to bits. The boat sailed only once, but in 1787 John Fitch, an American inventor, made the first successful steamboat with an engine driving a

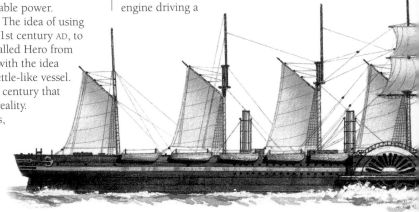

THE FIRST PASSENGER RAILWAYS

The first steam locomotives were built to haul coal trucks around mines. On 27 September 1825 a father and son, George and Robert Stephenson, ran the first passenger train from Darlington to Stockton in the north of England. Over 450 people rode in the train's open wagons that day, pulled by the Stephensons' locomotive *Active* (later renamed *Locomotion*), and the 13km/8 mile journey was completed in just 30 minutes. The railway age had begun.

▲ THE ROCKET
In Stephenson's famous *Rocket* the cylinder that drove the wheels was almost horizontal. This made it so powerful that it easily won the first locomotive speed trials in 1829.

▲ THE LIVERPOOL AND MANCHESTER
The 64km/40-mile-long Liverpool and Manchester railway, which opened on 15 September 1830, was the first real passenger railway. On the opening day, it also claimed the first railway casualty: Home Secretary William Huskisson was killed under the wheels of a locomotive.

series of paddles on each side of the boat. In 1790 Fitch started the world's first steam service on the Delaware River. In 1802, in Scotland, another steam pioneer William Symington (1763–1831) built a steam tug, the *Charlotte Dundas*. It was so powerful that it could pull two 70-ton barges.

The steamboat really arrived when American engineer Robert Fulton (1765–1815) made the first successful passenger steamboats in 1807. They carried people 240km/150 miles up the Hudson River between New York and Albany. This journey, which took four days by sailing ship, took Fulton's steamboats less than a day to complete.

Three years earlier, Cornish engineer Richard Trevithick had shown that heavy steam vehicles – or "locomotives" as they came to be called – could move more easily on rails. In 1804 he fired up the world's first steam railway locomotive at

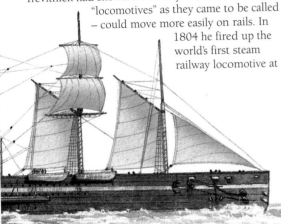

Pendarren ironworks in Wales. Even rails did not solve the problem at once, because Trevithick's locomotive cracked the cast-iron tracks. But the success of the concept was clear. Cast-iron rails were soon replaced with wrought-iron and, later, steel rails that could take much more weight. Within 15 years steam locomotives were running on short railways all over Britain. The age of steam travel had begun.

▲ HMS *THESEUS*
Steamships gained in power and reliability and, in the 1880s many navies began to build steam-power warships like HMS Theseus.

◀ THE GREAT EASTERN
In 1819 the New York-built Savannah, *a sailing ship equipped with a steam engine, made the first Atlantic crossing using steam power. The age of regular transatlantic steam passenger services began in 1837 with the launch of the* Great Western, *one of three giant steam ships designed by British engineer Isambard Kingdom Brunel. Brunel's* Great Eastern, *launched in 1858, was the biggest ship launched in the 1800s – 211m/692ft long and weighing almost 19,000 tons.*

▶ STEAM SPEED
Steam locomotives were the cutting edge of technology in Victorian Britain. Brilliant men such as James Nasmyth (1808–1890) went into locomotive design in the same way that talented designers are now drawn into electronic and space technology. As a result, steam locomotives rapidly became more and more efficient.

By the 1880s trains were running the 535km/330 miles from London to Edinburgh in little more than 7 hours, often hitting speeds of over 110kmh/70mph. Just 40 years earlier the journey had taken 12 days by coach.

Key Dates

- 1783 Claude d'Abbans sails the first steamboat on the Saone near Lyon in France.

- 1804 Richard Trevithick builds first steam-powered railway locomotive.

- 1807 Robert Fulton opens the first passenger steamboat service.

- 1819 The *Savannah* makes the first steam-powered crossing of the Atlantic.

- 1823 George and Robert Stephenson begin to build railway locomotives.

- 1825 Stockton and Darlington railway opens.

- 1830 Liverpool and Manchester railway opens.

Rays and Radiation

▲ SEE-THROUGH HAND
X-rays reveal the bones inside a living hand because they shine straight through skin and muscle, and are only blocked by bone.

IN 1864 SCOTTISH SCIENTIST James Clark Maxwell made the brilliant deduction that light is a kind of wave created by the combined effects of electricity and magnetism. He also predicted that light might just be one of many kinds of "electromagnetic" radiation. Scientists were keen to find out, and in 1888 German physicist Heinrich Hertz built a circuit to send big sparks across a gap between two metal balls. If Maxwell was right, the sparks would send out waves of electromagnetic radiation. But they might not be visible like light. So Hertz set up another electric circuit to detect them. The waves created pulses of current in this circuit, which Hertz saw as tiny sparks across another gap. By moving the receiving circuit, he worked out just how long the waves were. They proved to be much longer than light waves, and are now known as radio waves.

About the same time, others were experimenting with discharge tubes. Scientists had known for 100 years or more that a bottle from which air is sucked glows eerily if you put electrodes (electric terminals) into it and fire a spark between them. Discharge tubes gave a near-perfect vacuum (space without air), and the spark between the electrodes made the tube glow brightly. Sometimes even the

▲ FIRST X-RAY
In 1895, Röntgen shone X-rays through his wife's shoe to make a photo of the bones of her foot inside the shoe.

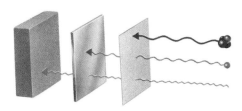

▲ RADIOACTIVITY
We now know that radioactivity is three kinds of particle shot out by atoms as they disintegrate naturally: alpha, beta and gamma particles. Each kind of particle has the power to penetrate different materials.

THE TV TUBE
The cathode-ray tube was not just behind the discovery of electrons and radioactivity. Until late 2007, most TV and computer screens were cathode-ray tubes. Though most screens in our homes today are LCD (liquid-crystal display), CRT screens remain popular in the printing and broadcasting industries, because of their superior fidelity and contrast.

▼ PRISM AND SPECTRUM
In the 1600s Newton showed that light is made of a spectrum, or range, of different shades. We now know that light itself is part of a much wider spectrum of electromagnetic radiation. The radio waves that beam out TV signals are just part of this spectrum.

▲ BAIRD'S TELEVISION ATTEMPTS
John Logie Baird (1888–1946) was the Scottish inventor who made television a reality. It had no single inventor, but it was Baird who made the first true TV pictures in 1926. Baird transmitted TV pictures by telephone line from London to Glasgow in 1928.

▶ THE CURIES IN THEIR LABORATORY
The Curies were among the greatest of all scientific experimenters. Their combination of brilliant insight and exact, patient work led them not only to discover the true nature of radioactivity – radiation from atoms – but to prove it too.

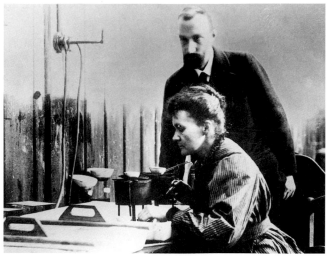

glass glowed. The glowing was named "cathode rays" because it seems to come from the negative terminal, or cathode. If the tube was empty, how was the spark crossing from one electrode to another? In 1897, J. J. Thomson guessed the spark was a stream of tiny bits of atoms, which he called electrons. For the first time, scientists saw that the atom is not just a solid ball, but contains smaller, subatomic particles.

Meanwhile, in 1895 the discharge tube helped Wilhelm Röntgen to discover another kind of radiation. Röntgen found that, even when passed through thick card, some rays from the tube made a sheet of fluorescent material glow. Although card could block out light it could not stop these new mystery rays, which he called X-rays. Within a few weeks he had taken a picture of the bones in his wife's foot by shining X-rays through it and onto a photographic plate.

In the same year French scientist Henri Poincaré was wondering why the glass in discharge tubes often glowed as well as the sparks. Perhaps radiation might be emitted not only by electricity but by certain substances too. Soon, Antoine Becquerel discovered this when he left uranium salts in a dark drawer on photographic paper. A few weeks later there was a perfect image of a copper cross that had

been lying on the paper. There was no light or electricity to form the image, so where was the radiation coming from?

Marie and Pierre Curie soon found the intensity of radiation was in exact proportion to the amount of uranium. They realized it must be coming from the uranium atoms themselves, and called this atomic radiation "radioactivity". In fact, not only uranium, but also many other elements are radioactive, including two new elements discovered by the Curies – radium and polonium. Since this crucial discovery many uses for radioactivity have been found, but so too have its dangers. Marie Curie herself died of cancer brought on by overexposure to radioactivity.

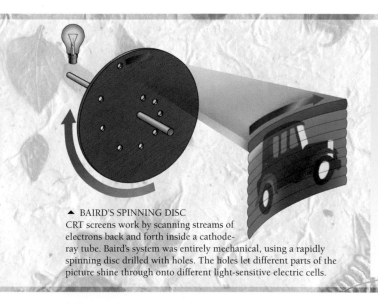

▲ BAIRD'S SPINNING DISC
CRT screens work by scanning streams of electrons back and forth inside a cathode-ray tube. Baird's system was entirely mechanical, using a rapidly spinning disc drilled with holes. The holes let different parts of the picture shine through onto different light-sensitive electric cells.

Key Dates

- 1864 James Clerk Maxwell says that light is electromagnetic radiation.

- 1888 Heinrich Hertz discovers radio waves.

- 1895 Wilhelm Röntgen discovers X-rays.

- 1897 J. J. Thomson discovers electrons.

- 1897 Antoine Becquerel discovers radioactivity.

- 1898 Marie and Pierre Curie discover the radioactive elements radium and polonium.

- 1898–1900 Ernest Rutherford finds that radioactivity is emissions of alpha, beta and gamma particles.

Space and Time

▲ MICHELSON
Albert Michelson (1852-1931) became the first American scientist to win the Nobel Prize in 1907.

In 1905, A TALENTED YOUNG scientist called Albert Einstein came up with his special theory of relativity. The theory is not easy to understand, but it has revolutionized the way in which scientists think about space and time. Its origins date back to 1610, when Galileo was thinking about how things moved and described a ship at sea. Shut yourself in a cabin, Galileo suggested, and you see fish in a fish tank swimming in all directions just as easily when the ship is moving as when it is at anchor. For the fish, the ship's motion is irrelevant. In the same way, when you walk around you are never aware that the ground beneath your feet is a planet whizzing through space at 100,000kmh/ 62,000mph. So we can only detect movement through space in relation to something else.

Half a century later, a Dutch astronomer called Owe Roemer added another dimension to the picture – time. Roemer realized that because the light took ten minutes to travel across space to the Earth, he was seeing the eclipse of Jupiter's moons in 1676 ten minutes after it actually

▲ EINSTEIN AND E=MC²
Einstein's theory of relativity is not just about space and time; it involves energy too. Energy is how vigorously something can move. Something moving fast clearly has a lot of energy, called kinetic energy. The energy of a heavy ball perched on a hilltop is called potential energy. Scientists knew that kinetic and potential energy are interchangeable – the ball might roll downhill, for instance.

Einstein went further and showed that mass, energy and movement are interchangeable. They are swapping over all the time – energy into mass, mass into movement and so on. Since light is the fastest moving thing, it clearly plays an important role in the relationship between energy, mass and movement. Einstein linked them in a famous equation: energy equals mass times the speed of light squared, or E=mc². This equation shows how a very little mass can give an enormous amount of energy.

TIME MACHINES
Ever since people realized that time is just a dimension, many have fantasized about the possibility of moving backwards or forwards in time. Stories such as H. G. Wells's *The Time Machine* and the films such as the *Back to the Future* series depict amazing time machines that can whisk you millions of years into the past or the future, or in some cases just a few minutes or days. Scientists are now beginning to think these may not be just pure fantasies. If time is just another dimension, like length and breadth, what is to stop us from journeying through time to visit the past or the future, just as we travel through space? Einstein himself said it was impossible, and though some scientists think we could do it by bending space–time in some way, no one has yet come up with any convincing ideas of just how it might be possible.

◀ TIME AND RELATIVE DIMENSION IN SPACE
The popular television series *Doctor Who* features a hero who can travel to other times and places in his TARDIS, which is disguised as a 1929 police telephone box. TARDIS stands for Time And Relative Dimension In Space. It is famous because it warps space and time, and is best known for being many times larger inside than it appears to be on the outside.

▶ THE FOURTH DIMENSION

Einstein's proof that everything is relative upsets our commonsense idea of time. We see time passing as one thing happens after another – as the hands tick round on a clock. It seems time can move in only one direction, from past to future. But many laws in science, such as Newton's laws of motion, work just as well whether time goes backward or forward. In theory, time could run backwards just like a video replay. Einstein's theory showed that this is not just theory, but reality. Many scientists now prefer to think of time, not as a one-way train, but as a dimension, like length, depth and breadth. The three space dimensions – length, breadth and depth – combine with the time dimension to make the fourth dimension of space–time.

occurred. In the same way, when we see a star four million light-years away, we see it as it was four million years ago. Someone elsewhere in the Universe would see the eclipse at a different time. So the timing of events depends on where you are. If this is true, how do you know which is the right time? Is it the time you set on your watch, or the time your friend on a distant planet sets? The fact is you do not know. You can only tell the time in relation to something else, such as the position of the Sun in the sky or the position of a distant star.

Despite this, 120 years ago most people were sure that behind all this relative time and space there was real, or "absolute", time and real movement. In 1887, two American scientists, Michelson and Morley, set out to prove it with an ingenious experiment. They reasoned that a beam of light moving the same way as the Earth should

whizz along slightly slower than one shooting past the opposite way – just as an overtaking bike passes you more slowly than one coming towards you at the same speed. So they tried to measure the speed of light in different directions. Any difference would show that the Earth was moving absolutely. Yet they detected no difference in the speed of light, in whichever direction they measured it.

Einstein then came to a startling conclusion, which he published as his theory of special relativity. It demolished the idea of absolute time and space for ever. Einstein showed not only that light is the fastest thing in the Universe – but that it always passes you at the same speed, no matter where you are or how fast you are going. You can never catch up with a beam of light. Einstein realized that every measurement must be relative, because not even light can help to give an absolute measurement.

◀ KILLING YOUR GRANDPARENTS

A famous argument against the possibility of time travel is about accidentally killing your ancestors. The argument asks, what if you went back in time to before your parents were born and killed your grandparents? Then neither your parents nor you could have been born. But if you were never born, who killed your grandparents? This kind of problem is called a paradox. Some scientists get round it with the idea of parallel universes, different versions of history that all exist at the same time, running in parallel.

Key Dates

- 1610 Galileo suggests the idea of relative motion.

- 1676 Owe Roemer realizes that light takes time to reach us across space.

- 1887 Michelson and Morley show that the speed of light is the same in all directions.

- 1900 Max Planck invents quantum theory to explain why radiation varies in steps rather than continuously.

- 1905 Albert Einstein publishes his theory of special relativity.

- 1915 Einstein publishes his theory of general relativity.

The Big Universe

▲ EDWIN HUBBLE
Hubble (1889–1953) was an exceptional man. He had trained at Chicago and Oxford in law, and taken up professional boxing, before turning to astronomy.

UP UNTIL THE 20TH century, astronomers thought the Universe was little bigger than our own Milky Way Galaxy, with the Sun at its heart. All the Universe consisted of, they thought, were the few hundred thousand stars they could see with the most powerful telescopes of the day. The largest estimates put the Universe at no more than a few thousand light-years across (one light-year is 9,460 billion km/ 5,876 billion miles, the distance light travels in a year). There were fuzzy spiral patches of light they could see through telescopes, but these were thought to be clouds of some kind. They were called spiral nebulae, from the Greek word for "cloud".

In 1918 an American astronomer called Harlow Shapley made an astonishing discovery. Shapley was working at the Mount Wilson Observatory near Los Angeles. He was studying ball-shaped clusters of stars called globular clusters through the observatory's powerful telescope. He wondered why they seemed to be concentrated in one half of the sky, and guessed that

this is because the Earth is not at the core of the Galaxy as had been thought – but right out at the edge, looking inwards. He also realized that if this is so, then the Galaxy must be much, much bigger than anyone thought – perhaps as big as 100,000 light-years across.

The discoveries that we are not at the heart of the Galaxy but at the edge, and that the Galaxy is gigantic, were in some ways as dramatic as Copernicus's discovery that the Earth is not at the heart of the Solar System. Even as Shapley was publishing his ideas, a new and more powerful telescope was being stationed

▲ THE ANDROMEDA GALAXY
The Andromeda Galaxy is the nearest major galaxy beyond our own, and the only one visible with the naked eye. But as Hubble's study of Cepheid variable stars within it showed, even this nearby galaxy is over two million light-years away. Thousands of other galaxies, which are visible only through powerful telescopes, are many billions of light-years away.

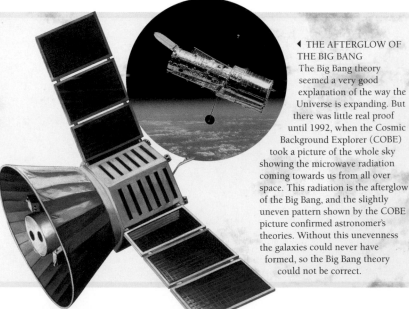

BIG BANG
Hubble's discovery that the Universe is getting bigger led to an amazing theory about the history of the Universe. If the Universe is expanding as Hubble showed, it must have been smaller at one time. Indeed, all the signs are that it was once very, very small indeed – perhaps smaller than an atom. The Universe began with an unimaginably gigantic explosion called the Big Bang. It was so big that the galaxies are still being flung out from it today.

◄ THE AFTERGLOW OF THE BIG BANG
The Big Bang theory seemed a very good explanation of the way the Universe is expanding. But there was little real proof until 1992, when the Cosmic Background Explorer (COBE) took a picture of the whole sky showing the microwave radiation coming towards us from all over space. This radiation is the afterglow of the Big Bang, and the slightly uneven pattern shown by the COBE picture confirmed astronomer's theories. Without this unevenness the galaxies could never have formed, so the Big Bang theory could not be correct.

▶ THE STORY OF THE UNIVERSE

By calculating back from the speed at which galaxies move, we can estimate that the Universe began about 13.8 billion years ago. Gradually, astronomers have been piecing together the history of the Universe, from the time that the first stars and galaxies formed, roughly 13 billion years ago, through the beginnings of the Earth some 4.5 billion years ago, the development of life 3.5 billion years ago, and the age of the dinosaurs 210–65 million years ago, down to the modern age.

at Mount Wilson. It enabled a young astronomer called Edwin Hubble to make even more astonishing discoveries.

Using the new telescope, Hubble began to look at the spiral nebulae – in particular the nebulae we now know as the Andromeda Galaxy. He could see that it was much more than a fuzzy patch of light, and actually contained stars. Among these stars he could see special stars called Cepheid variables, which are so predictable in their brightness that we can use them as distance markers. The Cepheid variables showed Hubble that Andromeda is several hundred thousand light-years away – far beyond the edge of the Galaxy.

Soon it became clear that many of the fuzzy patches of light in the night sky were other galaxies of stars, even farther away. Suddenly the Universe seemed much, much bigger than anyone had dreamed of. In 1927 Hubble made an even more amazing discovery. While studying the light from 18 galaxies, he noticed that the light from each one had a slightly different red tinge. He realized that this was because the galaxies are zooming away from us so fast that light waves are actually stretched out and become redder. Remarkably, the farther away the galaxies are, the faster they seem to be moving away from us. Hubble realized that this is because the Universe is expanding.

So within ten years the Universe which was thought to be just a few thousand light-years across was found to be many millions, and it was known to be growing bigger at an absolutely astonishing rate. Astronomers can now see galaxies 13 billion light-years away – zooming away from us at nearly the speed of sound.

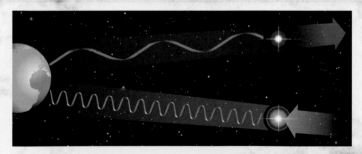

▲ RED SHIFT

We know galaxies are speeding away from us because their light is "red shifted". If a light source is rushing away, each light wave is sent from a little farther on – and so gets stretched out. As the light waves are stretched out, the light appears redder. The most distant galaxies have such huge red shifts that they must be moving very, very fast. Red shift is based on the observation by Austrian physicist Christian Doppler (1803–1853) that sound waves moving away are stretched out in the same way. The roar of a train coming towards you is high-pitched. As it zooms on past and away, the pitch drops as the sound waves become longer.

Key Dates

- 1918 Harlow Shapley shows that Earth is on the edge of the Galaxy.

- 1929 Hubble shows Andromeda is a galaxy beyond our own.

- 1927 Hubble realizes that other galaxies are flying away from us – and the Universe is expanding.

- 1927 Abbé George Lemaitre pioneers the idea that the Universe began in a Big Bang.

- 1948 Alpher and Herman suggest the Big Bang left behind weak radiation.

- 1964 Penzias and Wilson detect weak cosmic background radiation, providing evidence for the Big Bang.

Miracle Cures

▲ ALEXANDER FLEMING

The discovery of penicillin, the first antibiotic, by Scottish bacteriologist Alexander Fleming (1881–1955) was one of the great medical breakthroughs of the 20th century. For the first time doctors had a powerful weapon against a wide range of diseases.

IN 1900 DISEASE WAS A frighteningly normal part of life – and death. Few large families of children ever grew up without at least one of them dying. The introduction of vaccination began to save many people from catching diseases such as smallpox. Doctors could do very little once anyone actually became ill, except tend them and pray. To catch a disease such as tuberculosis or syphilis was very likely to be a death sentence.

The main reason for doctors' helplessness in the face of infectious (catching) diseases was the fact they had no idea what caused them. Then, in the late 19th century, thanks to the work of scientists such as Louis Pasteur, it finally became clear that it was tiny, microscopically small germs such as bacteria and viruses that were to blame.

Gradually medical scientists, especially those in Germany, began to realize that it might be possible to fight infectious disease with chemicals that targeted the germs but left the body unharmed. A very dedicated scientist called Paul Ehrlich believed that the key was to find chemical "magic bullets" that could be aimed at

▲ ERNST CHAIN
Along with Howard Florey, Chain continued the research into penicillin that had been started by Alexander Fleming. The value of the three men's work was recognized in 1945 when they were awarded the Nobel Prize in Medicine.

ANTIBIOTICS
Antibiotics work by attacking germ cells, but not body cells, and they have proved remarkably effective at treating a variety of bacterial diseases, including pneumonia, meningitis, scarlet fever, syphilis, tuberculosis and other infections. There are at least 70 useful antibiotics. Most are used against bacterial infections, but some attack fungal diseases and a few are designed to work against cancer. Diseases caused by viruses, however, cannot be treated by antibiotics in any way.

▼ HOW ANTIBIOTICS WORK
Antibiotics fight germs in a number of ways. Some antibiotics make the germ cell's skin leak vital nutrients or let in poisonous substances, but they have no affect on human cell skins. Others, such as penicillin, work by stopping the germ cell's tough skin from forming. Human cells do not have the same tough skins, so they are left unharmed. A third kind of antibiotic, including streptomycin and rifampicin, interferes with chemical processes inside the germ cell.

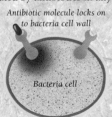

Antibiotic molecule locks on to bacteria cell wall

Bacteria cell

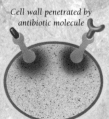

Cell wall penetrated by antibiotic molecule

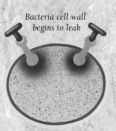

Bacteria cell wall begins to leak

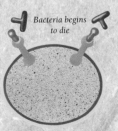

Bacteria begins to die

germs. With his colleague, Sahachiro Hata, Ehrlich worked to find such a cure for syphilis – a terrible disease that had killed millions of people over the centuries. In 1910 he discovered the chemical arsphenamine, which was sold under the name Salvarsan. It wiped out the germ that causes syphilis while leaving body cells virtually unharmed.

For the first time, doctors had a powerful weapon against a disease, and the search was now on for similar chemical treatments for other diseases. The early hopes were dashed, and it was not until the 1930s that scientists discovered a group of chemicals called sulfonamides that were deadly to a wide range of bacteria. In the meantime, a British scientist called Alexander Fleming had made a remarkable discovery.

In 1928 Fleming was working in his laboratory in St Mary's Hospital, London, when he noticed a strange thing. He had been culturing (growing) the staphylococcus bacteria in a dish and it had grown mouldy. What was remarkable was that the bacteria seemed to have died wherever the mould was. Fleming had a hunch that this mould, called *Penicillium notatum*, could be useful against disease.

Fleming himself was unable to find out if his hunch was true, but ten years later Howard Florey, Ernst Chain and others took up the idea and developed the first antibiotic drug, penicillin. "Antibiotic" means germ-attacking. Penicillin, one of the miracle drugs of the 20th century, has saved many, many millions of people from dying from a wide range of infectious diseases, including tuberculosis. Since then, thousands of other

▲ CLEAN BILL OF HEALTH
In the 1850s Austrian Ignaz Semmelweiss found that he could save women from dying in childbirth in hospital by getting his medical students to wash their hands to stop the spread of infection. Later, Joseph Lister introduced carbolic to kill germs in surgery. These antiseptic (germ-killing) techniques were not miracle cures, but they made hospitals, such as this smallpox hospital, much, much safer.

antibiotic drugs have been discovered. In the early 1940s, for instance, the American scientist Selman Waksman found the antibiotic streptomycin in soil fungi. Some antibiotics come from nature, mainly moulds and fungi, and some have been made artificially from chemicals. None has proved as effective and safe against such a broad range of diseases as penicillin.

◀ NEW DRUGS
In the past, drugs either occurred naturally or they were created in the laboratory. In future, some may be created in cyberspace, as chemists put computer models of molecules together with models of body cells to see how they react, which is what this chemist is doing. Computers may be able to trawl through millions of different ways of putting atoms together very quickly to find the perfect "magic bullet" that targets the disease precisely.

Key Dates

- 1867 Joseph Lister shows the value of antiseptic surgery.

- 1860s Louis Pasteur insists that many diseases are caused by germs.

- 1876 Robert Koch proves germs can cause disease.

- 1910 Ehrlich and Hata find Salvarsan is a cure for syphilis.

- 1928 Florey, Chain and others turn penicillin into the first antibiotic.

- 1942 Waksman discovers streptomycin.

- 1951 Frank Burnet discovers how the immune system attacks germs but not body cells.

Nuclear Power

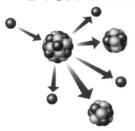

▲ NUCLEAR FISSION
In nuclear fission, an atom is split by the impact of a tiny neutron. As it splits into two smaller atoms, it releases a lot of energy and two more neutrons, which may split further atoms.

NO SCIENTIFIC DISCOVERY has been so awesome as that of nuclear energy, the energy in the nucleus of every atom in the Universe. Nuclear energy is not only the energy that makes nuclear weapons, it is the energy that keeps every star in the Universe burning. Until the 20th century, this vast power was undreamed of. Scientists knew that matter was made of atoms, but they thought atoms were no more lively than billiard balls. No one knew what energy really was.

Albert Einstein had a brilliant insight in his theory of special relativity of 1905. He showed that energy and matter are flip sides of the same basic thing, swapping back and forth all the time. His famous equation $E=mc^2$ gave this swap a real quantity. E is energy, and m the mass, or quantity, of matter; c is the speed of light, which is huge. If the mass of a tiny atom could be changed to energy, some scientists believed it would yield a huge amount of power.

At the same time, scientists such as Neils Bohr were probing the atom and finding that it is not just a ball. First, they found it holds tiny electrons whizzing around a nucleus, or core, of larger protons.

▼ NUCLEAR MUSHROOM
When a nuclear bomb explodes on the ground, a huge fireball vaporizes everything on the ground and turns it into a blast of hot gases and dust that shoots far up into the sky. When this blast reaches the stratosphere, one of the layers of the atmosphere that finishes 50km/30 miles from the earth's surface, it begins to cool and some of the gases condense into dust. As the dust begins to fall it billows out in a distinctive mushroom-shaped cloud. Often radioactive particles drop back to the ground.

THE MANHATTAN PROJECT

The bombs dropped on Hiroshima and Nagasaki were developed in a secret programme called the Manhattan Project by a team at Los Alamos in New Mexico. On 16 July 1945, the Los Alamos team exploded the first atomic bomb in the desert, to the amazement of spectators in bunkers 9km away.

The team achieved the critical mass of fission material (plutonium-239 and uranium-235) in two ways. One was to smash two lumps together from opposite ends of a tube, a system called "Thin Man". The other was to wrap explosive around a ball of fission material and smash it together ("Fat Man"). The Hiroshima bomb was a uranium-235 "Thin Man". The Nagasaki bomb was a plutonium -239 "Fat Man".

▲ J. ROBERT OPPENHEIMER
Oppenheimer (1904–1967) led the Los Alamos team but he later opposed hydrogen bombs. These are powerful nuclear bombs based not on the fission (splitting) of atoms, but on the fusion (joining together) of tiny hydrogen atoms.

▼ NAGASAKI
The effect of the nuclear bombs on Hiroshima and Nagasaki was so terrible that no one has used them in warfare again. The bombs obliterated huge areas of both cities and killed over 100,000 people instantly. Many of those who survived the initial blast died slow and painful deaths from the after-effects of radiation.

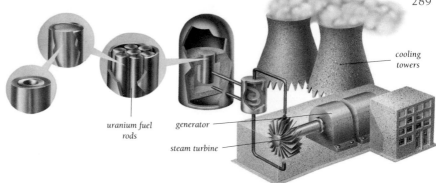

▶ NUCLEAR POWER
A nuclear bomb is an uncontrolled nuclear chain reaction. In a nuclear power station, the reaction is slowed down and sustained almost indefinitely to provide a huge amount of heat from just a small amount of uranium fuel. This heat boils water to make steam, which drives round the turbines (fan blades) that generate the electricity.

cooling towers

uranium fuel rods

generator

steam turbine

Then, in 1932, James Chadwick discovered a second kind of particle in the nucleus – the neutron.

At once, Italian atom scientist Enrico Fermi tried firing neutrons at the nuclei of uranium atoms. He found different atoms forming, and guessed that the neutrons had joined onto the uranium atoms to make bigger atoms of an unknown element, which he called element 93. But Fermi was wrong. In 1939, German scientists Otto Hahn and Fritz Strassman repeated Fermi's experiment. What they found was not a new element, but something even more astonishing – so astonishing that Hahn hardly dared believe it. It was another physicist, Lise Meitner who announced to the world what Fermi, Hahn and Strassman had done. They had split the uranium atom in two, making smaller atoms including barium. This splitting of the atom is called fission.

When the uranium atom split, it not only released a lot of energy, but also split off two neutrons. What if these two neutrons zoomed off to split two new atoms? These atoms would then, in turn, release two more neutrons, which

would split more atoms, and so on. Scientists soon realized this could become a rapidly escalating chain reaction of atom splitting. A chain reaction such as this would unleash a huge amount of energy as more and more atoms split.

Normally, chain reactions will not start in uranium because only a few uranium atoms are of the kind that splits easily, namely uranium-235. Most are tougher uranium-238 atoms. To make a bomb or a nuclear power plant, you need to pack enough uranium-235 into a small space to sustain a chain reaction. This is known as the critical mass.

During World War II, scientists in both Germany and the USA worked furiously to achieve the critical mass, since neither wanted to be last to make the atomic bomb. The Americans realized that another atom – plutonium-239 – might be used instead of uranium-235. At 3.45 p.m. on 2 December 1942, a team in Chicago led by Fermi used plutonium-239 to achieve a fission chain reaction for the first time. In August 1945, American fission bombs devastated the Japanese cities of Hiroshima and Nagasaki.

▲ NUCLEAR POWER PLANT
Nuclear reactions release huge amounts of energy, but they create dangerous radioactivity too. Radioactivity can make people very ill or even kill them. Many people suffered radiation sickness after the Hiroshima and Nagasaki bombs. Even nuclear power plants can have dangerous leaks. A serious nuclear accident occurred when the Chernobyl reactor, in Ukraine, went wrong in April 1986, spreading radioactive material over a vast area. The radioactive material produced by nuclear power stations must be stored safely for hundreds of years until it loses its radioactivity.

Key Dates

- 1905 Einstein reveals the theoretical power of the atom in special relativity.

- 1911 Rutherford proposes that atoms have a nucleus, circled by electrons.

- 1919 Rutherford discovers the proton.

- 1932 Chadwick discovers the neutron.

- 1939 Hahn and Strassman split a uranium atom.

- 1942 Fermi's team achieve the first fission chain reaction.

- 1945 July 16: Oppenheimer's team explode the first atomic bomb.

- 1945 August: US Air Force drop atomic bombs on Nagasaki and Hiroshima.

Lifeplan

EVERY LIVING THING – EVERY human, animal and plant – is made up from millions of tiny packages called cells. Inside each cell is a remarkable chemical molecule called DNA. It is the basis of all life. The DNA in human body cells not only tells each cell how to play its part in keeping the body alive, but it also carries all the instructions for making a new human being. The discovery of DNA's shape by James Watson and Francis Crick in 1953 was one of the major scientific breakthroughs of the 20th century, and the impact of their discovery on our lives has already been huge.

DNA (deoxyribonucleic acid) was discovered in 1869 by a Swiss student called Friedrich Miescher. Miescher was looking at pus on old bandages under a microscope when he saw tiny knots in the nucleus, or core, of

▲ DNA
DNA is one of the largest molecules known, weighing 500 million times more than a molecule of sugar. It is very thin, but very long – if stretched out it would be over 40cm/16in long. The molecule is usually coiled up, but it is made from two thin strands wrapped around each other in a twin spiral, or "double helix". It is rather like a long twisted rope ladder, with rungs made of chemicals called bases.

▲ FAMILY
Everyone has their own unique DNA, and it is so distinctive that it can be used to prove who you are, like a fingerprint. You get half your DNA from your mother and half from your father. There are sequences of bases in your DNA that are so similar to both your mother's and your father's that an analysis of your DNA proves who your parents are. DNA is also the reason why we all bear some resemblance to our parents.

the pus cells. His tutor Ernst Hoppe-Sayler analyzed these nuclear knots chemically and found they were acidic, so they called the substance nucleic acid. No one at the time had much inkling of its real significance.

Seventy-six years later, in 1945, American bacteriologist Oswald Avery was studying influenza bacteria when he noticed that DNA could turn a harmless bacteria into a dangerous one – as if it was giving instructions. In 1952 Alfred Hershey and Martha Chase

THE CHEMICALS OF LIFE
The study of the chemicals of life, such as DNA, is called organic chemistry, or biochemistry. It can also be called carbon chemistry because, remarkably, all life depends on chemicals that include atoms of carbon. There are literally millions of these carbon compounds, because carbon atoms are uniquely able to form links with other atoms. Some, such as proteins and amino acids, are more important than others.

▶ NICOTINE MOLECULE
Many organic compounds are based on a ring, or hexagon, of six carbon atoms. This is a model of the compound nicotine, found in the dried leaves of the tobacco plant. It is a poison used as an insecticide. It is also the chemical in cigarettes that makes people addicted to smoking.

▼ PROTEINS
Proteins are the basic material of all living cells. They are built up from different combinations of chemicals called amino acids. All these amino acids are present in each cell, like these cells from around human teeth. To make a protein, DNA must instruct the cell to make the right combination of amino acids.

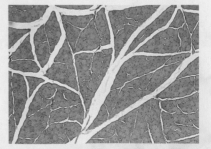

showed that this is just what DNA does. Once DNA's importance became clear, the race was on to find out how it worked. It was crucial to discover the shape of this long and complex molecule. In 1952 Rosalind Franklin, a young woman working at Imperial College in London, photographed DNA using X-rays, but could not figure out its structure. The young American Watson and Englishman Crick were then working on DNA at the Cavendish Laboratory in Cambridge. When they saw Rosalind Franklin's photographs, they suddenly realized that the DNA molecule is shaped like a double helix – that is, like a rope ladder twisted in a spiral.

After this great discovery, biochemists began to take DNA apart piece by piece under microscopes, then put it together again to find out how it gave instructions. The search focused on the four different chemicals making up the "rungs" of the ladder: guanine, cytosine, adenine and thymine. Erwin Chagraff found that these four "bases" only pair up in certain ways – guanine links only with cytosine; adenine only with thymine.

It soon became clear that the key to DNA lies in the order, or sequence, of the bases along each of the molecule's two long strands. Like the bits of a computer, the sequence of bases works as a code. The bases are like letters of the alphabet, and the sequence is broken up into "sentences" called genes. The code in each gene is the cell's instructions to make a particular protein, one of the basic materials of life. The complete gene code, or genetic code, was finally worked out in 1967 by American biochemists Marshall Nirenberg and Indian-American Har Khorana, earning them the Nobel Prize.

▲ STAYING ALIVE
Not only humans, but every living thing in the world has a DNA molecule in each of its body cells. This remarkable molecule tells the cell exactly what to do in keeping the living thing's body together, whether it is a bear or a salmon. It is also a complete copy of instructions for making an entirely new bear or salmon.

▲ THE GENETIC CODE
The key to the DNA code lies in the sequence of chemical bases along each strand, shown here in the form of a DNA fingerprint. These bases are a bit like letters of the alphabet, and the sequence is broken up into "sentences" called genes. Each gene provides the instructions to make a particular set of proteins.

Key Dates

- 1869 Miescher discovers DNA.

- 1945 Avery discovers that DNA issues life instructions to living things.

- 1952 Hershey and Chase show that DNA carries genetic instructions.

- 1953 Watson and Crick show that DNA has a double-helix (spiral) structure.

- 1954 Chagraff shows that DNA's four "bases" only join together in certain ways.

- 1961 Brenner and Crick show how so-called "letters" in the DNA code are formed by triplets of bases.

- 1967 Nirenberg and Har Khorana show how the genetic code works.

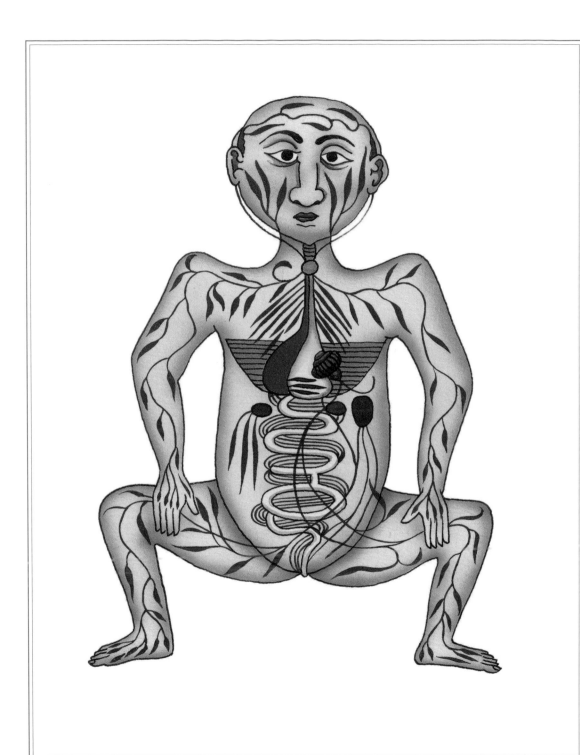

THE STORY
OF MEDICINE

By Brian Ward

From prehistoric skull-drilling to laboratory-grown body parts, humans have made great advances in medicine. This section shows how, over the ages, mastery of medicine has enabled humans to live longer, more comfortable lives.

The Arab World

During the period of the Byzantine Empire (AD300–1453), the works of Greek and Roman doctors were collected together. Some appeared in the languages used at the fringes of the empire, such as Persian and Syrian.

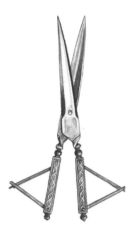

▲ SURGICAL SCISSORS
Scissors were developed as a more precise way than knives or scalpels to cut through tissue.

▶ AVICENNA
Avicenna was a Persian doctor working within the Arab Empire. His book, the Canon of Medicine, was used across the Middle East and Europe for centuries.

Meanwhile the Arab Empire was growing in power and influence. It conquered Persia and Syria. At first, the Arabs preferred their own traditional remedies, but as the power of the Islamic religion increased in the Arab Empire, many traditional treatments were lost. Doctors began to turn to ancient Greek ideas and translated Greek texts into Arabic. This meant that ancient Greek learning spread throughout the Arab Empire, into Europe and around the Mediterranean.

Important places of learning sprang up in Baghdad, Cairo and Damascus in the Middle East, and in Toledo, Cordoba and Seville in what is now Spain. Arab scientists and doctors published copies of the early medical works. Some of these were later translated into Latin and used in European medical schools from the 1200s.

Arab medicine did not contribute much new knowledge, but Arab writers made detailed descriptions of diseases and their diagnoses. Surgery suffered in early years, because dissection was banned, so little was known about anatomy. However, an Arab surgeon in Cordoba wrote a text on surgical techniques and others developed techniques for surgery on the eye and the internal organs. The Arabs were interested in alchemy (trying to transform cheap metals into gold, and searching for a source of eternal life). Their alchemical experiments led them to find many

MEDICAL PIONEERS

Not all of the medical scholars were Arabs. Many were Persians, Jews or Christians living within the Arab Empire. Rhazes was a Persian who put together a huge medical compendium. Maimonides was a Jewish doctor born in the 1100s. He became physician to the Saracen ruler Saladin. His extensive writings on medicine were based on Greek ideas.

◀ RHAZES
The Persian physician Rhazes was born about AD865. He wrote more than 200 books on a huge range of subjects. He was admired for his medical care of the poor.

▲ EYE SURGERY
Cataracts is an eye condition that clouds the lens of the eye and eventually leads to blindness. Arab physicians developed a technique for dislodging the clouded lens and pushing it clear of the field of vision. This allowed some degree of sight to be restored.

drugs by accident. Alchemists also developed techniques for purifying chemicals that are still used today. Arab pharmacists compiled long lists of herbal remedies, gathered from the places they conquered. Some describe more than 3,000 different drugs, some of which were very unusual. The real value of Arab writings, however, was how carefully they recorded information. These great works were painstakingly copied and circulated throughout the Arab Empire.

◀ MIXING MEDICINES
Persian and Arab apothecaries (pharmacists or dispensing chemists) developed a variety of methods for preparing medicines. These Persians are boiling ingredients over burning coals.

▼ PESTLE AND MORTAR
The simplest way to make up a herbal medicine was to grind its ingredients together using a pestle and mortar. This made a powder that could be mixed with water and drunk, or made into a paste or ointment. They are still in common use today.

▼ MEDICINE IN THE ARAB EMPIRE
The Arab Empire spread widely around the Mediterranean and the Middle East and adopted the traditional remedies of the regions it conquered. Arab scholars preserved ancient Greek and Roman traditions and wrote down the newest medical discoveries.

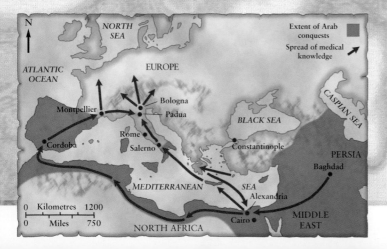

Key Dates

- AD620s Muhammad founds Islam.
- AD832 Baghdad is established as a place of learning.
- AD850 Muslim scholar at-Tabari compiles medical writings of Greece, Rome, Persia and India.
- c.AD865–928 Life of Rhazes.
- AD980–1037 Life of Avicenna.
- 1174 Maimonides is appointed as court physician to Saladin.
- 1236 Christians gain Cordoba.
- 1258 Mongol warriors sack Baghdad. Medical information preserved by the Arabs begins to flow back to the West.

Galen's Legacy

AFTER THE EMPEROR Constantine made Christianity the official religion of the Roman Empire, the power of Greek medicine and Galenic teaching began to fade. Once more, religion became more influential than practical medicine. Sickness was often seen as punishment from God for past sins. Prayer and pilgrimages to holy relics were the recommended cures for most diseases and cults of healing saints sprang up.

The Church's opinion of medicine was summed up by St Bernard, who lived from AD1090 until 1153. He said that going to the doctor was not a proper way to behave. Trying to cure a disease was seen as interfering with God's punishment. A dying person was more likely to call a priest than a doctor.

Christian saints became associated with different diseases. St Christopher dealt with epilepsy, St Roch was the patron saint of plague victims, St Apollonia looked after those with toothache and St Margaret kept women safe during childbirth.

However, the sick did receive some practical care. Many monasteries offered care of the sick. Hospitals were built across Europe, often alongside healing shrines (holy places). Special hospitals were built for lepers, who were treated with especial horror and considered 'unclean.'

Medical knowledge began to improve in the AD1000s, when a

▲ URINE GAZING
During the 1200s and 1300s, there were few ways to diagnose a disease. One method was to examine the patient's urine. Its appearance and even its taste were carefully noted.

▶ MEDICAL GIANTS
In this edition of Galen's works published in 1528, Galen is shown with two other medical geniuses. Hippocrates is on the left and Avicenna on the right.

FALSE BELIEFS

Throughout the Middle Ages, superstition formed part of medical practice. Herbals were books that listed the medicinal properties of plants. A few of these did have the promised effect, but most were useless. Bleeding, the use of leeches, enemas and deliberate vomiting were all recommended. Following the ideas of Hippocrates, these methods were thought to restore the balance of the humours.

◀ LUNGWORT
Many plants were used in medicine on the basis of their appearance. This practice was known as the doctrine of signatures. The leaves of lungwort were thought to look like the lung, so this plant was used to treat lung disease.

◀ ASTROLOGY
Astrology was thought to show a link between diseased body parts, different planets and star signs, and parts of the body. This is a chart showing planets' influences on the head.

▶ PURGING
Powerful drugs were given to cause vomiting. This purging and was believed to rid the body of poisons.

small group of doctors began work at Salerno, in Italy. They formed an influential medical school and revived ancient ideas, especially those of Galen. People assumed Galen's teachings were accurate, even though some were changed or missed out in translation and others had been wrong in the first place. Doctors treated their patients with diets and drugs, many of which were imported from the East.

Surgery became a separate branch of medicine and was carried out by barber-surgeons. Barber-surgeons provided a range of services. They cut hair, pulled out teeth, gave enemas (injected fluids into the rectum) and let blood.

At least one Greek technique was challenged. Hippocrates had recommended leaving open wounds to become septic. Henri de Mondeville, a French surgeon who lived from 1260 until 1320, had different ideas. He advised closing the wound as soon as possible and keeping it dry and covered to prevent infection. Thanks to de Mondeville, many limbs and lives were saved.

▲ LEECHES
Bloodletting was a treatment for most illnesses. People often used freshwater leeches to suck out the blood. Recently, the use of leeches has been reintroduced as a way to reduce serious bruising.

▼ CAUTERIZING IRON
To stop bleeding, medieval doctors used to apply a red-hot iron to coagulate (thicken) the blood. This caused agonizing pain. Cauterization was not very hygienic and many wounds became infected.

▼ POMANDER
In medieval times, people thought that foul smells spread disease. Many carried scented pomanders about with them to drive these smells away. The simplest pomanders were oranges stuck with aromatic spices called cloves.

▲ HOLY EYES
St Lucy of Syracuse became the patron saint of eye disease. According to legend, she plucked out her own eyes but they grew back. Many sick people still pray to saints.

Key Dates

- 1100–1300 Medical schools and hospitals are founded throughout Europe.

- 1100s Trotula joins the Salerno medical school. She writes the first complete work on women's health and another on skin disease.

- 1200s–1300s Physicians and surgeons begin to form into professional organizations.

- 1215 Pope Innocent III decrees that all doctors must be approved by the Church and bans lepers from the Church.

- 1260–1320 Henri de Mondeville recommends closing wounds.

Making a Diagnosis

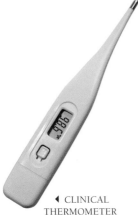

IAGNOSIS IS THE skill of identifying a disease. It is carried out by observing signs and symptoms of the illness. Until recently there were few medical tests to help a doctor identify a disease. Instead, doctors would talk to their patients, examine them and looked at how they behaved.

In Greece, at the time of Hippocrates, doctors tried to identify their patient's disease so they could reach their prognosis (say how the disease would develop). A doctor's reputation rested on how accurately

he predicted whether the patient would recover or die. Hippocrates taught that every single observation could be significant. Greek doctors used all of their senses in making their diagnosis. Touch, taste, sight, hearing and smell could all provide valuable clues. These principles still apply for modern doctors.

By Galen's time, taking the pulse had become a part of diagnosis. Galen gave instructions on how to take the

◄ CLINICAL THERMOMETER
The modern digital thermometer is quick and easy to use, and is also extremely accurate. It does not contain the poisonous mercury used in traditional thermometers, which were fragile and easily broken.

▶ USING THE STETHOSCOPE
The stethoscope introduced by Laënnec in 1819 was awkward to use, because it was rigid. Unlike the modern stethoscope, which has a bendy rubber tube, it was not easy to move around in order to detect sounds in different areas.

TOOLS OF THE TRADE
Diagnosis improved with the invention of instruments that allowed the doctor to find out what was going on inside the body. A whole range of new observations could be made, and these were added to the findings from old methods, such as interviewing the patient. Better measurements of pulse rate, blood pressure and temperature all helped towards accurate diagnosis.

◄ LAËNNEC'S STETHOSCOPE
In 1819 the French physician René Laënnec introduced the first stethoscope. This wooden device, almost 23cm/9in long, amplified the sounds of the chest.

▼ THE STETHOSCOPE TODAY
The modern stethoscope is a simple lightweight device. It allows doctors and nursing staff to listen to the sounds of the lungs and the heart. It often gives an early warning of illness.

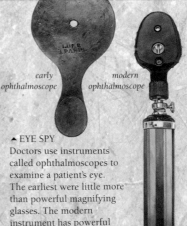

early ophthalmoscope   *modern ophthalmoscope*

▲ EYE SPY
Doctors use instruments called ophthalmoscopes to examine a patient's eye. The earliest were little more than powerful magnifying glasses. The modern instrument has powerful lenses and lights that allow the doctor to see right to the back of the eyeball.

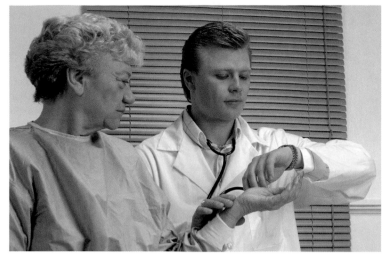

pulse. The findings could be described as 'fast' or 'normal.'

In the Arab world, diagnosis involved careful examination of the affected parts, checking the pulse and examining the urine. Arab doctors did not disclose their findings to anyone else in case they frightened the patient.

In most of Europe, diagnosis was rather haphazard, because disease was seen as a punishment from God. This meant its cause could not be questioned and the disease could not be treated, except with prayer. Sometimes the diagnosis was obvious to all, such as in cases of leprosy or plague, but even then the doctor was not able to cure the patient.

It was not until the 1700s that real advances were made in the art of diagnosis. In 1761, a Viennese doctor called Leopold Auenbrugger discovered that thumping on a patient's chest produced sounds which could indicate lung disease. The technique was reluctantly

accepted and is still in use today. However, most doctors did not perform physical examinations, and still formed their diagnosis by interviewing the patient. Auscultation (sounding the chest) improved with the invention of the stethoscope in 1816. This also allowed doctors to hear the heart properly, and diagnose different heart diseases.

Examination of the urine was a popular method of diagnosis for all sorts of disease. Its appearance, smell and even its taste were thought to reveal the state of the patient's health. Urine tests are still used in some forms of diagnosis today, for example to identify diabetes or pregnancy.

▲ COUNTING THE BEATS
Taking a person's pulse tells the doctor how fast the heart is beating. With each heartbeat, the arteries bulge slightly. The arteries at the wrist are very close to the skin surface, so the doctor can feel them bulge with his or her fingertip.

▲ UNDER PRESSURE
The sphygmomanometer is used to measure blood pressure. First the doctor puts an inflatable sleeve on the patient's arm. This is pumped up to close off the blood flow through the arteries. As the sleeve is slowly deflated, the device measures the blood pressure.

▼ BLOOD CHEMISTRY
Blood tests are used to measure changes in the chemical make up of the blood. These changes can indicate that a person is suffering from an infection, diabetes or some other hormonal disorder, or that a woman is pregnant.

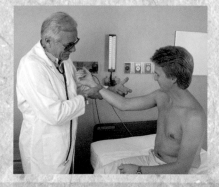

Key Dates

- 1714 Gabriel Fahrenheit invents the mercury thermometer.

- 1761 Leopold Auenbrugger publishes his findings on sounding the chest.

- 1819 René Laënnec introduces the first stethoscope.

- 1851 Hermann von Helmholtz invents the ophthalmoscope.

- 1868 Carl Wunderlich promotes widespread use of the thermometer.

- 1895 Wilhelm Röntgen discovers x-rays.

- 1896 Scipione Riva-Rocci invents the sphygmomanometer.

Germ-free and Pain-free

▲ KEEPING CLEAN
*Washing the hands is still
one of the most important
ways to limit the spread
of infection, both in
hospitals and in the home.
Modern surgical staff use
antibacterial soap to
prevent infection.*

▶ IGNAZ SEMMELWEISS
*Semmelweiss realized that
lack of hygiene was causing
many deaths among his
patients so he insisted on
rigorous washing. His views
were considered outrageous
and he was forced out of his
hospital in Vienna.*

SURGERY IN THE 1600s was a very dangerous business. There was no concept of hygiene. Surgeons worked in their normal clothes, which became splashed with blood. They used instruments in consecutive operations without any attempt at cleaning. Childbirth fever was a particular hazard, killing many women within a few days of giving birth. A Hungarian doctor, Ignaz Semmelweiss, realized that patients were more likely to suffer infection after being examined by medical students who had been carrying out dissections. He saw that when students had not visited the dissection rooms, infection did not occur. As a result, Semmelweiss insisted on high standards of hygiene in his hospital, and this cut the death rate dramatically. He

was violently opposed by many medical colleagues, however, and eventually had to leave his practice in Vienna.

At this time no one realized that microbes spread disease. It was not until the 1860s that Louis Pasteur discovered bacterial infection. The British surgeon Joseph Lister made the next major advance. He was alarmed at how many people died of severe bone fractures. Lister observed that if a bone was broken without penetrating the skin, infection seldom occurred. If a bone fragment punctured the skin, exposing it to the air, there was usually an infection, and this led to amputation or death.

When Lister found out about Pasteur's work, he realized that it was not air that caused the problem, but bacteria contaminating the wound. Lister had heard that carbolic acid could be used to kill bacteria in sewage, so he tried spraying a mist of diluted carbolic acid on wounds. His experiment had dramatic results. Out of his first 11 patients, only one died. This discovery was resisted at first, but as it became accepted it was possible to carry out

KILLING THE PAIN
Anaesthesia has a long history. The ancient Greeks used drugs to provide pain relief. By the 1800s, opium was widely used as a soporific (to make the patient sleepy). Alcohol was also used in surgery to help the patient relax. Ether and nitrous oxide were the first modern anaesthetics. They were introduced at about the same time and were both inhaled. Shortly afterwards, chloroform was introduced. After initial resistance, all three of these anaesthetics were enthusiastically accepted and became very widely used.

▼ WILLIAM MORTON
Morton was an American dentist who experimented with the effects of ether as an anaesthetic. In 1846 he anaesthetized a patient for the surgeon John Collins Warren.

▲ FIRST FAILURE
In 1848, Hannah Greener became the first person to die from the poisonous effects of chloroform. Greener had only had a minor operation to remove a toenail.

▼ CHLOROFORM MASK
Chloroform and ether were both applied by soaking a cloth mask. The mask's wire frame closely covered the nose and mouth so that the chloroform or ether fumes were breathed in by the patient.

routine operations with hardly any risk to the patient. Asepsis (keeping free from infection) was safer than allowing a bacterial infection to take hold and then trying to treat it with antiseptics. To achieve this surgeons tried to keep bacteria away from wounds by sterilizing their instruments and wearing masks and gowns.

At about the same time that asepsis was discovered, several doctors discovered how pain could be relieved by the use of anaesthetics. In 1846 the American dentist Thomas Morton showed how ether could be used to eliminate pain during surgery, while John Warren also experimented with the use of nitrous oxide (laughing gas). Nitrous oxide had been used for a while as a party novelty. Breathing in the gas made people collapse in fits of giggles. Chloroform was another form of anaesthetic. After John Snow gave it to Queen Victoria during the birth of Prince Leopold, its use became more widespread.

▲ STEAM SPRAY
Joseph Lister invented the carbolic steam spray. It produced a fine mist of mild carbolic acid in the operating room and killed bacteria. The death rate among Lister's patients fell from 50 per cent to 5 per cent.

◀ UNDER THE KNIFE
From the 1860s, operations were carried out in antiseptic conditions. A carbolic steam spray pumped an antibacterial mist into the room. Surgery was not only safer, it was more comfortable for the patient. Chloroform masks kept them unconscious during the operation.

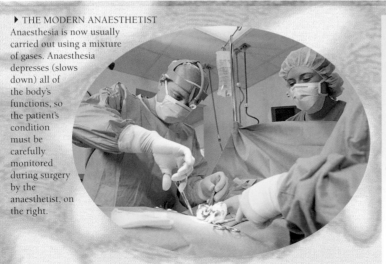

▶ THE MODERN ANAESTHETIST
Anaesthesia is now usually carried out using a mixture of gases. Anaesthesia depresses (slows down) all of the body's functions, so the patient's condition must be carefully monitored during surgery by the anaesthetist, on the right.

Key Dates

- 1800 Humphrey Davy reports that nitrous oxide can produce unconsciousness.

- 1831 Chloroform is discovered.

- 1844 Horace Wells uses nitrous oxide to anaesthetize a patient.

- 1846 William Morton uses ether to anaesthetize a patient.

- 1847 Ignaz Semmelweiss makes his staff wash their hands.

- 1865 Joseph Lister uses his carbolic steam spray in surgery.

- 1884 Cocaine is used as a local anaesthetic, pain-killing drug.

- 1886 Aseptic surgery begins.

Quacks and Charlatans

IT IS EASY FOR US to dismiss doctors in the past as being quacks or charlatans (people who swindled their patients by selling them useless cures). This was certainly true of some of them, but their strange activities need to be put into the context of the level of scientific learning of the time. For instance, it would not have been possible to convince Hippocrates or Galen about the existence of bacteria, or that bacteria cause disease, because it was only possible to see them through a microscope.

▶ QUACK MEDICINES
Salespeople drew attention to their wares by any means at their disposal. Many wore outrageous and eye-catching outfits, and they all perfected their own style of patter (sales talk).

Although surgery could sometimes be effective, most medicine was not able to cure disease. Doctors were forced to desperate measures in order to find cures. Sometimes a patient recovered by natural means, but then the experimental method used by the doctor would be accepted as a miracle cure. Prayer and the use of holy relics might be dismissed as quack medicine, but they are still widely used today, along with the laying on of hands (blessing the patient) and other forms of therapy based upon spiritual cure.

In Britain, quackery flourished in the 1700s. Outlandish cures were sold on street corners and at fairs and markets. During the 1800s people realized that quacks were exploiting the sick with cures and treatments that had no value at all.

Medical associations, such as the Royal Colleges in Britain, were set up. These professional organizations kept out charlatans and regulated the activities of doctors who were members. They also checked that the doctors were skilled enough to

FALSE HOPES
As medicine becomes more advanced, cures that were once promoted by respectable doctors are rejected as quackery. For example, spa baths were a popular treatment in Western Europe around 1900. They are now less popular, and many doctors would consider their use to be a form of quack medicine. However, they are still mainstream practice in parts of Eastern Europe.

▼ MUDBATHS
Baths in hot mud are widely used to treat diseases such as arthritis, especially in Eastern Europe. Elsewhere, mud treatments are considered harmless, but ineffective.

◀ ELECTRICAL CORSETS
Electricity was considered a magical cure-all in the 1700s and 1800s. Electrical currents were applied to parts of the body to cure a whole range of conditions.

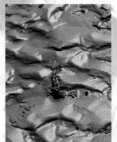

▲ FRANZ MESMER
The German physician Franz Mesmer developed techniques for what we now call hypnosis (putting someone into a trance). He called his discovery animal magnetism, and used it to treat patients who suffered from hysteria. His cures sometimes worked, even though they were scientific nonsense. Eventually, Mesmer was exposed as a fraud.

◀ MORISON'S PILLS
During the 1800s, James Morison's Vegetable Universal Pills achieved huge commercial success throughout Europe and the USA. Commonly known as Morison's Pills, they were said to cure all sorts of disease, but were found to be merely a mixture of powerful laxatives. This cartoon from the period pokes fun at people who believed in such unreliable cures. It suggests that the man has taken so many Morison's Pills that they have taken root in his stomach and made his skin sprout with grass!

perform their job. Gradually, laws were passed to stop products being sold with outrageous promises.

Lydia Pinkham's Vegetable Compound, introduced in 1873, was one of the most popular quack remedies – probably beccause it contained huge quantities of alcohol. This was sold first as a treatment for 'female weaknesses' and later as a cure for just about anything.

In the USA, quacks advertised cancer cures at high prices. These were aimed at desperate cancer sufferers, willing to pay almost any price for life. Quacks had to pay heavy fines if they were caught, but the practice still exists. Since the 1970s many people dying from cancer have visited Mexico to buy a so-called cure called laetrile, which is in fact poisonous. The same happens with AIDS, where unscrupulous dealers sell dubious pills and potions to those infected with HIV.

◀ FRANZ GALL
The German doctor Franz Gall developed the concept of phrenology. Phrenology is a form of diagnosis based on examining the skull. Gall claimed that skull shape revealed the functions of parts of the brain. He 'read' the skull by feeling for bumps. Phrenology survived for many years, but it is no longer considered to have any use to medicine.

▼ PHRENOLOGY
This porcelain head is marked with the regions identified by Franz Gall. Each area was identified with an aspect of a person's personality or how they behave, such as secretiveness or wit.

Key Dates

- 1700s Benjamin Franklin praises air bathing (sitting naked near an open window).

- 1775 Franz Mesmer develops his theory of animal magnetism.

- 1780 James Graham opens his Temple of Health in London.

- 1810s Franz Gall develops the concept of phrenology.

- 1970s Laetrile is promoted as a cure for cancer.

- 1991 The American Cancer Society declares laetrile is poisonous, but it remains on sale, especially on the Internet.

Public Health

▲ CHOLERA
This image from the 1800s shows cholera in the form of a spectre that descends on the Earth to claim its victims. More than 7,000 Londoners died in an outbreak in 1832.

PUBLIC HEALTH is not a new idea. The Romans understood the need for clean water supplies and built huge aqueducts to bring in water to the hearts of their cities, along with water pipes and public baths. They also constructed elaborate sewage systems to remove waste from their cities. The Romans were not even the first to build aqueducts. The Etruscans had started to build them in 312BC.

Ancient Chinese and Indian religious writings had recommended good diet and hygiene to protect health, but in medieval Europe, all of this was forgotten. The Church frowned on washing, as it seemed too much like a bodily pleasure. There was no concept of hygiene, and sewage and rubbish were just thrown out into the street. It is no coincidence that during this period Europe was ravaged by plague, leprosy, tuberculosis (TB, also known as consumption),

typhoid and cholera. People thought that these diseases were spread by miasma (unpleasant smells). This idea probably did encourage some disposal of waste. The miasmic theory of infection persisted into the 1800s, until the effects of bacteria were finally demonstrated.

The cholera epidemics had already brought matters to a head. For centuries the River Thames had been London's sewer and source of drinking water. It was black and stinking, and finally everyone had had enough. The government commissioned a report from a civil servant called John Chadwick, which turned out to be the most influential document ever prepared on the subject of public health. It was published in 1842. The report described the probable causes of disease in the poorer parts of London, and also suggested practical ways to solve the problem. These public health measures included supplying houses with clean running water and proper sewage drainage.

Not long after this came the first proof of the risks from contaminated water, during a terrible cholera outbreak in 1854. John Snow, a London doctor, realized that many cholera cases were clustered in a small area near Broad Street. Investigation showed that they all drew their water from a public pump. Snow removed the pump handle, and within a few days the epidemic stopped. Even so, it took several years for the medical profession to accept that cholera was not spread by foul air, but by drinking water contaminated by sewage.

CLEAN SOLUTIONS

Flushing toilets and clean running water in the home remained novelties into the 1800s. Before then, people had to visit public pumps and taps for their water. In the late 1800s local authorities began to demolish the worst slums and replace them with better housing. By the 1900s children's health was improving. Schools provided meals for the poorest, and medical inspections allowed disease to be detected early on.

▶ FOUL WATERS
Dr John Snow started as a surgeon in Newcastle-upon-Tyne, England, and moved to London in 1836. After halting the cholera epidemic he recommended improvements in sewerage.

▶ WATER CLOSET
Flushing toilets, such as this one from the 1880s, were a great improvement in public health. The first toilets were often elaborately decorated and were almost works of art.

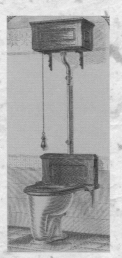

▲ AMERICAN SINK (1888)
The kitchen of the 1800s was not always very hygienic. Hot water on tap was a rare luxury. Cleanliness depended on having enough servants to scrub all the work surfaces and floors, which often carried germs.

▶ LONDON LIVING CONDITIONS
During the 1800s, living conditions for the poor were atrocious. They lived in cramped housing without proper sanitation. These people are going through the rubbish on the river. Such conditions provided an ideal breeding ground for disease.

▼ BUILDING A SEWER
Repeated outbreaks of disease finally led to the building of sewers, such as this one being dug in London in 1862. These enormous mains sewers were connected to outfalls far down the River Thames, where the tides could sweep the sewage away.

▲ ROYAL VICTORIA HOSPITAL, MONTREAL
Many hospitals were built in the 1800s, such as this one in Canada. These were often magnificent buildings, but as there were still few effective medical treatments, many patients came to hospital to die.

Key Dates

- c.1700BC King Minos of Crete has a flushing toilet in his palace.

- 312BC The Etruscans build the first aqueduct.

- AD300s Two-seater toilet, shaped like a temple, in use in Greece.

- c.1590 John Harrington invents a flushing toilet.

- 1770–1915 Development of the modern water closet, or toilet.

- 1854 John Snow shows dirty water is the cause of cholera.

- 1880s Most British cities have sewage treatment plants, after the Public Health Act of 1875.

Alternative Therapies

SOME PEOPLE TOTALLY reject modern medicine. Christian Scientists, for example, believe that prayer and faith can cure all disease. Jehovah's Witnesses reject only some aspects of conventional medicine, such as transfusions.

Not all people reject traditional treatment for religious reasons. Some people find that their condition cannot be cured by orthodox (traditional) medicine, so look for an alternative. Also, while many people still respect a doctor's advice so much that they would never dream of questioning it, others may be

sufficiently well-informed about their illness to wish to take treatment into their own hands.

In the 1990s there was increased interest in alternatives to traditional medicine. There is a difference between alternative therapies, in which a person rejects conventional medicine and seeks some other form of therapy, and complementary medicine, in which patients take extra steps as well as the treatment prescribed by their doctor. Most doctors accept

▲ CAMOMILE
Extracts of camomile are widely used for pain relief in homeopathic medicine. Homeopaths use tiny quantities of drugs that produce similar symptoms to those of the condition they wish to treat.

▶ MOXIBUSTION
One type of acupuncture is moxibustion, in which cones of herbs are burned on the skin at points on some of the meridians (channels) described by Chinese medicine.

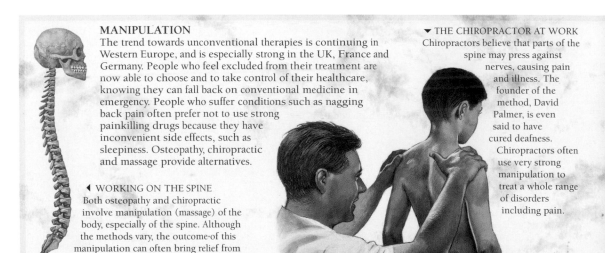

MANIPULATION
The trend towards unconventional therapies is continuing in Western Europe, and is especially strong in the UK, France and Germany. People who feel excluded from their treatment are now able to choose and to take control of their healthcare, knowing they can fall back on conventional medicine in emergency. People who suffer conditions such as nagging back pain often prefer not to use strong painkilling drugs because they have inconvenient side effects, such as sleepiness. Osteopathy, chiropractic and massage provide alternatives.

◀ WORKING ON THE SPINE
Both osteopathy and chiropractic involve manipulation (massage) of the body, especially of the spine. Although the methods vary, the outcome of this manipulation can often bring relief from back pain. Family doctors often recommend these practitioners to their patients.

▼ THE CHIROPRACTOR AT WORK
Chiropractors believe that parts of the spine may press against nerves, causing pain and illness. The founder of the method, David Palmer, is even said to have cured deafness. Chiropractors often use very strong manipulation to treat a whole range of disorders including pain.

that their patients may use complementary therapies and do not mind as long as these do not interfere with conventional treatments. In Britain, 40 percent of family doctors routinely refer patients to complementary therapists. Alternative therapies, though, can mean that a sick person delays going to their doctor and this can make their problem much more difficult to treat.

Some of these therapies are difficult to define. Herbal treatments, for example, can be a form of conventional medicine if they are known to contain medically active ingredients. Where their effectiveness is not proven, they are classed as alternative or complementary therapies.

Acupuncture is an ancient Chinese healing technique where needles are inserted into the body. Science dismissed this technique as quackery until, in recent years, it was found that acupuncture at certain points has a powerful painkilling effect. Acupuncture is especially helpful for lingering pains that do not respond to drugs.

What is common to all forms of complementary and alternative medicine is that they have no scientific explanation. Some believe that they work because of the placebo (inactive drug) effect. Placebos given to patients in medical trials often work as well as the real drugs, probably because the patient really believes that they will.

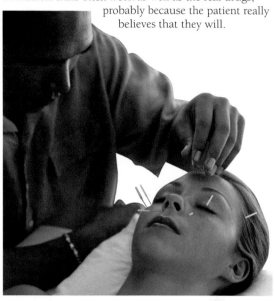

▲ ACUPUNCTURE
Scientific research has shown that acupuncture, the Chinese practice of inserting needles into the skin, really does kill pain. Serious operations have been performed in China with no other form of painkiller except acupuncture.

▸ AROMATHERAPY
Smells have a powerful effect on the body and on mood. Aromatherapy depends on massaging the body with scented oils, or on breathing in the fumes of heated oils. This helps the patient to relax and may have an effect on some illnesses.

◂ SHIATSU
This is a technique to relieve pain that evolved in Japan during the 1900s. Practitioners of shiatsu use their fingers to press hard on acupuncture points, and also use massage and meditation to treat their patients.

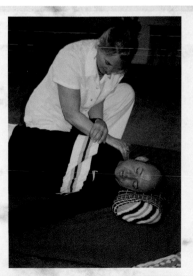

▸ FEET FIRST
Reflexology is based on the idea that different areas on the feet represent different parts of the body. Massage and stimulation of these areas can help treat illness and generally improve health.

Key Dates

- 300BC First descriptions of acupuncture in the *Nei Ching*.

- AD1601 Acupuncture discussed in detail by Yang Chi-chou.

- 1796 Samuel Hahnemann says that 'like cures like' and develops homeopathy in Germany.

- 1874 American doctor Andrew Still introduces osteopathy.

- 1895 Chiropractic is developed in the USA by David Palmer.

- 1900s Shiatsu is developed.

- 1930s Reflexology is introduced by Eunice Ingham.

Clubs, Maces, Hammers and Flails

THE EARLIEST KIND of weapons were clubs, maces and hammers. People could hold them in their hands. They could not break down and nothing could go wrong with them. The club is the oldest weapon. The earliest clubs were lumps of stone picked up from the ground. Prehistoric people used them as both tools and weapons. Clubs could be used to crush up seeds for food. They could be used as weapons to hunt animals or to fight with enemies. In South Africa, there are wall paintings made around 6000BC showing two human figures with long heavy sticks that look like clubs. People also made clubs from long, heavy animal bones or thick lengths of wood taken from trees, bushes or plants.

When people learned how to make bronze, iron and steel, they used these metals to make stronger weapons. Using metal, the simple club was turned into a mace. A mace had a weighted, spiked

▲ CLUBS AND MACES AT HASTINGS
The Bayeux tapestry showing Norman cavalry, armed with maces and clubs, at the Battle of Hastings in 1066.

▲ THE MACE
This elaborately crafted mace is a weapon of war but may also serve as a symbol of political or military status.

or pointed end. This could be used to batter through an enemy's shield or armour. It could be used in hand-to-hand fighting or by soldiers on horseback. Today in the USA a ceremonial mace, made of ebony and silver, is used in the House of Representatives. In Britain, the sceptre carried by the queen on special occasions is also a kind of mace.

The war hammer was like an ordinary carpenter's claw hammer, but had only one claw. This was a kind of spiked pick. The shaft, or handle, of a war hammer was up to a metre in length. A soldier using a hammer could reach out from his saddle to strike his enemy. Using the sharp claw of the hammer, the soldier could then puncture his enemy's metal helmet. This kind of blow to the head could be fatal, killing instantly.

The flail was first used by farmers to thresh corn. It was made into a weapon which is a mixture of mace and club. Between one and three lengths of chain were fixed to one end of a thick metal stick. Weighted spikes were attached to the end of each length of chain. When the flail was used, the chains whipped through the air, and struck the enemy in several places at once.

SIMPLE WEAPONS FOR CLOSE COMBAT

In its most primitive form, a club or contact weapon extends the reach of a person in close combat and replaces their feet or fists as weapons. It can be made from any spare wood or timber. Later the use of metal and the positioning of the weight at one end made these contact weapons much more effective in battle.

◀ THE SHILLELAGH
This Irish chieftain holds a shillelagh, a type of club made from hard wood like blackthorn or oak. Clubs are the simplest of contact weapons. In a more sophisticated version, they are still used today in the form of police night sticks.

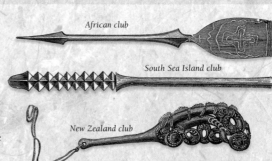

African club

South Sea Island club

New Zealand club

▲ CLUBS FROM ACROSS THE WORLD
Clubs made from wood, bone and stone with both ritual and warlike functions can be found throughout the world. Some combine two materials, so a wooden haft may be weighted with stone. Another method is to pour molten lead into a hole made in the top of the club. Leather strips may be added to the handle to improve grip, or a loop for the user's wrist.

◀ THE ROUT OF SAN ROMANO
This detail from a painting by the Italian Renaissance artist Uccello shows horsemen wielding maces, hammers and bows.

▲ HAMMER VERSUS MACE
Even though medieval knights wore complicated battledress, they still fought with simple weapons. In this picture you can see how the hammer and mace were used, and how powerful they look.

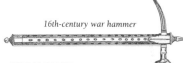

16th-century war hammer

▲ WAR HAMMER
The spike on the war hammer was designed to penetrate metal. The flat end was used for smashing in helmets.

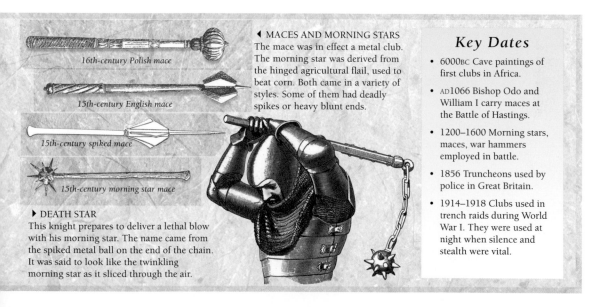

16th-century Polish mace

15th-century English mace

15th-century spiked mace

15th-century morning star mace

▶ DEATH STAR
This knight prepares to deliver a lethal blow with his morning star. The name came from the spiked metal ball on the end of the chain. It was said to look like the twinkling morning star as it sliced through the air.

◀ MACES AND MORNING STARS
The mace was in effect a metal club. The morning star was derived from the hinged agricultural flail, used to beat corn. Both came in a variety of styles. Some of them had deadly spikes or heavy blunt ends.

Key Dates

- 6000BC Cave paintings of first clubs in Africa.
- AD1066 Bishop Odo and William I carry maces at the Battle of Hastings.
- 1200–1600 Morning stars, maces, war hammers employed in battle.
- 1856 Truncheons used by police in Great Britain.
- 1914–1918 Clubs used in trench raids during World War I. They were used at night when silence and stealth were vital.

Axes and Throwing Weapons

THE AXE WAS FIRST USED as a woodsman's tool for felling trees. The first axes, like the first clubs, were made from sharp stones or flints. They were simply cutting tools. Later they were fixed to shafts or handles, which made them more powerful. They could be swung first to put more force behind the blow.

Axes were first made by tying sharp flints into forked or split branches. When people learned how to use bronze, iron and steel, they made stronger, sharper axes. By the time of the Iron Age, axe heads could be cast with a socket to fit the handle. Then the blade was hammered and ground to a sharp edge. Axes are still made in the same way today.

Axes have always been symbols used by powerful kings and rulers. The double-headed bronze axe was used as the symbol of the Minoan civilization in Crete. Pictures of the axe were used in wall paintings and as decoration on pottery.

The hand axe had a short handle. It could be used to hack the enemy in hand-to-hand combat. Soldiers could also throw the axe,

◄ **DECORATIVE AXE HEADS**
The simple wedge shape of an axe head has often been decorated for war or ritual throughout the world.

◄ **KNIGHT WITH AXE**
Medieval knights often rode into battle armed with a heavy battleaxe. This had a sharp blade and a spike. The axe was attached to the knight's arm with a chain. These axes could cause terrible injuries to both men and horses.

although this meant they might lose it. A good example of a fighting axe was the tomahawk used by Native North Americans. Tomahawks were first made of stone, then later of steel brought by traders. They were used for hunting and fighting. The tomahawk had a long handle which gave it a powerful swing. British soldiers fighting in North America in the 18th century adopted the tomahawk for their own use.

The last time an axe was used in combat in Europe was at the battle of Waterloo in 1815 between the

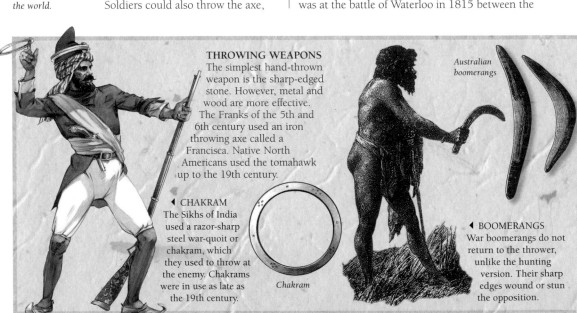

THROWING WEAPONS
The simplest hand-thrown weapon is the sharp-edged stone. However, metal and wood are more effective. The Franks of the 5th and 6th century used an iron throwing axe called a Francisca. Native North Americans used the tomahawk up to the 19th century.

Australian boomerangs

◄ **CHAKRAM**
The Sikhs of India used a razor-sharp steel war-quoit or chakram, which they used to throw at the enemy. Chakrams were in use as late as the 19th century.

Chakram

◄ **BOOMERANGS**
War boomerangs do not return to the thrower, unlike the hunting version. Their sharp edges wound or stun the opposition.

▼ NORSE RAIDERS
Norse raiders disembark from their longships and race into action armed with their single-headed war axes. These iron-bladed weapons were often elaborately decorated.

French and the British, together with the Prussians. During the battle, French troops used axes to break down the door of the farm at Hougoument, which was being held by the British infantry.

The axe is still in use today. In some armies, it is the badge of the assault pioneers. These are soldiers who do engineering work. The badge shows crossed axes. Firefighters also use axes which look rather like ancient war axes. They have spikes and blades and are easy to hold and use in one hand.

▼ THROWING KNIFE
The leaf-shaped throwing knife was a war weapon used throughout Africa from Nigeria through the Congo to the Sudan. As it turned through the air in flight the blades of the throwing knife were intended to strike the victim in a sawing action. The disadvantage of a throwing weapon was that if it missed, it could be thrown back.

African throwing knife

◀ WAR BLADE
This African throwing knife had a steel, double-edged blade. The short handle was bound with grass or a leather thong to give the warrior a good grip. The knife was designed purely as a weapon, unlike an everyday knife, and could not be used off the battlefield for day-to-day tasks or hunting.

Key Dates

- 2000–1700BC Double-headed axe used as symbol for the civilization of Minoan Crete.

- 700BC Evidence that slings were used in Assyria.

- AD400–500 Francisca throwing axes found in England.

- 700–1100 Single- and double-bladed axes used by Norse raiders.

- 900–1400 Heavy, long-handled battleaxes used by knights.

- 1700s Iron-bladed tomahawks manufactured for North America.

- 1800s Chakrams in use in India.

Slings, Bows and Crossbows

THE SLING, LIKE the longbow and crossbow, is a "stand-off" weapon. This lets a soldier attack his enemy while remaining out of reach himself. Slings were used in early sea battles. Piles of sling stones were discovered at Maiden Castle, Dorset, where the Celtic defenders fought the Romans in AD44.

▲ DAVID AND THE GIANT GOLIATH
The shepherd David defeated the Philistine warrior Goliath by stunning him with a sling stone.

Bows are among the most ancient weapons in the world. Ancient cave paintings, dating from 10,000 and 5000BC, from Castellon in Spain show figures of men using bows for fighting. Bows have been found in Denmark dating from 2000 to 1500BC and in Egypt from around 1400BC.

Though the bow was used in war, it was also used for hunting. Many of the skills of the hunter were also those of the warrior. Experienced archers could fire accurately from horseback or chariot.

In the 16th century, Henry VIII of England ordered that young men should work at shooting their bows every Sunday after the morning service at church. Most bows were made from yew wood.

The triumph of the English and Welsh longbow was in three battles against France: Crécy on 26 August, 1346; Poitiers on 19 September, 1356; and Agincourt on 25 October, 1415. English and Welsh archers were able to keep the French mounted nobles under a constant rain of arrows from 270m/885ft. As horses and riders crashed to the ground, others became entangled with them and they all became easy targets.

When muskets and rifles were first invented, the longbow, in the hands of a skilled archer, was still more accurate It was not until the American Civil War of 1861–65 that firearms became more effective. Muskets were adopted by armies simply because it was easier to train soldiers to use them.

◀ TAKING AIM
A crossbowman takes aim. He operated the trigger, which held back the string with a hook called a nut, with his right hand. If the weapon was used to hunt game a stone was used in place of the bolt.

◀ TAKING COVER
A crossbowman takes cover with his weapon and equipment stowed in a shield carrier.

STAND OFF WEAPONS

The crossbow and longbow allowed ordinary foot soldiers to engage enemies at long range. This meant that mounted knights and foot soldiers could be killed before they could use their swords, lances or axes. Both longbows and crossbows could penetrate metal at short range, which meant that they could bring down a knight in full battledress.

 Longbow with six arrows

 Longbow

 Range of 255m/835ft

Crossbow with one bolt

Crossbow Range of 360m/1,180ft

▲ SHOOTING RANGE
The expert longbowman could fire up to six aimed arrows in a minute to a range of about 255m/835ft, or twelve less accurately.

On the other hand, the skilled crossbowman had a longer range at 360m/1,180ft, but a far slower rate of fire. He could only shoot one bolt a minute.

Using the Crossbow

Spanning

Fitting the bolt

Taking aim

▲ THREE STAGES
It took much longer to load a crossbow than to aim and fire an arrow. There were three stages to loading and firing a crossbow. Spanning was the first stage. It involved pulling the bow string back and locking it. Then the bolt was fitted into the slot. Finally the bow was aimed and fired. With mechanical assistance as many as four bolts could be fired in a minute.

▼ LONGBOWS IN ACTION
English and Welsh longbowmen protected by a palisade of stakes fire at advancing French knights.

Some armies used men armed with crossbows. The crossbow is a short bow attached to a piece of wood or metal called a stock. The bowstring was pulled back by hand or mechanically and held in place by a hook and trigger mechanism. The short arrow, or bolt, was fitted into a slot and aligned with the string. The crossbowman had only to aim and operate the trigger.

The first description of a crossbow appears in a book called The Art of War by the Chinese military thinker Sun Tzu, writing in 500BC. In 1139 Pope Innocent II tried to ban the use of the crossbow against Christians because of the terrible injuries it caused. Richard I of England died in 1199 from gangrene caused by a crossbow bolt.

Forked steel tip

Barbed arrowhead

▲ ARROWHEADS
Archers used different shaped arrowheads. Barbs and forks were popular. Barbs ensured that the arrow stayed lodged in the target and made withdrawal difficult. The forked steel tip was used in the Far East.

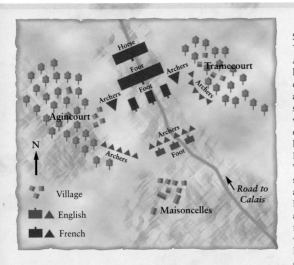

◄ LONGBOWS SAVE THE DAY
The Battle of Agincourt was the last great victory of the longbow against mounted soldiers. Wet weather slowed down the French knights and the English and Welsh archers stopped two attacks before Henry V's forces attacked from the rear. The French were defeated and lost about 5,000 of their men.

Key Dates

- 10,000–5000BC Cave paintings in Spain show archers in battle.

- 500BC Sun Tzu writing about military doctrine mentions crossbows.

- AD1100 Crossbows widely used in Europe.

- 1199 King Richard I of England killed by a crossbow at Chaluz in France.

- 1200s Longbow enters wide use in England and Wales.

- 1914–1918 Crossbows used for firing grenades in the trench warfare during World War I.

Daggers and Knives

SMALL, LIGHT AND EASY TO CARRY, daggers and knives are hand-held weapons. Daggers and knives make very good secret weapons as they can be used in complete silence. They were used on their own for hand-to-hand fighting, or for throwing.

Although the dagger design was based on the knife, there is an important difference between the two. The knife is a simple tool, sharp along one edge of the blade, it may have a relatively blunt point. It can be used for everyday tasks like cutting up meat for example, as well as being used as a weapon. A dagger, is double-edged and tapers along its length to a sharp point. It may have a guard between the blade and the handle to protect the user's hand. It is always classified as a weapon.

The earliest daggers were made from flint. Early daggers were also made from sharpened wood or bone. Daggers made from bronze, iron and steel lasted longer.

◀ SWORD AND DAGGER
A knight fully suited up and equipped with sword and dagger. The sword was suitable for hacking and the dagger for thrusts to gaps in the metal.

▶ MURDER WEAPON
Lurking in the shadows, an assassin armed with a stiletto awaits his victim. This dagger was easy to conceal and deadly if it penetrated a vital organ.

Stiletto

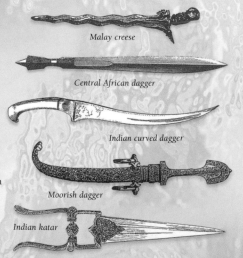

DAGGER DESIGN

As a weapon, a dagger or knife was inexpensive and very effective in even unskilled hands. It could be used for agricultural or domestic work if necessary. A dagger consists of the blade, the cross guard that protects the user's hand and knuckles, the grip or handle and the pommel. In a fight, the pommel at the base of the grip could be used in the same way as a hammer on an opponent's head. Dagger designs vary from country to country. The Indian katar or push dagger was designed to be used in a punching action.

Pommel

Grip or handle

Blade

◀ A BLADE FROM THE BRONZE AGE
This Swedish dagger dates from around 1350–1200BC and shows all the basic design principles of a hand-held edged weapon. It has a separate riveted hilt, distinct pommel and double-edged blade with fullers or blood grooves. Later designs would have a full-length tang, an extension of the blade, built into the handle. This gave the dagger greater strength and better balance.

Malay creese

Central African dagger

Indian curved dagger

Moorish dagger

Indian katar

▶ A DUEL
Duels were considered a respectable way to settle an argument. The stiletto is used here to block the sword thrust.

In the 14th and 15th centuries, sword fighters used daggers with their swords. A swordsman would hold the dagger in his left hand to block and deflect his enemy's sword. He would then make a thrust with the sword in his right hand.

Swordsmiths were the people who made swords and daggers. The daggers they made were almost works of art. They had beautiful inlays and precious and semi-precious metals and jewels set in the handles. In the Middle Ages the Saracens of Damascus in Syria developed a method of hammering layers of steel together. This made blades of swords and daggers very hard and sharp and created a pattern rather like watered silk, known as Damascene.

In the 20th century the dagger and the knife are still used by soldiers in combat. In World War I the US Army was issued with the Fighting Knife Mk 1 which protected the user's knuckles with a guard which could be used as a "knuckle duster". Modern combat knives are more like multi-purpose tools, with a saw edge, screwdriver and wire cutter as well as a sharp knife blade.

▲ TOLEDO, CITY OF STEEL
This Spanish city was known for its beautifully designed swords, daggers and armour, which were manufactured for many centuries and exported through Europe.

▶ SWORDBREAKER
A 17th-century Italian swordbreaker was a dagger made for special use in a sword fight. It was designed to trap an opponent's sword thrust in its notched blade. The dagger would not be used just to parry a sword thrust. A vigorous twist of the wrist could either break the thin blade of the trapped sword, or wrench it from the user's hands.

Cross guard

Notched blade

Key Dates

- 2000BC Bronze daggers were manufactured throughout Europe.

- 500BC First Iron Age weapons produced and used widely.

- AD1600s–1700s Stiletto manufactured in Italy. It was copied and used throughout Europe.

- 1700s–1900s Dress daggers worn as part of military or political uniforms.

- 1820s Bowie knife invented in USA by Jim Bowie. Its classic design forms the model for most modern sheath knives.

- 1940s–2000s Combat knives issued to soldiers as multi-function tools.

Swords and Scimitars

ONE OF THE MOST ANCIENT weapons in the world, the sword is now a symbol of rank for officers on ceremonial parades. Tools shaped like swords were used in farming work and to cut down trees. Like other working tools they were adapted to use in fighting. The kukri from Nepal is an ancient weapon that remains in service today with Gurkha regiments of the British army. Its broad, curved blade is ideal for chopping and even digging, but it is also a very good weapon for close combat.

Early swords were used to slice rather than to thrust. For many centuries European swords had a short, straight blade which tapered to a point. It was sharp on both edges. They were first made in bronze, later iron and finally steel. The short Roman steel

▲ VIKING WEAPON
A Viking sword from the 10th century. Its hilt is covered with silver leaf.

sword called a gladius was about 50cm/ 20in long. It was like a long, wide-bladed dagger. The gladiators who fought in the Roman circus or arena with these swords got their name from the gladius.

Swords in the Middle Ages were longer. They were about 80–90cm/30–35in long with a cross-shaped handle and tapering blade. Long swords could be used to thrust at the enemy but most soldiers fought by hacking at each other. Swords could be used by soldiers on foot or horseback.

Very strong men used the two-handed sword, which was very long, with a broad blade. Swordsmen used both hands to fight with it. Scottish chieftains in the mid-16th century used a long, double-edged, two-handed sword called the claidheamh múr, or claymore.

◀ TWO-HANDED
Medieval knights in close combat. One of them is armed with a hand-and-a-half, or two-handed sword.

SWORDS

Swords today are made from steel and have been made from bronze, stone and even wood. Although no longer used in war, in many cultures they remain the symbol of power and status within military organizations. Sword fighting techniques vary according to the design of the blade. The Japanese prefer a chopping action, while the thin-bladed rapier is best suited to a thrust.

▲ SWORD SKILLS
A Japanese samurai warrior from the 15th century. Samurai warriors usually wore two swords and a distinctive headdress.

▶ SAMURAI WEAPON
The Japanese traditionally used single-edged daggers and swords of different lengths. The traditional long-bladed sword is called a katana.

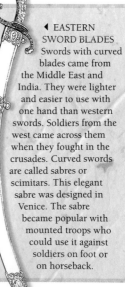

◀ EASTERN SWORD BLADES
Swords with curved blades came from the Middle East and India. They were lighter and easier to use with one hand than western swords. Soldiers from the west came across them when they fought in the crusades. Curved swords are called sabres or scimitars. This elegant sabre was designed in Venice. The sabre became popular with mounted troops who could use it against soldiers on foot or on horseback.

◀ DEATH AT DAWN
A Victorian print shows the victor of a duel armed with a rapier. His victim's weapon shows the guard or side rings designed to protect the hand.

▶ HEAVY BLADE
An Asian warrior armed with a bow and broad-bladed sword. The sword has the weight closer to the tip, which makes it ideal for a chopping action.

Knights and soldiers discovered the sword-making techniques of the Middle East during the crusades. This led to improved sword design in the west. Soldiers in the Middle East used a curved sword called a scimitar. These had long, narrow blades and very sharp edges.

The guard in front of the sword handle was made to protect the fighter's hand. Around 1600, Venetian sword makers produced a new guard design called the basket hilt. This was a curved, perforated guard that protected the whole hand. The basic design is still used today on many modern ceremonial swords.

The mounted soldiers of the cavalry charged towards their enemy with their swords pointing forward for a straight thrust. However, long swords became difficult to use once the soldiers were fighting close to each other. There was no room to make a good stroke. The sabre was developed as a cavalry weapon. It had a short, curved blade and was used to slash and thrust. The blade cut as it went up and as it came down.

In Renaissance Europe, noblemen and courtiers wore weapons almost as fashion accessories. Rapiers were very popular. These were light, very narrow swords with elaborate guards. The fashion lasted from about 1530 through to 1780.

Key:

English
1 E. Howard
2 T. Howard
3 Constable
4 Surrey
5 Dacre
6 Sir E. Stanley

Scots
7 Home
8 Crawford
9 D'Aussi
10 James
11 Argyll and Lennox

Map labels: Twizel Bridge, Heaton Mill, Route of Surrey's march, English route from Twizel and Heaton Mill, R. Till, Etal Castle, Bar Moor, Ford Castle, Pipers Hill Monument, Branxton, Scottish Artillery, From Doddington

Kilometres 0 1
Miles 0 1

▲ THE BATTLE OF FLODDEN 1513
This battle, between the English and the Scots, took place in Northern England. The Scots fought with the two-handed claymore sword.

Key Dates

- 1300BC Bronze swords used in war.
- 650–500BC Iron swords in use.
- AD900s Viking double-edged swords used in Viking raids all over Europe.
- 1300s Curved Turkish sabres in use as a cavalry weapon.
- 1500s Rapiers in use.
- 1500s Scottish two-edged swords in use.
- 1600s Venetian basket-hilt swords in use throughout Europe.
- 1850 Kukri in use with Nepalese soldiers.

Spears, Poles, Pikes and Halberds

PREHISTORIC HUNTERS used spears to kill animals for food. They were more powerful and accurate than simple stones and could be thrown from safe distances. The earliest spears were simply straight saplings (very young trees) which were sharpened at one end. In the Far East, bamboo wood was used. It was light and strong and could be hardened in a fire to give a very sharp point. Flint, stone or metal points fixed on to a spear made it even more effective.

There were soldiers armed with spears in most ancient armies. Another name for the throwing spear is javelin. Throwing

▲ THE QUARTERSTAFF
This was the simplest weapon ever made. It could be cut from saplings. In Europe in the Middle Ages, the staff was used more in competitions and brawls than in war.

spears have one drawback. Once they have been thrown at the enemy, you cannot get them back. In fact, the enemy may use them to throw at you. The Romans solved this problem by inventing a spear called a pilum. This had a long, thin neck near the point. When the spear hit a target, it snapped at the neck. Then it could not be used by the enemy.

Longer, heavier stick weapons were used to fight with rather than to throw. In medieval times, country people used large sticks called staffs for walking. Various types of blades were attached to these to make weapons for both cavalry and

▶ PIKE WALL
Pikemen in the 17th century lined up to form a barrier for cavalry. This tactic gave musketeers time and space to reload their weapons behind the pike wall.

POLE ARMS
The advantage of pole arms like spears, pikes or halberds is that the user can stab, chop or even entangle his enemy at a safe distance. Peasants often fitted a pruning bill to the shaft of a quarterstaff to make simple pole weapons during revolts and insurrections.

◀ PIKEMAN
A pikeman in the splendid uniform of the 17th century. In addition to his helmet, he might also have a breastplate for extra protection. Pikes had been used as early as 350BC, when the Macedonians had pikes nearly 5m/16ft long.

English halberd

Bill

Italian linstock

German glaive

English gisarme

infantry troops. A spear point would make a lance, used by cavalry. Knife blades and axes were also used, as well as billhooks, which were tools for cutting hedges. A trident was made by attaching a sharp-pointed fork (like a pitchfork). Halberds were long poles with a spear point and an axe head mounted behind it. Pikes were long, heavy pole weapons with long blades of various designs.

In the 14th and 15th centuries, the Swiss developed specialized pike tactics. Using a pike that consisted of a 6m/20ft shaft and a 1m/3ft iron shank, Swiss soldiers marched in columns which had a front line of 30 men but could be 50 to 100 men deep. The massed pikes could stop a cavalry attack. Many rulers and generals hired Swiss pikemen to fight in their battles. Today, the Pope's Swiss Guard, armed with pikes, is all that is left of this force.

The bayonet fitted to the muzzle of modern army rifles is based on the pike. Bayonets were first used by soldiers with muskets. Although muskets were effective firearms, they took time to reload. By fitting long pointed blades, called bayonets, to their muskets and forming themselves into a hollow square with bayonets pointing outwards, soldiers could break up a cavalry attack and protect each other while they reloaded.

◀ SWISS GUARD
The Swiss Guard at the Vatican still carry pikes and wear uniforms similar to those worn in the 15th and 16th centuries.

▶ CLOSE COMBAT
Two soldiers fighting with halberds. One tries to use the curved beak to trip his enemy while the other uses the spike as a spear.

▶ ON THE MOVE
An Etruscan warrior armed with a sword and throwing spear. The classic tactic for these lightly-armed men was to throw their spears, then to run forward as the spears were in flight. By the time the spears reached their target, the Etruscan soldier was within sword reach. The enemy was hit twice in one move.

▲ ISLAND WEAPONS
Spears have been used throughout history in many different cultures. This islander from New Caledonia in the Pacific Ocean is ready to throw one spear and holds two more in reserve.

Key Dates

- 600BC Greek hoplites use short throwing spears.

- 350BC The sarissa (light spear) used in Macedonian phalanx formations.

- 200–100BC Roman foot soldiers use the pilum, or heavy javelin.

- AD900–1400 Lances used by knights for jousting and war in Europe.

- 1400s Pole axe enters service.

- 1400–1599 Halberd widely used.

- 1600s Pikes enter service.

- 1815 Cavalry lances adopted by Britain from France.

Ancient Firearms

IREARMS ARE WEAPONS that use gunpowder and shot. The earliest firearms in the west were made around the beginning of the 15th century. They worked rather like mini cannons and were small enough to be carried by a soldier on foot or on horseback. They looked rather like the modern hand-held flare used to signal an emergency at sea. They had a short barrel attached to a handle.

By the late 15th and early 16th centuries, the standard firearm was about one and a half metres long with a barrel, stock and butt. The stock supported the metal barrel and the butt rested in the crook of the firer's shoulder when the gun was being used.

The arquebus was a bigger weapon, often used mounted on a simple tripod. It usually needed two people to operate it. One aimed it and the second put a lit taper into the touch hole or vent. The soldiers who had to carry these heavy weapons were very keen for craftsmen to make them lighter and easier firearms. The matchlock was the first improvement. This weapon was fired using a fuse or length of cord which had been soaked in a chemical called saltpetre. This made it burn slowly. The cord was coiled into a curved lever called a serpent. A shallow pan filled with gunpowder had a thin tube leading into the barrel of the weapon. To operate the matchlock, the soldier lit the cord, opened the spring-loaded cover to the pan and

▲ MATCHLOCK
The matchlock was used in Europe until the 18th century and in parts of India until as late as the 20th century.

▶ MOUNTED FIREPOWER
The wheellock was ideal for mounted soldiers who would need to keep one hand free.

HANDGUNS
Improved metal technology and designs made hand guns more reliable and easier to carry. Tactics for infantry and cavalry changed to suit these firearms. Weapons were still made by craftsmen. After the Napoleonic wars, muskets and guns began to be mass produced.

Mould

Inside a rifled gun barrel

Bullet spinning from the barrel

▲ POWDER HORN
Gunpowder was stored in a powder horn to keep it dry. Many of them were made from hollow animal horns. They had a spout through which an exact measure of powder was dispensed.

▶ HAND MADE
The lead ball fired by muskets was easily made using a simple mould. Once the molten lead had hardened, the handles of the mould were opened and the new ammunition was ready. Soldiers made their own ammunition as needed.

Shot

▲ RIFLING
Rifling was a system of grooves inside the barrel of a firearm which gave the bullet a spin as it left the barrel. This made the gun more accurate. Rifled weapons were still rare in the early 19th century. Now rifling is used in every modern gun.

◀ MUSKETEERS
Musketeers armed with the heavy Spanish-style matchlock weapon that required a fork rest for easy handling. This weapon was used by armies throughout Europe from about 1567 for over 100 years and the musketeers were an elite within the army.

▶ WHEELLOCK
This firearm used a spring-loaded wheel and pieces of iron pyrites to produce sparks which ignited the gunpowder at the moment of firing. But they were expensive and not in common use.

then pulled the trigger. This brought the burning cord, or match, down into gunpowder, which exploded.

The matchlock was not a practical weapon for a soldier mounted on horseback who needed to have one hand on the reins. So the wheellock was developed. It worked rather like an old-fashioned cigarette lighter. When the trigger was pulled the pan of gunpowder was uncovered. A metal wheel rubbed against a lump of iron pyrites and produced a stream of sparks. A mounted soldier could carry two or three short-barrelled wheellock pistols in holsters on his saddle or tucked into the tops of his riding boots. The snaphaunce, miguelet and flintlock were later firearms. They used flint and steel to produce a spark. The flintlock was in use until the mid-19th century. A trained soldier could fire a shot every 20 seconds from a smoothbore flintlock musket, but the weapon was inaccurate beyond 80m/260ft.

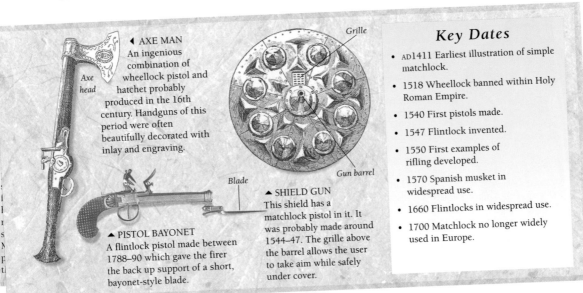

◀ AXE MAN
An ingenious combination of wheellock pistol and hatchet probably produced in the 16th century. Handguns of this period were often beautifully decorated with inlay and engraving.

Axe head

▲ PISTOL BAYONET
A flintlock pistol made between 1788–90 which gave the firer the back up support of a short, bayonet-style blade.

Blade

Grille

Gun barrel

▲ SHIELD GUN
This shield has a matchlock pistol in it. It was probably made around 1544–47. The grille above the barrel allows the user to take aim while safely under cover.

Key Dates

- AD1411 Earliest illustration of simple matchlock.
- 1518 Wheellock banned within Holy Roman Empire.
- 1540 First pistols made.
- 1547 Flintlock invented.
- 1550 First examples of rifling developed.
- 1570 Spanish musket in widespread use.
- 1660 Flintlocks in widespread use.
- 1700 Matchlock no longer widely used in Europe.

Helmets and War Hats

SOLDIERS HAVE ALWAYS worn helmets of some kind to protect their heads and eyes in combat. They came in all shapes and sizes, to suit the kind of weapons soldiers were likely to come up against. Ancient helmets were designed to protect soldiers from attack by cutting weapons such as swords or thrusting weapons such as spears or arrows. Some helmets were simple round metal hats. Others were more like iron masks. The ancient Greeks invented the nosepiece. This was a strip of armour running from the brim of the helmet along the bridge of the nose. It was still in use in the 17th century. The Romans preferred helmets with deep cheek pieces. These were hinged flaps that hung down the sides of the helmet, covering the ears and cheeks, but leaving the front unrestricted. This made it easier for the wearer to see clearly as he was fighting.

In the 11th century, the Normans wore conical helmets with nosepieces. They also wore a chain mail hood which completely covered the ears and back of the neck. This gave them added protection.

▲ SAXON HELMET
This helmet from the 7th century comes from the Saxon burial ground at Sutton Hoo. It is inlaid with silvered bronze.

PROTECTING THE HEAD

Since the head incorporates the brain and face with important organs such as the eyes, ears, nose and mouth, it has always been protected in war. Helmets were made from bronze, iron or steel. Today they are made from modern plastics and polymers, which are light but very strong.

◀ THE GREAT HELM
By the mid-14th century the helm was the most widely used helmet by mounted knights. A visor pulled down to protect the face. Helms often sported elaborate crests at the top showing the owner's coat-of-arms. Today's motorcycle helmets resemble the helm.

Assyrian war hat

Hoplite helmet

Assyrian helmet

▲ ANCIENT HELMETS
Helmets began as simple metal hats. Later, hinged flaps were added to give protection to the cheeks, nose and neck without making it too difficult for the soldier to see or move. The flaps were often decorated.

◀ SPEED OR STRENGTH
During the crusades of the 11th and 12th centuries, European knights, who wore heavy suits and helmets, met Saracen warriors who wore lighter mail coats and small helmets that fitted close to their heads.

The most magnificent helmets were made during the medieval period in Europe. Ordinary foot soldiers had simple armour including a plain helmet but royalty and noblemen had splendid battledress. The helmets were engraved and inlaid and were made with angles to deflect sword blows and a hinged visor that protected the wearer's eyes. A three-dimensional model of the family crest was often set on top. These elaborate helmets were like badges to show the nobility of the wearer.

By the time of the English Civil War (1642–1651), helmet design had changed. There was neck and earflap protection, a hinged peak and a face guard. The helmet was known as a "lobster-tail pot" because it looked like a lobster shell.

When the helmet was revived in World War I, the British army adopted the style of the brimmed war hat worn by archers at the Battle of Agincourt (1415). It was called the "kettle".

▶ LOBSTER POT
The pot or lobster-tail pot helmet worn by Parliamentarian cavalry in the Civil War gave them their nickname of "Roundheads".

▶ MEDIEVAL HELMETS
Armourers in the Middle Ages produced headgear for wealthy and discriminating customers. Some of the designs were very fanciful. Others had carefully constructed angles and shapes which could deflect sword or mace blows.

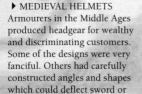

English, 13th century

French, 15th century

French, 12th century

French, 13th century

German, 15th century

Key Dates

- 1700–1100BC Bronze helmets in use in Mycenae.
- 55BC–AD100 Roman cavalry and infantry helmets introduced.
- 1000–1100 Norman helmets with nosepiece.
- 1300s Basinet hinged helmet.
- 1350s Helms in use by European knights in battle and in tournaments.
- 1400s Kettle-hat or war hat.
- 1500s Nuremberg close helmets.
- 1600s Pot or lobster-tail pot helmet worn by Cromwell's Roundhead army in the English Civil War.

Animals at War

ELEPHANTS, HORSES, DONKEYS, bullocks and camels have all been used to fight wars. Most of them were used to carry soldiers or pull wagons. Elephants were used rather like modern tanks. An elephant could trample enemy soldiers, while archers riding in a large basket on its back could pick off targets with their arrows.

▼ HANNIBAL'S TANKS
The most famous elephants in war belonged to Hannibal the Carthaginian general. In 216BC he brought them from Spain to fight against Rome at the battle of Cannae in southern Italy.

WAR BEASTS
Elephants are not aggressive by nature but could be used to frighten troops who had never seen them before. A panicking elephant could trample its own soldiers. In India, handlers called mahouts carried a spike. If their elephant went out of control, they killed it.

◀ ELEPHANT POWER
The elephant has three natural weapons: its great weight, its huge tusks and its powerful trunk.

▼ ELE-FIGHTER
The Indians put armour on their elephants as well as fighting towers on their backs.

▲ THE HEAVY BRIGADE
Elephants were used on the front line of battle to frighten the enemy infantry and to block cavalry charges. Like modern tanks, they were protected from close range attack by special groups of foot soldiers.

One of the earliest battles to use war elephants was fought at Arbela, now modern Irbil, in 331BC. The Persian leader Darius led an army, including 15 war elephants, against Alexander the Great of Macedonia. Alexander's troops were frightened of the elephants at first, but so well-disciplined that they did not run away but fought and won the battle.

War elephants had been used in India by the Hindus from around 400BC. They were as important as chariots on the battlefield. At the battle of Hydaspes in India in 327BC, Porus, the Rajah of Lahore, led elephants against Alexander. This time, Alexander's horses were frightened by the elephants. However, his foot soldiers attacked the elephants with battleaxes.

The animals panicked and the Macedonians won. The most famous war elephants belonged to Hannibal, the Carthaginian general. He fought against Rome in the Second Punic War (218–203BC). The elephants were used in several battles but Hannibal was eventually beaten.

Elephants were first seen in England in AD43 when the Romans used them to invade. War elephants were still in use in India during the 18th century. They had iron plates fixed to their heads and were driven forward like four-legged battering rams to break down the gates of the town of Arcot in 1751. They panicked when they were fired at by muskets and stampeded.

▲ CAMEL ARMY
The camel has been used for transport in battle in the Middle East. It has lots of stamina and can move fast. Camels can also travel a long way without much food or water. Here, camel-mounted soldiers use lances and swords in a lively battle.

◀ OVER THE ALPS
Hannibal marched with his elephants across the Pyrenees and the Alps to attack Imperial Rome. When he set out from Saguntum in 218BC, he had 50,000 infantry, 9,000 cavalry and about 80 elephants. By the time he reached the Po valley in northern Italy six months later, only a few elephants were still alive. Hannibal had lost 30,000 infantry and 3,000 cavalry.

Key Dates

- 327BC Battle of Hydaspes. Alexander the Great meets Indian elephants.

- 275BC Battle of Beneventum, Italy. Carthage uses elephants for the first time against Rome.

- 218BC Hannibal crosses the Alps.

- 202BC Battle of Zama. Hannibal defeated and his elephants taken.

- 190BC Battle of Magnesia. Syrian war elephants panic and confuse their own troops.

- AD43 Roman Emperor Claudius uses elephants to invade Britain.

Horses in Battle

HORSES MADE IT POSSIBLE for armies to move around quickly. They could pull wagons and siege weapons or carry loot and possessions. On the battlefield, they could be ridden by scouts or messengers taking news to and from the generals planning the battle. Large horses, working together as heavy cavalry, were unstoppable on the battlefield.

The first people to use the horse in war were the Assyrians around 800BC. They used them as cavalry, to pull chariots and for hunting. The Romans bred from European, Middle Eastern and African stock to produce racehorses, hunters, chargers and harness-horses.

The saddle with stirrups, which were probably invented in China, reached Europe in the 2nd century AD and transformed mounted operations forever. They made it easier to ride a horse. A Roman soldier on foot could cover about 8km/5 miles a day. When he was on a horse, he could travel twice as far as that.

The horse also made it possible for groups of people to move far away from their home lands. In the 13th century, the Mongols roamed from Central Asia as far as Vietnam, the Middle East and Europe.

There were two kinds of cavalry, the light and the heavy. The difference between them was based on the size of the horse. Most ancient armies had both light and heavy cavalry. About two-thirds of the Mongol riders

▲ PARTING SHOT
Horse archers from Parthia, an ancient country now part of Iran, used to pretend to retreat then turned and fired their arrows backwards to take the enemy by surprise.

◀ A LIGHT SKIRMISH
Persian light cavalry troops, carrying round shields and armed with lances and maces, fight a running battle.

HORSES AT WAR
Horses have been used in war for centuries. They can pull wagons and guns as well as being ridden. They are strong and fast, but can be stopped by long-range weapons.

▶ BAREBACK WARRIOR
The fast, lightly-armed Numidian cavalry played an important part in the victories of Hannibal during the Punic Wars with Rome. They fought and rode bareback.

◀ HEAVY DUTY
German knights in the heavy battledress worn in medieval battles. This protected both horse and rider.

▼ JOUSTING TOURNAMENT
*Today, tournaments and battles are
re-enacted by "knights" on horseback.*

▶ AT THE
CHARGE
*The horse wears
a kind of helmet
known as a
chauffron.
Its spike is almost
as much of a
weapon as the rider's lance.
Both are pointed towards
the enemy when the
horse charges.*

were light cavalry. They had small, fast horses, wore protective helmets and carried bows and arrows. The heavy cavalry had big, strong horses, wore chain mail or heavy leather clothing and were armed with lances.

Armies in medieval Europe had only foot soldiers and knights on horseback. To carry a knight in full armour the horse had to be big and strong. The knights were a kind of heavy cavalry. By the 16th century the armies of Europe had concentrated on heavy cavalry. The French called them gendarmerie and the Germans called them Schwarzreiter or "Black Riders". It was when they fought with Turkish armies in the 17th century that Europeans began to see how useful a light cavalry could be and to set up light brigades of their own. The Hungarian light cavalry, called hussars, wore Turkish-style uniforms.

The heavy cavalry wore helmets and breastplates, rode large horses and carried a pistol and heavy sabre. The light cavalry had no armour and rode horses chosen for their speed. The riders carried two or even three pistols and a light sword.

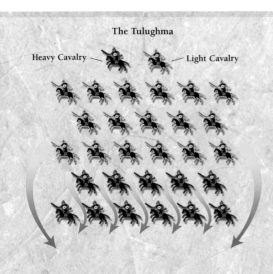

The Tulughma

Heavy Cavalry — Light Cavalry

◀ MONGOLIAN
WAR TACTICS
The Mongolian army used light and heavy cavalry and many different tactics. This one is the tulughma. The heavy brigade led the charge and broke up enemy lines. At the same time they protected the ranks of light cavalry behind them. When the enemy ranks were broken, the lighter horses ran through or round their own heavy ranks.

Key Dates

- 500BC Persians employ lancers and horse archers.

- 53BC Parthian horse archers defeat Romans at Carrhae (modern Iraq).

- AD100s Stirrup introduced to Europe.

- 200–400 Horse archers and lancers used by Romans.

- 977–1030 Mahmud of Ghazni uses cavalry horse archers in north India.

- 1000–1200 Crusaders use Moslem mercenaries called Turcopoles.

- 1396–1457 French cavalry, gendarmes, in action.

- 1500–1600 German "Black Riders" in action in Europe.

Chariots and War Wagons

or horses, the archer riding beside him was free to concentrate on fast and accurate firing at the enemy. Not all chariots were two-man vehicles. If there was only one rider, he would tie the reins around his waist to keep his hands free so he could use his weapons. Some chariots, pulled by three or four horses, could carry several men, armed with a variety of weapons. Used all together, chariots could break up ranks of enemy infantry. Some later chariots had the protection of armour. They may also have had blades or scythes fitted to the hubs of their wheels to prevent enemy infantry or cavalry approaching too close. The drawback with chariots, like many wheeled vehicles, was that they could bog down in mud and it was hard for them to cross rough ground.

Between 1420 and 1434 the Hussites, a group of people from Bohemia

CHARIOTS WERE A CLEVER WAY to combine speed and action. Most of them were pulled by horses. The driver was called a charioteer. For the armies of ancient Egypt, Assyria, Persia, India and China, chariots were the weapon of surprise, racing in and out of battle. Most chariots held two people, the driver and the bowman. With the driver to handle the horse

▲ ROMAN CHARIOT
The chariot was not used a great deal in war. It was a popular sight at the public Games held in Rome and other major cities of the Empire.

▶ EGYPTIAN TACTICS
An Egyptian courtier on a hunting trip fires his bow and arrows from a moving chariot. The same skills would be used in war.

▲ WARRIOR QUEEN
Boudicca, chieftain of the British tribe called the Iceni, used war chariots in her battles against invading Romans.

WHEELS OF WAR
Chariots were first used in the Bronze Age in the 15th century BC in the Middle East. They could be pulled by two to four horses, but the larger number were harder to control. They could move easily on the flat deserts of Egypt and around the Euphrates, but they were not ideal transport in muddy, broken or rocky terrain. The war wagons used by the Hussites in Europe in the 15th century AD were almost like the first tanks. They were formed into circles like mobile forts. Soldiers fired cannons and muskets from the shelter of the wagons.

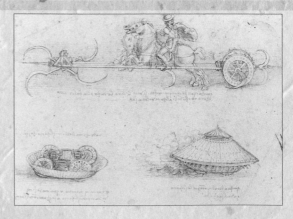

▲ LEONARDO'S TANKS
Leonardo da Vinci, the genius of the Renaissance, had many ideas that were ahead of his time. This sketch shows armoured vehicles of various kinds. They look like early versions of modern tanks.

▼ GUN CARRIAGES
In 15th-century Europe, horses and carts were used to haul heavy cannons around the battlefield. This meant that the guns could be taken to positions where they could be most use. As artillery troops became more mobile they could do more harm to the enemy.

German cavalry at bay. There were 350 wagons in a Wagenburg, linked together with chains and sometimes dug in. Within the circle of wagons were 700 cavalrymen and 7,000 infantry. Gaps closed with chains, posts and spikes could be opened to allow the Hussite cavalry out to attack. When the Hussites brought in cannon mounted on special wagons, the German cavalry refused to attack them any more because they were too dangerous.

(now the Czech Republic), fought with the Germans. The Hussites were followers of the religious reformer John Huss. Their army, commanded by Jan Zizka, used armoured carts. The wagons were formed into a circle of wagons called a Wagenburg, or wagon castle. Behind the wagons, crossbow archers and musketeers kept the

Some historians have suggested that the Hussite Wagenburg was the first tank in history as it combined fire power, protection and movement.

▲ CHARIOTS OF MARBLE
Many artists have made paintings and sculptures of chariots. This Roman sculpture of a chariot and a pair of frisky horses is in the Vatican Museum.

Key Dates

- 1400BC Chariots used by Egyptians.
- 331BC Persian chariots armed with scythes at Battle of Arbela.
- 327BC Indian chariots used at Battle of Hydaspes.
- 225BC Last use of chariots by Celts in Battle of Telamon, Italy.
- AD60 Boudicca uses chariots against the Romans in Britain.
- 378 Romans use wagons to defeat Goths at Adrianople (modern Turkey).
- 1420–34 Fighting wagons used by Jan Zizka and the Hussites.

Cavalry Weapons

THE WEAPON USED BY A MOUNTED soldier reflected his skills as a rider. The Mongol cavalry riders of Genghis Khan could ride without reins, which meant they were able to use a bow while in the saddle. The lance or spear could be used in one hand. It was long enough for a rider to reach enemy foot soldiers. Cavalry normally rode straight at their enemy using the speed and impetus of the horse to add weight to the lance thrust. The cavalry lance became popular in medieval Europe and continued to be used in battle by horsemen in Poland and Hungary. Polish Lancers used it against the French during the Napoleonic Wars in 1800–1815. Medieval knights used the lance in battle, and honed their skill in tournaments. The knight's horse also became a target, so craftsmen began to make armour for horses.

Horse armour was called bard. At its simplest it was made up of the chauffron, a plate covering the front of the horse's skull, and the peytral which covered the breast above the front legs. Full protective gear included the crupper and the flanchard. The crupper covered the horse's rump. The flanchard was an oblong plate fixed to the base of the saddle. It protected the horse's flanks and closed the gap between the crupper and peytral.

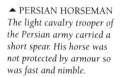

▲ PERSIAN HORSEMAN
The light cavalry trooper of the Persian army carried a short spear. His horse was not protected by armour so was fast and nimble.

▲ SAMURAI BOWMAN
Japanese samurai warriors did not only use swords. Many were also masters of the longbow. A mounted archer on a trained horse had two advantages. He could move fast and he could fire his weapon from a distance, out of the range of his enemy's swords and lances.

THE HORSE AT WAR

The horse changed combat forever. On horseback, soldiers could travel further and transport more equipment. They could also cover more ground on the battlefield. Stirrups gave the riders more control over their mounts, leaving their hands free for fighting in battle.

◀ MONGOLIAN PONY
Tough, fast little Asian ponies provided transport and mare's milk for the Mongol warriors as they crossed Europe.

▲ HARD RIDING
Medieval horse armour protected the animal without slowing it down. The rider's legs covered its bare flanks in battle.

▲ A GREAT TEAM
Chain mail protects this horse's neck. The weight of horse, man and metal at the gallop swept them through the ranks of the enemy's foot soldiers.

▼ TOURNAMENT
When jousting for sport, knights used blunted lances so that they would not harm each other.

Chauffron

Blunted lance

Knight's insignia

European cavalry troopers had been using straight swords from Roman times. When fighting in the Middle East, European soldiers came across the curved sword, which was used as a pattern for the curved cavalry sabre. This was ideal for the slashing backstroke.

The wheellock pistol was developed in the 16th century. It was designed to be used with one hand so that the rider could shoot while keeping full control of his horse. Because of the noise, flashing and smoke, horses had to be trained to carry men through gunfire.

▶ GOING WEST
In 1190 the Mongol emperor Genghis Khan led his great army westwards. It was divided into groups of 10,000 men called hordes. The hordes were named after different shades. Ogodai, Monkai, Kublai Khan and Tamerlane were later Mongol leaders who continued to expand deep into eastern Europe, reaching almost as far as Austria.

Western Christendom
Golden Horde
Blue Horde
Byzantium
White Horde
Kwarzim
Mongol Union
China
Gobi Desert
Sung
Moghul Empire
N

0 — Kilometres — 3000
0 — Miles — 2000

〰〰 Great Wall of China
← Conquests of Genghis Khan
← Conquests of Ogodai
← Conquests of Monkai and Kublai Khan
← Conquests of Tamerlane

Key Dates

- 400s BC Persian mounted archers.

- 400BC Spartan cavalry armed with short javelins.

- 330s BC Alexander the Great uses mounted lancers.

- 200s BC Hannibal uses Numidian mounted lancers.

- 1200s Mongol hordes, mounted on horseback, invade Europe.

- 1300s–1500s Jousting lances in use.

- 1400s Heavy horse armour introduced.

- 1600s Sabres introduced as cavalry weapons.

Castles and Fortifications

THERE ARE NUMEROUS EXAMPLES of prehistoric and ancient fortifications throughout the world. The people who built them often used natural features such as hills, cliffs and crags or rivers, lakes and swamps to enhance their strength. Where these features were not present, people created them, making ditches, mounds and later walls and towers. Sometimes castle builders used earlier sites. For example, at Porchester in Hampshire in the 1120s, Henry I built a motte-and-bailey castle using the square fortifications of an earlier Roman Saxon fort.

The outlines of square Roman forts can be seen throughout Europe. These forts were called castra, which is where we get the word castle. Castra were built

▶ THE MEDIEVAL CASTLE
This typical castle has crenelated walls, which meant the defenders could shoot through the gaps.

Crenellation

Gatehouse

Drawbridge

Portcullis

◀ SCOTTISH CASTLE
Caerlavarock Castle, Scotland, is a classic moated castle. The pattern of stone bricks on the top of the round towers is known as machicolation. It is to protect soldiers inside the towers as they fight off an attack. The moat which surrounds the walls gives even more protection. The castle was hard to storm.

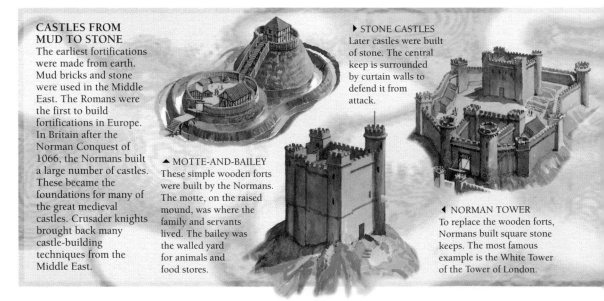

CASTLES FROM MUD TO STONE
The earliest fortifications were made from earth. Mud bricks and stone were used in the Middle East. The Romans were the first to build fortifications in Europe. In Britain after the Norman Conquest of 1066, the Normans built a large number of castles. These became the foundations for many of the great medieval castles. Crusader knights brought back many castle-building techniques from the Middle East.

▲ MOTTE-AND-BAILEY
These simple wooden forts were built by the Normans. The motte, on the raised mound, was where the family and servants lived. The bailey was the walled yard for animals and food stores.

▶ STONE CASTLES
Later castles were built of stone. The central keep is surrounded by curtain walls to defend it from attack.

◀ NORMAN TOWER
To replace the wooden forts, Normans built square stone keeps. The most famous example is the White Tower of the Tower of London.

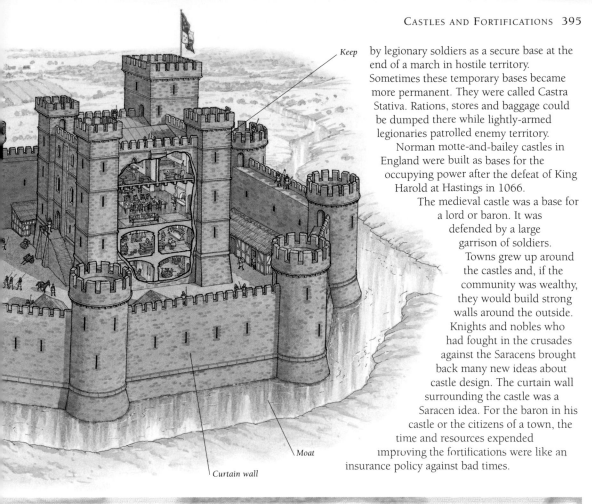

Keep

Moat

Curtain wall

by legionary soldiers as a secure base at the end of a march in hostile territory. Sometimes these temporary bases became more permanent. They were called Castra Stativa. Rations, stores and baggage could be dumped there while lightly-armed legionaries patrolled enemy territory.

Norman motte-and-bailey castles in England were built as bases for the occupying power after the defeat of King Harold at Hastings in 1066.

The medieval castle was a base for a lord or baron. It was defended by a large garrison of soldiers.

Towns grew up around the castles and, if the community was wealthy, they would build strong walls around the outside. Knights and nobles who had fought in the crusades against the Saracens brought back many new ideas about castle design. The curtain wall surrounding the castle was a Saracen idea. For the baron in his castle or the citizens of a town, the time and resources expended improving the fortifications were like an insurance policy against bad times.

◀ WELSH CASTLES
In the 13th century, King Edward I of England built a large number of castles in Wales. This was to strengthen his grip on the country. The Welsh people did not care for English rule. Craftsmen were brought from all over England to help in the building work. Edward's wife and queen, Eleanor, gave birth to their first son, the future Edward II, at Caernarfon Castle. He became the Prince of Wales, the first English man to hold the title.

Key Dates

- 2500BC Ur of the Chaldees, first fortified city, built (in modern Iraq).
- 701BC Jerusalem fortified.
- 560BC Athens fortified.
- 1058–1689 Edinburgh Castle.
- 1066–1399 Tower of London.
- 1181–89 Dover Castle.
- 1196–98 Chateau-Gaillard built by Richard I in France.
- 1200s Krak des Chevaliers, a Crusader castle, built in Syria.
- 1538–1540s Henry VIII builds forts along England's south coast.

Towers, Keeps and Gates

To DEFEND THEIR CASTLES people built tall towers and keeps. Standing at the top, they could see enemy ships or army columns a long way off. This gave the people in the castle time to prepare for attack. When the enemy arrived at the castle walls, the lookouts on the tower could see down into their camps or siege weapons and fire missiles at them. Towers can be square or round, but always have very thick walls.

Towers are safe places to hide when an enemy attacks. In the 9th and 10th centuries, Vikings raided England and Ireland. To defend themselves, Irish people built high towers in villages or near monasteries. These stone-built towers had no outer protection. They had arrow slits or embrasures and a simple door built high up the wall that could only be reached using a ladder.

After the Norman Conquest of England, Norman barons built many castles. They were mostly of the motte-and-bailey kind. A curtain wall stood around the bailey. Towers were built at the corners of the wall and at intervals along the sides. Soldiers could use the towers as safe bases. The towers had a thicker belt of stone at the base. This was called a batter. It was meant

◀ LOOK OUT
The high towers of Ireland were built as refuges from invading Vikings. They were not intended to hold out against a long siege but were good look-outs and safe places to hide.

▶ BAMBURGH CASTLE
Bamburgh Castle Keep, in Northumberland, England, dates from 1200. The keep was the strongest part of a castle.

THE KEY TO THE CASTLE

The gate was the most vulnerable part of a castle because it was the point of entrance. When it was open, attackers could force their way in, and the castle could be captured very quickly. It was very important that the opening could be closed quickly. An iron gate called a portcullis could be dropped into place in seconds. The drawbridge only needed to be lifted a short way to prevent the enemy crossing the moat.

▶ DRAWBRIDGE
The drawbridge was made from very thick wood. It could be raised very quickly. It was operated by a system of weights which worked in the same way as a see-saw.

◀ PORTCULLIS
The portcullis was operated by a winch. The guards could release it quickly, and let it crash down under its own weight. Spikes on the bottom of the portcullis could trap attackers caught underneath it.

to strengthen the towers against battering rams and make it difficult to mine through the walls.

The gate was the weakest part of the castle. It was protected by a gatehouse and a portcullis. Some gatehouses had two portcullises. Attackers could be lured through the open gate only to find their way barred by an inner portcullis or gate hidden around a corner. Once the attackers were inside, the defenders would lower the outer portcullis and trap them. The passage between the gates became a stone tunnel. In the roof of the tunnel were slots known as "murder holes". Defenders could shoot arrows, drop rocks or pour boiling liquids through the holes on to their trapped enemies.

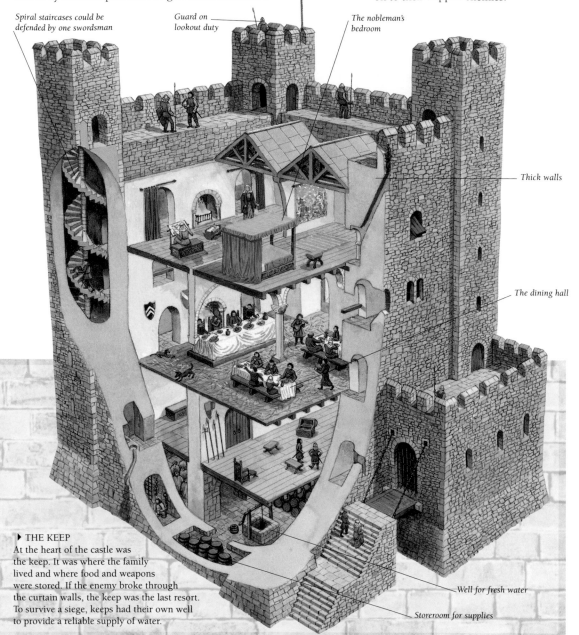

Spiral staircases could be defended by one swordsman

Guard on lookout duty

The nobleman's bedroom

Thick walls

The dining hall

▶ THE KEEP
At the heart of the castle was the keep. It was where the family lived and where food and weapons were stored. If the enemy broke through the curtain walls, the keep was the last resort. To survive a siege, keeps had their own well to provide a reliable supply of water.

Well for fresh water

Storeroom for supplies

Walls

CASTLE WALLS were built to a set pattern. Surrounding the castle was a curtain wall. This could be 5–8m/16–26ft thick and wide enough for people to walk along. On top of the wall was the parapet. The parapet was a wall about 50cm/1½ft thick. In some castles they were built only at the top of the outer face of the wall. Others had them on both sides. They were about two metres high, so that they completely concealed and protected any soldier standing guard on the curtain wall.

Along the parapets were regular gaps which were low and wide enough for an archer to shoot at enemies. The gaps were called crenellations. The sections of raised wall between the gaps, which protected the archer, were called merlons.

At intervals in the wall and in towers of the castle, the builders cut narrow windows from which archers

▲ KEEPING THE NIGHT WATCH
Castles were defended day and night. Norman soldiers on the parapet check on the sentries manning the gatehouse and the curtain wall below.

could fire. These were called embrasures. When soldiers began to use cannon, the embrasures were made larger to fit the muzzles of the guns. Circular holes were cut at the base of arrow slits so that both the artillery men and the archers could fire from the same embrasure. This embrasure was known as a "cross-and-orb". Larger embrasures were covered by hinged shutters when they were not being used. From the outside, an embrasure looked like a narrow slit. On the inside, it opened up so that an archer could lean to one side and shoot at targets to the left or right. A variation on this design was the balistraria, a cross-shaped slit for crossbows.

If an enemy force reached the base of a wall the defenders had to lean out to attack them. This would leave them open to attack by enemy archers. The castle builders invented machicolation, which was made to

SLITS AND EMBRASURES

The walls and crenellations of castles were pierced with holes called embrasures. These were made so that the soldiers could fire arrows or crossbow bolts at their enemy below. Later, castle walls were pierced with loopholes for cannon and muskets. The hole was shaped to fit the kind of weapon being fired through it. On the inside face of the wall the sides of the embrasure were angled so that an archer or musketeer could shoot at targets to one side.

▼ ARCHER'S SLIT
The earliest kind of slit was made to fit arrows. Arrow slits also let light and air in to the inside of the castle and through the curtain walls.

▲ CROSSBOW EMBRASURE
This design was used by crossbow archers. It allowed them to aim at targets to the left or right of them, or even to track a moving target before firing their bolts.

▼ LOOPHOLE
When cannons began to be used, arrow holes were changed to fit them. A round hole was cut at the base of a narrow slit.

◀ CARCASSONNE
This walled city in southern France looks much the same today as it did in medieval times. It was so strongly defended, the only way an enemy could capture the city would be to starve the citizens.

▲ WINDSOR CASTLE
The towers on each side of the gatehouse at Windsor have machicolations at the top.

protect the defenders. This was a battlement wall built out on stone supports. It had embrasures that faced downwards so that defenders could drop rocks and stones on their attackers.

Henry VIII made many changes in the design of fortresses. To fight off the threat of French invasion in the mid-16th century he built a number of forts along the south coast of England. Their walls were not high, but low and massive. This was to provide a wide platform for cannons and large guns to stand on. As the power and range of cannons got better, the walls of fortifications became wider and lower.

◀ WALLS WITHIN WALLS
The Roman general Scipio, also known as Africanus, built a wall with seven forts around the Spanish city of Numantia. He then besieged the city for eight months in 133BC. Its 4,000 citizens finally gave in after Scipio had blocked off the river access.

▶ CITY WALLS
In ancient times cities were often under threat of attack and invasion. It was common to build fortified walls around the city for protection. This imposing wall surrounds the Moroccan city of Essaouira.

Key Dates

- 1451BC Walls of Jericho stormed.
- 598BC Nebuchadnezzar destroys the walls of Jerusalem.
- 493BC Piraeus, the port of Athens, made secure with fortifications.
- 478BC Athenian city walls restored.
- 457BC Athenian long wall built.
- 393BC Conon rebuilds long walls at Athens following their destruction by the Persians.
- AD93–211 Walls of Perge (southern Turkey) built by Septimus Severus.
- 447 Ramparts of Constantinople rebuilt after earthquake.

Defending Borders

▲ THE GREAT WALL
Large enough to be seen from space, this famous earthwork in China took centuries to build.

Most fortifications in ancient history have normally protected families and their retainers in castles, or citizens behind curtain walls with fortified gates. When the movement of large numbers of people threatens a civilization, bigger walls have to be built. The Great Wall of China and Hadrian's Wall in England are two very famous examples of land barriers made to defend whole territories.

The Great Wall of China was built over four distinct periods. The building of earthworks in 476–221BC was followed by the Great Wall of Qin Shi Huangdi (221–206BC). The Great Wall of Wu Di (140–86BC) and other emperors was finally finished as the Great Wall of the Mings (AD1368–1644). The Great Wall of China was originally built to delay Mongol attacks along the north frontier long enough for the main force of the Chinese army to get to the threatened area and defeat the enemy.

The Roman Emperor Hadrian toured northern Britain in AD122 and ordered the construction of a physical barrier against the lawless tribes in Caledonia (modern Scotland). At first, the barrier was made from

▶ HADRIAN'S WALL
Named after the Roman Emperor Hadrian, the wall was originally a wooden palisade with a bank and ditch. It was later rebuilt as a stone-faced wall 5m/16ft high and 2.5m/8ft thick. Small forts called milecastles were placed at every mile/1.5km along the wall.

Roman legionary

THE WORLD'S EDGE
The Romans and the Chinese had huge empires to guard. Just beyond their borders were people ready to invade. To mark and defend their borders, they built long walls or earthworks. A system of signals allowed sentries to alert the garrisons if raiders tried to cross the wall. Then soldiers could quickly get to the site to drive them off.

◀ LEGIONARY FROM AFRICA
Roman soldiers were recruited from all parts of the enormous empire. They were often sent on duty far away from their home country. This was to make sure they did not desert.

▲ WALLS AROUND WALLS
The Romans used walls and ramparts as weapons in their siege tactics, closing off a city or fort from any outside assistance or supplies and starving it into surrender. This is the siege of Massilia laid by Julius Caesar in 49BC. Massilia is modern-day Marseilles.

◀ MILE CASTLES
Protected from the Picts (the painted people) from the north by Hadrian's Wall, small towns grew up around the mile castles along the Wall. There were shops and markets, taverns and baths. Many of the Roman legionaries who manned the Wall married and settled down in the towns.

timber and turf. In its final form, Hadrian's Wall was just a stone wall. It ran from Wallsend on the east coast to Bowness in the west, a distance of about 118km/ 73 miles. The wall used natural features such as crags to give it extra height. It varied from 2.3m/7½ft to 3m/10ft in width and was 4.5m/15ft high with a crenellated parapet 1.5m/5ft above that. There were milecastles along the wall at regular intervals of one Roman mile (1,481m or 4,860ft) and two guard turrets between them. The milecastle was in a kind of gateway with a garrison of about 16 soldiers. The turrets may have been shelters for soldiers on guard or signal stations. Ten forts were built to house the garrison for the wall.

Hadrian's Wall was an effective military obstacle, and, like similar Roman barriers, it marked the limits of the Roman Empire. Beyond it were barbarians.

▶ JERUSALEM
The walls of the Holy City have been stormed and fought over ever since biblical times. Jerusalem is a city divided into the Jewish western area and the Arab territory in the east. The last battle took place in 1967 during the Six Day War between the Arabs and the Israelis.

◀ BUILDING THE GREAT WALL
During the Ming period, the wall was made from dressed ('finished') stone and brick. It was about 10m/30ft at its widest and varied in height from 7.5m/25ft to 12m/40ft. The parapet added an extra 1.5m/5ft. The top of the wall was wide enough for horses to gallop five abreast. Every 200 paces – about 150m/ 500ft – there were towers 3.5m/12ft high which straddled the wall. Crossbow archers could cover the gap between the towers north and south of the wall. Signal flags or beacons were used to pass messages between towers.

Key Dates

- 476–221BC Various earth walls built in northern Chinese provinces.

- 221–206BC Emperor Qin Shi Huangdi orders earth walls to be joined together to make the first Great Wall of China.

- AD100 Romans build walls (called limes germanica) across Germany and Romania.

- AD122 Emperor Hadrian orders wall to be built at northern edge of Roman Empire.

- 700s King Offa of Mercia, England, builds a dyke to separate England from Wales.

Under Siege

▲ OUT OF RANGE
Building a castle on a hill site with a moat and a narrow, easily guarded entry road makes it very hard for an enemy to capture it.

A SIEGE IS WHAT happens when an enemy army surrounds a castle or a city, planning to capture it. They can attack, or they can wait until the people inside get too hungry and surrender. A strong, well-stocked castle or fortified town could easily withstand a siege if their besiegers ran out of food. The defenders of a castle or even the wall around a town were higher up than the besiegers so they could see what the enemy was doing. They were also protected by a wooden palisade or a stone wall. From behind these walls, sniper archers could pick off the attackers as they came to the foot of the wall.

If the attackers reached the wall, they tried to make a hole in it so that they could get into the castle or city. Another way to get in was to climb the wall using ladders and grapnel hooks. This was dangerous, because the defenders waited until an attacker was half way up the ladder then pushed it away from the wall.

To attack the enemy camp the soldiers of the castle could use many of the weapons that the besiegers had been using. Each side lobbed rocks or cannon balls at

one another. If a battering ram was used, the defenders might try to set fire to it. Another way to disarm it was to use huge tongs hanging from a crane to grab the ram and pull it up inside the castle or curtain walls.

Castles often had secret passages leading to a hidden exit called a "sally port". This could be further down a river or along the coast and from here the defenders might make their escape if the siege became too severe. Sally ports were also very strong doors from which the defenders could launch quick raids on their attackers. The plan was to destroy the enemy's siege weapons, generally by setting them alight. The defenders would also capture prisoners and steal food stocks.

▶ HOT RECEPTION
As storming ladders are raised against a castle, defenders fight back by pouring boiling liquid on the shed protecting a battering ram crew.

HOLDING OUT
Siege was not always easy for the besiegers. If the castle was well defended and the people inside had lots of water and food supplies, they could sit out any number of attacks. If the siege went on for a long time, the besiegers could run out of food themselves, or die from disease and be forced to stop the siege.

◀ SIEGE SEE-SAW
The tenelon was a crane or see-saw with a basket on one arm. Troops inside the basket could be hoisted over the walls.

▲ WHO'S WINNING?
Every kind of siege weapon is used against the defenders in this castle keep. They are fighting back but seem to be outnumbered and may be running out of food. One of the soldiers is lowering a basket and water pot for supplies.

◀ A CASTLE FALLS
Battering rams, scaling ladders and towers can all be seen in action in this medieval siege. It is the end of the siege. The walls have been finally breached after heavy bombardment and the besiegers are within the walls.

◀ ROMAN SIEGE
The Roman army were very successful at sieges. They invented many techniques and siege engines. In this scene, the besiegers are attacking on three points. A ram batters at the tower. Soldiers advance under cover of their shields locked into the testudo, or tortoise, formation. Some have reached the wall and are scaling it. A tenelon hoists men on to the far tower. The defenders crowd the battlements, but they only have rocks to throw at the enemy.

Key Dates

- 415–413BC Siege of Syracuse. Athenians fail to take city.

- AD70 Siege of Jerusalem, part of the Jewish Wars of the Roman Empire.

- 1189–91 Siege of Acre (Israel), part of the Third Crusade.

- 1487 Siege of Malaga.

- 1544 Siege of Boulogne.

- 1565 Siege of Malta, part of the wars of Islam. Turkish army try to capture Malta from Christian forces. They fail.

- 1688–89 Siege of Londonderry.

Siege Attack

T HE ROMANS HAD A VERY SUCCESSFUL method of siege attack. First, they would take a good look at the target fort or city to see if a siege would be practical. They would then surround their objective with an outer belt of soldiers so that it could not be relieved by friendly forces and set about systematically destroying it. Several specialist weapons were needed to do this. The most important was the siege tower.

Historic pictures of siege towers often show something that looks like a mobile multi-level building. The height varied. The three iron-clad towers used by the Romans in the Siege of Jerusalem in AD70 were 10m/30ft high with catapults on top. The towers were fitted with drawbridges that were lowered to span the gap to the castle wall. The military engineers Gaston de Bearn and William de Ricou, employed by the

Crusaders in 1099 in another siege of Jerusalem, designed two towers of about the same height as the ones the Romans used.

The earliest descriptions we have of siege weapons come from around 400 to 200BC. Among them were those developed by the engineer Diades, who worked with Alexander the Great. Diades developed two unusual siege weapons, which do not seem to have been copied by future generations. The first one was a mural hook, also known as a crow. It was slung from

Siege tower

Animal skin covering

Battering ram

▶ ANCIENT ATTACKERS
Babylonian siege machines batter down the walls of an enemy fortress while archers fire on the walls.

▲ SIEGE GRIFFIN
A fantasy siege engine designed to be winched towards the enemy as it fires the cannon from its mouth. The ramp in the chest would be lowered for the assault.

SIEGE TOWERS
In order to reach the top of the walls and take on the defenders soldiers had to be at the same height and within range. Mobile siege towers could be pushed forward until the soldiers inside them could fire at the enemy and eventually cross simple drawbridges on to the walls.

Mantlet

◀ ALEXANDER
Alexander the Great was a fine general. He laid many sieges. The best known was the Siege of Tyre, a fortified town. It lasted for seven months.

▲ MOBILE SHIELD
The mantlet was either a row of fixed hurdles, or in this example a mobile shield which could be wheeled close to the enemy wall to give cover to archers.

a wooden gantry like a ram but it had a huge double clawed hook. This was used to pull down the battlements along the top of a city or fortress wall. The second was the telenon, a kind of crane. A large box or basket hung from it. Soldiers got into the basket and were swung on to the enemy's walls to attack.

Smaller items were also used. Scaling ladders were lightweight ladders, sometimes with hooks at the top. The besiegers used these to assault the walls. The soldiers would run forward, fix the ladders in position and scramble up them.

Grapnels or grappling hooks were hooks attached to a length of rope. Soldiers would throw the grapnel so that it hooked over the parapet of the wall and then climb up the rope.

While the soldiers were climbing the walls, archers would keep shooting from behind their mantlets to keep the enemy occupied. Otherwise the defenders would just cut the ropes or push away the ladders.

▼ GOING IN
The drawbridge on an Assyrian siege tower crashes onto the enemy wall as the assault party storms in.

Another way to get inside was by using a trick. In the Trojan War between the Greeks and the Trojans, the Greeks pretended to give up. They gave the city of Troy a large wooden horse as a parting gift. The Trojans took it inside the city, not realizing that there were Greek soldiers hiding inside the horse. Once inside the city walls, the Greeks jumped out and, after some fighting, they took the city and won the war.

◄ ENGINEERS AT WAR
The Romans were masters of the planning and building work as well as the tactics of a siege. The siege of a large city was like a major engineering operation. Large numbers of timber structures had to be made very quickly and put into position. Sieges could go on for many years so any building had to be quite sturdy.

Key Dates

- 612BC Nineveh (modern Iraq), capital of the Assyrian Empire, besieged and destroyed.

- 1346-47 Siege of Calais. Town officials prepare to die following surrender.

- 1429 Siege of Orleans relieved by Joan of Arc.

- 1453 Siege of Constantinople. Turks take the city ending the Holy Roman Empire.

- 1871 Siege of Paris. Citizens driven to eat zoo animals.

Bombardment

BEFORE SOLDIERS had cannons, bombardment weapons were built based on natural forces. Classical and medieval siege weapons worked on one of three principles: spring tension, torsion or counterweight. Spring tension weapons were like giant crossbows. They used springy wood that bent easily, such as ash or yew.

▲ GETTING YOUR OWN BACK
In this medieval picture, trebuchets are used to lob the severed heads of prisoners over the walls of a castle.

Torsion means twisting. Torsion weapons were powered by twisted rope. The tighter it was wound up, the more power there was when it was released. This method could be used to fire stones or javelins. The Romans of the 3rd century AD nicknamed one of their torsion weapons onager, meaning "wild ass". This was because of the violent kick of the machine's arm when the rope was released. They used a rope made from human hair for this weapon as it was very elastic.

The ballista was a little like a crossbow. The tension was produced by bending two lengths of wood held in coiled cord or braided hair.

The counterweight weapon or trebuchet reached Europe from China around AD500. It was like a giant see-saw with a heavy weight at one end and a sling at the other. A stone or other missile was placed in the sling which was tied down so the heavy weight was in the air. When it was released, the weighted end would drop and lob the stone.

Stones were not the only thing that the trebuchet threw. Burning materials were hurled over the walls to try to start fires. Corpses of humans and animals were also thrown. This was to spread infection and to bring down the spirits of the defenders.

Looking at these weapons today, they seem crude and simple. However, in medieval Europe, with its poor roads and simple carpentry tools, building a weapon such as a trebuchet or a catapult and bringing it into action was a very impressive feat.

▶ WILD ASS
The onager or wild ass was developed about the 3rd century AD. It earned its name from the violent kick from the throwing arm when the ratchet was released.

Throwing arm   Release lever
Hair rope
Sling

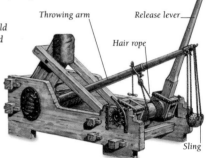

GUIDED MISSILES
Before gunpowder, muscle power was used to throw missiles at the enemy. Soldiers had to be very strong to stretch or twist the ropes and springs or lift the heavy counterweights that gave catapults and trebuchets their power.

▲ ARCHIMEDES
A Sicilian scientist, Archimedes designed weapons for the defenders of Syracuse during the siege of 213–212BC. His engines were very effective against the Roman fleet.

▶ GREEK FIRE
Siege machines could be adapted to throw 'Greek fire', a mixture of chemicals, over the walls to burn the enemy.

◀ MASS ATTACK
This machine was designed to fire a barrage of arrows or javelins at one time. It was probably not very accurate.

◀ BALLISTA
The Romans developed the ballista, a weapon to launch missiles at the enemy. It worked rather like a crossbow and could be adapted to suit various kinds of ammunition. A light field ballista such as this could fire stones or javelins.

▼ CATAPULT
Protected by a mantlet, three soldiers tighten the tension on a catapult while a fourth prepares a stone for launching. The largest catapults could fire a 22.5kg/5½lb stone as far as 365m/1,200ft.

▶ ROMAN INVASION
In AD43, the Romans invaded Britain in the south. They got as far north as the Plautian frontier, named after the Roman leader Plautus. Maiden Castle in Dorset was the site of a battle between the Britons and the Romans. At this battle, catapults and ballista were used by the Roman army. There had been a fort of some kind on this site since the Stone Age, but by the time the Romans came, it was well fortified by ramps, walls and dykes.

Irish Sea

North Sea

Plautian Frontier Zone

Camulodunum (Colchester)

R. Thames

N

Maiden Castle

Gesoriacum (Boulogne)

Noviomagus (Chichester)

0   Kilometres 150
0   Miles   100

Key Dates

- 400–200BC Catapult introduced into Rome from Syria.

- 211BC Mounted crossbow, possibly designed by Archimedes, in use to defend Syracuse.

- AD100 Greeks build a catapult with an iron frame.

- 101–107 Ballista used by Romans in the Dacian wars (central Europe).

- 300 Onager in use with Romans. It was still used in medieval times.

- 1250s Trebuchet in extensive use.

- 1000–1400 Spring engines used in medieval Europe.

Ramps, Rams and Mining

So THAT THEY COULD BRING their weapons in closer to the enemy, besieging troops built ramps outside the walls of the city or castle. Ramps or causeways were needed to cross ditches or moats filled with water. Ideally more than one ramp would be built so that the enemy would not know where the main assault was going to fall. The Romans pioneered the technique of building a ramp, known as an agger, from hurdles, packed earth and stone.

Once the besieging forces had filled in the moat and built a ramp up to the enemy's walls, the battering ram was wheeled into position. The battering ram was one of the oldest siege weapons. It was made from a heavy tree trunk hung on chains from a timber frame. The whole thing was covered by a wooden shelter called a penthouse. The roof and walls of the penthouse were often covered with animal hides that were kept wet as a protection against fire.

The battering ram could have a metal knob, sometimes in the shape of a ram's head, that was mounted at the front end of the tree trunk. By swinging the ram and driving it against the wall, the soldiers operating it would, with time and effort, make a hole.

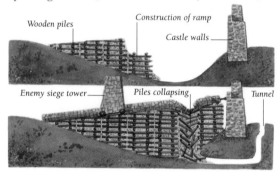

Wooden piles — *Construction of ramp* — *Castle walls* — *Enemy siege tower* — *Piles collapsing* — *Tunnel*

▲ ROMAN RAMP
The agger or ramp is protected by flanking towers. Soldiers work on the ramp under long protective sheds.

▶ UNDERMINING
Defenders could destroy a ramp by digging a tunnel under its wooden piles and setting fire to them to make the ramp collapse.

BATTERING TO VICTORY
The battering ram was the heavyweight siege weapon used to smash holes in the walls of a castle or town. There were many different designs. It was an accepted rule in Roman siege tactics that once the ram had been brought into action, the defenders within the fort or town could expect no mercy when the walls finally came down. So a ram was a frightening weapon in more ways than one.

◀ DEMONSTRATION
This picture shows how an 11th-century ram worked. In a real battle, the ramming crew would be protected from fire and missiles by a penthouse.

▲ GREEK BATTERING RAM
This wheeled tower is a two-in-one weapon. The ram batters the wall while the arm above it pulls down the castle battlements.

▶ RAM TOWER
Rams could be carried on the shoulders or mounted on wheels. This ram tower was pushed forward on wheels or rollers until it was within range of the castle wall. The gantry structure allowed the crew to develop a good, powerful swing with the ram.

◀ HOOKING A RAM
A hook mounted on a crane grabbed the siege weapon, which could be lifted and dropped until it broke up.

Mining was another way to break through a city or castle wall. First, the attackers would build an easy-to-move shelter and put it against the wall. Protected under the shelter, the soldiers could begin to knock down the wall. They supported it with wooden beams so that it did not fall down too soon. When enough of the wall had been weakened in this way, a fire would be lit under the beams. When the beams had been weakened by the fire, the wall collapsed, and the besieging forces could then storm across the gap that had been created. The soldiers inside the castle could dig their own mine beneath the attackers' mine shaft. They could try to make the enemy's mine collapse, or fight underground.

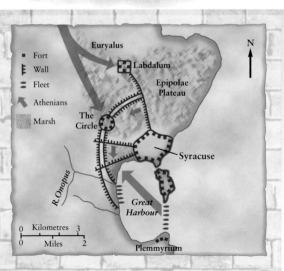

▶ SYRACUSE
The map shows the Siege of Syracuse in 415BC by the Athenians. They built the square fort at Labdalum and a circular fort with surrounding siege walls. But Syracuse held out and inflicted Athens' greatest defeat. The Athenians lost nearly 200 ships and 40–50,000 soldiers.

Euryalus

N

■ Fort
Ɛ Wall
⊒ Fleet
➔ Athenians
▨ Marsh

Labdalum

Epipolae Plateau

The Circle

R. Onopus

Syracuse

Great Harbour

0 Kilometres 3
0 Miles 2

Plemmyrium

Key Dates

- 429–427BC Plataea, in Greece, besieged using ramps and defeated by Spartans.

- 415–413BC Siege of Syracuse (Sicily). Archimedes, born in Syracuse, designs some of the defensive machinery.

- 52BC Siege of Alesia in Gaul. Vercingetorix the Gaulish leader finally surrenders to Romans.

- AD72 Siege of Masada, Jerusalem. Romans build ramps to get over the huge walls of the fortress. Many defenders kill themselves rather than be captured.

Gunpowder Arrives

▲ POWDER RECIPE
The formula for gunpowder – one part sulphur, six parts saltpetre and two parts charcoal – was first written down by the Englishman Roger Bacon around 1242.

SOLID GUNPOWDER turns quickly into gas when burnt. If it is loose, gunpowder produces a flash, a cloud of white smoke and not much noise. If it is enclosed, the noise and the explosive force increases. This produces energy which can be used to push a solid object along a tube, or to blow up a building. The first use of gunpowder

in battle in Europe was by the British at the Battle of Crécy (1346). King Edward is said to have had three to five guns which were called roundelades or pots de fer because of their bottle or pot shape. Early weapons fired stones or arrows similar to crossbow bolts.

Cannon design did not change much over three hundred years. Gunpowder was poured into the open end or muzzle, and then packed down with a rammer. The packed gunpowder was secured in place with wadding, which was rammed home. A cannon ball was then loaded. Loose gunpowder was poured down the touch hole, a small hole at the closed end of the cannon. It was lit using a slow match, a length of rope soaked in saltpetre, which would burn slowly. The explosion that followed pushed the cannon ball out of the gun muzzle. It could reach ranges of between

Penthouse

▶ WHEELED CANNON
Protected by a penthouse this cannon sits on a simple frame that allows the crew to move it around the castle to fire stones at the enemy battlements. The cannon is held in place with guy lines and pegs which absorb the recoil when it fires and ensure it is correctly aligned.

Cannon

Wooden frame

EXPLOSIVES
Gunpowder was first used in Europe for weapons in the 14th century. It had been used in China since the 11th century to fuel battlefield rockets. It was more powerful than ropes, counterweights or springs, but gave off great clouds of smoke.

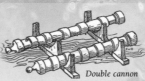

Double cannon

▶ HAND MORTAR
A 16th-century short-barrelled weapon used for lobbing shot into enemy ranks.

◀ DOUBLE SHOT
These cannons are on a static mount and would be fired in quick succession against a wall or gate – almost like a double-barrelled weapon.

Hand mortar

▲ HAND CANNON
The hand cannon was first used in 1364 and was the first step towards hand guns as we know them today. The gunner had to support his heavy firearm with a forked pike to keep it steady.

▶ SNAKE GUN
This drawing by the artist Dürer shows a cannon called a serpentine as it was thought to look like a snake or serpent. Many early cast cannon were shaped to look like serpents.

Serpentine

200m/650ft and 700m/2,300ft depending on the size of the cannon and the ball. By the 1860s, ranges for a 5.5kg/12lb cannon ball fired using a 1.1kg/2½lb charge had increased to 1,500m/5,000ft.

The ninth Siege of Constantinople by the Turks from April to May 1453 is the first example of the power of cannon. Constantinople was then the capital of the Eastern Roman Empire. It was ruled by Constantine XI. The Turkish leader was Sultan Muhammed II. A Hungarian engineer called Urban made a very long bronze cannon for the Turks.

◀ ENGLISH GUNS
One gunner raises the mantlet as the other prepares to light the touch hole to fire the stone ball.

▲ CANNON WITH COVER
Early cannon were built in a similar way to beer barrels. Lengthways cast iron strips were bound with iron hoops and mounted in a static wooden carriage.

It measured 8m/26ft and was capable of throwing a 660kg/1,450lb stone 1.6km/1 mile. Loading and firing took some time, so the weapon could only fire seven times a day. After 12 days of heavy bombardment, the Turks had broken through the walls of the city. Constantinople fell on May 29, 1453.

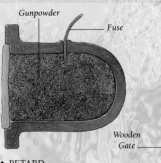

Gunpowder

Fuse

Wooden Gate

▲ PETARD
The petard was an explosive device designed to blast wooden gates. It was used by army engineers of the 15th and 16th centuries. It looked rather like a cut-down cannon. It was about 30cm/12in long, 25cm/10in wide, weighed about 27kg/60lb and had a touch hole and open muzzle.

▼ USING THE PETARD
The petard was attached with its muzzle pressed up against the wooden gate and then the fuse was lit. This was a dangerous thing to do, particularly if the fuse was too short or burned too fast. If the device detonated too soon, the user could be caught in the explosion – literally hoist by his own petard.

Key Dates

- 1242 Roger Bacon writes down the formula for gunpowder.

- 1324 Cannon believed to have been used at siege of Metz, in France.

- 1342 Reports of cannon at siege of Algeciras, Spain.

- 1346 Confirmed use of cannon at the battle of Crécy, France.

- 1450–1850 Most cannon were cast in bronze, iron or brass.

- 1500 Metal shot had replaced stone.

- 1571 At the battle of Lepanto, Greece heavily gunned galleys were used.

War at Sea

▲ OAR POWER
There were many kinds of warship design. This is a Greek galley with a single bank of oars.

▼ OARS AT WORK
There were three layers of galley slaves in a trireme. To be effective they had to be able to row in time, so they probably used a drum to keep the time. Clearly the best position was on the top row.

THE MEDITERRANEAN Sea was central to the ancient world. Its name means "in the middle of the earth". Many countries depended on it for food and trade. Whoever controlled the sea, therefore, had power over all the countries which surrounded it.

The Mediterranean has hardly any tides. Ships were not dependent on the tide coming in to launch and could not become stranded when the tide went out. The sea became part of the battlefield. Fighting methods and weapons were much the same as they were on land. The key to sea fighting was transport. Fast boats with a reliable power source usually won the battle. The Greeks, Romans, Persians and Carthaginians all developed warships which could deliver troops quickly to the scene of the battle. As each would try to stop the other, they adapted land weapons for use at sea, such as grappling hooks, siege towers and catapults.

A good general used sea power to help his land battles. The tactics developed by the ancient sea

SEA POWER
Most warships relied on banks of galley slaves to row them into action. Some ships had sails that could be used when the wind was blowing in the right direction.

◀ XERXES
This Persian king came to power in 486BC and launched a massive land and sea assault on Athens and her allies in 480BC but he was defeated.

▶ THE BATTLE OF SALAMIS
This classic sea battle was fought in 480BC between the Athenians led by Themistocles and the Persians under Xerxes.

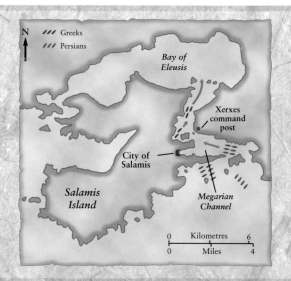

N

/// Greeks
/// Persians

Bay of Eleusis

Xerxes command post

City of Salamis

Salamis Island

Megarian Channel

| 0 | Kilometres | 6 |
| 0 | Miles | 4 |

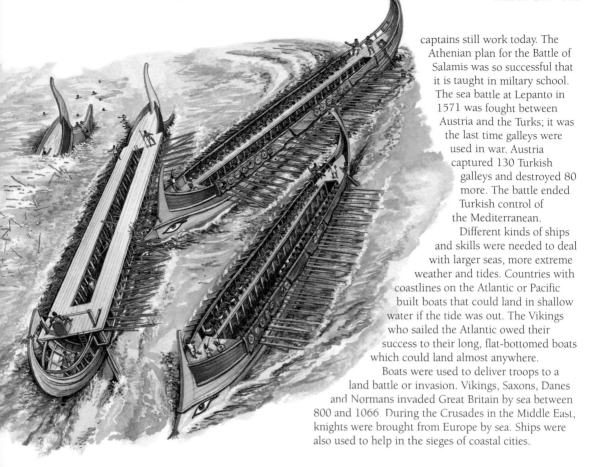

captains still work today. The Athenian plan for the Battle of Salamis was so successful that it is taught in miltary school. The sea battle at Lepanto in 1571 was fought between Austria and the Turks; it was the last time galleys were used in war. Austria captured 130 Turkish galleys and destroyed 80 more. The battle ended Turkish control of the Mediterranean.

Different kinds of ships and skills were needed to deal with larger seas, more extreme weather and tides. Countries with coastlines on the Atlantic or Pacific built boats that could land in shallow water if the tide was out. The Vikings who sailed the Atlantic owed their success to their long, flat-bottomed boats which could land almost anywhere.

Boats were used to deliver troops to a land battle or invasion. Vikings, Saxons, Danes and Normans invaded Great Britain by sea between 800 and 1066. During the Crusades in the Middle East, knights were brought from Europe by sea. Ships were also used to help in the sieges of coastal cities.

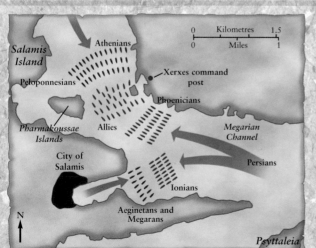

◄ TACTICS
The Persian fleet of 1000 ships had trapped the 370 Greek triremes in the Megarian Channel. The Greeks retreated northwards, luring the Persians into the narrow waters near Salamis. Once there, the Persian fleet could not move. The Greeks turned and went on the attack. They sank 300 Persian galleys and lost only 40 ships of their own.

Key Dates

- 480BC Battle of Salamis. Greeks beat Persians.

- 31BC Battle of Actium. Caesar Octavian defeats Mark Antony in Roman Civil War.

- AD1340 Battle of Sluys between French and English as part of 100 Years War. Warships become battlefields.

- 1571 Battle of Lepanto. Austrians beat Turks.

- 1588 England defeats Spanish Armada.

Sail or Oar?

I N THE ANCIENT WORLD, trading ships used sails and windpower to move around the seas. Captains of warships could not rely on winds and tide alone. They used manpower as well. Greek, Roman, Turkish and Spanish ships used massed oarsmen. Others, such as the Anglo-Saxons, Norsemen and Normans, used a combination of sail and oars. The French and British preferred sail-powered vessels and improved their design through the centuries.

The Greeks were first with the oar-driven warship. They used vessels called triremes which had three rows of oars and 150 rowers. Athenian sailors developed a way of fighting using their rowing skills. They would approach an enemy ship at full speed, come alongside and at the last minute pull in their oars. This smashed

◀ ARMED GALLEY
A Roman sculpture shows the banks of oars with armed soldiers at the ready on deck.

▲ THE MARY ROSE
Henry VIII's flag ship was armed with cannons low down which could fire broadsides.

A HARD LIFE
Few people wanted to row a galley. Criminals in countries such as Italy or Spain in the 15th and 16th centuries were often condemned to the galleys as a punishment. Prisoners of war were also made to row in their enemy's galleys.

▶ OARS AT WORK
There were three layers of galley slaves in a trireme. To be effective they had to be able to row in time, so a drum was used to beat out the rhythm.

▲ GALLEY SLAVES
Chained to their benches in the dark, hot, smelly hull of their boat, galley slaves could be worked until they died. Their bodies would then be thrown over the side.

◀ MEDITERRANEAN GALLEY
Fast, light, unarmed boats were used to transport troops. If the boat was sunk in battle, the soldiers and the rowers were picked up by their own side and the boat was abandoned.

▶ FLOATING BATTLES
Spanish and English ships engage in battle in 1372 as part of the Hundred Years' War. The warships sailed very close together and the soldiers fought across the decks as if on land.

all the oars on the enemy ship, which were still sticking out.

The oarsmen in the galleys were normally slaves. Some were convicted criminals, but many were prisoners of war. By the time of the Battle of Lepanto (1571) the Turks had smaller galleys called galiots with 18 to 24 oars, and the Venetians had developed a large vessel called a galleas. Galleys were equipped with sails so that with good winds they could operate without using the oarsmen.

The Scandinavian raiders who roamed as far away as the Mediterranean and Black Sea used both wind and manpower. Under Bjarni Herjolfsson, a Viking longboat reached North America in AD985. The Vikings could row their long, narrow boats when there was no wind or they were close inshore. Because the vessels were light and almost flat on the bottom they could land on gently shelving coasts or even mud flats.

By the 14th and 15th century, all warships in northern Europe relied on wind power. The sailors working in the tidal, stormy waters of the English Channel and North Sea needed to be highly skilled.

Under Henry VIII ship design began to change. By the time of the Armada, British warships were sleek and low. They were about 35m/115ft long and 10m/30ft wide and were called galleons. Like the galley, they were ships built specially for war. New designs in sails and rigging made the vessels even more seaworthy. The galleon was able to make long distance voyages and so it became the vessel used by navigators and explorers.

▲ FAST AND FURIOUS
Vikings used their fast boats to make lightning raids. They were able to sail as far as America. The chance of plunder and easy pickings made the risky journey worthwhile.

Viking warrior

Key Dates

- 241BC Lilybaeum. After a long siege, Rome defeats Carthage, and Carthaginians lose 120 ships.

- AD655 Battle of the Masts. Moaviah governor of Syria attempts to capture Constantinople from the sea.

- 841 Vikings reach Dublin.

- 1027 Normans land near Naples and establish stronghold.

- 1281 Mongol invasion of Japan defeated by "divine wind" or "kamikaze".

- 1588 Spanish Armada in running battles with the English fleet along the south coast of England.

Ramming and Grappling

B EFORE GUNPOWDER ALLOWED SHIPS to stand off at a distance and bombard one another, warships used light siege weapons, archers and slingers. The siege weapons could kill and injure people and damage sails and rigging. The archers and slingers acted as snipers, picking out targets on the enemy ships. Ramming could cause major damage. From the Greeks in 600BC to the Spanish Armada of 1588, galleys powered by oars were fitted with a long ramming beak. The trick was to drive this into the hull of the enemy ship.

▲ GREEK FIRE
Fire can be used as a weapon at sea. "Greek fire", an inflammable chemical, was used by Byzantine ships around the 4th century.

▲ SHIP RAM
This massive bronze-cased ram could easily pierce the hull of an enemy ship if it struck broadside.

The Romans introduced a new weapon in 260BC at the Battle of Mylae in Sicily. The corvus or "crow" was a hinged gangplank with a weighted hook. It could be swung out over an enemy ship and dropped so that it was stuck in the deck. Then a boarding party raced across the corvus on to the enemy ship. The Romans won at Mylae and took control of the Mediterranean.

Grappling irons, hooks with heavy chains, were later used in sea battles to assist boarding. Once the ships were alongside and the boarding parties in action, the fight became a land battle at sea, with hand-to-hand combat. Medieval ships showed this in their design with crenellated wooden "castles" in the bow and stern.

WAR AT SEA
Before gunpowder changed war, ships could ram the enemy, or slice off their oars. Other weapons were the corvus and twin-hulled siege vessels which could carry fighting towers.

◀ DECORATIVE RAM
This finely worked prow with its ram shaped like a row of swords shows the quality of the work on classical warships.

▲ ROMAN SEA BATTLE
Some sea battles between the Romans and Carthaginians were on a huge scale, with ships locked together as boarding parties fought.

▲ FIRE SHIP
This ingenious little ship is designed to carry a tub of burning tar into the middle of an enemy fleet at anchor. It could damage rigging and sails and had the potential to sink ships much larger than itself. The English sent fire ships like this one against the Spanish Armada when it was at anchor.

▶ CROWS AND TOWERS
The Romans developed a grappling weapon called a corvus, the Latin word for crow. It looked rather like a crow's big beak. It was a hinged gangplank with a hook which sank into the enemy ship's deck. Special twin-hulled siege vessels could carry fighting towers to the enemy.

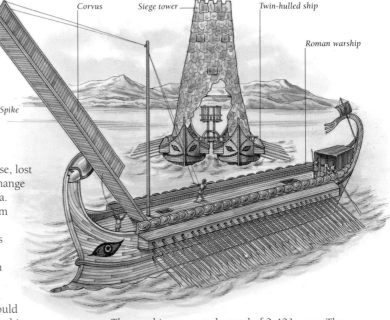

Corvus — Siege tower — Twin-hulled ship

Roman warship

Spike

This is why the front of a ship is known as the forecastle or fo'c'sle.

The English warship the Mary Rose, lost off Portsmouth in 1545, marks the change from ancient to modern warfare at sea. When she was recovered in 1982 from the mud into which she had settled, her weapons included both longbows and cannon. The ship was designed without castles but with gun ports on the lower decks. Heavy broadside cannons stood on these gun decks. When they opened fire, their shot would damage the hulls and masts of enemy ships.

In the running battle with the Spanish Armada in 1588, the English Royal Navy demonstrated that modern ship design, skilled sailors and good weather could shift the odds to the benefit of a smaller force. The Spanish had 20 great galleons, 44 armed merchant ships, 23 transports, 35 smaller vessels, four galleases (a double-sized heavily armed galley) and four galleys.

The warships mounted a total of 2,431 guns. The English had 68 ships in Plymouth, a London squadron of 30 ships and a further squadron of 23 in the eastern English Channel. Aside from seafaring skills and ship design, their strength lay in their 1,800 heavy cannon, mostly long-range cannons called culverins.

In running battles up the Channel the English finally prevented the Spanish from landing in England.

◀ ARMADA
Before dawn on July 28, 1588, the English sent fire ships into the Spanish fleet off Flanders as part of their running battle with the Armada. It forced the Spanish to cut their anchor cables. In the great sea battle that followed, only a storm prevented the English fleet from capturing or destroying 16 of the most damaged Spanish ships.

Key Dates

- 480BC Battle of Salamis, Greece. Greeks defeat Persians.

- 262BC Battle of Mylae, Sicily. Romans win and take control of the Mediterranean Sea.

- 241BC Battle of Lilybaeum, Sicily. Romans defeat the Carthaginians.

- 31BC Battle of Actium, Greece. Romans defeat Cleopatra and the Egyptians.

- AD1571 Battle of Lepanto. Christian Allies defeat Turks.

- 1588 Defeat of the Spanish Armada by the English.

Sailing to War

CARRYING SOLDIERS AND THEIR WEAPONS, vehicles, horses and food by sea and landing them on an enemy shore is called an amphibious operation. Amphibious means able to work on land and in water. In ancient times, this was a simple operation. Coasts weren't always defended and boats were flat enough to land directly on sand or shingle shores.

As ships became bigger, they had to remain off shore and troops transferred to smaller boats before they could land. Horses could swim ashore on their own, but artillery and wagons posed an extra problem. In bad weather these operations could be dangerous and so sailors and soldiers looked for sheltered anchorages where they could land and unload in safety.

One of the earliest recorded amphibious operations were the Punic Wars of 264–241BC between the Carthaginians, who lived in what is now Tunisia, and the Romans, in modern Italy. Both sides transported men and horses across the Mediterranean. The Carthaginian general Hannibal even took about 80 war elephants by ship from North Africa into Spain.

There were earlier operations. The most famous is described in Homer's Iliad, an epic poem that includes both myth and fact. To lay siege to Troy (a city located in what is now Turkey) the Greeks, under Agamemnon, had to sail across the Aegean Sea. Archaeological evidence of both Troy and the Trojan Wars dates the sea crossing to around 1200BC.

BATTLES BY LAND AND SEA

Islands could not be attacked without the use of ships. Sometimes the landings were the beginning of a long campaign. They could be part of the siege of a fortified port, or the means of escape for a battle fought on the coast. Vikings used their boats like a modern "getaway car", raiding a settlement and escaping quickly.

▲ HELEN OF TROY
The wife of the king of Sparta was so beautiful that her face was said to have "launched a thousand ships". She was kidnapped by Paris of Troy, which began the Trojan Wars.

▲ NATURAL LIFT
A Sumerian warrior uses an inflated animal skin as a float to help him to cross a fast-flowing river.

◄ TROOP CARRIERS
Boats like this one were used to ferry troops across the Mediterranean to fight battles on land.

At Marathon in September 490BC a Persian invasion fleet landed a force of 20,000 on the Greek coast near Athens. They were defeated by the Athenians, who numbered only 11,000, but despite heavy losses they were able to reach their ships and escape.

In Europe there was usually no need for soldiers to travel by sea. The waves of raids by the sea-going Saxons between AD205 and 577 and the Viking raids between AD800 and 1016 reached eastern England and northern France. They were not so much amphibious operations as military "smash and grab raids". The Anglo-Saxons and the Vikings eventually settled in the territories they had been raiding.

For island countries, such as Britain, that might be threatened by enemy landings, it was a good idea to build watchtowers and fortifications at the docks and other likely landing sites.

▲ THE NEW WORLD
In the 16th century, Spanish and Portuguese explorers sailed west and invaded large areas of South America.

▼ INVASION
In 1066, William of Normandy transported 9,000 men with all their horses and equipment for his invasion of England.

◀ THE BATTLE OF MARATHON
In 490BC Persia invaded Greece. The Persian leader Darius worked his way down from modern-day Turkey in the north, with a force of 150,000 men in ships. He landed an army 20,000 strong near Marathon. The Greeks met them on the coastal plain with about 11,000 soldiers and lost only 192 to the Persians' 6,400.

Key Dates

- 490BC Battle of Marathon. The Greeks defeat the Persians.

- 415BC Athenians land in Sicily and besiege Syracuse.

- 54BC First Roman invasion of Britain.

- AD43 Second Roman invasion of Britain.

- 400s Raids on England by Jutes, Angles and Saxons.

- 700s–800s Vikings raid Europe.

- 1027 Normans land in southern Italy.

- 1066 Normans invade England.

War Games

ETWEEN THE YEAR 1700 AND THE PRESENT DAY, the ways in which wars are conducted have changed beyond all recognition. Flintlock muskets have been replaced by automatic machine guns, and horses have been replaced by metal-shelled tanks and assault helicopters. Change has been most rapid during the last hundred years. World War I was fought mostly hand-to-hand, but the main battles of the Gulf War were fought using missiles and planes.

The introduction of steam power and petrol engines meant that soldiers did not have to rely on animals for transport, which could get tired or injured. The ships that relied on the wind for power were replaced by vessels that moved at greater speeds against winds and currents when powered by steam.

Metal plating, that had protected knights in the Middle Ages, found new uses protecting ships, land vehicles and even aircraft. New lighter, stronger, and even fire resistant materials were developed. These new materials were initially used to provide clothing to protect crews, but were later also used for fire fighters and the emergency services.

Before World War I people were optimistic about science. They believed that technological advances would make life safer, healthier and easier. In part this has been true, but science has also been used for war. Destruction on a huge scale has now become a reality. But though the two world wars led to the development of weapons of mass destruction (nuclear, chemical and biological weapons), they were also the spur for life-saving medical techniques.

▲ GRENADE
A hand grenade is a small bomb that can be thrown by hand. The Mills bomb was the first modern grenade, used by the British Army from 1915.

▼ KEY DATES
The panel charts the development of modern weapons, from early developments in gun design, to the introduction of stealth technology in modern aircraft.

▼ FORTIFICATIONS
As the technology of warfare has developed, the means of defending against ever-changing weaponry has altered dramatically.

PISTOLS AND ARTILLERY

The Gatling gun

- **1784** Invention of the Shrapnel shell.
- **1807** Forsyth patents the percussion ignition.
- **1835** Lefaucheux patents the pin-fire cartridge.
- **1835** Colt patents his revolver design.
- **1883** Maxim patents fully automatic machine gun.

- **1901** British 10-pounder cannon introduced.
- **1914–1918** World War I: long-range artillery in use.
- **1934** First general-purpose machine gun introduced.
- **1939–1945** World War II: self-loading rifle developed; recoilless guns, rocket artillery and anti-tank guns in use.
- **1947** Kalashnikov designs the AK47 assault rifle.
- **2002** A high-energy laser beam shoots down an artillery shell during a US military test.

Colt automatic pistol

FIGHTING ON THE LAND

- **1850** Morse Code invented.
- **1858** First aerial photography.
- **1865** First antiseptics used.
- **1882** Armoured steel developed.
- **1914–1918** World War I: land and sea camouflage developed.
- **1916** September: first tanks used in World War I.
- **1925** French demonstrate the half-track vehicle.
- **1939–1945** World War II: aerial photography and infra-red technology developed.
- **1943** Infra-red night-vision viewer used.

- **1944–1945** German missiles launched against Britain.
- **1944** June 6: D-Day, the largest amphibious operation in history, takes place.
- **1991** Iraqi SCUD surface-to-surface missiles launched in the Gulf War.
- **2002** Development of the Pulsed Energy Projectile (PEP), a kind of non-lethal stun gun.

World War II Sherman tank

▼ AVIATION
The development of military air power has been one of the most important changes to modern warfare. Controlling the skies above any battlefield has become critical to modern tactics, and critical to military success. Aircraft are now more deadly than ever. They can fly faster and for longer, and over greater distances carrying more weaponry than ever before.

The 1940s saw the rapid development of the aircraft as the jet turbine replaced the piston engine. New planes could fly further and with more weapons than had ever been possible before.

Radio communications began at the end of the 1800s as a laboratory experiment. One hundred years later it had become an essential part of the equipment of war. The world wars showed how important communication was, and scientists developed the technology to meet the demands of soldiers.

Helicopters had existed in a basic form before World War II, but by 1945, engineers in the United States and Britain were designing new, more powerful versions of these rotary wing craft. By the end of the 1900s the helicopter had become a life saver, lifting sailors from the sea or survivors from burning buildings.

The soldiers of the developed world are no longer troops sent just to fight. They have also become peace-keepers, attempting to prevent brutal wars. Fast communications allow them to keep their leaders informed about developments on the ground on an hour by hour basis.

▲ MOBILITY
The ability to move large numbers of troops and equipment quickly and easily is an essential part of any successful campaign.

▼ TECHNOLOGY
Warfare has always pushed back technological boundaries, from the first tanks to stealth bombers like this B-2 bomber.

FIGHTING ON THE SEAS

- **1805** Battle of Trafalgar.

- **1863** The steam-driven submersible *David* attacks Federal iron-clad ship.

- **1904** *Aigret*, first diesel-powered boat.

- **1906** Launch of HMS *Dreadnought*.

- **1914–1918** World War I.

- **1916** May 31: Battle of Jutland.

- **1939–1945** German U-boats use "wolf pack" tactics against Allied shipping.

- **1941** May 27: sinking of the *Bismarck*.

- **1942** June 4–7: Battle of Midway.

- **1944** June 6: D-Day.

- **1954** *USS Nautilus*, the first nuclear-powered submarine, is commissioned.

- **1961** *USS Enterprise* is first nuclear-powered carrier.

- **1966** Soviet Osa-class missile-armed craft enter service.

- **1990–1991** Osa-class craft see action in the Gulf War.

US Knox-class frigate

REACHING FOR THE SKIES

F86 Sabre

- **1903** Wilbur and Orville Wright make the first powered flight.

- **1907** September 29: first helicopter lifts a man off the ground into the air.

- **1912** Machine gun fired from aircraft for first time.

- **1914–1918** World War I.

- **1914** October 5: first aircraft to be shot down.

- **1939–1945** World War II: first strategic bombing.

- **1945** August 6 and 9: atomic bombs dropped on Japan.

- **1945** December 3: the first jet landing and take-off from an aircraft carrier.

- **1950** First jet-versus-jet victory in the Korean War.

- **1955** B-52 enters service with the United States Air Force.

- **1957** The first space satellite is launched.

- **1977** December: first flight of Lockheed Martin F-117.

- **1989** July 17: first flight of Northrop Grumman B-2A Spirit stealth aircraft.

- **1991** Gulf War: F-117 Nighthawk, B-52 Stratofortress and 300 helicopters are used in one of the largest air assaults of all time.

Pistols and Rifles

▲ RIFLEMAN
A 19th-century French soldier carries a bolt-action rifle.

YOU CAN SEE PISTOLS every day in most countries because police officers carry them. In thrillers and westerns, the heroes and villains are usually armed with pistols. You have probably seen lots of pistols, but do you know how they work?

There are two sorts of pistols. A revolver has a cylindrical magazine with six rounds of bullets. Newer pistols are self-loading, with a detachable box magazine that fits into the handle and can hold up to 14 rounds of ammunition. Rifles are bolt-action, semi-automatic or automatic weapons, and have a magazine that holds between 5 and 30 rounds. An automatic weapon automatically places the next round in the chamber for firing, so fires repeatedly when the trigger is pulled.

▶ RIFLES
British soldiers of the late 19th century use their massed firepower to compensate for the short range and inaccuracy of their flintlock muskets.

The most famous revolvers are the "Six Guns" used in the 1800s in the United States. These were famous as they enabled the user to fire six shots in quick succession. In World War I (1914–1918) and World War II (1939–1945), British troops used the .455in Webley MarkVI revolver or the .38in Enfield Number 2 Mark1.

The Germans used the Luger pistol as it was easy to reload. It was named after Georg Luger, a designer at the Ludwig Löwe factory in Berlin. It weighed 850g/2lb, had an eight-shot magazine and fired a 9mm round.

The US Army carried the .45in Colt 1911 self-loading pistol throughout both world wars, the Korean War and the Vietnam War. It weighs 1.11kg/2½lb and has a seven-round magazine. The Belgian 9mm Browning High Power was first manufactured in 1935. It weighs 1.01kg/2¼lb when loaded and has an effective range of 50–70m/160–230ft. Its magazine holds 13 rounds in two staggered rows – a feature copied in later designs.

The British used the bolt-action .303in Short Magazine Lee Enfield (SMLE) rifle during World War I and for

---

A SOLDIER'S TOOLS

The rifle and pistol have always been the tools of the infantryman. They are light and portable, and have become more accurate and faster firing. Cavalry, artillery and support troops such as engineers also carry these weapons, primarily for self-protection rather than attack. The rifle and pistol cartridge have also allowed the weapons' mechanical feed to be improved.

▲ THE US ARMY RIFLE
In the years before the American Civil War, the US Army used a .58in rifle. Rifling made the bullet more accurate by spinning it, causing the bullet to fly straighter. The bayonet was used in close-quarter fighting.

▲ SHORT MAGAZINE LEE ENFIELD (SMLE) BOLT-ACTION RIFLE
This compact rifle was 1.132m/3¾ft long, weighed 3.96kg/8¾lb and had a ten-round magazine. It was used by the British Army from 1907 to 1943. More than three million were made in Britain, India and Australia.

▲ BOLT ACTION
The Mauser action had five rounds. They could be loaded into the breech, the back part, by moving the bolt.

▲ THE AUTOMATIC
The US Colt 1911A1 (right) and Browning 1903 are two classic self-loading pistols. Their ammunition is in a magazine in the pistol grip.

▲ THE MI6
The MI6 is now widely used throughout the world. It was first used by the US Army in Vietnam. At that time the M16 was revolutionary because it fired a 5.56mm round, was made from plastics and alloys and weighed only 3.18kg/7lb.

much of World War II. The German 7.92mm Karabiner 98K was a very accurate weapon but only had a five-round magazine. The US Garand M1 rifle and M1 carbine were popular self-loading rifles during World War II as they were tough and reliable.

Two weapons have dominated armed conflicts since 1945; the US 5.56mm M16 Armalite rifle weighing 3.18kg/7lb, and the Soviet-designed 7.62mm AK47 weighing 4.3kg/9½lb. Both can fire on full automatic at 700 (M16) and 600 (AK47) rounds per minute (rpm).

▲ THE ENFIELD L85A1 RIFLE
This is the main rifle issued to British troops. It weighs 3.8kg/8½lb and is 785mm/31in long. On automatic it fires 5.56mm rounds at 700 rounds per minute (rpm). The Enfield L85A1 has been used in action in the Persian Gulf, in Kosovo and in Northern Ireland.

▼ THE SNIPER'S HIDE
In World War II, snipers built camouflaged positions called hides in which they could observe and shoot at the enemy. They were often concealed for long periods in the hides, which needed to be well built and weatherproof. This hide has an angled roof covered in turf.

A turf roof conceals the hide.

The hide is deep enough to allow the sniper to stand.

▲ THE SNIPER
A soldier is camouflaged to blend into the woodland. He aims his Accuracy International L96A1 7.62mm sniper's rifle. It is fitted with an optical sight.

Key Dates

- 1807 Dr Forsyth patents the percussion ignition.

- 1812 Pauly patents the first cartridge breech-loader.

- 1835 Lefaucheux patents the pin-fire cartridge.

- 1835 Colt patents his revolver design.

- 1849 The Minié rifle replaces smooth-bore rifles.

- 1886 French adopt the first small-bore smokeless-powder cartridge.

- 1888 Britain adopts Lee–Metford bolt-action repeater.

- 1939–1945 Self-loading rifle developed.

Automatic Weapons

▲ THE GARDNER
This early water-cooled, hand-cranked machine gun is mounted on an adjustable tripod. Its ammunition is fed into the chamber from the top.

THE FIRST MACHINE GUN dates back to 1718, when Puckle's gun was developed in Britain. It was a large hand-cranked revolver on a stand that fired seven rounds per minute (rpm). The Gatling gun was also hand-cranked. It fired at a rate of 100–200rpm. It was developed in the US in 1862 and used in the American Civil War.

The first successful automatic machine gun was the 7.92mm Maxim gun designed by the American (Sir) Hiram Maxim. It used the energy of the exploding cartridges to operate the mechanism and fired at 500rpm. This rapid firing rate heated up the barrel, so it was cooled by a water-filled jacket. The British used the Maxim gun in action in 1895.

The French Hotchkiss machine gun used the gases of the exploding cartridges to operate its mechanism. It had a heavier barrel designed not to need a water jacket, but that

cooled in the air. Ammunition was fed in on a cloth belt, where other similar weapons used metal belts.

The belt-fed British Vickers .303in machine gun was designed in 1891 and was not withdrawn from service with the British Army until 1963. The World War II German MG42 was a 7.92mm general-purpose machine gun (GPMG). Stamping and spot welding speeded its manufacturing process. It had a top range of 2,000m/6,500ft and fired 1,550rpm. Features of its design were copied in the postwar Belgian FN MAG and in the US M60 machine guns.

The first sub-machine guns (SMGs) fired

◀ THE GATLING GUN
The hand-cranked Gatling gun, used here by British soldiers, was introduced in 1862. Designed by Dr Richard Gatling, it had between six and ten barrels. It saw action in the American Civil War and was formerly adopted by the US Army during the Spanish-American War. Later models were mounted on a light artillery carriage.

SUB-MACHINE GUNS (SMGS)
The first sub-machine gun to go into service was the Italian Villar Perosa, which was used in World War I. SMGs fire pistol-calibre ammunition such as 9mm or .45in at the same rate as a conventional machine gun. They are not accurate over long ranges, but are ideal in situations where intense close- range firepower is required.

▶ THE STEN MK II SMG
This 9mm SMG weighs 3kg/6½lb empty and fires at 550rpm. Over two million were made in World War II.

◀ THE AK47
The AK47 assault rifle fires a 7.62mm round, which is halfway between a rifle round and a pistol round.

◀ THE TOMMY GUN
The Thompson M1 was the simplified World War II version of this SMG. It had a 30-round box magazine and weighed 4.74kg/10½lb empty.

▶ THE UZI SMG
The Uzi is a 9mm SMG developed in Israel. It weighs 3.5kg/6¾lb empty and fires at a rate of 600rpm.

pistol-sized ammunition and could be carried by one person. They were developed at the end of World War I. The .45in Thompson (Tommy) gun, designed in the 1920s in the US, became notorious in the US gang wars of the 1920s. It was widely used by British and American troops in World War II.

The World War II German MP38/40 was the first sub-machine gun to have a folding metal butt. This feature reduced its size from 833mm/32¾in to 630mm/25in. It fired at 500rpm and had a 30-round magazine.

Modern SMGs are compact and lightweight weapons. They are a common weapon for bodyguards as they can be carried inside jackets or briefcases.

▲ HELICOPTER MOUNTED
Machine guns were first fitted to helicopters by the French in the 1960s. They are now used by helicopters to protect the aircraft when flying into "hot" landing zones or to attack enemy infantry.

▲ VEHICLE MOUNTED
A Belgian 7.62mm MAG machine gun is mounted on a vehicle in the desert. The MAG is in service in many countries and can be mounted on a tripod for long-range fire, or on a built-in bipod for shorter ranges.

▶ THE M60
The poor reliability of the US 7.62mm M60 general-purpose machine gun in Vietnam earned it the nickname of "the Pig". It has since been modified and improved and is widely used across the world.

▼ BEATEN ZONE
A machine gun fires long bursts over long ranges, spreading its bullets in to a cone-shaped area called a "beaten zone". It is fatal or very risky for soldiers to enter this bullet-swept zone.

Machine guns are very effective defensive weapons when used in pairs. Two machine guns can be positioned so that they fire from the side across the path of an aproaching enemy. This arrangement makes their fire overlap, creating two overlapping "beaten zones". This combined fire power creates a doubly dangerous area for the enemy.

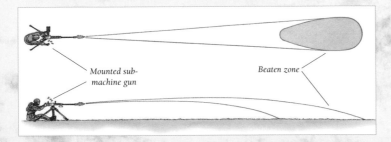

Mounted sub-machine gun

Beaten zone

Key Dates

- 1883 Maxim patents fully automatic machine gun.

- 1896 United States order Browning-Colt gas-operated gun.

- 1926 Czech ZB/vz26 light machine gun designed.

- 1934 MG34 introduced, the first general-purpose machine gun.

- 1942 MG42 creates the basis for many post-war designs.

- 1947 Kalashnikov designs the AK47 assault rifle.

- 1961 US Army evaluates Armalite rifle.

Artillery – Cannons and Mortars

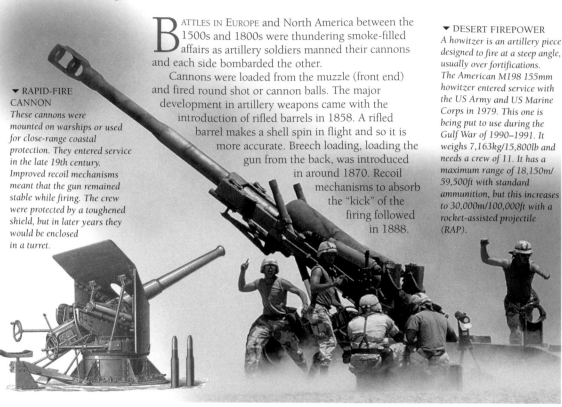

BATTLES IN EUROPE and North America between the 1500s and 1800s were thundering smoke-filled affairs as artillery soldiers manned their cannons and each side bombarded the other.

Cannons were loaded from the muzzle (front end) and fired round shot or cannon balls. The major development in artillery weapons came with the introduction of rifled barrels in 1858. A rifled barrel makes a shell spin in flight and so it is more accurate. Breech loading, loading the gun from the back, was introduced in around 1870. Recoil mechanisms to absorb the "kick" of the firing followed in 1888.

▼ RAPID-FIRE CANNON
These cannons were mounted on warships or used for close-range coastal protection. They entered service in the late 19th century. Improved recoil mechanisms meant that the gun remained stable while firing. The crew were protected by a toughened shield, but in later years they would be enclosed in a turret.

▼ DESERT FIREPOWER
A howitzer is an artillery piece designed to fire at a steep angle, usually over fortifications. The American M198 155mm howitzer entered service with the US Army and US Marine Corps in 1979. This one is being put to use during the Gulf War of 1990–1991. It weighs 7,163kg/15,800lb and needs a crew of 11. It has a maximum range of 18,150m/ 59,500ft with standard ammunition, but this increases to 30,000m/100,000ft with a rocket-assisted projectile (RAP).

BIG BOYS

Before aircraft that could drop large bomb loads had been developed, artillery was used to bombard fortifications or defend important locations such as ports and capital cities. The bigger the calibre (diameter of the barrel), the bigger the shell and so the greater the volume of explosives that could be enclosed in the gun. Big shells were therefore more destructive.

▶ US ARMY BREECH-LOADING HOWITZER
This siege howitzer is mounted on a turntable and has a hoist for loading.

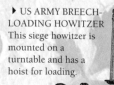

▲ RAILGUNS
Railways have been used to carry heavy guns and mortars since the American Civil War. The world's biggest guns were the German guns used in World War II.

▼ MODERN MORTAR
A soldier loads a British 81mm mortar with a high-explosive (HE) bomb. On the left a second soldier kneels ready with another bomb to ensure a rapid rate of fire.

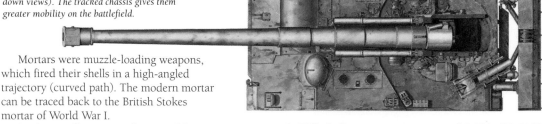

▲ SELF-PROPELLED GUNS
*The US 155mm M109 SP gun (above) and the US
203mm M110A SP howitzer (right: side and top-
down views). The tracked chassis gives them
greater mobility on the battlefield.*

Mortars were muzzle-loading weapons,
which fired their shells in a high-angled
trajectory (curved path). The modern mortar
can be traced back to the British Stokes
mortar of World War I.

Modern artillery ranges from World War II weapons
such as the huge 80cm German K(E) Gustav railway
siege gun to the tiny Japanese 70mm battalion gun Type
92. The K(E) Gustav fired a 4,800kg/10,600lb shell to
47km/29 miles. It had a crew of 1,500 men. The
Japanese gun, with a crew of five, fired a 3.7kg/8lb shell
to 1,373m/4,500ft.

World War II mortars included the massive German
60cm Karl, which was also used to bombard
Sevastopol, as well as Warsaw. It fired a 1,576kg/

3,474lb shell to a maximum range of 6,675m/21,900ft.
It was mounted on a tracked chassis, but this gave it
very limited mobility and it crawled along at only
10kmh/6mph. Karl mortars had a crew of 18. There
was also the little British 2in mortar. It weighed
4.1kg/9lb, fired a 1.02kg/2¼lb bomb to a maximum
range of 456m/1,496ft and had crew of two.

Recent developments include the M982 Excalibur,
an artillery shell with a range of 40km/25 miles, which
is guided by GPS (Global Positioning System).

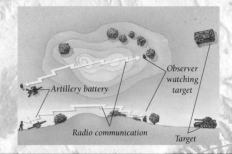

Key Dates

- 1784 Invention of Shrapnel shell.
- 1858 French adopt rifled artillery.
- 1870 Breech loading widely used.
- 1884 French develop smokeless gunpowder.
- 1888 Konrad Hausser develops long-recoil cylinder.
- 1899 Maxim "Pom Pom" automatic cannon in use.
- 1914–1918 World War I: long-range artillery developed.
- 1939–1945 World War II: recoilless guns, rocker artillery and anti-tank guns.

▲ TRAJECTORIES
Mortars and howitzers have a
high-angled trajectory and can
lob shells over obstacles. Field
artillery has a flatter trajectory.

▶ INDIRECT FIRE
An artillery battery may not see
its target when it fires. It can be
instructed to adjust its fire by
an observer who watches where
the shells fall.

Artillery – Pack Guns

▲ FIELD PIECE
Horse-drawn artillery consisted of the gun, the limber that contained the ammunition and charges, and the team of horses.

IN JULY 1999 the last Royal Tournament was held in London, England. It marked the end of the annual Royal Navy field gun race between crews from Portsmouth and Plymouth. The crews dismantled a Victorian 10-pounder mountain gun and raced across a series of obstacles before re-assembling it and firing a blank shell. It was an exciting test of strength and co-ordination. Pack howitzers like the 10-pounder were designed to be dismantled and carried by men or five mules across mountainous or rough terrain. If the pack artillery could then be assembled on a mountain ridge, their fire could dominate the roads through the valleys below.

The 10-pounder was used in India on the North-west Frontier between 1901 and 1915. It fired a 4.5kg/10lb shell out to 5,500m/18,000ft.

▸ ITALIAN PACK GUNS
Alpine mountain troops move their guns to new positions in World War I. Pack guns could be broken down into about four sections for ease of transport.

The gun became famous as the "screw gun" because its barrel broke down into two sections that were screwed together when it was assembled for firing.

The 10-pounder was replaced by the 3.7in pack howitzer that soldiered on during both World Wars. The howitzer's maximum weight was 2,218.2kg/4,890lb and it fired a 9.08kg/20lb shell out to 5,490m/18,000ft.

During World War II, the US 5mm M1A1 pack

MOVING ABOUT

Pack howitzers, or mountain artillery, and light anti-aircraft guns were designed to be dismantled so that they could be carried by troops or mules to remote mountaintop positions. Today's light guns can be carried by helicopter, which is faster and more reliable.

◂ MUSCLE POWER
Royal Navy sailors at the Royal Tournament in London, demonstrating how the British 10-pounder mountain gun can be dismantled and reassembled.

▲ ANTI-AIRCRAFT GUN
A Soviet-made, Iraqi ZPU-4 23mm anti-aircraft gun in a coastal position. It was captured in 1991 in Kuwait at the end of the Gulf War.

▲ CIVIL WAR CANNON
The breech-loading cannon used in the 1860s in the United States were very similar to those used during the Napoleonic Wars.

howitzer proved a very effective weapon for airborne forces. It was originally designed for carriage by six mules. The M1A1 fired a 6.24kg/13¾lb high-explosive shell out to 8,930m/29,300ft and weighed 588.3kg/1,297lb. The 105mm M3 howitzer was a bigger version of the M1A1 and weighed 1132.7kg/2,497lb. It could fire a 14.98kg/33lb shell out to 6,633m/21,760ft.

Postwar mountain artillery has been dominated by the Italian OTO Melara 105/14 Model 56 105mm howitzer. It was introduced in 1957 and since then more than 2,500 have been built. The Model 56 has been used by more than 17 countries. Its design is so good that it has been effectively copied in India with a 75mm pack gun howitzer. The Model 56 can be broken down into 11 parts that can be transported by mules or even carried on soldiers' backs for short distances. It weighs 1,290kg/2,845lb and can fire a 19kg/42lb high-explosive shell out to 10,600m/34,775ft.

The use of helicopters, and the widespread need for air mobility, make the requirement for light guns and pack howitzers almost universal. They can be transported slung beneath helicopters and brought into action very quickly.

The guns of the future will be constructed from new materials, many of which are currently used in modern aircraft design. These materials are strong but much lighter than steel and alloys.

▲ PACK HOWITZER
The Italian 105mm Model 56 pack howitzer in action. The shield can be removed to save weight. The howitzer's hinged trail legs can be folded, making the gun easier to transport.

▼ ANTI-AIRCRAFT FIRE
Anti-aircraft gun crews developed the skill of aiming just in front of a moving aircraft. This meant that the shell, with its time fuse, exploded as the aircraft flew into the blast and fragments. Radar now makes the job faster and easier.

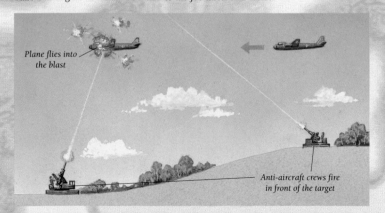

Plane flies into the blast

Anti-aircraft crews fire in front of the target

Key Dates

- 1901 British 10-pounder introduced.
- 1901-1915 The 10-pounder used on Indian North-west Frontier.
- 1914–1918 World War I: anti-aircraft guns used.
- 1932 Swedish 40mm Bofors anti-aircraft gun appears.
- 1936 German 8.8cm Flak 36 anti-aircraft gun developed.
- 1939–1945 World War II: American 75mm M1A1 pack howitzer used.
- 1957 Italian 105mm Model 56 pack howitzer appears.

Bombs, Rockets and Torpedoes

ROCKETS PROPELLED by gunpowder are a common sight across Britain on 5 November (Guy Fawkes' Night) and in the United States on 4 July (Independence Day). People watch as the rockets streak into the sky and burst into a shower of glittering stars. Rockets were originally used by the ancient Chinese as a weapon. They called them "fire arrows".

Later, in the 1800s, the British employed rockets against the French during the Napoleonic Wars. They were used in 1815 by a Royal Artillery troop at the battle of Waterloo. American and European armies experimented with them throughout the 1800s.

▲ TRENCH WARS
British troops on the Western Front in World War I, with a stock of mortars.

▶ STINGER SAM
The US low-altitude surface-to-air missile (SAM) has a maximum range of about 4,000m/13,000ft and a maximum speed of Mach 2.2. It has a 3kg/6½lb high-explosive warhead.

The self-propelled, or "fish", torpedo developed in the late 1800s revolutionized naval warfare. In World War I rockets were fitted to British fighter planes to attack German Zeppelin airships.

The first aerial bombs were used in World War I when pilots threw hand grenades at enemy troops. By the end of the war British bombers, such as the Handley Page 0/400, were carrying 600kg/1,300lb bombs to attack targets in Germany.

From World War II to the present day, bombs have been either high-explosive (HE) or incendiary devices. HE bombs are designed to explode on the surface or to penetrate reinforced concrete. Incendiary bombs burn at great heat and include napalm, a jellied fuel that splashes over a wide area. Cluster bombs are small HE bombs that are scattered from a larger container over a much wider area.

World War II rockets included the huge liquid-fuel German V-2, which was designed by Werner von Braun.

FLYING BOMBS

Aircraft and artillery use rockets and bombs to deliver high-explosive or incendiary payloads to target areas. Torpedoes launched from ships and submarines or dropped from the air proved very effective against ships of all sizes in World War II. Rockets have become a more effective weapon and are now launched from helicopters as well as from ships.

Safety pin and ring   Striker

Explosive

Detonator

5-second fuse

◀ HAND GRENADE
The British Mills bomb No 36 hand grenade was introduced in 1915. It uses a mechanism with two safety features; a pin and also a handle.

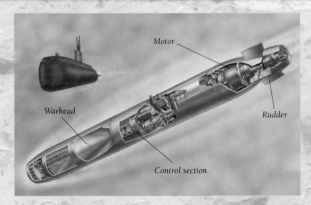

Motor

Warhead

Rudder

Control section

▲ TORPEDO
A torpedo consists of a warhead, fuel supply, motor and rudder. Modern weapons also have wire guidance systems and warheads like those of an anti-tank weapon. When the warhead explodes it can penetrate deep into a ship's hull.

◀ MULTIPLE ROCKET LAUNCHER
The US Multiple Rocket Launcher System (MRLS) was used in action during the Gulf War of 1990–1991. Its tracked chassis allows it to move rapidly around the battlefield, and it can reload in a few minutes.

Warhead

It weighed 13.6 tons and had a range of more than 300km/185 miles. Another World War II rocket was the crude but effective solid-fuel 8in rocket projectile (RP) fired from Allied aircraft.

Postwar rockets include intercontinental guided missiles with nuclear warheads, air-to-air missiles for combat aircraft, and anti-tank missiles with ranges of between 3,000m/10,000ft and 5,000m/16,000ft.

Robert Whitehead and Giovanni Lupis developed the first torpedo in 1866. It took its name from a Caribbean electric-ray fish. Torpedo boats were designed to carry the new weapon, and ships designed to destroy torpedoes, known as "destroyers", were in turn developed. The torpedo

Computer   Fuse

▲ SMART BOMB
The US Paveway laser-guided bomb follows the reflected laser energy bounced back from its target. Laser-guided bombs were first used in the Vietnam War.

made battleships vulnerable to attack by smaller vessels and submarines. In World War II torpedoes were also launched from aircraft. Modern torpedoes, with sophisticated guidance systems and warheads, are still carried by submarines. Torpedoes are also designed to seek and destroy submarines.

▶ ANTI-AIRCRAFT MISSILE
The British Rapier surface-to-air missile was first used during the Falklands War in 1982. It has a top speed of 650m/2,100ft per second and a range of 7,000m/23,000ft.

▶ ALFRED NOBEL
Swedish scientist Alfred Nobel (1833–1896) developed a range of high explosives. These included dynamite (1863) and nitrocellulose (1888), from which smokeless propellant was developed. Nobel's explosives changed warfare in the 20th century.

▲ CLUSTER BOMB
The cluster bomb unit (CBU) dropped from aircraft contains smaller bombs, or submunitions, that are ejected to scatter across the ground. The CBU is used against soldiers in open or unarmoured vehicles.

Key Dates

- 1860–1880 Hale rockets in use in Britain and US.

- 1890 Whitehead develops torpedo.

- 1903 Russian rocket engineer Konstantin Tsiolkovsky develops liquid-fuel rockets.

- 1944–1945 German V-1 and V-2 cruise missiles and ballistic missiles launched against Britain.

- 1981–1986 Air-launched cruise missiles enter service with US Air Force.

- 1991 Iraqi SCUD surface-to-surface missiles launched in the Gulf War.

Anti-tank Weapons

▲ EXPLOSION
A Swedish BILL anti-tank missile explodes above the turret of a target tank.

ANTI-TANK GUNNERS need to have the cool nerve of an old-style big-game hunter. As the enemy tank crashes towards them, perhaps firing its machine guns, the anti-tank crew must wait until their enemy is in range and then fire at its most vulnerable point.

As soon as tanks had appeared on the Western Front in World War I, all the combatants began to think of ways of stopping or destroying these machines by using anti-tank weapons.

The Imperial German Army developed a powerful bolt-action anti-tank rifle firing a .50in bullet. Most armies, however, relied on the crews of field guns to shoot it out with these early tanks. Anti-tank rifles were used by the British and Soviet armies in the opening years of World War II, but thicker armour and new weapons soon made them obsolete.

The true anti-tank gun, which was developed in the 1920s and 1930s, fired a very hard shell at high velocity. Early guns were between 37mm and 57mm in calibre. As World War II progressed the guns grew bigger, and the Germans used the 88mm anti-aircraft gun as a very effective anti-tank gun. The Russians used a huge 100mm gun.

The major change in anti-tank weapons came with the development of the shaped charge and short-range rockets. The shaped charge penetrated all conventional armour, while there was no recoil with a rocket projectile. The weapon that combined rocket and shaped charge was the American 2.36in rocket launcher M1. It was nicknamed the "Bazooka" after the musical instrument played by the US comedian, Bob Burns.

▲ INFANTRY ANTI-TANK
Anti-tank weapons may have a crew, for example the M40 106mm recoilless rifle or the TOW or Milan missiles, or they may be single-shot one-man weapons such as the M72 or the RPG-7.

PENETRATION

Most infantry anti-tank weapons have a shaped charge warhead. This consists of explosives shaped around the outside of a copper cone. When the warhead explodes the energy of the explosion is pushed inwards and forwards, creating a jet of molten metal and gas. A slug of metal at the front then melts its way through the skin of the tank.

◀ CARL GUSTAV
Canadian soldiers use the Swedish 84mm recoilless anti-tank weapon called the Carl Gustav. It can fire a wide range of ammunition.

▲ BILL
The launcher of the revolutionary Swedish BILL missile is fitted with a thermal imaging (TI) sight. It can detect the heat generated by the engine of a tank or fighting vehicle and use it as a target. This technology can also be used just as a night-vision device by troops on reconnaissance missions during darkness.

▸ FAIRCHILD A-10
The Fairchild A-10 has the official title Thunderbolt II, but is known as "the Warthog" by its crews. It has a powerful multi-barrel 30mm GAU-8 cannon in the nose and can also carry anti-tank missiles and bombs.

At the close of the war the Germans had looked at the concept of an anti-tank guided weapon (ATGW), which they designated the X-7. It had a range of 1,000m/3,300ft, weighed 10kg/22lb and would be guided to its target by signals passed along a light wire that was on a spool on the launching mount. The X-7 was reported to be capable of penetrating 200mm/8in of armour.

Most modern ATGWs are wire guided

because this is a reliable system that cannot be jammed by the enemy. Warhead design has changed as armour has improved, and now consists of two or even three shaped charges that detonate in succession. In 1979 Sweden produced a missile designated BILL, which explodes above the tank sending its shaped charge jet through the thin top armour. These two designs, called "tandem warheads" and "top attack", indicate the direction that anti-tank weapon technology will take in the 21st century.

◂ TANK DESTROYER
A British Alvis Striker firing a wire-guided Swingfire anti-tank missile. The Swingfire has a maximum range of 4,000m/13,000ft.

▾ LAW
The M72 LAW is a telescopic rocket launcher that weighs 3.45kg/7½lb. It has an effective range of 220m/720ft. It was first used in action in the Vietnam War, and later by the British in the Falklands in 1982.

▾ DESTRUCTION
An Iraqi tank destroyed by American A-10s during the Gulf War. The tank has almost blown apart because the ammunition and fuel inside have exploded. Internal explosions are a constant worry for all armoured vehicle crews.

Key Dates

- 1918 German 12mm anti-tank rifles in use.
- 1927 First dedicated anti-tank guns developed.
- 1942 "Bazooka" rocket launcher developed in US.
- 1943 German PaK 43/41 anti-tank gun enters service.
- 1956 French introduce Nord SS10 wire-guided missile.
- 1972 Euromissile Milan produced.
- 1973 Egyptians use Sagger guided missiles in Sinai.
- 1979 Swedish BILL developed.

Transport

WHEN ARMIES GO to war they use similar forms of transport to ordinary people – car, train, ship and aircraft. For centuries they relied on human or animal power for transport. Oxen, horses and mules pulled wagons and guns; and troops carried heavy loads in packs.

Ships were vital for island nations such as Britain because they could transport troops overseas and, if necessary, evacuate them. In World War II amphibious operations became highly specialized, with landing craft designed to put troops and vehicles ashore on open beaches.

The steam locomotive made troop transportation faster and allowed large numbers of troops and equipment to be moved around. The American Civil War (1861–1865) demonstrated the importance

of a reliable railway system. Railway lines and particularly bridges became a key target for raids by troops and, later on, by aircraft.

At the beginning of World War I vehicles such as taxis and buses were used to move troops quickly. Later, trucks became more readily available. Huge numbers of trucks were used in World War II, increasing the need for fuel supplies. After D-Day in June 1944 a fuel pipeline was laid from Britain to northern France across the Channel. It was codenamed PLUTO, which stands for Pipe Line Under The Ocean.

Among the wheeled vehicles produced in World War II the ¼-ton

◀ MOTORBIKE
A German Afrika Korps BMW R75 motorcycle combination, armed with an MG34 machine gun, roars through the Libyan desert in 1942.

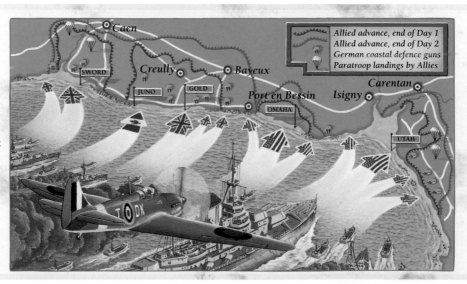

AMPHIBIOUS OPERATIONS
World War II saw the development of specialized landing craft to carry vehicles, troops, and stores for amphibious operations. Before 1942 soldiers went ashore from small boats, ships or modified freighters. In the Pacific, the US Marine Corps used tracked amphibious APCs to carry marines ashore.

Allied advance, end of Day 1	
Allied advance, end of Day 2	
German coastal defence guns	
Paratroop landings by Allies	

Caen
SWORD Creully Bayeux
JUNO GOLD Port en Bessin Isigny Carentan
OMAHA
UTAH

◀ EXTRA PROTECTION
An Israeli M113 APC, in desert camouflage, is fitted with extra armour and carries a .50in Browning machine gun. APCs have enough internal space to make them ideal weapons carriers for missiles, AA guns or spare ammunition. They are also used as ambulances and for radio communications.

▼ HUMVEE FIREPOWER
A TOW anti-tank missile streaks away from its launcher, which is mounted on an HMMWV, a wheeled utility vehicle known to US soldiers as a "HumVee". The rugged, stable and reliable HumVee is popular with US service personnel because it is easy to drive.

Jeep remains the most enduring symbol. The US produced 639,245 Jeeps before the war ended, and the Jeep continued to serve in many armies into the 1960s. In World War II the US-designed DUKW, a six-wheeled amphibious truck, was used during amphibious operations to ferry stores from ships to the shore. Despite their age, DUKWs are still being used by the British Royal Marines for training missions.

Most armies now use 4-ton trucks and light ¼-ton vehicles. However, some specialized Alpine regiments still use mules to carry heavy equipment such as mortars, howitzers and ammunition up narrow mountain tracks.

◀ D-DAY LANDINGS
Landings at beaches in Normandy, codenamed Utah, Omaha, Gold, Juno and Sword, began at 06.30 on 6 June 1944. By midnight 57,000 US and 75,000 British and Canadian troops and their equipment were ashore.

▲ LANDING CRAFT
US soldiers approach Omaha Beach in Normandy in June 1944. They are in a Higgins boat, a landing craft designed to carry soldiers.

◀ DUCK
The DUKW, a wartime amphibious truck, was nicknamed the "DUCK". It is still in service with the UK's Royal Marines for use in training missions.

Key Dates

- 1885 Four-wheel motor carriage developed.

- 1914 French use 600 taxis to transport troops at the Marne.

- 1925 French demonstrate the half-track vehicle.

- 1927 British Army tests mechanized warfare tactics.

- 1940 Germans conduct trials for an amphibious invasion of Great Britain.

- 1943 US DUKW used in combat.

- 1944 D-Day, the largest amphibious operation in history, takes place in northern France.

Communications

▲ CARRIER PIGEON
A homing pigeon carries simple messages in a capsule attached to its leg.

IN A FAST-MOVING GAME such as a football match, information can mean the difference between victory or defeat, communicating tactics and positions. In wartime, this sort of communication is even more critical – the lives of thousands of soldiers are at risk. Ships, aircraft and many other military units report their positions, which allows a commander to build up a picture of the battle.

For centuries messages were sent either verbally or as a written despatch and carried by foot or horseback. Beacons positioned on high hills were lit if there was a threat of enemy invasion or attack. Signal flags used at sea were a key to the British victory at Trafalgar on 21 October 1805. In 19th-century India and South Africa, where the air was clear and the sunshine constant, devices called heliographs used reflective mirrors to flash Morse code signals.

The Morse code could also be used with signal lamps; this method of communication was particularly effective at sea. The telegraph, which allowed Morse messages to be sent over long distances, was first used in the American Civil War (1861–1865).

▲ FIELD RADIO
A modern field radio is light and reliable. It may even have a built-in security system that makes it impossible to decode a message without the correct equipment.

CODES AND SIGNALS
Signal systems were initially visual ones, using flags, light or even smoke. They allowed people to communicate beyond the range of the human voice. Telegraph, telephone and radio increased the range. However, the danger of interception by the enemy made it essential that signals should be in code.

A	J	S
B	K	T
C	L	U
D	M	V
E	N	W
F	O	X
G	P	Y
H	Q	Z
I	R	

◀ SEMAPHORE
The British Army and the Royal Navy used this system of signals before radio had been developed. The advantage of semaphore is that flags don't operate from an electronic system that can break down.

A B C D E F G H I J K
L M N O P Q R S T U
V W X Y Z Error Interval Numeral Attention

▲ MORSE CODE
Invented by Samuel Morse in 1850, this "dot and dash" code was the key to the telegraph system. It was first used operationally during the Crimean war.

◀ WARTIME RADIO
French troops with American uniforms and equipment operate a radio during fighting in Germany in 1945.

▶ CONCEALED
Men of the US Army's 82nd Airborne Division during the invasion of Grenada in 1983. The soldier carries the radio in a medium pack to conceal it.

The telephone was in widespread use by 1880 and was used in the Boer War (1899–1902) and the Russo-Japanese War (1904–1905). In World War I, field telephones were developed and telephone cables were laid quickly to connect headquarters with the artillery batteries.

The first radios were cumbersome and required a wagon and team of horses to transport them. In 1915, an observer used a radio in a hot air balloon over the Dardanelles in Turkey. During the interwar years radios became small enough to fit in a backpack.

Most military radios operate in the very high frequency (VHF) range between 30 and 200megahertz (MHz) and in the high frequency (HF) range between 1 and 30MHz. Anyone with a radio receiver tuned to the right frequency could listen to a radio conversation, and so codes were introduced. However, even if a message

was encoded the station could be jammed by a powerful signal. One technique for ensuring security and avoiding jamming was "burst transmission". A message would be prepared and then sent in a few seconds to another station that would display it on a screen. In the 1980s radios were designed that could change frequencies at random intervals. If the receiving station was correctly tuned it would follow the "hops" and so a conversation could take place without interruption.

The latest development in radio communications are satellites. They receive radio signals and re-broadcast them, allowing messages from remote locations to be transmitted reliably over huge distances.

▲ SUNLIGHT
A British soldier uses a signal mirror to contact a circling helicopter. It is a silent but effective communications tool.

▶ THE ENIGMA CODE
During World War II the Germans used a variety of codes. Most of them used a machine to jumble up the letters of the message. The British, assisted by the French, Poles and Americans, were able to break the German codes. This literally saved Britain from starvation because some of these codes were for the U-boats, which were sinking ships carrying food and fuel to Britain. The code machines were like very complex typewriters.

Key Dates

- 1850 Morse Code invented.
- 1858 Heliograph invented.
- 1876 Telephone invented.
- 1892 First detected radio signal.
- 1901 Transatlantic radio link established.
- 1921 Teleprinter developed.
- 1925 Short-wave, crystal-controlled radio invented.
- 1926 Enigma coding machine developed.
- 1949 Transistor invented.
- 1960 Microchip first used.

Protecting the Soldier

▲ THE HELMET
The helmet, such as this M1 steel helmet, is the oldest and most effective protection for a soldier.

ARMOUR HAD PROTECTED soldiers when firearms were awkward and heavy and the sword was still used in warfare. However, armour was no longer worn once firearms improved and freedom of movement had become more important.

Like the "hard hats" worn by construction workers on building sites, the steel helmets introduced in World War I were intended to protect soldiers from objects falling on their heads. Such objects are normally shrapnel, the tiny fragments that fall from the sky when a shell explodes. During World War I protection was introduced for snipers – soldiers who use powerful rifles with telescopic sights to shoot at an unwary enemy or important targets such as officers. This protection was very unwieldy and heavy, and resembled the breastplates of medieval soldiers.

Following the use of poison gas by the Germans on the Western Front in World War I, gas masks or respirators were produced. The first masks were simply cotton pads worn with goggles, but by the end of the war respirators were not only more effective but also more comfortable to wear. Modern masks use charcoal filters. Charcoal is a very useful filter against impurities, hence its use in domestic water filters. It is also used in soldiers' protective uniforms.

▲ A BOLD NEW ERA
Explosive reactive armour (ERA) comes in bolt-on slabs. It explodes outwards when hit, counteracting the penetration of charges.

PROTECT AND SURVIVE

As weapons became more effective and more lethal, soldiers looked for ways of improving their protection. Soldiers who were fighting a defensive battle dug themselves in, built log or sandbag fortifications or, even better, reinforced concrete ones. The difficulties came when they were in the open. Thick steel plates gave protection, but their weight meant that soldiers could move only short distances at low speed.

In the 1980s and 1990s new materials have allowed soldiers to move freely with protection from shell fragments and bullets. Fireproof materials, used in tank and aircraft crew overalls, protect the wearer against flash burns from exploding fuel tanks. In bad weather troops now have the comfort of breathable waterproofs.

British helmet, World War I

British paratrooper's helmet, 1944

British helmet Mk III, 1944

US M1 steel helmet, World War II

British Mk 6 helmet, 1986–2009

Current US Lightweight Helmet (LWH)

◀ EVACUATION OF CASUALTIES
US soldiers carry a casualty on a litter to a Blackhawk helicopter. Helicopters were first used for flying wounded from the battlefield during the Korean War and have become a vital link in the casualty evacuation chain. Nicknamed "Dust Off" in the Vietnam War, helicopters could literally take an injured man from deep in the jungle and fly him to a modern hospital. He could be admitted to a fully equipped operating theatre in less than an hour. Many troops who would have died in earlier times because of a lack of prompt and thorough medical support now survive terrible battlefield injuries.

In World War II protective jackets with overlapping steel plates were produced to protect American bomber crews from the shrapnel from German anti-aircraft (flak) guns. The jackets were called "flak jackets".

Today's body armour is made from materials such as Kevlar, which is light and strong. Its woven form is used for jackets and even boots; it can also be bonded into a plastic for used in helmets. These new materials can protect a soldier, even at close range, from shots from hand guns and even rifles.

In the confined spaces of aircraft, warships and armoured vehicles, fire has always been a major threat. In World War II, leather jackets and gloves, as well as goggles, provided some protection. The crews on warships wore steel helmets and anti-flash hoods made from an asbestos-based fabric.

The development of artificial fire-resistant fabrics such as Nomex has allowed gloves, flying overalls, jackets and trousers to be made from a material with a high level of protection. Tanks and aircraft now have fire detection systems that operate instantly, swamping potential fires with a gas that cuts off the oxygen.

▶ GUARDIAN ANGLE
If the armour on a fighting vehicle is sloped, this increases the distance through which a projectile has to pass before it breaks through to the interior. If a projectile strikes at an oblique angle it may even ricochet and fall away harmlessly.

Material that is 8mm/⁵⁄₁₆in thick when vertical is 11mm/⁷⁄₁₆in thick when tilted

8

11

Key Dates

- 1856 Bessemer steel produced.
- 1865 First antiseptics used.
- 1882 Armoured steel developed
- 1914–1918 World War I: steel helmets introduced to protect soldiers from shrapnel.
- 1920s Gas masks and respirators introduced after the use of poison gas in World War I.
- 1939–1945 World War II: penicillin, plastic surgery and blood transfusions introduced.
- 1970s Explosive reactive armour, ceramic armour, Kevlar and Nomex developed.

▲ TOUGH TRAIN
A Soviet armoured train captured by the Germans in World War II. Armour protected the crew, but the train was vulnerable if the tracks were destroyed or damaged.

AFVs

▲ WAR CAR
The first armoured car, the Charron Girardot et Voigt, was built in France in 1904.

A S FAR BACK AS 1482 the idea of an armoured fighting vehicle (AFV) appeared in sketches drawn by Leonardo da Vinci. It was moved by muscle power, with the crew operating geared hand cranks and firing muskets through slits. However, it was the British War Office that saw the first true AFV in 1902 when the Simms "War Car" was demonstrated. It used a petrol engine to drive a wheeled vehicle at a maximum speed of 18kmh/ 11mph. It was protected by 6mm/¼in of plating and armed with two machine guns and a one-pounder gun.

The Belgians and British Royal Navy used armoured cars with machine guns in 1914. However, the mud of the Western Front was unsuitable for wheeled vehicles. Armoured cars were used in the Middle East by the British when fighting against the Turks.

The interwar period saw the development of six- and even eight-wheeled armoured cars and the half-track. This vehicle had tracks at the rear of its chassis and wheels at the front. It had the cross-country performance of a tank but could be driven like a truck. The German Sdkfz 251 and American M3 half-track were widely used in World War II.

◀ APC
This M113 Armoured Personnel Carrier (APC) is fitted with TOW anti-tank missile launchers. APCs are used in both wartime conflicts and civil disturbances.

PROTECTION AND MOBILITY
Armour protection is used for combat vehicles and also to protect VIP (Very Important Person) cars and vehicles used by the media in hostile locations. Protection may be quite basic, consisting of plates and panels, or it may be a system that is both bulletproof and mineproof.

◀ UP IN SMOKE
A Swedish APC burns after being hit by an anti-tank weapon in a demonstration on an army range. APCs contain fuel, hydraulic fluid under pressure and ammunition, so internal fire can be catastrophic. This vehicle had its rear doors closed, but the explosion has blasted one open. Fire suppression systems need to operate quickly for soldiers to survive a fire. Recently, if not under fire, troops have sat on the roof of their moving APC in case it hits an anti-tank mine, catches fire and explodes.

▲ BRITISH SAXON APC
The 4x4 Saxon is effectively an armoured truck. It weighs 9,940kg/22,000lb, can carry ten people and has a top speed on roads of 96kmh/60mph. It has been used in Northern Ireland and Bosnia to transport troops under armour.

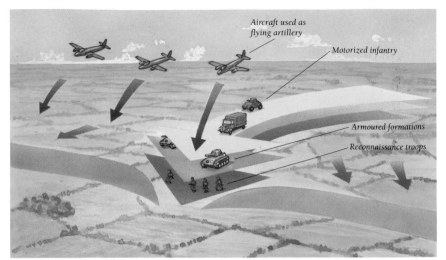

Aircraft used as
flying artillery

Motorized infantry

Armoured formations

Reconnaissance troops

◀ MILITARY
FORMATION
*The armoured tactics
pioneered by the Germans in
1939–1942 used aircraft as
flying artillery. At the front
were reconnaissance troops,
followed by armoured
formations and backed by
motorized infantry in
trucks. The tanks were
massed to punch through
enemy fortifications.
The infantry secured the
flanks as the armoured
troops plunged deeper into
enemy territory.*

After the war the M3 was used by the Israeli Army up to 1967. The half-track also allowed infantry to keep pace with fast-moving tanks. Artillery mounted on tracked chassis could bombard enemy positions before the infantry and tanks attacked.

Before D-Day on 6 June 1944, the British developed several special tanks, nicknamed "Funnies". They included tanks that could clear paths through minefields, lay special matting roads across shingle beaches or lay bridges over ditches. Another of these special tanks was the Armoured Vehicle Royal Engineers (AVRE) that could fire an 18kg/40lb demolition bomb

210m/690ft against German fortifications. An armoured engineer vehicle that can lay bridges or bulldoze rubble is now a standard vehicle in most major armies.

Since the end of World War II AFVs have been developed as armoured ambulances, recovery vehicles, mobile workshops, headquarters, nuclear biological and chemical (NBC) detection vehicles and troop carriers. They are wheeled like the French VAB or fully tracked like the American M113. The wheeled APCs are widely used in United Nations peace-keeping operations because they give protection against rifle and machine gun fire as well as shell fragments.

▲ FRENCH PANHARD ERC
Armed with a 90mm gun, the French ERC Sagaie armoured car has a top speed of 95kmh/59mph on roads. Its six wheels give it a better cross-country performance than a normal four-wheeled vehicle. The ERC saw action during the Gulf War of 1990–1991 against Iraq.

Key Dates

- 1904 First armoured car.

- 1914 Armoured car shoots down German Taube aircraft.

- 1919–1922 Armoured cars used in Ireland against the IRA.

- 1920 Rolls Royce armoured car introduced; it serves until 1941.

- 1931 First cast turrets introduced by France for the D1.

- 1932 Japanese field first diesel-powered armoured vehicle.

- 1936 Torsion bar suspension introduced by the Germans.

- 1944 Tetrach light tanks land by glider in Normandy, France.

Camouflage

EXAMPLES OF CAMOUFLAGE exist all around us in nature. Birds, fish and other animals have self-protection in the form of patterns that help them blend into the background of vegetation, sky, water or sand.

The earliest military camouflage consisted of the dark-green tunics and black buttons adopted by the British rifle regiments during the Peninsula War of 1808–1814. The British had learned camouflage and field craft from the experience of fighting the American colonists and Native Americans in North America in the late 18th century. The red coats of the British stood out clearly in battle, making them easy targets.

In 19th-century India, British troops dyed their white tropical uniforms with tea to produce a shade of brown that Indians called *khaki*, meaning dusty. These "khaki" uniforms helped the troops to blend into the dry terrain as they fought against tribes on the North-west Frontier.

In World War I camouflage, a word taken from the French *camouflet* meaning "smoke puff", became a serious technique. The French Army used conscripted artists to devise colorations to conceal artillery and vehicles. Some of these were in fantastic shapes and shades, and also included nets with strips of cloth that could be draped over buildings, guns and vehicles.

▲ GREEN AND BROWN
A British soldier in the black, green, brown and buff camouflage that was introduced in the early 1970s. It is designed to mimic the shadows and highlights of natural vegetation. It is effective in tropical and temperate terrain, and has been adopted by the Dutch and Indonesian armies.

▲ DESERTED
A soldier in the desert with his helmet garnished with nylon "scrim" to break up its outline. His equipment and clothing have softened with use and do not present hard unnatural lines and shapes.

MEN AND MACHINES
Camouflage conceals soldiers, vehicles and buildings. It may consist of paint patterns, netting, painted screens, planted vegetation or even fake buildings and vehicles. Good camouflage fools the naked eye, but special cameras and night-vision equipment will penetrate ordinary camouflage. Special nets and paints have in turn been developed to counter this technology.

▶ WAR PAINT
A soldier with some of the elaborate patterns that can be painted to break up the shape and coloration of the human face. Grass has been added to his helmet.

▲ HELMET COVERS
US military helmets with cotton drill desert camouflage covers. This spotted pattern is known to US service personnel as "chocolate chip cookie" camouflage. The rubber band around the helmet is used to secure vegetation for camouflage.

▲ SNOW DAY
In the course of an exercise in the 1980s in northern Canada, Canadian Army Special Forces slog through the snow in white camouflaged uniforms and backpack covers. They have affixed white tape to their weapons to break up the outline.

▼ SLOGGING
US soldiers armed with M16 rifles and carrying rucksacks slog through the dust. They are wearing camouflaged uniforms. Their Kevlar helmets have cloth covers made from the same material.

The development of aircraft and aerial photography during the two World Wars made camouflage essential. Elaborate deception schemes included building fake vehicles and constructing huts with lighting that operated by itself at night.

By the end of the 20th century new methods of detection took camouflage out of the simple visual detection range. These methods included night-vision equipment and thermal imaging, enabling the viewer to see the heat generated by humans or equipment. Modern camouflage can conceal the shade, shape, heat and radar signature of aircraft, ships and tanks.

◀ FOOLING THE EYE
A USAF Rockwell B-1A bomber in "viscam", the visual camouflage designed to make the bomber blend into the background over which it is flying. Although electronic aids such as radar and thermal imaging can be very accurate, pilots and soldiers also rely on their eyes to double check.

▼ JETS OVER THE DESERT
Two F-15 Eagles are in flight with a chase plane over the desert. The Eagles are painted in pale "air superiority" camouflage that is designed to blend into the sky.

Key Dates

- 1775–1783 American War of Independence: use of field craft by colonists.

- 1808–1814 Peninsular War: the British riflemen wear dark-green camouflaged tunics.

- 1857–1858 Indian Mutiny: white uniforms dyed "khaki".

- 1914–1918 World War I: land, sea and air camouflage developed.

- 1939–1945 World War II: aerial photography and infra-red technology developed.

- 1970s Black, green, brown and buff camouflage introduced.

Battleships

Nelson was one of the greatest naval commanders. One of the secrets of his victories was an efficient system of flag signals.

A CAPITAL SHIP IS A major naval warship. Today's capital ship is probably a submerged submarine with nuclear missiles aboard, or an aircraft carrier. Yet for centuries the capital ship was a battleship such as HMS *Victory,* which was powered by sail and armed with cannons along its hull.

Sea war in the 18th and 19th centuries was a test of sailing skills, stamina and courage. The gunners learned to load and "run out" the cannons and fire them as quickly as possible to ensure that there was a steady barrage against enemy warships. The wooden-hulled ships were very strong, and when soaked with salty seawater they did not burn easily.

The change came in the mid-19th century with the development of steam propulsion, armour plating and breech-loading guns. In 1859 the French launched the first steam-powered iron-clad battleship, *La Gloire.* It was armed with 36 163mm guns. Within two years the British had launched the *Warrior,* an iron-clad ship with superior protection and armaments.

During the American Civil War the indecisive battle between the iron-clad battleships *Merrimack* and *Monitor* in 1862 gave some clue about the outcome of future naval battles.

The battle of Tsu Shima (Toshima) on 27 and 28 May 1905 pitted Russian battleships against Japanese ones. The battle ended with a decisive victory for the Japanese naval forces. The Russian defeat at Tsu Shima led ultimately to defeat for the Russian forces in the Russo-Japanese War.

◀ ABOARD THE *MONITOR*
The battle of Hampton Roads, Virginia, on 8–9 March 1862, saw the Confederate armoured steam frigate *Merrimack* fight an inconclusive battle with the USS *Monitor.* The *Monitor* had 11in guns in a revolving turret.

Muzzle —

▶ US CANNON
This 19th-century muzzle-loading ship's cannon has simple gearing on its wooden carriage, which allows the muzzle to be lowered or raised.

FROM WOOD TO IRON
Steam power and armour plate made the new iron-clad warships "wolves among a flock of sheep" when they first appeared in a world dominated by wooden sailing ships. An "arms race" developed with new and more sophisticated iron-clad ships being built throughout Europe in the 19th century.

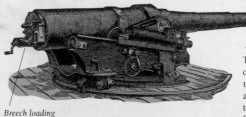

Breech loading

— Muzzle

◀ A US 8IN GUN
This gun could be used aboard capital ships or for defending the coast. It is breech loading and is mounted on a turntable trackway to allow it to rotate fully through 360 degrees.

▼ BATTLE OF TRAFALGAR
The Battle of Trafalgar was fought on 21 October 1805 off the Spanish coast. It involved 27 British and 33 French and Spanish ships. The battle was a victory for the British under Nelson.

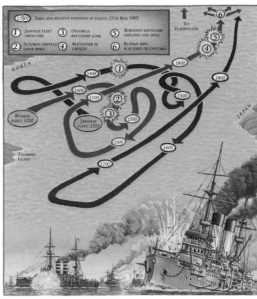

▲ BATTLE OF TSU SHIMA
This battle between the Imperial Russian Baltic fleet and the Imperial Japanese fleet took place off Korea between 27 and 28 May 1905.

At the beginning of the 20th century the launch of HMS *Dreadnought* in 1906 marked a further change in the design of capital ships. It was armed with 10 12in guns and 27 12-pounder guns. By this time battleships had a speed of 18 knots and weighed 15,000 tons.

▲ SEA BATTLE
In a sea battle in 1862, during the American Civil War, the *Merrimack (right)* fights it out with the USS *Monitor*. This battle saw the first operational use of armoured steam-powered craft in war.

Key Dates

- 1805 October 21: Battle of Trafalgar.

- 1859 French launch the first steam-powered, iron-clad battleship, *La Gloire*.

- 1862 March 8–9: Battle of Hampton Roads.

- 1864 August 5: Battle of Mobile Bay.

- 1866 July 20: Battle of Lissa.

- 1898 May 1: Battle of Manila Bay.

- 1905 May 27–28: Battle of Tsu Shima.

- 1906 Launch of HMS *Dreadnought*, first modern "big gun" warship.

20th-century Battleships

THE BATTLE OF JUTLAND in 1916 during World War I was fought between the capital ships of the Royal Navy and the Imperial German Navy. The outcome was indecisive.

In the interwar years several countries attempted to reduce the weight of capital ships and the size of their fleets. However, both the Japanese and the Germans were building warships in secret, and they entered World War II with powerful modern ships. The Germans saw their ships as a powerful weapon to attack Allied merchant shipping. As a result, German warships, such as the 50,000-ton battleship *Bismarck*, became a priority target for the Royal Navy. The *Bismarck* was sunk on 27 May 1941 after being pounded by the guns of the battleships HMS *King George V* and HMS *Rodney*.

The development of aircraft carriers and submarines made capital ships very vulnerable. The Japanese battleships *Yamato* and *Mushashi*, the largest and most heavily protected ships of their class in the world, displaced 64,000 tons each. They were armed with nine 18in guns and twelve 6in guns. They had

▲ NIGHT SALVO
A US battleship fires a battery salvo at night.

crews of 2,500 men and carried six spotter aircraft. The *Yamato* and the *Mushashi* were sunk by torpedo and dive-bomber aircraft from US carriers on 7 April 1945 and 24 October 1945 respectively. Earlier, HMS *Prince of Wales*, which had fought against the *Bismarck*, was sunk by Japanese aircraft on 10 December 1941.

Battleships fired huge shells, which were effective in the bombardment of coastal defensive installations prior to an amphibious landing. During World War II battleships were used on D-Day and to support the US Marine Corps landings throughout the Pacific.

Today the title of capital ships has passed to aircraft carriers and nuclear submarines armed with ballistic

▶ CLOSE IN SUPPORT
This US Navy 20mm Phalanx system is radar controlled. The gun fires at 1,000–3,000rpm. Its very hard depleted-uranium rounds are designed to destroy surface-skimming anti-ship missiles such as the Exocet. The Phalanx has a maximum range of 6,000m/20,000ft. It can rotate through 100 degrees in one second, and elevate up to 68 degrees in one second. The gun has a 989-round ammunition drum that can be reloaded in 10–30 minutes.

CAPITAL SHIPS
Capital ships, the big warships around which naval fleets are formed, were originally big-gun battleships. Today's surface fleets and task forces are based around the aircraft carrier. Carriers and submarines are nuclear powered, which gives them the ability to stay at sea almost indefinitely and to travel huge distances.

▶ PRESTIGE
Capital ships were the focal point of the great navies of the 20th century. In peacetime these great ships would travel the world "showing the flag", visiting the ports of other nations whom their government wished to impress. In wartime capital ships were the flagships for the admirals in command of battle fleets.

▲ DRESSED OVERALL ▼
These armoured, steam-powered warships are "dressed overall" with signal flags displayed as decoration. Modern warships have a more streamlined appearance.

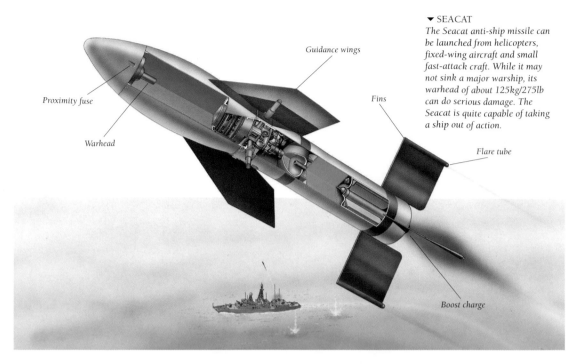

▼ SEACAT
The Seacat anti-ship missile can be launched from helicopters, fixed-wing aircraft and small fast-attack craft. While it may not sink a major warship, its warhead of about 125kg/275lb can do serious damage. The Seacat is quite capable of taking a ship out of action.

Guidance wings

Proximity fuse

Warhead

Fins

Flare tube

Boost charge

missiles (SSBNs). The United States Navy has the largest number of SSBNs in the world.

In March 1992 the US Navy decommissioned the last operational battleship in the world, the USS *Missouri*. The 45,000 ton *Missouri* was launched in

1944 and served in the Pacific during World War II and later in the Korean War. The *Missouri* was armed with nine 16in guns. These were last used in action as recently as 1991 when the battleship bombarded Iraqi positions in Kuwait during the Gulf War.

▼ BROADSIDE
A Missouri-class battleship lets rip a broadside with her 16in guns. The guns have a maximum range of 41,600m/136,000ft and fire an 850kg/1,870lb shell. The US Navy was the last force to use battleships in action.

Key Dates

- 1914–1918 World War I.
- 1914 November 1: Battle of the Coronel.
- 1914 December 8: Battle of the Falklands.
- 1916 May 31: Battle of Jutland.
- 1939 December 13: Battle of the River Plate.
- 1941 May 27: Sinking of the *Bismarck*.
- 1944 June 6: D-Day.
- 1945 April 7: Sinking of the battleship *Yamato*.
- 1992 *Missouri* decommissioned.

Smaller Fighting Ships

▲ PATROL
A warship fires one of its Harpoon missiles.

THERE WAS SHOCK and surprise among senior naval officers in both Europe and North America when the first torpedo boat was launched in 1878. It was the 19 knot British-built *Lightning,* with a torpedo tube in its bow. This compact torpedo boat had the speed and fire power to race after larger ships and to sink or damage them.

Japanese torpedo boats proved very effective against the Russians in the Russo-Japanese war during night-time action at Wei-Hai-Wei in 1895 and again at Port Arthur on 8 February 1904.

In World War I the Royal Navy deployed coastal motor boats (CMBs) and motor launches (MLs) in the narrows of the English Channel.

▶ PATROL
US warships patrol, their masts cluttered with radar and radio antennae.

During World War II the German motor torpedo boats were designated *S-Boot,* or *Schnellboot* meaning "fast boat". They were known by their crews as *Eilboot (E-Boot)* meaning "boat in a hurry". Several classes of *S-Boot* were built. Most were powered by three-shaft Daimler–Benz or MAN diesel engines and had a maximum speed of 39–42 knots with a range of 350km/200 miles.

World War II armament was varied, but for most of the war it consisted of two 2cm anti-aircraft (AA) guns and two 21in torpedo tubes. From 1944, defensive armament was upgraded and became one 4cm and three 2cm AA guns, or one 3.7cm and five 2cm AA guns. Larger types of ship could also carry six or eight mines in place of reloading torpedoes.

During World War II, John F. Kennedy, the future President of the United States, commanded a US Navy patrol torpedo (PT) boat in the Pacific. The boat

INDIVIDUAL SHIPS
The anti-ship missile and torpedo have given smaller craft a powerful punch, making them a dangerous enemy for larger, slow-moving naval vessels. Modern materials and improved engine design give these craft a performance similar to racing speedboats. They are able to dart towards larger, slower ships, launch their missiles and retreat very quickly.

▼ SAETTIA
An Italian Saettia-class small-missile craft has a crew of 33, a maximum speed of 40 knots and weighs 400 tons fully loaded.

▼ PATRA
A French Patra-class craft has a crew of 18, a maximum speed of 26 knots and weighs 147.5 tons fully loaded.

▼ SPICA
A Swedish Spica II-class torpedo attack craft has a crew of 27, a maximum speed of 40.5 knots and weighs 230 tons fully loaded.

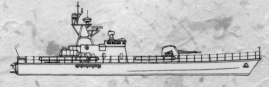

◀ PATROL BOAT
Small nations with coastlines to protect make extensive use of patrol craft such as this one. These boats are used to police maritime borders and for anti-piracy and anti-smuggling operations.

was powered by three petrol engines which gave it a maximum speed of 40 knots.

The surface-to-surface missile was developed after World War II and gave small craft new hitting power. The postwar Soviet Osa ships were capable of speeds up to 38 knots and were armed with four SS-N-2A "Styx" missiles. Nearly 300 Osas were built and were used to equip 20 navies throughout the world. Osas saw action in the Middle East in the 1973 Yom Kippur War between Israel and her Arab counterparts, and also in the Gulf War in 1990–1991.

Patrol boats are ideal for landing small groups of special forces. These sorts of attacks are usually undercover, amphibious attacks. Patrol boats are also widely used in peacetime for search and rescue missions, fishery patrols and anti-piracy operations.

◀ KNOX
A US Knox-class frigate has a crew of 300, a maximum speed of 27 knots and weighs 4,260 tons fully loaded. It is armed with guns, torpedoes and missiles. Knox class frigates are no longer in service with the US navy, but are still used by smaller nations.

▼ TESTS
Verifier, a British Aerospace trials craft, launches a Sea Skua anti-ship missile during evaluation trials. Missiles such as the 145kg/320lb Sea Skua with its 9kg/20lb warhead, although originally designed as an airborne anti-ship missile, give even the smallest craft a considerable punch.

Key Dates

- 1878 *Lightning* 19-knot torpedo boat launched.

- 1914–1918 World War I: Royal Navy coastal motor boats and motor launches reach 35 knots.

- 1939–1945 World War II: German E-boats reach 42 knots.

- 1958 Soviet Komar class missile-armed craft enter service.

- 1966 Soviet Osa class missile-armed craft enter service.

- 1973 Soviet Osa class craft see action in the Middle East.

- 1990–1991 Osa class see action in the Gulf War.

Submarines

THE FIRST SUBMARINE attack was carried out by the semi-submersible steam-driven craft called *David* during the American Civil War. It damaged a Federal iron-clad ship with a spar torpedo. No one would have guessed that this crude underwater craft would be the forerunner of the most sophisticated and powerful weapons that the world has ever known.

Electric and oil fuel motors made fully submersible boats practical. In 1886 Lt Isaac Peral of Spain built an electrically powered boat. The following year the Russians built a boat armed with four torpedoes. In 1895 the streamlined *Plunger* was built in the United States by John Holland. On the surface it used a steam engine to charge the batteries which powered it when moving underwater.

The German U-boats in World War I showed how submarine warfare could be a strategic weapon in attacking commercial shipping as well as launching tactical attacks on enemy warships.

On 8 August 1914, the U-15 fired a torpedo at the battleship HMS *Monarch*. Although the torpedo missed, it was the first time that an automotive torpedo had been fired against an enemy from a submarine.

In World War II the Germans capitalized on this experience by concentrating U-boats into "wolf packs" to attack British convoys in the North Atlantic. The Allies were able to defeat the U-boats by breaking the coded signals transmitted to them and by using improved detection systems and weapons. In the Pacific, the US Navy waged a highly effective submarine campaign against Japanese commercial and naval ships.

In the postwar years nuclear power changed submarines forever. Now they could, in theory, stay submerged for indefinite periods of time. The first

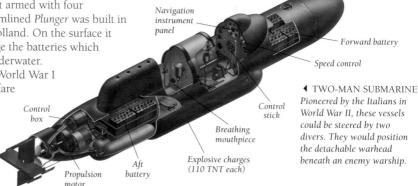

Navigation instrument panel

Forward battery

Speed control

◄ TWO-MAN SUBMARINE
Pioneered by the Italians in World War II, these vessels could be steered by two divers. They would position the detachable warhead beneath an enemy warship.

Control box

Control stick

Breathing mouthpiece

Explosive charges (110 TNT each)

Propulsion motor

Aft battery

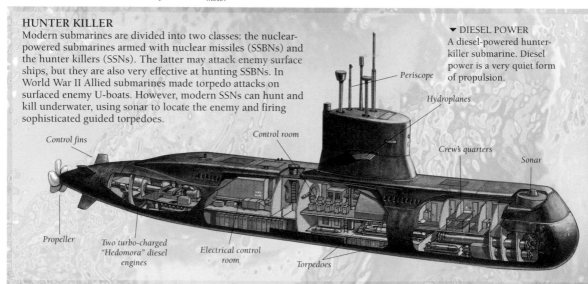

HUNTER KILLER
Modern submarines are divided into two classes: the nuclear-powered submarines armed with nuclear missiles (SSBNs) and the hunter killers (SSNs). The latter may attack enemy surface ships, but they are also very effective at hunting SSBNs. In World War II Allied submarines made torpedo attacks on surfaced enemy U-boats. However, modern SSNs can hunt and kill underwater, using sonar to locate the enemy and firing sophisticated guided torpedoes.

▼ DIESEL POWER
A diesel-powered hunter-killer submarine. Diesel power is a very quiet form of propulsion.

Periscope

Hydroplanes

Control room

Crew's quarters

Sonar

Control fins

Propeller

Two turbo-charged "Hedomora" diesel engines

Electrical control room

Torpedoes

nuclear submarine was the USS *Nautilus*. It was commissioned in 1954 and could dive to more than 200m/650ft. In 1959 the launch of the USS *George Washington* marked the arrival of the world's most formidable weapon. This nuclear-powered submarine was armed with Polaris nuclear missiles that could be launched while the boat was submerged.

On 2 May 1982, off the Falklands, the submarine HMS *Conquerer* torpedoed and sank the Argentinian heavy cruiser *General Belgrano*. Despite the use of very efficient anti-submarine tracking systems and weapons, submarines remain a powerful weapon because of the secret nature of their operations.

▶ BOMBER
An SSBN is known in the Royal Navy as a "bomber". Its missiles are housed in launch tubes astern of the fin, or conning tower.

Type A3 Polaris missile

Periscopes and radar mast

Bridge (for surface use)

Communications room

Machine control room containing nuclear reactor control panels

Electrical generating plant

Nuclear reactor (top secret)

Missile compartment

Navigation area

Torpedo tubes

▲ ATOMIC SUBMARINE
First developed by the US, the nuclear-powered submarine is the most powerful warship in history. It is armed with intercontinental nuclear missiles which can be fired from underwater.

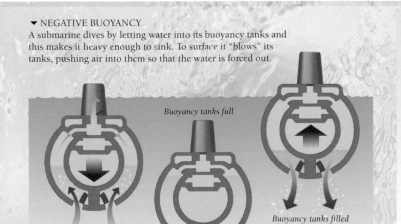

▼ NEGATIVE BUOYANCY
A submarine dives by letting water into its buoyancy tanks and this makes it heavy enough to sink. To surface it "blows" its tanks, pushing air into them so that the water is forced out.

Buoyancy tanks full

Buoyancy tanks flood, and submarine sinks

Buoyancy tanks filled with air, expelling the water, and the submarine surfaces

Key Dates

- 1863 October 5: steam-driven submersible *David* attacks Federal iron-clad ship.

- 1895 USS *Plunger*, the first battery-powered boat.

- 1904 *Aigret*, first diesel-powered boat.

- 1914–1918 World War I German U-boats wage war against Allied commercial shipping.

- 1939–1945 World War II German U-boats use "wolf pack" tactics against Allied shipping.

- 1954 USS *Nautilus*, the first nuclear-powered submarine, is commissioned.

Aircraft Carriers

▲ VERTICAL
A Royal Navy Harrier takes off in the Falklands in 1982.

EARLY AIRCRAFT WERE FRAGILE and underpowered. They were still a dangerous and risky form of transport when US airman Eugene Ely made the first successful flight from a platform rigged on the deck of a US Navy cruiser in 1911. Two months later the intrepid Ely also made a landing onboard a ship. He had effectively become the first carrier pilot, although at that time aircraft carriers had not been conceived.

In 1913 HMS *Hermes* pioneered aircraft carrier design with its short flying-off deck and three aircraft. A U-boat sank her in 1914, but her successor, completed in 1919, was a true aircraft carrier. During World War I the British used seaplane carriers from which aircraft were lowered into the sea.

The interwar years saw a rapid development in carrier design and capability. HMS *Ark Royal*, which was commissioned in 1938, incorporated all the latest features: arrester wire to halt incoming aircraft, net crash barrier, batsmen to guide pilots and catapults to launch aircraft. In 1939 Britain had ten carriers. In 1941 Japan had eleven and the US had three. By the end of the war the US Navy had over 100 in action.

At Taranto in 1940, 21 Swordfish aircraft from the

Royal Navy carrier HMS *Illustrious* attacked ships of the Italian Navy, severely damaging three battleships. The Japanese are believed to have based their attack at Pearl Harbor on 7 December 1941 upon Taranto. They committed 360 aircraft armed with torpedoes and bombs, and sank or immobilized eight battleships, three cruisers and other craft. The US Navy carrier fleet, which was at sea at the time of the attack, formed the nucleus of a new Pacific fleet.

In May 1942, the US Navy fought the Battle of the Coral Sea against the Japanese. It was the first sea battle fought entirely by aircraft attacking ships. In June 1942,

▲ TAKE-OFF
A RNAS Sopwith Pup fighter aircraft takes off during trials in World War I.

LARGE AND SMALL

In the 20th century aircraft carriers have grown from simple "flat tops" to virtual cities at sea. The USS *Nimitz*, for example, has a crew of more than 6,000 with 50 aircraft as well as helicopters. In World War I HMS *Hermes* was the first aircraft carrier and had only three aircraft. *Hermes* was sunk by a U-boat; even today aircraft carriers are vulnerable to submarine attack.

▲ LAUNCHING
This McDonnell Douglas Hornet is preparing to take off.

◀ SIZE
A huge US carrier is guided into dock by small tugboats.

▲ ARRESTING
A McDonnell Douglas Hornet hits an arrester net.

▲ FIGHTER POWER
McDonnell Hornet fighters aboard a US carrier. The Hornet's six Phalanx missiles can be used against six targets simultaneously.

the Battle of Midway was another complex air and sea action. These two battles cost the Japanese six of their ten carriers, and the US Navy four of the original eight.

After 1945, further enhancements were incorporated into carrier design. The addition of helicopters allowed carriers to launch operations against enemy submarines and also to land marines to secure coastal positions. The angled flight deck allowed aircraft to take off while others were landing. In 1961 the USS *Enterprise* was completed – at 75,700 tons it was the largest aircraft carrier ever built. It could carry 100 aircraft and, being nuclear powered, had a cruising range the equivalent of 20 times around the world.

In 1967 the British decided to phase out fixed-wing aircraft in preference for the Vertical Short Take-Off and Landing (VSTOL) BAe Sea Harrier. The upward-angled ski-slope deck made take-offs easier for Harriers, and subsequently both Italy and Spain have adopted this less expensive option of a carrier equipped with Harriers. In the mid-1970s the Soviet Union began building carriers equipped with VSTOL Yakovlev Yak-36MP "Forger" aircraft and helicopters.

Carriers were involved in the Korean War, at Suez in 1956, in Vietnam, in the Falklands and in the Gulf War of 1990–1991.

▼ CARRIER POWER
This US Navy Kitty Hawk class conventionally powered carrier has a crew of nearly 6,000. It can carry up to 50 aircraft including F-14 Tomcats and F-18 Hornets as well as helicopters.

▼ BATTLE GROUP
A modern naval battle group is built up around a carrier, with supporting vessels to provide cover against enemy aircraft, surface vessels and submarines. The carrier's combat aircraft can attack ships and installations at a safe range from the group.

Key Dates

- 1913 HMS *Hermes* commissioned.

- 1940 November 11: Fleet Air Arm air attack on Italian fleet at Taranto.

- 1941 December 7: Japanese carrier aircraft attack US Navy in Pearl Harbor.

- 1942 May: Major carrier action in Battle of the Coral Sea.

- 1942 June 4–7: Battle of Midway.

- 1961 USS *Enterprise* is the first nuclear-powered carrier.

- 2014 Launch of HMS *Queen Elizabeth*, the largest warship ever built for the Royal Navy.

Early Fighter Planes

▲ RED BARON
The German fighter ace Baron Manfred von Richthofen was killed in 1918. He commanded a squadron called the "flying circus".

THE EARLY PILOTS were often wealthy and enterprising sportsmen, so the idea of shooting at each other in war was considered to be ungentlemanly. However, it was not long before pilots carried rifles and pistols when flying, and took pot shots at each other. The first true fighter action took place during World War I on 5 October 1914, when a French Voisin V89 brought down a German Aviatik aircraft with its machine-gun fire.

The interrupter gear invented by the Dutchman Anthony Fokker allowed German aircraft to fire forwards through the arc of their propeller. This meant that fighter pilots could aim their aircraft at enemy planes.

▶ FOKKER TRIPLANE
The German World War I Fokker Dr-I fighter had a maximum speed of 200kmh/125mph and was armed with two 7.92mm Spandau machine guns.

Between 1914 and 1918 aircraft speeds increased from 170kmh/105mph to 270kmh/165mph. The first fighter flew at a height of 4,000m/13,000ft, but by the end of the war they were up to 6,000m/20,000ft.

One of the most successful British fighters was the SE-5a. It had a maximum speed of 66kmh/41mph and was armed with a single synchronized Vickers or Lewis machine gun. The German D1 Albatross had a maximum speed of 55kmh/34mph and was armed with twin 7.92mm Spandau machine guns.

The interwar period saw the development of the all-metal aircraft with wing-mounted machine guns and also cannon that fired explosive rounds. By 1939 the Messerschmitt Bf-109E had a top speed of 572kmh/355mph, and by 1945 the 109G with a 1,900hp inline engine had a top speed of 689kmh/428mph. Armament was a 30mm cannon and two 7.92mm machine guns.

The World War II Allied fighters, the Supermarine Spitfire, and the North American P-51 Mustang were classic types. The Mustang, fitted with extra fuel tanks, had a

FIGHTERS OF THE WORLD WARS

Early fighters were slow scout aircraft with simple armament. By the beginning of World War II they were all-metal monoplanes with cannon as well as machine guns. By the close of the war the first jet fighters were in action and many aircraft were equipped with radar.

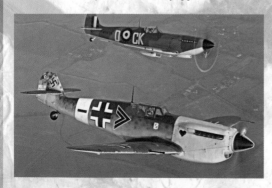

◀ BATTLE OF BRITAIN
A Spitfire with a postwar Merlin-engined Messerschmitt Me-109 photographed during the film *The Battle of Britain*. Spain used the Messerschmitt 109 after the war but put in new engines to improve its performance.

▲ P-38 LIGHTNING
With a top speed of 666kmh/414mph the Lockheed Lightning, introduced in 1941, was armed with four machine guns and a 20mm cannon. It could carry 1,800kg/4,000lb of bombs.

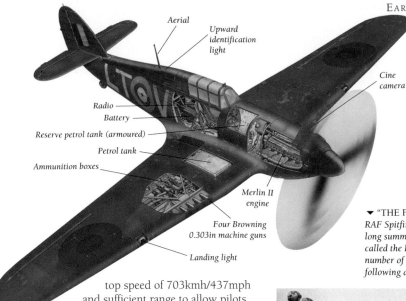

Aerial

Upward
identification
light

Cine
camera

Radio

Battery

Reserve petrol tank (armoured)

Petrol tank

Ammunition boxes

Merlin II
engine

Four Browning
0.303in machine guns

Landing light

◀ HAWKER HURRICANE
*Armed with eight .303in
machine guns, the Hurricane
was older and slower than the
Spitfire. However, it shot down
more German aircraft during
the Battle of Britain than the
Spitfire did. Hurricane pilots
concentrated on attacking the
slower, more vulnerable
bombers, while Spitfires fought
with the escorting
Messerschmitt 109 fighters.*

▼ "THE FEW"
*RAF Spitfire pilots wait on an airstrip in the
long summer air battle of 1940 that was
called the Battle of Britain. The small
number of pilots were nicknamed "The Few"
following a speech by Winston Churchill.*

top speed of 703kmh/437mph
and sufficient range to allow pilots
to escort bombers to Berlin and back.
The Spitfire went through 21 different marks between
1936 and 1945, becoming a more powerful and more
heavily armed fighter with each version. The Spitfire
MIX, powered by a Rolls-Royce 1,660hp Merlin engine,
had a top speed of 657kmh/408mph and was armed
with .303in machine guns and 20mm cannon.

Some of the fighters continued in service into the
1950s and 1960s as ground-attack aircraft. Those
fighter aircraft that are still flying today are in the hands
of aviation enthusiasts.

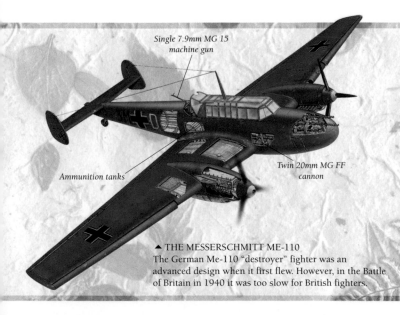

Single 7.9mm MG 15
machine gun

Ammunition tanks

Twin 20mm MG FF
cannon

▲ THE MESSERSCHMITT ME-110
The German Me-110 "destroyer" fighter was an
advanced design when it first flew. However, in the Battle
of Britain in 1940 it was too slow for British fighters.

Key Dates

- 1910 Rifle fired from an aircraft
  for first time.
- 1912 Machine gun fired from
  aircraft for first time.
- 1913 37mm cannon fired from
  an aircraft.
- 1914–1918 World War I.
- 1914 October 5: first aircraft to
  be shot down.
- 1917 Royal Aircraft Factory
  SE-5a introduced.
- 1939–1945 World War II.
- 1944–1945 Me-262, the world's
  first jet fighter.

Jet Fighters

D URING THE 1930s aircraft powered by jet propulsion featured in science fiction comics, together with men from Mars and moon rockets. However, both the British and the Germans were conducting research in this field before World War II. The first jet to fly was the German He-178 in 1939, followed by the British Gloster Meteor which flew fitted with jet engines in 1941. The two aircraft never met in combat, but science fiction became reality in 1944 when RAF Meteors took to the air to chase and shoot down German V-1 flying bombs.

▲ FLYING HIGH
An F-15 Eagle pilot in the cockpit

Deliveries of the world's first operational jet-powered fighter, the German Messerschmitt Me-262 *Schwalbe* (Swallow), began in May 1944. However, these were initially configured as bombers and the fighter did not enter service until later that year. It had a maximum speed of 869kmh/540kph and was armed with four 30mm cannon and 24 5cm R4M rockets. Me-262s took a heavy toll of US Army Air Forces (USAAF) bombers during 1945. On the Allied side, the Gloster Meteor had a top speed of 660kmh/410mph and was armed with four 20mm cannon.

The Korean War saw the first jet versus jet action when US Air Force F-86 Sabres, F-80 Shooting Stars and US Marine Corps F9F Panthers fought with Chinese MiG-15s. The first victory went to a US Air Force (USAF) F-80 Shooting Star on 8 November 1950 against a Chinese MiG-15 over the Yalu river.

Jet fighters have been in action, either in air combat or attacking ground targets, in most parts of the world since the 1950s. Over North Vietnam, in the conflicts between India and Pakistan, the Arab–Israeli wars, the Gulf Wars between Iran and Iraq and between the Coalition Forces and Iraq, US-designed aircraft have fought with Soviet aircraft. In the Falklands in 1982 British Harriers were pitted against US and French-designed aircraft. Soviet jet aircraft were used in ground attack operations during the Afghan war.

Among the most versatile jet fighter aircraft are the Russian MiG-21 and the American McDonnell Douglas F-4 Phantom, which have fought in

◀ FIGHTING FALCON
The American F-16 Fighting Falcon multi-role fighter is made by General Dynamics, and is in service in more than 14 countries worldwide. Painted in striking livery, it is flown by the USAF Thunderbirds display team.

A NEW BREED OF WAR PLANE
Immediately after World War II there was a move to design and build jet fighters. US and Chinese jets clashed in the Korean War in 1950–1953. Although missiles such as the Sidewinder have been widely used in combat, the 30mm cannon is still a very effective weapon and can be used against ground targets.

◀ MIRAGE 5
The French Dassault fighter has a top speed of 1,912kmh/1,188mph. Operating in a ground-attack role the Mirage can carry bombs, rockets or missiles.

▼ PHANTOM
The F-4 Phantom has been built in larger numbers than any Western combat aircraft since World War II.

▲ F86 SABRE
The first woman to fly faster than sound, Jacqueline Cochran, achieved the record in a Sabre on 18 May 1953.

▲ HAWK
The British BAe Hawk is a versatile combat aircraft that can also be used as a trainer.

Weapons system
ranging radar

IFF aerials
(identification
friend or foe)

Koliesov lift
engines

▼ FORGER
*The Russian Yak-38, or "Forger", was a vertical
take-off combat aircraft that first flew in 1971.*

▼ HARRIER
*The BAe Harrier has proved an effective
fighter and ground-attack aircraft in the
Falklands and in the Gulf War.*

GSh-23L
cannon pack

Vietnam and the Middle East.

In many of these combats the AIM-9 Sidewinder heat-seeking air-to-air missile has been the key weapon. The AIM-9 heat-seeking missile takes its inspiration from nature. The sidewinder snake locates its prey by detecting their body heat with special sensors in its head. The AIM-9 Sidewinder missile detects the heat from the engine exhausts of its target.

▲ EAGLE
*A missile-armed USAF McDonnell Douglas F-15 Eagle multi role
fighter moves into position to refuel in-flight.*

▼ EUROFIGHTER
Built by a consortium of Spain, Germany, Italy and the UK, the Eurofighter Typhoon first flew on 29 March 1994. The project has been hampered by political problems because Germany has reduced its requirement and has argued for a less expensive aircraft now that the Cold War has ended.

Key Dates

- 1939 German Heinkel He-178 jet fighter flies.
- 1944 German Me-262 enters service.
- 1944 British Gloster Meteor in action against V-1 flying bombs.
- 1944 Lockheed Shooting Star enters service with USAAF/USAF.
- 1945 December 3: de Havilland Vampire makes first jet landing and take-off from a carrier.
- 1950 First jet versus jet victory in Korean War.
- 1966 August 31: Hawker Harrier makes first hovering flight.

Early Bombers

▲ LANCASTER
The British bomber was used in the "Dam Buster" raids against Germany.

T HE POTENTIAL FOR AIRCRAFT to operate as a platform for delivering bombs to enemy targets was realized as early as 1911. In that year the first bombs were dropped from an aircraft during the Italo-Turkish war.

In World War I bombers started as scout planes in which the crew had taken a few grenades to lob at the enemy lines. Bombers grew from these small single-engined two-seater aircraft to types such as the British Handley Page 0/400. Around 550 of these twin-engined bombers were built. When they attacked German military and industrial targets, they flew in formations of 30–40 aircraft.

The German Gotha GIV and GV bombers attacked targets in London and southern England in World War I. They carried between 300kg/660lb and 500kg/1,100lb of bombs, had a crew of three and were capable of 175kmh/110mph with a range of 600km/370 miles.

In the interwar period there was considerable fear that bombers carrying bombs loaded with poison gas would attack large cities, causing huge casualties. The German Air Force was re-formed secretly after World War I, and the sleek Heinkel He-111 and Dornier Do 17, both described as airliners, were re-engineered as bombers for World War II. The He-111 carried 2,500kg/5,500lb of bombs and the Do 17 1,000kg/2,200lb. The Junkers Ju 87 became notorious as the Stuka dive bomber

◀ HANDLEY PAGE 0/400
With a crew of three the RAF Handley Page 0/400 could carry up to 900kg/2,000lb of bombs. It was armed with up to five .303in Lewis machine guns.

BOMBERS OF THE WORLD WARS

In the two World Wars the payload and range of bombers increased dramatically. At the beginning of World War II the German He-111 was carrying 2,500kg/5,500lb of bombs at 420kmh/260mph. By the close of World War II the four-engined Avro Lancaster was carrying 6,350kg/14,000lb of bombs at 462kmh/287mph for 2,575km/1,600 miles.

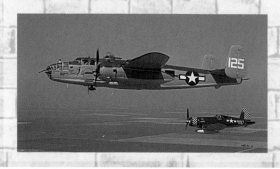

◀ B-25 MITCHELL
A US Mitchell medium bomber escorted by a Vought F-4U Corsair carrier-based fighter. The Mitchell could carry 1,400kg/3,000lb of bombs. Several of the planes have been restored in the US.

▲ LANCASTER
The RAF Avro Lancaster entered service in March 1942 and became the mainstay of the bombing campaign against Germany. By 1944 there were 40 Lancaster squadrons in action.

▲ B-17 FLYING FORTRESS
The B-17 could carry 2,700kg/6,000lb of bombs at 503kmh/313mph.
By the end of the war over 4,700 were in front line service with the USAAF.

and the Ju 88 made the transition from bomber to heavily armed fighter.

On the Allied side bombers grew in size, range and bomb load. In 1939, the Vickers Wellington could carry 3,000kg/6,600lb of bombs. By 1945 the Avro Lancaster was able to carry 6,350kg/14,000lb of bombs to 2,670km/1,660 miles. The USAAF Boeing B-17 had a maximum bomb load of 5,800kg/12,800lb and a range of 5,310km/3,300 miles. The Consolidated B-24 Liberator carried up to 3,600kg/8,000lb of bombs at 483kmh/300mph.

Supporters of strategic bombing say that it made a major contribution to the Allied victory in World War II. However, despite the importance of bombing, history has shown that victory is only guaranteed when ground forces enter enemy territory and occupy it.

▼ DRESDEN 1945
German authorities sort through bodies in the ghastly aftermath of the attack on Dresden. Attacked by 773 RAF bombers by night and by the USAAF during the day, roughly 20sq km/8sq miles were destroyed by fire. In the overcrowded city more than 100,000 died in the firestorm.

Key Dates

- 1911 Bombs first dropped in the Italo-Turkish war.

- 1914–1918 World War I: tactical and rudimentary strategic bombing established.

- 1936–1939 Spanish Civil War: tactical bombing perfected.

- 1939–1945 World War II: first strategic bombing.

- 1942 Pressurized B-29 Superfortress flies.

- 1944–1945 German Arado 234 jet bomber in action.

- 1945 Atomic bombs dropped on Japan by B-29s.

Modern Jets and Stealth

THE CLOAK OF INVISIBILITY is a feature of many ancient myths. Although it may not be a reality, new techniques in aircraft design have made them very hard to detect by systems such as radar. These features are known as "stealth", and all modern combat aircraft now have some stealth features. Stealth in aircraft design is the attempt to minimize the ways in which aircraft can be detected by ground or airborne defensive systems.

In its earliest form, camouflage paint was a stealth feature, but the echo from radar would show the location of the most ingeniously camouflaged aircraft. One technique for defeating early radars was to fly very low and so hide the aircraft among the clutter of radar echoes. Modern radars can now discriminate between clutter and moving targets, so the next move was to design an aircraft that gave very little or no radar return. This was achieved by giving the aircraft as few surfaces as possible

from which a radar beam could bounce off and so give an echo. In addition to the design of the aircraft's profile, it was coated with a radar-absorbent material that would further reduce or limit the echo. If there is no discernible radar echo, the heat from the engines

▲ NIGHTHAWK
*The Lockheed F-117A
Nighthawk first saw action in
1989 in Panama and later in
1991 in the Gulf. An F-117
was shot down over the former
Yugoslavia in 1999.*

▶ STEALTH
*The Lockheed/Boeing F-22
Raptor, the current fighter
for the USAF, has "stealth"
features within its design.*

MODERN DEVELOPMENTS

Radar and thermal detection systems have made combat aircraft vulnerable, even if they are flying low and at night. Since radar reflects off flat hard surfaces, any aircraft with a less angular shape and a "radar-absorbent" coating is less likely to be detected. The engines produce hot gases that can be picked up by radar. However, these gases can be cooled or screened before they pass into the air.

Nuclear warhead

Tercom guidance system

*F-107 WR-400
turbofan jet engine*

Folding wings

▼ BLENDED WING
Boeing is experimenting with blended wing body (BWB) designs, aiming to increase fuel efficiency and reduce noise. Such craft have no clear dividing line between the wings and the main body.

▶ SCALE MODEL
A wind-tunnel model of an American experimental combat aircraft. Computer models are used to evaluate new designs.

▲ CRUISE MISSILE
The German V-1, the earliest cruise missile, was slow and fairly inaccurate. In the late 1970s the United States produced a cruise missile that could be launched from land, sea or air. It has a guidance system that is very accurate and can fly a circuitous route to its target.

▶ BOEING B-52
The veteran USAF B-52 strategic bomber has been used since 1955. It can carry up to 22,680kg/50,000lb of air-launched cruise missiles or 51,454kg/113,437lb conventional bombs.

▶ SPIRIT
The Northrop Grumman B-2A looks back to the German Gotha flying design which was developed at the close of World War II. The B-2A can carry 22,680kg/50,000lb of ordnance at 764kmh/475mph and has a range of 11,000km/6,900 miles before needing to refuel.

The classic stealth aircraft is the US Lockheed F-117 fighter, which was used in action in 1989 as a bomber in the invasion of Panama and later in attacks on Iraq in 1991. An F-117 was shot down during the air attacks on Serbia in 1999.

The Northrop Grumman B-2 Spirit is a dedicated stealth bomber. It is capable of carrying 16,920kg/37,300lb of ordnance over a maximum range of 9,815km/6,100 miles.

The USAF Advanced Tactical Fighter initiative took place in the 1990s. It was a competition between the Lockheed/General Dynamics YF-22 and the McDonnell Douglas YF-23, two fighters with stealth features. The Lockheed aircraft was also briefly dubbed SuperStar and Rapier, but is now designated the F-22 Raptor. It entered service in December 2005.

of a modern aircraft can still be detected. The solution to this problem is to position the engines so that the hot gases from them flow over the top of the wings. The gases are cooled as they pass over special ceramic plates.

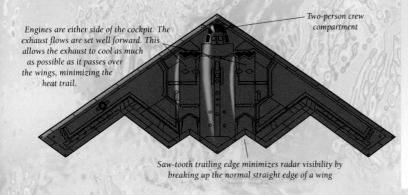

▼ STEALTH TECHNOLOGY
Although stealth is associated with aircraft, it has also been employed in the design of modern combat ships and even in tanks. Ships and tanks can be detected on radar and thermal imaging, so their exhausts need to be screened and any radar reflective surfaces have to be softened.

Engines are either side of the cockpit. The exhaust flows are set well forward. This allows the exhaust to cool as much as possible as it passes over the wings, minimizing the heat trail.

Two-person crew compartment

Saw-tooth trailing edge minimizes radar visibility by breaking up the normal straight edge of a wing

Key Dates

- 1951 Canberra bomber is the first jet to fly across the North Atlantic non-stop.

- 1955 B-52 enters service with the USAF.

- 1977 December: first flight of Lockheed Martin F-117.

- 1983–1984 US stealth research ship *Sea Shadow* built.

- 1989 July 17: first flight of Northrop Grumman B-2 Spirit.

- 1991 March 14: Smyge Swedish stealth patrol craft launched.

- 2005 December 15: F-22 Raptor goes into service.

Airborne Troops

▲ PARACHUTE
The light fabric of a parachute traps air, slowing down the descent of the soldier or paratrooper.

I T IS HARD FOR US to realize how unusual paratroops seemed when they first appeared in World War II. Most soldiers had never been in an airliner, so men who arrived by parachute from aircraft seemed almost as fantastic as spacemen. The Soviet Union pioneered airborne forces in the interwar years. However, it was Nazi Germany that made first use of them in World War II.

Airborne troops could be delivered to the battlefield either by parachute or in gliders. Troop-carrying gliders carried between 10 and 29 troops and could also be used to transport vehicles and light artillery. They were particularly effective when an operation called for a formed group of men to attack a target such as a bridge or coastal artillery battery. The problem with paratroops was that they could be scattered over a large area if they jumped too high.

The German attack on the island of Crete in May 1941 involved 22,500 paratroops and 80 gliders. The airborne forces suffered very heavy losses: 4,000 were killed, 2,000 wounded and 220 aircraft were destroyed. Hitler declared that "the day of the paratrooper is over".

The British and Americans were quick to learn from the Germans mistakes, and airborne forces were used on D-Day in Normandy in June 1944. Airborne forces were also in Sicily in 1943, in Normandy in 1944, and at the Rhine crossings in 1945. In Burma in 1943, British and Commonwealth troops known as Chindits were landed by glider deep inside Japanese lines. They drew Japanese forces away from the front lines in India.

After World War II, the French made extensive use of paratroops in Indochina (Vietnam) between 1948 and 1954. However, in May 1954 at Dien Bien Phu they were defeated

▸ PARATROOPER
A British paratrooper in World War II. The buckle in the middle of his chest operates as a quick release for the parachute harness.

▲ JUMPING FOR FUN
A sports parachutist exits from an aircraft in the "spread stable position". Before he pulls the release on his parachute he will enjoy a period of "free fall".

AIRBORNE OPERATIONS
Attacks by paratroops and glider-borne soldiers in World War II were sometimes a gamble because these lightly equipped soldiers could be defeated by ground troops with tanks and artillery. If friendly ground forces could link up with them, airborne troops could sieze and hold key positions such as bridges, fortifications and causeways. They could help to keep up the momentum of an attack.

▸ TRANSPORT
Transport aircraft can carry trucks and vehicles that can be unloaded if a suitable airfield has been captured and secured.

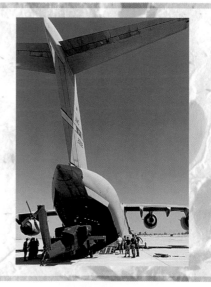

▲ DROP ZONE
Parachutes float down and collapse in a mass military drop. The flat area allocated for such an operation is called a drop zone, or DZ. Helicopters put down soldiers on a landing zone, or LZ.

when they set up an airborne base deep inside Viet Minh lines. They lost 11 complete parachute battalions in the fighting.

On 5 November 1956 French and British paratroops landed at Port Said to recapture the Suez Canal, which had been nationalized by the Egyptians.

Today, helicopters mean troops no longer need to parachute from aircraft. However, airborne forces are still considered an elite group within all national armies.

▲ SEALS
These Seals, US Navy Special Forces troops, are wearing harnesses that clip on to a ladder. They are being lifted by a Chinook helicopter.

▶ HOW A PARACHUTE WORKS

The umbrella shape of the parachute, called a canopy, is made from silk and, later, nylon. It traps air and so slows the descent of the parachutist or cargo. A small hole in the middle canopy allows air to escape and prevents the parachute from swinging from side to side.

Modern square parachutes are called "ram air". They can be steered allowing the parachutist to land with very great accuracy. The latest development is a remotely controlled steerable canopy that can be used by special forces in remote locations to take delivery of cargo. The load is dropped at a great height.

Key Dates

- 1797 Parachute invented.

- 1927 Italians are first to drop a "stick" of paratroops.

- 1930s Soviet forces develop paratroops.

- 1939–1945 Airborne operations in Europe and Far East.

- 1941 German airborne attack on island of Crete.

- 1944 British and Polish landings at Arnhem.

- 1953–1954 Battle of Dien Bien Phu in Vietnam.

- 1956 French and British paratroops capture Suez Canal.

Doomsday Weapons

▲ GAS DRILL
British soldiers wear anti-gas uniforms during a gas drill in 1939.

FOR CENTURIES WARS HAVE caused destruction on a large scale. However, it was not until the 20th century that the term "weapons of mass destruction" (WMD) came into use to describe chemical, biological and nuclear weapons. Yet biological and chemical weapons are some of the oldest in existence.

In ancient times armies poisoned wells with dead animals or used disease-bearing rats to spread infection around besieged cities.

The first modern use of chemical weapons was in World War I. On 22 April 1915 the Germans released chlorine in support of an attack against the British and French at Ypres. In World War I most of the

types of war gases that now exist were developed – these caused temporary choking and blistering on the skin or poisoned the blood. The blistering agent was called mustard gas because of its mustard-like smell.

By the end of World War I these gases had been contained in artillery shells. The shells were fired as part of a conventional high-explosive barrage when soldiers attacked.

▶ RESPIRATOR
These US troops are equipped with the ABC-M17 respirator, which is a hood that fits over the head.

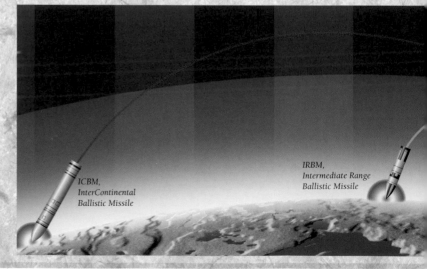

WEAPONS OF MASS DESTRUCTION

Nuclear, biological and chemical weapons are particularly horrible because the damage they cause can be vast and almost open-ended. Viruses and germs used in biological weapons reproduce themselves, and the radiation following a nuclear explosion remains a hazard for centuries. The harmful effects are not restricted to a specific area, and can be spread by the weather over a wide area. These factors distinguish such weapons from conventional explosives, whose effect lasts for just one detonation in a localized area.

ICBM, InterContinental Ballistic Missile

IRBM, Intermediate Range Ballistic Missile

▼ FIRST ATOMIC BOMB
The first atomic bomb, codenamed "Little Boy", was dropped on Hiroshima on 6 August 1945. It had the power of 20,000 tons of TNT. It killed 78,150 people and destroyed 10sq km/6sq miles of the city.

▲ BALLISTIC MISSILE
A US ballistic missile lifts off during a test launch. With improved guidance, missiles are very accurate and capable of hitting small targets such as enemy missile silos.

The chemists of Nazi Germany produced the most effective chemical agent when they discovered nerve gas poisons. Called Tabun, Sarin and Soman, they affected the human nervous system and killed within a few minutes. The Nazis never used this weapon because they feared that the Allies also possessed it and would retaliate; in fact the Allies did not have the weapon.

Iraq used mustard and nerve gases in 1984 during the Iran–Iraq war (1980–1988). They caused 40,000 deaths and injuries to the unprotected Iranian troops.

Atomic weapons were developed by a team of Europeans and Americans led by Robert Oppenheimer in the US in World War II. They worked by releasing the energy from splitting the atom of uranium ore. The drive for this programme had been the fear that German physicists might be developing a similar bomb. The first atomic bomb test took place in New Mexico on 16 July 1945. On 6 August an atomic bomb codenamed "Little Boy" was dropped on the Japanese city of Hiroshima. Three days later a device codenamed "Fat Man" was dropped on the city of Nagasaki. The explosions were the equivalent of the detonation of 20,000 tons of high explosives. In Hiroshima over 70,000 people died or disappeared: in Nagasaki the figure was 40,000.

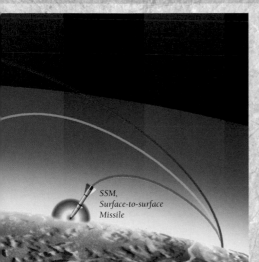

SSM,
Surface-to-surface Missile

◄ MISSILES
Missiles are called "ballistic" because their flight is curved like that of a long-range shell.

▼ CRUISE MISSILE
An artist's impression of a nuclear capable cruise missile as it homes in on its target.

Key Dates

- 1915 April 22: German chemical attack on Western Front.

- 1939–1945 German researchers develop nerve gases.

- 1945 August 6: atomic bomb dropped on Hiroshima.

- 1945 August 9: atomic bomb dropped on Nagasaki.

- 1949 USSR detonates its first atomic bomb.

- 1952 Britain detonates its first atomic bomb.

- 1966–1973 US forces use Agent Orange defoliant in Vietnam.

REFERENCE

◀ ANCIENT JAPAN

Japanese fishermen pursue a whale through high seas in this typically stylized image. Early people in northeastern Japan relied on fish and other seafood for much of their diet. Whale meat was an important food source to them.

Ancient Civilizations

The first civilizations tended to develop in areas with fertile land, a good water supply and an even climate. This was because people had to develop efficient farming methods, and ways of storing and trading food, before they could build large cities. The type of soil, the distance from water sources, whether the ground was high or low, and the climate, all affected the nature of the civilization that emerged in any given area. In North Africa and the Middle East, great rivers such as the Nile in Egypt and the Tigris and Euphrates in Mesopotamia (in present-day Iraq) allowed the development of increasingly complex civilizations. Natural barriers, such as mountains or deserts, limited the growth of some civilizations, such as the Greek city states. By contrast, the landscapes of Central and South America were important in creating and defining the unique cultures that developed there.

HELLENISTIC AGE
Alexander the Great (356-323BC) was a brilliant general who built up a huge empire, including Macedonia, Greece, Egypt and Persia.

THE ETRUSCANS
From 800–100BC, the Etruscans built a series of cities between the Arno and Tiber rivers in western Italy.

NORTH AMERICAN PEOPLE
The Hopewell civilization in North America began in around 200BC.

EARLY MEXICANS
The Olmecs ruled north-central Mexico between 1200–900BC.

CENTRAL AMERICAN SUCCESS
The Maya civilization lasted between 300BC–AD900. Maya cities were built in southern Mexico, Guatemala, Honduras and Belize.

AFRICAN CIVILIZATIONS
Many civilizations and kingdoms developed on the huge continent of Africa. That of Benin flourished from 1100 to 1897.

PEOPLE OF THE ANDES
The civilization of Chavin de Huantar in the high Andes mountains reached its peak 850–200BC.

ANCIENT ROME
The mighty Roman Empire developed from the city of Rome in central Italy. It was at its largest extent in AD117.

ANCIENT EGYPT
On the fertile Nile Delta in northern Africa, the ancient Egyptian civilization flourished between 3100BC and 333BC.

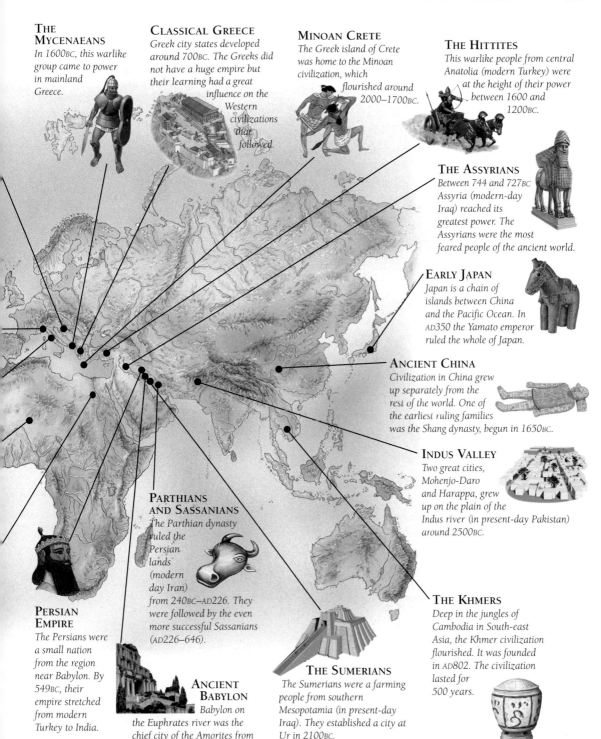

THE MYCENAEANS
In 1600BC, this warlike group came to power in mainland Greece.

CLASSICAL GREECE
Greek city states developed around 700BC. The Greeks did not have a huge empire but their learning had a great influence on the Western civilizations that followed.

MINOAN CRETE
The Greek island of Crete was home to the Minoan civilization, which flourished around 2000–1700BC.

THE HITTITES
This warlike people from central Anatolia (modern Turkey) were at the height of their power between 1600 and 1200BC.

THE ASSYRIANS
Between 744 and 727BC Assyria (modern-day Iraq) reached its greatest power. The Assyrians were the most feared people of the ancient world.

EARLY JAPAN
Japan is a chain of islands between China and the Pacific Ocean. In AD350 the Yamato emperor ruled the whole of Japan.

ANCIENT CHINA
Civilization in China grew up separately from the rest of the world. One of the earliest ruling families was the Shang dynasty, begun in 1650BC.

INDUS VALLEY
Two great cities, Mohenjo-Daro and Harappa, grew up on the plain of the Indus river (in present-day Pakistan) around 2500BC.

PARTHIANS AND SASSANIANS
The Parthian dynasty ruled the Persian lands (modern day Iran) from 240BC–AD226. They were followed by the even more successful Sassanians (AD226–646).

PERSIAN EMPIRE
The Persians were a small nation from the region near Babylon. By 549BC, their empire stretched from modern Turkey to India.

ANCIENT BABYLON
Babylon on the Euphrates river was the chief city of the Amorites from around 1900BC.

THE SUMERIANS
The Sumerians were a farming people from southern Mesopotamia (in present-day Iraq). They established a city at Ur in 2100BC.

THE KHMERS
Deep in the jungles of Cambodia in South-east Asia, the Khmer civilization flourished. It was founded in AD802. The civilization lasted for 500 years.

World Exploration

The desire to know the world in which we live has led many brave people to explore wild regions, risking their lives in the pursuit of discovery. Throughout history, trade has been the main driving force of exploration. It was the search for a new trade route to China and India that sent Vasco da Gama into the Indian Ocean, and Christopher Columbus across the Atlantic. Many explorers set out seeking fame and fortune. Others were motivated by religious conviction, feeling it was their duty to convert other races to Christianity. Today, there are few places on Earth that have not been fully explored, except for the high mountains of Tibet and the ocean floor.

AROUND THE WORLD
In trying to find a westerly route to the Spice Islands in Indonesia, the Portuguese sailor Ferdinand Magellan and his crew became the first people to circumnavigate the Earth.

EXPLORING CANADA
In May 1497, the Italian adventurer John Cabot set sail from Bristol, England. A month later he landed in Newfoundland off the coast of Canada.

THE NEW WORLD
Early explorers returned from Central and South America with stories of vast temples and huge amounts of gold. In 1521, a Spanish lawyer called Hernán Cortés made his fortune by seizing the Aztec capital city of Tenochtitlán and capturing its ruler.

HEYERDAHL'S VOYAGE
The Norwegian explorer Thor Heyerdahl set out to prove that the Polynesians could have come originally from South America. He built a raft, like those used by early settlers, and sailed from Peru to the South Pacific.

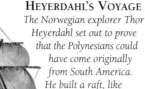

THE VOYAGE OF COLUMBUS
An Italian named Christopher Columbus devoted his life to finding a sea route to Asia by sailing west across the Atlantic Ocean. Financially supported by Queen Isabella of Spain, he set out in 1492, and after 36 days at sea, he found what we now call the Bahamas.

VIKING EXPEDITIONS

In AD 992, Leif Eriksson set out from the Viking colony of Greenland, heading west. He sailed via Baffin Island to a place in eastern Canada he called Vinland.

THE NORTH-EAST PASSAGE

In 1878, Nils Nordenskjold tried to find a route northeast from Europe to the Pacific Ocean. He set out from southern Sweden on board his ship the Vega. In 1879 he finally sailed into the Pacific Ocean.

DEVOTED TO TRAVEL

Ibn Battuta was born in 1304. He spent a total of 28 years voyaging around the Islamic Empire, as well as much of Europe, South-east Asia and China.

MARCO POLO

The explorer Marco Polo was born in Venice. He claimed to have stayed in China for 20 years from 1271.

THE SILK ROAD

Merchants from Europe, the Middle East, central Asia and China road along the Silk Road to buy and sell goods.

DR LIVINGSTONE

The missionary and doctor, David Livingstone, went to Africa to convert the local people to Christianity. Once there, however, he journeyed extensively and helped to transform European knowledge about Africa.

ROUTE TO INDIA

The Portuguese navigator Vasco da Gama was the first European to reach India by sea. Between 1497 and 1498 he sailed around the coast of Africa, eventually arriving in India.

INTO AFRICA

From the 1760s Europeans explored northern and central Africa, mapping the Nile and Niger rivers and the Sahara Desert. The south, however, remained largely unexplored by Europeans until the late 1800s.

COOK

Between 1768 and 1779, James Cook of the British Royal Navy explored much of the Pacific Ocean, including Eastern Australia, which he called New South Wales.

2 million–1BC

	2 million–12,000BC	12,000–10,000BC	10,000–3000BC
EUROPE	**1 million years ago–400,000BC** First known settlement of *Homo erectus* in Europe. **400,000–30,000BC** Neanderthals and "modern" humans are living side by side in Mesopotamia. **30,000–12,000BC** Europe freezes in the Ice Age. Artists make great cave paintings in France and Spain.	**12,000–900BC** The great ice sheets begin to thaw as temperatures increase. Sea levels rise. 	**10,000–5000BC** Cave paintings in Spain show men armed with bows in combat. **6000–4000BC** Farming spreads to eastern Europe, probably from Turkey. **4000–2000BC** Stone circles and other megalithic monuments become common in western Europe.
AFRICA	**2–1 million years ago** Early hominids, the first human-apes, are alive in Eastern Africa. **1 million years ago–400,000BC** *Homo erectus*, a type of early human, use stone hand axes as a multi-purpose tool. **400,000–30,000BC** *Homo sapiens*, humans, appear in various places south of the Sahara.		**6000–4000BC** The climate of what is now the Sahara Desert is very wet. Cattle herding is common in many parts of the region. **3100BC** The kingdom of Egypt is founded. King Narmer unifies the Upper and Lower kingdoms of Egypt and becomes the first pharaoh. The ancient Egyptians worship many gods.
ASIA	 **2–1 million years ago** *Homo erectus* is established in both Java and China and has probably mastered the use of fire. **400,000–30,000BC** Neanderthals and "modern" humans are living side by side in Mesopotamia.	**12,000–9000BC** The dog is domesticated in the Middle East. The first pottery is produced by the Jomon civilization in Japan. 	**9000–6000BC** Farming is established in the Fertile Crescent in the Middle East. **6000–4000BC** Trading towns such as Çatal Hüyük, Turkey, begin to develop. **5000BC** The Sumerians, a farming people, settle in southern Mesopotamia. **2900BC** Earliest known writing, cuneiform, is developed in Mesopotamia.
AUSTRALASIA	**30,000BC** Human settlement of Australia probably begins. **29,000BC** People are living in Tasmania, which is linked to the Australian mainland by a land bridge. **25,000BC** Puritjarra Rock Shelter near the Cleland Hills, Northern Territory, is occupied. **24,000BC** Signs of human occupation near Lake Mungo, New South Wales.	**10,000BC** The population of native Australians is about 300,000 people. 	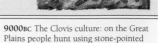
AMERICA	**30,000–12,000BC** The first settlement of North America begins as men and women cross the Bering land bridge from Siberia. 	**12,000–9000BC** People in Chile build houses from wood and skins – the first evidence of shelters in the Americas.	**9000BC** The Clovis culture: on the Great Plains people hunt using stone-pointed spears. **4000–2000BC** The farmers of Mexico domesticate the maize plant. Other crops spread to North America.

2500–2000BC	2000–1500BC	1500–1000BC	1000–500BC	500–1BC
2000BC– First iron working transforms tools and weapons. **2000BC** The Minoans of Crete build a palace at Knossos. **2000BC** Celtic tribes worship their own groups of gods.	**2000–1700BC** The Minoan Civilization in Crete is at the height of its success. **1900BC** Cretans use potter's wheel. **1800** Flint daggers made in Sweden. **1600** Bronze weapons used in Sweden and Greece.	**1400BC** Phoenician sailors explore the Mediterranean. **1450BC** The Mycenaean civilization on the Greek mainland invades and conquers the Minoans of Crete. **1200BC** Decline of the Mycenaean civilization.	**900BC** Greeks begin to trade in the Mediterranean. **753BC** According to legend, Rome is founded by Romulus and Remus. **700BC** Greek city states develop. **509BC** Rome made a republic	**490BC** Battle of Marathon fought between the Greeks and the Persians. Greeks defeat an enemy once thought to be unbeatable. **146BC** Greece comes under Roman rule. Many Greek gods are renamed by the Romans. **27BC** Augustus becomes the first Roman emperor.

2686–2181BC Old Kingdom in Egypt. The pharaohs build up their power and are buried in pyramids.	**2040–1786BC** Middle Kingdom of Egypt. **1786–1567BC** Invasion forces sent to Egypt from Syria and Palestine.	**1570–1085BC** New Kingdom. Egyptian pharaohs rule once more and the civilization flourishes. **1490BC** Egyptians sail to Punt on the East African coast.	**1083–333BC** The Egyptian empire collapses. Egypt divides into separate states. **500BC** Hanno, from Carthage, in modern Tunisia, explores the coast of Africa.	**333–323BC** Egypt becomes part of Alexander the Great's empire.

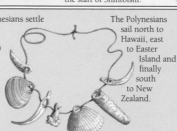

2500BC Ur in Mesopotamia becomes a major city. **2500BC** The first cities are built on the plain of the Indus River in Pakistan. **2500BC** First fortified city, Ur of the Chaldees, in modern Iraq. **2166BC** Birth of Abraham, founder of the Jewish nation.	**1700BC** Ur declines, and Babylon gains in strength **1680BC** The Hyksos, a group of Asian settlers, introduce horse-drawn chariots to Egypt. **1500BC** Hindu beliefs spread throughout northern India.	**1469BC** The first record of a battle, at Megiddo, between Egypt and the Canaanites. **c.1200BC** Zoroaster lives in Persia.	**900BC** Hindu beliefs are written down in the four *Vedas*. **605–562BC** Reign of King Nebuchadnezzar. He builds the fabulous hanging gardens in Babylon, the most sophisticated city in the Near East. **660BC** Legendary date of the unification of Japan and the start of Shintoism.	**500BC** In China, Sun Tzu writes the first book on military theory. **500BC** Silk Road opens. **500BC** Mahavira founds Jainism. **c.500s BC** Life of Lao-Tzu, legendary founder of Taoism. **551–479BC** Life of Confucius. **485–405BC** Life of Buddha.

	2000BC Islands of the South Pacific are uninhabited.	**1000BC** Polynesians settle in Tonga and Samoa. Over the next 2000 years the Polynesians slowly spread out across the South Pacific Ocean.	The Polynesians sail north to Hawaii, east to Easter Island and finally south to New Zealand.	

2300BC Farming leads to permanent settlement in villages in Mexico. **2300BC** Use of pottery in Mexico and Guatemala.	**c.2000BC** First evidence of metal working in Peru. **c.2000–1500BC** Pottery spreads among farmers in Peru. **c.2000–1000BC** The beginning of Mayan culture in Mesoamerica (Central America). Farmers begin to settle in villages.	**1800–900BC** The Initial Period in Peru. People settle in permanent villages, and there is evidence of social and religious organization. Pottery spreads. **1500BC** Agriculture reaches the southeast and later, the midwest of North America. **1200–900BC** The Olmec people of Mexico build the region's first large cities.	**850–200BC** The Chavin de Huantar civilization in the high Andes mountains reaches the peak of its success.	**200BC** Beginnings of Hopewell civilization in North America. **200BC** Many small, independent cultures develop in the valleys of the Andes. **300BC–AD200** Maya cities established in Mexico, Honduras and Guatemala.

AD1–1000

	AD 1	AD 100	AD 200	AD 300	AD 400
EUROPE	AD80 The Colosseum is built in Rome.	AD117 Emperor Trajan conquers Dacia (Romania). Empire is at its largest extent. AD165–167 Plague spreads throughout Europe.	AD200 The Roman road system covers all parts of the Empire.	AD300s First Barbarian invasions of Roman Empire. AD324 Christianity becomes the official religion of the Roman Empire. AD395 The Roman Empire is divided. The eastern empire becomes the Byzantine Empire.	AD408–410 The Goths under Alaric besiege Rome and sack it on August 24, 410. AD400–500 Throwing axes found in England.
AFRICA	AD44 Morocco is conquered by Rome. AD70 Christianity reaches Alexandria on the Mediterranean coast of Egypt.	AD193–211 A Libyan, Septimus Severus, becomes Roman emperor.	AD238 Revolt begins in North Africa against Roman rule.	AD320–650 The Ethiopian kingdom of Axum, East Africa, grows.	
ASIA	AD25 The Later Han period begins in China. The Emperor moves the capital to Luoyang. AD30 The first Christian churches are founded.	AD100s Mahayana Buddhism emerges in India and spreads to China AD105 A Chinese official develops the paper making process.	AD220 Power struggles weaken the court and the Han empire collapses. AD250 Rise of the Yamato culture in Japan.	AD350 The Yamato emperor rules the whole of Japan. AD399 Fa Hsien travels from China to India and Ceylon.	
AUSTRALASIA					AD400 Polynesians reach Easter Island in the east and the Hawaiian Islands in the north. They may have come from South-east Asia or even possibly crossed the Pacific on their rafts from Peru in South America.
AMERICA		AD150 The city of Teotihuacan (near modern day Mexico City) in Central America flourishes. By AD600 over 150,000 people live there.	AD200 (or before) There is evidence of maize being grown by the mound-building people of North America.	AD300–800 Classic phase of Maya civilization flourishes in Mexico, Guatemala and Honduras.	AD400 Hopewell civilization declines. 

AD 500	AD 600	AD 700	AD 800	AD 900	AD 1000

AD500 Saxon raids on Britain from north Germany.

AD700s–1000s Norse raids on Britain and Europe.

AD700–1100 Double-bladed axes used by Viking raiders.

AD778 Battle of Roncesvalles. The Franks under Charlemagne beaten by Basques and Gascons.

AD800s Vikings spread their Norse religion throughout northern Europe.

AD992 The Viking Leif Eriksson discovers Newfoundland and names it Vinland.

AD1054 Christianity splits into Roman Catholic and Orthodox churches.

AD1066 The Battle of Hastings. William of Normandy invades and seizes power in Britain.

AD1095–99 The First Crusade. European Christian armies fight for the Holy Land.

AD639–642 Arabs occupy Egypt

AD698–700 Arabs conquer Carthage and Tunis. The north African coast is converted to Islam.

AD700–1200 Kingdom of Ghana develops in West Africa.

AD700s Arab merchants develop a trade route with rich Saharan trading cities. They exchange tools and weapons, copper and horses for gold, ivory, skins and slaves.

AD900 West Africa: increase in trade and prosperity in Hausaland, a region on the Lower Niger.

AD538 The first Buddhists to settle in Japan arrive from Korea.

AD570–632 Life of Muhammad, the founder of Islam.

AD600s Islam spreads throughout the Middle East.

AD604 In Japan Prince Shotoku introduces government based on Chinese models.

AD635–642 Muslims conquer Syria, Egypt, and Persia.

AD680 Decisive split between the Sunni and Shi'ah Muslims.

AD710 The Yamato period ends in Japan and the state capital moves to Nara.

AD711 Muslims invade Spain. The empire expands to include northeastern India.

AD802 The Khmer empire, in modern Cambodia is founded under King Jayavarman II.

AD881 King Yasovarman I builds the earliest surviving Khmer temple.

AD1099 The first Christian crusaders visit Palestine.

AD500 South Pacific Islanders eat sweet potatoes, a plant that comes from the Americas.

AD1000 Polynesian Maoris settle in New Zealand.

AD500–1000 Civilizations of Huari and Tiahuanco in Mexico.

AD615 The great Maya leader Lord Pacal rules in the city of Palenque in Mexico.

AD650 The city of Teotihuacan begins to decline. It is looted and burned by unknown invaders around AD700.

AD850 The Toltecs of northern Mexico begin to create the city-state of Tula.

AD900 Most Maya cities in Central America are in decline.

AD900–1200 Cities in the northern Yucatan (in Mexico) flourish under the warlike Toltecs from Tula.

AD980–90s Vikings settle in Greenland and explore parts of North America.

AD1011–1063 The Mixtecs are ruled by the leader Eight Deer, in the area of Oaxaca, central Mexico. The Mixtecs are master goldsmiths.

AD1050–1250 Cahokia is a major region of civilization in Mississippi in North America.

1100–Present

	1100	1200	1300	1400	1500
EUROPE	**1100–1300** Medical schools are founded throughout Europe. **1199** King Richard I of England killed by a crossbow at Chaluz in France.	**1215** The Pope decrees that all doctors need church approval. **1200s** Longbow enters wide use in England and Wales. **1258** Medical texts preserved by the Arabs flow back to the West.		**1419** Henry "the Navigator" establishes a school of navigation in Portugal. **1492** Christopher Columbus crosses the Atlantic.	**1517** Roman Catholic Church splits as the Reformation gives rise to Protestant churches. **1543** Copernicus shows that the Earth circles the Sun. **1543** Vesalius accurately illustrates human anatomy.
AFRICA	**1100–1897** Kingdom of Benin, West Africa.	**1200–1500** Kingdom of Mali, West Africa. **1270–1450** Great Zimbabwe is capital of Shona kingdom.	**1350–1600** Kingdom of Songhai, West Africa. **1300s** The city of Timbuktu becomes a prosperous area for trade across the Sahara Desert.	**1480s** Portuguese cross the equator and sail around the Cape of Good Hope. **1482** The Portuguese open a trading post for exporting slaves to the New World.	
ASIA	**1100s** Islamic invaders bring new medical practices to India. **1187** Muslim leader Saladin retakes Jerusalem and overruns most of the crusader kingdoms. **1189–92** Third Crusade recaptures Acre from Saladin.	**1211** Ghengis Khan begins invasion of China. **1234** Mongols overrun northern China. **1271–95** Marco Polo visits China. **1291** Acre, the last Crusader stronghold in Palestine, is lost.	**1368** Mongols thrown out of China by the Ming dynasty.	**1405–33** Zheng He, from China, leads expeditions to South-east Asia. **1444** Final crusade. **1498** Vasco da Gama, from Lisbon, Portugal, sails to India.	**1500s** European settlers bring European medical ideas to India. **1549** Xavier, a Spanish Jesuit, goes to Japan as a missionary. **1594–97** Barents, a Dutch mariner, explores the Arctic Ocean.
AUSTRALASIA	**1000–1600** Statues on Easter Island.				**1520–21** Magellan crosses the Pacific on his round-the-world voyage.
AMERICA	**1100s** Incas start to dominate central Peru.		**1325** Aztecs found the city of Tenochtitlán on the spot now occupied by modern-day Mexico City.	**1450s** Incas build Machu Picchu. **1492** Columbus finds the West Indies. **1497** Cabot finds Newfoundland.	**1502** Amerigo Vespucci finds the Americas. **1513** Balboa sights the Pacific Ocean. **1519–33** Spanish conquer the Aztecs of Mexico. **1535–36** Cartier journeys up the St Lawrence River.

1600	1700	1800	1850	1900	1950

1610 Galileo spies Jupiter's moons through a telescope.

1628 Harvey shows how the heart circulates blood.

1661 Boyle describes the chemical elements

1668 Newton establishes 3 laws of motion.

1752 Franklin shows lightning is electricity.

1783 The Montgolfier brothers' balloon carries two men aloft.

1789 Lavoisier writes the first list of elements.

1789 French Revolution.

1804 Trevithick builds the first steam locomotive.

1830 Faraday and Henry find that electricity can be generated by magnetism.

1850 Morse code invented.

1871 Paris Commune.

1876 First detected radio signal.

1914–18 World War I

1917 Russian Revolution.

1926 Enigma coding machine developed.

1939–45 World War II

1945 Cold War begins.

1947 Kalashnikov designs the AK47 assault rifle.

1960 Microchip first used.

1989 End of the Cold War.

1710–1810 More than seven million Africans sent to the Americas as slaves.

1795–1806 Park, from Scotland, explores the River Niger.

1841–73 Livingstone, from Scotland, explores southern and central Africa.

1844–45 Barth, from Germany, explores the Sahara Desert region.

1874–77 Stanley, a missionary from Wales, sails down the Congo river.

1601 Yang Chi-chou writes his ten-volume Ch'en/Chiu Ta-Ch'eng, describing acupuncture.

1600s The first medical descriptions of Chinese medical practice reach the West.

1699 Guru Gobind Singh forms the Khalsa (Sikh comunity).

1725–29 Bering, from Denmark, crosses Siberia.

1734–42 Teams of explorers map Siberian coasts and rivers.

1878 Nordenskjold, from Finland, discovers the Northeast Passage.

1945 Atomic bomb dropped on Hirsohima, in Japan.

1945–62 Chinese Revolution.

1915–75 Indo-China War.

1945–62 War in South-east Asia.

1966–73 Vietnamese War between USA and Communist Viet-Cong.

1978–1982 Islamic Revolution.

1991 The Gulf War between the forces of NATO and Iraq involves one of the largest air assaults of all time.

1605 Jansz explores Queensland.

1642–43 Tasman discovers New Zealand.

1770 Cook lands in Australia.

1802–1803 The Australian coast is surveyed by English navigator, Mathew Flinders.

1828–62 Australian interior explored.

1911 Amundsen reaches South Pole.

1947 Thor Heyerdahl makes his Kon-Tiki expedition from Peru to the South Pacific.

1967 Discovery of Lystrosaurus fossils in Antarctica.

1603–15 Chamblain explores Canada and founds Quebec.

1610–11 Englishman Henry Hudson searches for the Northwest Passage.

1680–82 La Salle, from France, sails down the Mississippi River.

1700s Iron-bladed tomahawks manufactured for North America.

1800s Several scientific expeditions explore the Amazon.

1830 Joseph Smith translates the Book of Mormon.

1835 Colt patents his first revolver design.

1861–65 American Civil War.

1908 Ford's Model T is the first mass-produced car.

1908 Peary, from the United States, reaches the North Pole.

1956–1960 Cuban Revolution led by Fidel Castro.

1961 Cuban Missile crisis.

1961 USS Enterprise is the first nuclear-powered aircraft carrier.

1963 JF Kennedy is assassinated.

People and Places

A

Abbasids, dynasty of Muslim caliphs (rulers), who ruled the Arab world from AD749 until 1258.

Abu Bakr, the first caliph (ruler) of the Muslim empire, who succeeded Muhammad in AD632.

Agincourt, site of the battle in France in 1415, at which English and Welsh longbowmen defeated the French.

Ahura Mazda, the supreme god in the Zoroastrian religion.

Alexander the Great, king of Macedonia from 336 to 323BC, who created a huge empire that included the Middle East, Near East and north-western India.

Allah, the Islamic name for God.

Altamira, site in Spain known for its prehistoric cave paintings.

Amritsar, Sikh holy city in north-western India founded by Guru Ram Das, where the sacred Golden Temple was built between 1574 and 1581.

Amundsen, Roald, Norwegian explorer, who was the first to successfully voyage along the North-west Passage in 1903–06, the first person to reach the South Pole in 1911.

Angkor Wat, site of the temple city in Cambodia that was built from 1113 as the capital of the Khmer empire.

Appian Way, the first of the major Roman roads, constructed, in Italy, in 312BC.

Arbela, site of the battle in the Middle East at which Alexander the Great's army defeated the Persians in 331BC.

Archimedes, Greek citizen of Syracuse (*c*.285–212BC), the world's first true scientist, who used mathematical theories and practical experiments to prove his discoveries.

Armstrong, Neil, American astronaut who became the first human to set foot on the Moon in 1969.

Asgard, the realm of the gods in Norse mythology.

Asoka, ruler of the Mauryan empire from 269 until 232BC, who established Buddhism as the state religion.

Athens, the most important of the ancient Greek city-states, at the height of its power in the 5th century BC.

Auenbrugger, Leopold, Austrian doctor who, in 1761, proved that sounding the chest reveals information about the state of the lungs.

Augustus, the first emperor of Rome (27BC–AD14), who founded the Roman Empire to replace the Roman republic.

B

Babylon, city on the Euphrates river in Lower Mesopotamia (modern Iraq) that was the capital of the Babylonian Empire from about 1700BC.

Baekeland, Leo, inventor, in 1909, of Bakelite, the world's first entirely synthetic plastic.

Baird, John Logie, Scottish pioneer who demonstrated practical television in 1926.

Balboa, Vasco da, Spanish explorer and soldier who was the first European to see the Pacific Ocean, after crossing central America in 1513.

Barents, Willem, Dutch explorer who tried to find the North-east passage round the north of Russia to the Pacific Ocean in several voyages (1594–7).

Becquerel, Antoine, French scientist who discovered radioactivity in 1897.

Benz, Karl, German engineer who offered the first petrol-engined car for sale in 1888.

Bering, Vitus, Danish explorer who crossed Siberia and voyaged around the northern Pacific Ocean along the coasts of Siberia and Alaska between 1725 and 1741.

Bougainville, Louis, French navigator who led the first French voyage around the world (1766–79), and after whom the Papua New Guinean island of Bougainville was named.

Boyle, Robert, Irish scientist (1627–91) who said that everything in the material world is made of elements and compounds.

Brahman, the supreme Hindu god.

Bruce, James, British explorer who, in 1770, discovered Lake Tana, source of the Blue Nile (a tributary of the Nile).

Burke, Robert O'Hara, Australian explorer who, with William Wills, was the first to cross Australia from south to north in 1860–61. Both men died on the return journey.

Burton, Richard, British explorer who, in 1857, set out to find the source of the Nile with John Speke and explored the lakes of East Africa.

C

Cabot, John, Italian-born explorer who discovered Newfoundland, off the coast of Canada, in 1497 and claimed it for England.

Canaan, the land promised to the Jews by God (modern Israel).

Carthage, an ancient town in modern-day Tunisia, which was the most important Phoenician and, later, Roman colony in North Africa.

Cartier, Jacques, French explorer who, in 1534, explored the St. Lawrence estuary in Canada and then sailed upriver to Montreal.

Catholic, at first, the universal Christian Church which, in 1054, split into Western and Eastern (or Orthodox) branches; today, it usually refers to the Roman Catholic Church headed by the Pope in Rome.

Celts, people who lived in central and western Europe during the Iron Age, just before these areas were occupied by the Romans.

Champlain, Samuel de, French explorer who founded Quebec in 1608–9.

Chandragupta, founder of the Mauryan Empire in 322BC, which extended over much of modern India and Pakistan.

Charlemagne, Frankish king who, during the AD770s, took control of most of western Europe and was crowned first emperor of the Holy Roman Empire in AD800.

Clark, William, American soldier and explorer who, with Meriwether Lewis, led the first expedition (1804–6) across the North American continent to reach the Pacific Ocean.

Columbus, Christopher, Italian-born Spanish explorer who, in 1492, became the first modern European to sail across the Atlantic Ocean and reached the West Indies in the Caribbean.

Confucius, Chinese philosopher who lived from 551 to 479BC and whose peaceful teachings formed the basis of Confucianism.

Constantine the Great, Roman emperor who, in AD312, granted toleration of Christianity, which soon became the official religion of the Roman empire.

Constantinople, capital of the Byzantine empire until its capture by the Turks in 1453 (modern Istanbul).

Cook, James, British naval officer and explorer, who sailed round New Zealand and mapped the eastern coast of Australia, explored Antarctica and discovered Hawaii.

Copernicus, Nicolas Polish astronomer who, in 1453, showed that the Earth revolves around the Sun and not the Sun around the Earth.

Coral Sea, an arm of the Pacific Ocean, off northern Australia, where an American aircraft-carrier force inflicted the first naval blow to the Japanese in World War II.

Cortés, Hernán, Spanish soldier who conquered the Aztec empire in Mexico at Tenochtitlán, the Aztec capital, in 1521.

Crécy, site of the battle in France in 1346, at which English and Welsh longbowmen defeated the French.

Crete, Greek island that was home to the Minoan civilization in around 2000BC and was ruled at various times by Greeks, Romans, Turks and Arabs; it was the site of a major airborne German assault and victory in May 1941.

Crick, Francis, British scientist who, along with James Watson, discovered the double-helix structure of DNA in 1953 and helped to pave the way for modern genetics.

Culpeper, Nicholas, English herbalist who wrote the first modern herbal in 1649.

D

Damascus, major Muslim city in Syria, where high-grade steel weapons were made in the Middle Ages.

Dardanelles, strait in north-west Turkey that links the Mediterranean and Black Seas, and where Allied Forces suffered a grim defeat in 1915.

Darius I, king of Persia (522–486BC), who extended his kingdom to include parts of Egypt and India, but who failed to conquer Greece and was defeated at Marathon in 490BC.

Darwin, Charles, English naturalist who published his controversial theory of evolution, *The Origin of Species*, in 1859.

Demeter, Greek goddess of farming and harvests.

Dezhnev, Semyon, Russian explorer who sailed around the eastern tip of Siberia in 1648.

Dias, Bartolomeu, Portuguese explorer who rounded the Cape of Good Hope and reached the Indian Ocean in 1488, thus finding a sea route to the East.

Dien Bien Phu, village in Indochina (modern Vietnam) gained by Communist forces in 1954, thus marking the end of French colonial rule.

Dionysus, Greek god of wine.

Domagk, Gerhard, German scientist who developed Prontasil, one of the first antibacterial drugs, in 1932.

Dordogne, region in south-west France where important Cro-Magnon finds have been made.

Drake, Francis, English explorer who led the second voyage round the world between 1577 and 1580.

Duat, the underworld in ancient Egyptian religion.

E

Einstein, Albert, revolutionary physicist, who published his theories of special relativity and general relativity in 1905 and 1915 respectively.

Ely, Eugene, American aviator who made the world's first successful take-off from and landing on a ship in 1911.

Empedocles, Greek philosopher who, in the 400s BC, described the four humours (elements) that make up the body.

Eric the Red, Viking explorer who sailed from Norway in AD982 and reached Greenland via Iceland.

Euclid, Greek mathematician who taught at Alexandria and wrote his *Elements of Geometry* in about 300BC.

Eyre, Edward, Australian explorer who walked along the south coast of Australia from Adelaide to Albany in 1840–41.

F

Fa Hsien, Chinese monk who visited India and Sri Lanka in AD339 to study Buddhism.

Falkland Islands, British colony in the south Atlantic Ocean and the scene of a short war in 1982, when British troops expelled the Argentine forces that had occupied the islands.

Faraday, Michael, English chemist and physicist (1791–1867) and pioneer in the field of electricity.

Fleming, Alexander, Scottish bacteriologist who discovered penicillin in 1928, paving the way for modern treatment of infectious diseases.

Franklin, John, English explorer and the first to try to find the North-west Passage round the north of Canada, starting in 1845 but dying in the ice during 1847.

Frobisher, Martin, English explorer who reached Baffin Island off the north-western coast of Canada in 1576, while seeking the entrance to a north-western passage to the Pacific Ocean.

G

Gagarin, Yuri, Soviet cosmonaut who, in 1961, was the first man in space.

Galilei, Galileo, Italian scientist (1564–1642) who was the first to use a telescope to examine the night sky and whose astronomical achievements included the discovery of four of Jupiter's moons.

Gama, Vasco da, Portuguese explorer who was the first modern European to reach India by sea in 1497–98.

Gautama, Siddhartha, generally known as the Buddha (enlightened one), the founder of the Buddhist system of belief around 500BC

Ghengis Khan, ruler of the Mongols, who conquered northern China in 1234.

Great Zimbabwe, site of the city in Zimbabwe that was the capital of one of the first civilizations of southern Africa.

Guru Nanak, the Indian founder of the Sikh religion, who lived from 1469 until 1539.

H

Hall, Charles, American explorer who made three attempts to reach the North Pole on foot, and died on the last in 1871.

Halstaat, the first stage of the Iron Age in Europe, from the 600s to the 500s BC, named after an Iron Age archaeological site in Austria.

Hammurabi, king of Babylon (1792–1750BC), who conquered Mesopotamia and is best known for his Code of Laws, which included the first code of practice for doctors.

Han Wu Di, emperor of China (140–87BC), who extended the Han empire to its greatest extent after defeating the northern nomads.

Hanno, Phoenician explorer who sailed around the coast of West Africa in 500BC.

Hartog, Dirk, Dutch explorer who, on a journey to the East Indies, sailed too far south and discovered Western Australia in 1615.

Harvey, William, English physician who described how the heart pumps blood around the body in 1628.

Hausser, Konrad, the designer of the first effective long-recoil mechanism for artillery in 1888.

Henry the Navigator, prince of Portugal and founder of a school of scientific navigation, who financed voyages of discovery along the coast of West Africa during the 1400s.

Hillary, Edmund, New Zealand explorer and mountaineer who, along with Tenzing Norgay, became the first to scale Mount Everest in 1953.

Hipparchus, Greek who compiled a catalogue of the stars and became the first truly great astronomer, though much of his work was based on records left behind by the ancient Babylonians.

Hippocrates, Greek citizen of the island of Kos who lived from 460 to 377BC and who is known as the 'father of medicine' for his works and writings on the accurate diagnosis and treatment of disease.

Hiroshima, Japanese city on which the first atomic bomb was dropped in August 1945.

Holland, John, American engineer who developed the world's first practical submarines in the 1890s.

Homer, supposed writer of the *Iliad* and *Odyssey*, Greek epic poems about the Trojan War and its aftermath.

Hubble, Edwin, American astronomer whose discoveries in the 1920s led to the 'big bang' theory of the universe.

Hudson, Henry, English explorer who, in 1610, sailed into the bay in northern Canada that is now named after him, but his crew later mutinied and returned home without him.

Hunter, John, Scottish surgeon of the 1700s, who transformed surgery into a science.

I

Ibn Battuta, Islamic explorer who traversed the limits of the Islamic world (1325–53), as far west as Mali in West Africa and as far east as Xiamen in China.

J

Jansz, Willem, Dutch explorer who sailed south from the East Indies in 1605 and discovered what is now known as Queensland, in north-eastern Australia.

Jayavarman II, founder of the Khmer empire in South-east Asia, who ruled from AD802–850.

Jenner, Edward, English physician who revolutionized the prevention of disease in 1796 when he successfully inoculated a boy against smallpox.

Jericho, the earliest-known town, where the first domesticated cereals were grown; also the scene of a famous siege during the Israelite conquest of Canaan.

Jerusalem, holy city for Jews, Christians and Muslims and the site of the Jewish Great Temple built by King Solomon.

Jesus of Nazareth, a Jew born around 7 or 6BC, who Christians believe was the son of God and whose life, death and teachings are the foundations of the Christian Church.

Jolliet, Louis, French explorer who, along with Jacques Marquette, charted the upper parts of the Mississippi River in 1672.

Julius Caesar, the last leader of the Roman republic, a great soldier, who conquered Gaul, launched raids into Germany and Britain, and was killed in 44BC.

Jutland, site of the greatest naval battle of World War I, fought in May 1916 off the west coast of Denmark.

K

Knossos, city in Crete that was the heart of the Minoan civilization until about 1450BC.

Korea, country in Asia, and site of a major war between 1951 until 1954, in which jet-powered fighter planes were first used against each other.

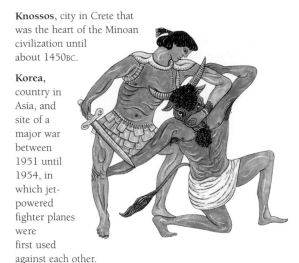

L

Lao-tzu, the Chinese founder of Taoism, a philosophy based on following a natural path through life.

Lascaux, cave in the Dordogne region of France known for its prehistoric cave paintings and engravings of animals.

Lavoisier, Antoine, French chemist who helped to prove that all materials are made up of basic elements.

Leeuwenhoek, Antonie van, Dutch scientist who made the first practical microscope in 1671, through which he identified microbes which he called 'animalcules'.

Leif Eriksson, son of Eric the Red, Viking explorer, who sailed from Greenland in AD992 to establish a small settlement at Vinland in eastern North America.

Leonardo da Vinci, Italian engineer, inventor, architect and artist, who was a true master of many fields.

Lepanto, site of a naval battle off the coast of Greece, at which, in 1571, the Austrians defeated the fleet of the Turks.

Lewis, Meriwether, American administrator and explorer who, with William Clark, led the first expedition (1804–06) across North America to reach the Pacific.

Lindbergh, Charles, American aviator, who made the first non-stop solo transatlantic flight (from New York to Paris) in 1927.

Livingstone, David, Scottish doctor and missionary who explored southern and eastern Africa and discovered Victoria Falls (1852–6); after disappearing in the region of the Great Lakes, he was found by Henry Stanley.

Luger, Georg, Austrian who, in 1899, designed an automatic pistol, used by the Germans in the two World Wars.

Luther, Martin, German religious reformer whose condemnation of the Roman Catholic Church in 1517 led to the Reformation and the establishment of Protestantism.

M

Magellan, Ferdinand, Portuguese-born navigator who captained the first round-the-world voyage in 1519; on the way he discovered what is now called the Magellan Strait and named the Pacific Ocean. When he died in 1521 Juan de Elcano completed the voyage.

Mahavira, Indian founder of the Jain religion in the 500s BC.

Makkah, also spelt Mecca, holy Islamic city in modern-day Saudi Arabia that was the birthplace of the prophet Muhammad.

Malpighi, Marcello, Italian physician of the 1600s who contributed to the understanding of blood circulation by his discovery of the capillaries that link arteries and veins.

Marathon, site in eastern Greece of a battle at which the Greeks successfully defended themselves from Persian invasion in 490BC.

Marconi, Guglielmo, Italian-born scientist who sent the world's first radio message in 1895.

Marquette, Jacques, French explorer and missionary who, along with Louis Jolliet, charted the upper parts of the Mississippi River in 1672.

Maxim, Hiram, American-born British magnate who invented the first fully-automatic machine gun in 1883.

Meadowcroft Rock Shelter, site in Pennsylvania of the first known settlement in North America.

Mercator, Gerhardus, Dutch mapmaker who, in 1552, created a projection of the world that accurately represented the surface of a sphere (the Earth) on a flat plane (map).

Mesopotamia, the fertile area of land between the Tigris and Euphrates rivers in the Middle East, where the world's first civilizations emerged.

Midgard, the middle world in Norse mythology, where humans live.

Midway, Pacific islands, off which American aircraft-carriers defeated the Japanese navy in June 1942.

Moses, prophet who brought the Jews out of Egyptian captivity in about 1466BC, and to whom God revealed the Ten Commandments.

Muhammad, also spelt Mohammed, prophet born in Makkah in AD570 and founder of the Islamic religion.

N

Nagasaki, Japanese city on which the second atomic bomb was dropped in August 1945.

Nebuchadnezzar II, king of Babylon from 605 to 562BC, best known for creating the Hanging Gardens of Babylon, one of the Seven Wonders of the ancient world.

Nelson, Horatio, British naval hero and commander who defeated the French and Spanish navies at the Battle of Trafalgar in October 1805, but died during the battle.

Newton, Isaac, English scientist and mathematician who came up with his famous theory about gravity in 1666, and who also made important scientific discoveries about motion and the nature of light.

Nightingale, Florence, British nurse who pioneered modern nursing methods during the Crimean War (1853-56) on the Black Sea coast of Ukraine.

Nineveh, city near the River Tigris in Mesopotamia that was the capital of the Assyrian Empire from the 880s BC until its destruction in 612BC.

Nordenskjöld, Nils, Finnish explorer, first journeyed round the North-east Passage into the Pacific Ocean (1878–79).

Norgay, Tenzing, Nepalese mountaineer who, along with Edmund Hillary, became the first to scale Mount Everest in 1953.

Normandy, part of northern France and site of the D-Day campaign which began in June 1944 when Allied troops landed on the Normandy coast, marking the start of the liberation of German-occupied territory.

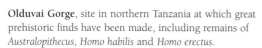

O

Odin, also known as Wotan, the primary god of Norse mythology.

Offa, king of Mercia in north-western England in the AD700s, who built Offa's Dyke to protect his kingdom from Welsh raids.

Olduvai Gorge, site in northern Tanzania at which great prehistoric finds have been made, including remains of *Australopithecus*, *Homo habilis* and *Homo erectus*.

Oppenheimer, Robert, American nuclear physicist who led the development of the atomic bomb during World War II.

P

Park, Mungo, Scottish explorer who drowned while exploring the River Niger in West Africa (1795–1806).

Pasteur, Louis, French scientist who, in the 1860s, established how bacteria cause infection and who developed pasteurization, a technique for destroying microbes with heat.

Peary, Robert, American admiral and explorer who led the first expedition to the North Pole in 1909.

Pericles, Athenian statesman (443–429BC), who lifted the city-state to a peak of political and economic power, and began the construction of the Parthenon and other buildings on the Acropolis in 447BC.

Persepolis, city in south-west Iran, founded by Darius I and the capital of the Persian Empire from about 835BC.

Pilate, Pontius, Roman governor of Judea who condemned Jesus of Nazareth to crucifixion in about AD30.

Pizarro, Francisco, Spanish soldier, who conquered the Inca Empire of Peru in 1532.

Planck, Max, German physicist who published his quantum theory in 1900, revolutionizing scientific understanding of atomic processes.

Plate, River, also known as the Río de la Plata, river in Argentina in whose estuary the German pocket battleship *Graf Spee* was trapped by British forces in 1939 and deliberately sunk by her captain.

Polo, Marco, Italian explorer who claimed to have visited China and the Mongol Empire in the 1200s.

Priestley, Joseph, English chemist who identified oxygen in the 1700s.

Ptolemy, Egyptian astronomer who lived in Alexandria (AD90–170) and whose Earth-centric picture of the universe went unchallenged until the 1500s.

Puritjarra Rock Shelter, early site in the Northern Territory for inhabitation of Australia.

Pythagoras, Greek philosopher and mathematician, born in Samos in 560BC.

Pytheas, Greek mariner of Massilia (Marseilles) who, in 330BC, sailed round the coast of Spain, Gaul and through the English Channel, to reach 'Thule' (either southern Norway or Iceland).

R

Re, ancient Egyptian sun god.

Rome, city in the western part of central Italy that was the capital of the Roman empire.

Ross, James, Scottish explorer who discovered the magnetic north pole in 1831 and charted much of the coast of Antarctica in 1841.

S

Saladin, Muslim leader in the Middle East, who recaptured Jerusalem from the Christian Crusaders in 1187.

Sargon, king of Assyria at the peak of the Empire's power in the late 700s BC, who founded the capital city of Khorsabad (in modern Iraq).

Scott, Robert, English polar explorer, who led the second expedition to reach the South Pole in 1912, but died on the way back to the coast.

Shiva, one of the three main gods of the Hindu religion, responsible for both the preservation and the destruction of life.

Snow, John, British doctor who traced the cause of the London cholera outbreak of 1842 to contaminated water supplies.

Solomon, Jewish king known for his wisdom, who completed the construction of the Great Temple in Jerusalem in about 960BC, which had been begun by his father, King David.

Stonehenge, site in southern England of a large prehistoric stone circle.

T

Thule, name of what the ancients regarded as the northernmost land of the world, probably Norway or Iceland.

Torres, Luis, Spanish explorer who, in 1607, proved that Australia was an island by finding the strait that separated it from New Guinea.

Troy, a city in eastern Turkey which the Greeks besieged in the Trojan War (1200BC).

V

Valhalla, the heaven of the brave in Norse mythology.

Vishnu, one of the three main Hindu gods, responsible for preserving the universe.

W

Waterloo, site of the battle in Belgium at which, in 1815, Napoleon was finally defeated by the British and Prussians.

Watson, James, American scientist who, along with Francis Crick, discovered the double-helix structure of DNA in 1953 and helped to pave the way for modern genetics.

Wegener, Alfred, German scientist who, in 1923, first put forward the theory of continental drift and who also suggested that there was once one giant supercontinent.

Whitehead, Robert, British engineer who developed the first effective locomotive torpedoes from the 1860s.

William I, Duke of Normandy, who became King of England after defeating the Anglo-Saxon King Harold at the Battle of Hastings in 1066.

Willoughby, Hugh, English explorer who reached Novaya Zemlya off the northern coast of Russia in 1554.

Wills, William, Australian explorer who, along with Robert O'Hara Burke, was the first to cross Australia from south to north in 1860–61, but both men died on the return journey.

Wright, Wilbur and Orville, American brothers and aviation pioneers who achieved the world's first powered and sustained flight in a controllable heavier-than-air craft during December 1903.

X Y Z

Xavier, Francis, Spanish missionary who journeyed to India and then on to Japan, which he reached in 1549.

Yamato, ruling clan of Japan in about AD350, who organized the first unified control of the Japanese islands.

Yangtze Delta, region at the mouth of the Yangtze river in China, where rice was first cultivated around 5000BC.

Zeus, supreme god in Greek religion.

Zheng, king of Qin (246–210BC) and, later, Emperor Qin Shi Huangdi of China (221–210BC), who created the first great Chinese empire and started building on the first Great Wall of China.

Zheng He, Chinese explorer who led seven voyages of discovery into South-east Asia and the Indian Ocean between 1405 and 1433.

Zoroaster, Persian priest who lived around 1200BC and whose teachings form the basis of the Zoroastrian religion.

Glossary

A

alchemy
An early form of chemistry, which looked for a way to change base metals into precious ones, and for the secret of eternal life.

alignment
Term used to describe objects that are lined up neatly. A stone alignment is a long row of standing stones, often lined up to correspond with the movements of the Sun, Moon or stars.

alloy
Material made by mixing two or more metals. The most common alloy in prehistoric times was bronze, made from copper and tin.

amphitheatre
A circular or oval open-air theatre, with seats arranged around a central area.

anaesthetic
Substance that prevents feeling in all or part of the body.

anatomy
The study of the structure of the body – where everything is and how it fits together.

antibiotic
A drug, typically based on a natural substance, that attacks germs.

aqueduct
A manmade channel to supply water.

archaeologist
A person who studies the buildings, tools, pots and other remains of past societies.

armada
A fleet of battleships.

artillery
Large weapons that need transport to move them around the battlefield and a crew to operate them.

astrolabe
Navigational instrument once used to measure the height of the Sun at noon, thus giving a ship's latitude.

Australopithecine
A hominid of the genus *Australopithecus*, alive more than a million years ago.

Ayurveda
A series of Indian religious texts dating back to about 2000BC.

B

bacterium
Member of a group of microbes (bacteria) that cause many common infections.

bayonet
A blade fitted on to the end of a musket, named after the French town of Bayonne.

Bronze Age
Period in which the use of bronze for making tools and weapons became well established (3000–1000BC).

burial mound
Artificial earth mound containing human graves.

C

city-state
A city that is also an independent state or country.

civilization
A settled society that has developed writing, organized religion, trade, grand buildings and government.

clone
A perfect genetic replica of a living thing.

constellation
One of the patterns of stars that astronomers use to find their way around the night sky. The pattern is visual and there is no real connection between the stars in a constellation.

crusade
A military expedition launched from Christian Europe to attempt to recover the Holy Land from Muslim rule.

cuirass
Protection for the front and back of the upper body, originally made from leather.

cuneiform
A type of writing that uses wedge-shaped figures, carved with a special tool. It developed in Mesopotamia from about 3000BC.

D

decimal system
A numerical system based around the number 10, first developed by Hindu mathematicians in AD662.

diagnosis
Identification of a disease from its symptoms.

E

earthwork
A bank or rampart of earth, often built for protection.

emplacement
Position of an artillery gun on the battlefield or outside a besieged castle.

epidemic
A widespread outbreak of an infectious disease.

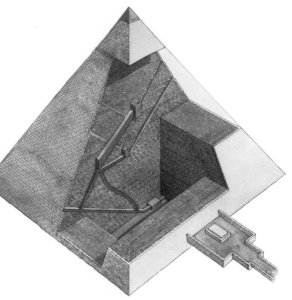

evolution
The gradual change of living species over time.

F

fossils
Part of an animal or plant that is preserved in stone.

G

genus
A group of animals or plants that have characteristics in common. A genus normally has more than one species in it.

glacier
A slow-moving river of ice.

glaze
Layer of material spread on to a pot before firing to create a hard, waterproof finish.

H

hieroglyphics
Ancient Egyptian picture writing.

hominid
Member of the family Hominidae, which includes humans and australopithecines.

Homo erectus
Upright-walking member of the human genus *Homo*, which lived over 500,000 years ago.

Homo habilis
Early member of the human genus *Homo*, alive in Africa about 1.7 million years ago.

Homo sapiens
The modern human species, which developed around 100,000 years ago, and to which we belong.

hoplite
A heavily-armed infantry soldier from ancient Greece.

hunter-gatherers
People who live on meat which they hunt and plants which they gather.

I

Ice Age
Period when the temperature was much lower than today, and large parts of the Earth's surface were covered in ice.

infantry
Foot soldiers with hand-held weapons.

Iron Age
Period during which iron became the main metal used for tools and weapons, from about 2000BC.

irrigation
The use of manmade channels to water farmland.

J

jousting
Sporting combat between two knights on horseback.

L

land bridge
Area of land connecting two landmasses that are now separate.

latitude
Imaginary horizontal lines that circle the Earth and are measured in degrees north or south of the Equator.

La Tène
Style of abstract art produced by the Celts, dated around 450–50BC.

legion
The main unit of the Roman army, made up of Roman citizens.

longitude
Imaginary vertical lines that circle the Earth and are measured in degrees east or west of a line called the prime meridian, which runs through Greenwich in England.

M

medieval
Term describing people, events and objects from the Middle Ages.

megalith
Large stone, standing alone or used as part of a tomb, stone circle or other monument.

Mei Ching
Chinese book about the pulse by Wang Shu-ho, published in AD280.

Mesolithic
The Middle Stone Age. The period during the Stone Age when people improved their hunting techniques and began to make smaller stone tools.

Middle Ages
Period in history that lasted from around AD800 to 1400.

mummy
A preserved dead body, like those of ancient Egypt.

myths
Stories told by ancient peoples. Myths often describe the activities of gods and goddesses and were frequently used to explain natural events such as thunder.

N

Neanderthal
Early hominid, shorter and stockier than humans, that lived in Europe and the Middle East and died out around 35,000BC.

Neolithic
The New Stone Age. The period when people began to farm but were still using stone tools.

nirvana
Name of the perfect state of existence that Buddhists seek to reach.

nomads
People who move around as a group in search of food, water and land for grazing animals.

Northern Hemisphere
The half of the Earth that lies north of the Equator.

O

obelisk
A tall, four-sided tapering pillar with a pyramid-shaped top.

obsidian
Naturally occurring glass-like substance formed in volcanoes. Used in prehistoric times in the same way as flint for making tools.

oracle
A means by which ancient peoples could contact the gods to ask for advice or find out about the future.

ore
Rock containing deposits of metal.

P

pack ice
Ice floating on a sea or ocean that has become packed together in huge sheets.

Palaeolithic
The Old Stone Age. The period when human life first emerged. This time was typified by a hunter-gatherer way of life and by the use of simple stone tools.

palaeontologist
A person who studies fossils.

papyrus
A kind of paper made from layers of papyrus reeds.

pharaoh
A title for the later kings of ancient Egypt. The word pharaoh means "great house."

philosophy
A set of beliefs and values held by an individual or group.

pommel
The weighted end of the handle of a broad sword, used to deliver a hammer blow in battle.

prehistory
The period before there were any written records.

prophet
Someone through whom God speaks.

Q

quadrant
Navigational instrument, consisting of a quarter-circle marked in degrees. It was used by sailors to calculate the angle of the Sun and thus to work out the ship's latitude.

quantum theory
The idea that, on a subatomic level, energy is always broken into tiny chunks or quanta.

Qur'an
The holy book of Islam as spoken by Muhammad.

R

radiation
The spread of energy as particles or waves, for example X-rays, light or gamma rays.

Ragnarok
The final battle foretold in the Norse religion.

rampart
Wide earth mound built to fortify a castle or town.

Rastafarianism
Religion of the West Indies ordaining a belief in the Old Testament but worshipping Haile Selassie, emperor of Ethiopia from 1930 until 1974.

reincarnation
The belief that when a person dies, he or she will be reborn in another body.

relief
A carving that stands out or is raised from the surface.

republic
A country or state, such as ancient Rome, ruled by elected representatives of its people.

ritual
A ceremony in which the order of events, and the words used, rarely change over the years.

S

saltpetre
A name for the mineral potassium nitrate. It is used to make gunpowder, explosives, matches and fertilizers.

samurai
A word first used to describe the imperial guard of ancient Japan. Later it was used to describe a high born warrior class in general.

Sanskrit
The language of the earliest Hindu writings.

seal
An engraved disc used to leave an impression on soft wax. Official government documents are often sealed.

Seven Wonders
A list of seven magnificent structures found in the ancient world. They include the Hanging Gardens of Babylon and the Great Pyramid at Giza in Egypt.

Shi'ah and Sunni
The two primary branches of the Islamic religion which developed from AD680.

Shinto
The major religion established in Japan during the 6th century AD.

shrine
A sacred place or container where religious objects or images may be kept.

Silk Road
The ancient overland trading route between China and Europe.

South Pole
The southernmost point of the Earth's axis of rotation, which lies in Antarctica.

Southern Hemisphere
The half of the Earth that lies south of the Equator.

Spanish Armada
An armada is a fleet of battleships. The Spanish Armada was sent by Philip of Spain to invade England in 1588. It was defeated.

Stone Age
Term describing any period when people made their tools out of stone.

superpower
A country possessing immense economic and military power, such as the USA or the former USSR.

Swiss Guard
Group of Swiss soldiers chosen to guard the Pope. The tradition was begun by Pope Julius II in the early 1500s. Today, a Papal Swiss Guard is still used to guard the Pope.

T

Torah
Hebrew name for the first five books of the Bible.

tournament
Armed contest between knights, fought for respect and ceremony.

trade
The process of buying and selling goods.

transfusion
Passing a liquid, often someone else's blood, into the bloodstream.

transplant
An organ or piece of tissue put into a patient's body which has been taken from another living thing.

tribe
A group of people descended from the same family or sharing the same language and culture.

trident
large fork with three prongs used as a weapon.

Trireme
Warship used by ancient Greeks. Its name comes from the Greek words for "three" and "oars", because it was powered by men rowing in three ranks.

tsar
The title of the hereditary emperor and ruler of Russia. Also sometimes written as czar.

Z

Ziggurat
A pyramid-shaped temple built by the ancient Babylonians.

Index

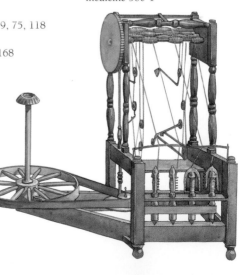

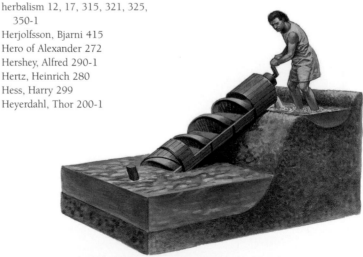

This edition is published by Armadillo, an imprint of Anness Publishing Ltd,
108 Great Russell Street, London WC1B 3NA; info@anness.com

www.annesspublishing.com; twitter: @Anness_Books

If you like the images in this book and would
like to investigate using them for publishing,
promotions or advertising, then please visit
www.practicalpictures.com for more information.

Publisher: Joanna Lorenz
Produced by Miles Kelly Publishing Limited
Project Editors: Nicole Pearson, Richard McGinlay
Designers: Joyce Mason, Ann Samuel
Production Controller: Ben Worley

The publishers would like to thank the following artists who contributed to
this book: Julian Baker (Baker Illustrations); Andy Beckett (Illustration Ltd);
Mark Beesley; Mark Bergin; Richard Berridge, (Spec Art); Vanessa Card; Rob
Chapman (Linden Artists); James Field (SGA); Wayne Ford; Chris Forsey;
Mike Foster Malting Partnership); Terry Gabbey (AFA); Roger Gorringe
(Illustration Ltd); Jeremy Gower; Peter Gregory; Ron Hayward; Gary Hinks;
Sally Holmes; Richard Hook (Linden Artists); Iamnee; Rob Jakeway; John
James (Temple Rogers); Kuo Chen Kang; Aziz Khan; Stuart Lafford (Linden
Artists); Ch'en Ling; Steve Lings (Linden Artists); Kevin Maddison; Janos
Marrfy; Shane Marsh (Linden Artists); Rob McCaig; Chris Odgers; Alex Pang
(SGA); Helen Parsley (JM & A Associates); Terry Riley Studio; Andrew
Robinson; Chris Rothero (Linden Artists); Eric Rowe (Linden Artists); Martin
Sanders; Peter Sarson; Mike Sanders; Rob Sheffield; Don Simpson (Spec
Art); Sue Stitt; Guy Smith (Mainline Design); Nick Spender (Advocate);
Clive Spong (Linden Artists); Stuart Squires; Roger Stewart; Ken Stott; Steve
Sweet SGA; Mike Taylor (SGA); Catherine Ward; Ross Watton (SGA); Mike
White (Temple Rogers); Alison Winfield; John Woodcock.

PHOTOGRAPHIC ACKNOWLEDGEMENTS

PREHISTORIC PEOPLES: AKG Photo 18bl/ Erich Lessing 19b, 48tr; Ancient
Art and Architecture Collection 51b; English Heritage Photo Library 54tr,
62c, 65t, 68tr; E.T. Archive 26br, 28br; Hutchison Library/ Mary Jellife 21b,
45b/ Southwell 71bl; The Stock Market 36bl, 38br.

ANCIENT CIVILIZATIONS: AKG London 121tl/ Paul Almasy 87tl/ Erich
Lessing 81bl/ Jean-Louis Nou; AKG Berlin 90br; iStock 112t, 117tl; Mary
Evans Picture Library 108tr.

WORLD RELIGIONS: The Bridgeman Art Library 153tr, 179bc/ Dinodia
Picture Agency, Bombay 160cr/ The National Museum of India 150br/
Victoria and Albert Museum 147tr; Corbis 185tl/ Dave Bartruff 173cr/
Bennett Dean; Eye Ubiquitous/ Bettmann 186tl/ Kevin Fleming 177bc/
159tr/ Lindsay Hebberd 149tl/ Earl & Nazima Kowall 160br/ Lake County
Museum 186cr/ Charles & Josette Lenars 160bc/ Daniel Laine 168br/ Denis
O'Regan 187br/ David H. Wells 172br; Sonia Halliday Photographs 181bc,
183tr; iStock 182tr; Robert Lesley 184bl; Judy McCaskey 139bc; Clare
Oliver 166c, 167tr, 167bc; Panos Pictures/ Piers Benator 180br/ Alain le
Garsmeur 155bl/ Kaveh Kazemi 142bc.

EXPLORATION AND DISCOVERY: Corbis 252bl; Hutchison Library 226br,
228cr/A. Zvoznikov 222cr/ R. Francis 224br/ N. Haslam 226tr/ E. Parker
226bl/ C. Pasini 232c/ A. Singer 230bl/ N. Smith 243bl; Popperfoto 239b,
240br, 242bl/ Reuter 242tr; The Stock Market 230tl.

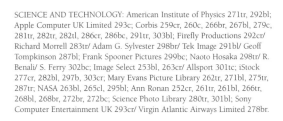

SCIENCE AND TECHNOLOGY: American Institute of Physics 271tr, 292bl;
Apple Computer UK Limited 293c; Corbis 259cr, 260c, 266br, 267bl, 279c,
281tr, 282tr, 282tl, 286cr, 286bc, 291tr, 303bl; Firefly Productions 292cr/
Richard Morrell 283tr/ Adam G. Sylvester 298br/ Tek Image 291bl/ Geoff
Tompkinson 287bl; Frank Spooner Pictures 299bc; Naoto Hosaka 298tr/ R.
Benali/ S. Ferry 302bc; Image Select 253bl, 263cr/ Allsport 301tc; iStock
277cr, 282bl, 297b, 303cr; Mary Evans Picture Library 262tr, 271bl, 275tr,
287tr; NASA 263bl, 265cl, 295bl; Ann Ronan 252cr, 261tr, 261bl, 266cr,
268bl, 268br, 272br, 272bc; Science Photo Library 280tr, 301bl; Sony
Computer Entertainment UK 293cr/ Virgin Atlantic Airways Limited 278br.

THE STORY OF MEDICINE: Bridgeman Art Library 329tr; British School of
Shiatsu-Do (London) 355bl; Corbis 333cl, 340c, 342tl, 360bl /AFP 357cr/
Nathan Benn 349tl; Bettmann 327tr, 329cl, 332cr, 344cr, 345tr, 347bl,
347bc, 350bl, 351tl/ Hulton-Deutsch Collection 341bl, 342bl/ Buddy Mays
313bc; Lisa M McGeady 355cr; Roger Ressmeyer 359bl; Mary Evans Picture
Library 367tl, 368br, 324bc, 325tl, 336bl, 338tl, 353tr; Ann Ronan Picture
Library 326ca, 348bc, 360tr; Science Photo Library/ Hank Morgan 362c.

ANCIENT WEAPONS: AKG London 382tr/ Erich Lessing 367tl; E.T Archive
382tr, 392tl, 411tr, 417bl/ British Museum 390br; Mary Evans Picture
Library 405bl, 415tr, 415bl, 419tr.

MODERN WEAPONS AND WARFARE: Imperial War Museum 447bc;
Popper-Hanke Collection 433bc; Popperfoto 462cr, 469bc; Solo Syndication
Ltd 430bl; Science Photo Library 436br. With special thanks to Will Fowler
for supplying the following images: 423cl, 425tr, 425c, 426br, 428bc, 428br,
429tl, 430br, 431cr, 432c, 433tl, 433cr, 433bl, 434tl, 434br, 436c, 437cr,
438cr, 440tl, 440cr, 444bl, 444br, 441cl, 441bl, 441bc, 442c, 443tl, 443bl,
444cl, 444bl, 444br, 445cr, 445bl, 446tr, 447tl, 447tr, 447bl, 448cr, 449bl,
450bl, 450br, 451bl, 452tl, 453tl, 459bl, 462cr, 462bc, 462tl, 462br, 466br,
467cl, 467bl, 470c, 470br, 470bl, 472br, 474bc, 474tl, 474br, 466br, 467cl,
467bl, 470c, 470br, 470bl, 472br, 474br, 477tl, 477bc.

All other pictures from Dover Publications and Miles Kelly archives.

Manufacturer: Anness Publishing Ltd, 108 Great Russell Street, London
WC1B 3NA, England
For Product Tracking go to: www.annesspublishing.com/tracking
Batch: 2844-23732-1127